ECONOMIC IMPERIALISM

The Economic Approach Applied Outside the Field of Economics

D1265473

ECONOMIC IMPERIALISM

The Economic Approach Applied Outside the Field of Economics

Edited by

GERARD RADNITZKY and
PETER BERNHOLZ

A Professors World Peace Academy Book

Paragon House Publishers
New York

Published in the United States by
PARAGON HOUSE PUBLISHERS
2 Hammarskjöld Plaza
New York, New York 10017

A Professors World Peace Academy Book.

Library of Congress Cataloging-in-Publication Data

Economic Imperialism.

  "A Professors World Peace Academy book."
  1. Economics—Methodology.   I. Radnitzky, Gerard.
II. Bernholz, Peter.   III. Professors World Peace
Academy.
HB71.E24   1986   330'.072   86-12337
ISBN 0-943852-11-0
ISBN 0-943852-18-8 (pbk.)

CONTENTS

PREFACE

Since the dawn of civilization, economic thinking has played a central role in human affairs. As production and economies have become more and more complex, a specialized activity has slowly emerged that turned into a specific discipline in the eighteenth century and since then has become increasingly important. Economic science is rightly considered to be the best developed of the social sciences. However, the contemporary attitude towards economics is divided. On the one hand, economics is considered the "dismal science." Book titles such as B. Ward's *What's Wrong with Economics?* (London, 1972) are symptomatic of this stance. On the other hand, there is considerable optimism about the possibilities inherent in economics—that is, if the methods of economics are applied to problems *outside* the traditional subject matter of economic study. Thus, R. B. McKenzie and Gordon Tullock write: "This new field of research is, we think, more exciting, more interesting, and even more relevant than the traditional applications to traditional economic problems" (*The New World of Economics. Exploration into the Human Experience* [Homewood, IL 1975, 1977, 1981], p. ix). The popularity and impact of the "economic approach" is increasing. Yet, this is a sociological fact and, as such, it does not necessarily tell us anything about the merits and limitations of that approach. The label "economic approach" has for many—more wrongly than rightly—become associated with the so-called Chicago School, of which Gary S. Becker is a main proponent. The critics have often viewed the extension of economics, in particular the extension of microeconomic theory to all human affairs, with misgiving. They have accused the Chicago School, Public Choice, the Economics of Law, and similar approaches or extensions of economic theory, of "disciplinary imperialism" and of not being aware of the boundaries of the realm of valid application of economic thinking. The best way of forming an opinion about the possibilities that the economic approach may have to offer is to try it out. Thus, the purpose of this collection of papers is to provide a sample of its application to various areas of human life. "Economic approach" is taken in the wide sense of any application of the tools of economic analysis.

All life is problem solving. All problem solving contains cognitive components. Even practical problems involve cognitive problems. In all nature there is a scarcity of resources, and normally individuals have competing goals. One basic difference between "life" and non-living matter is that an organism must do something in order to maintain itself as a system at a certain level of complexity, as a "going enterprise," while non-living matter need not. That means that an organism must "act" even if choice in the strict sense is not involved. Man, however, is a choosing animal, a chooser *par excellence*. Acting rationally, using appropriate means to achieve one's ends and also critically examining one's ends, involves essentially taking into account "costs" and "benefits," whereby "costs" and "benefits" are taken in the widest sense. Since resources are always scarce—last not least our limited lifetime—rational conduct is governed by principles of economics. Hence, it is plausible that new and important knowledge can be gained by applying the perspective of economics, the methods and conceptual tools of economics—some of them suitably generalized—to fields of inquiry that have traditionally been thought to lie outside the competence of economics. However, in order to be successful and to lead to substantial cognitive progress, this application has to be accompanied by methodological reflection on the merits and limitations of the tools that are either imported from economics or are an extension of economic concepts. It involves a critical analysis of the explanatory power and the unifying potential of the economic approach and of economics as a general social science that aims at explaining and predicting the behavior of living systems in general, of groups and associations, and of the functions and workings of institutions and organizations in the environment. The economic approach obviously competes, and sometimes collaborates, with approaches used by other disciplines. It uses certain assumptions like that of rational behavior, the scarcity of available resources, competing ends, and the interdependence of feedback systems with limited information available to the many interacting participants.

The fields to which the economic approach or perspective has been applied over the last thirty or forty years include politics, sociology, ethnology, law, biology, psychology, and so forth. In this volume a number of scientists and scholars, each of whom has gained an international reputation in his special field of study, explore the potential of the economic approach to human behavior in various areas outside the traditional fields of economics. Such a wide range of studies applying the economic approach to various areas of human life that lie outside the traditional realm of economics have never before been assembled in one place. Each chapter focuses on a different field of study, and the chapters are unified through the economic approach. All the papers are original and with the exception of Peter Bernholz's paper, which will be published simultaneously in a special journal, they are here published for the first time. The papers are original also in the sense that they do not intend merely to review the development of the economic approach in the various fields of study concerned; they make themselves an original contribution. The book is primarily intended for all those interested in the possibilities of the economic approach, but it is intended also for advanced undergraduate and postgraduate students of the various fields of inquiry that form the subject matter of the volume, i.e., for students of political science, law, sociology, psychology, contemporary history, the general philosophy of science and the special methodology of economics. Readers from other disciplines may also find it interesting and useful because it is often surprisingly instructive to examine a problem, especially a familiar problem, from an entirely fresh angle. For the benefit of the hurried reader, each of the chapters has been provided with an abstract, and the *abstracts* have been gathered and placed in the prefatory material.

Part *I* consists of three papers that introduce the reader to the economic approach. Part *II* applies the approach to the study of history, including contemporary history and voting behavior. Part *III* focuses on key problems of sociology, on the evolution of certain institutional, in particular, legal frameworks, and on the attitude towards life time. Part *IV* uses the economic approach in the study of the social aspects of science and the methodology of research. Part *V* applies the economic approach to problems of political science and to politics: to conflict, autocracy, and the central problems of the constitution of a democracy.

The volume is the result of a workshop that led up to a colloquium held in Vienna at the Hotel Ambassador 7–10 June 1984. The colloquium was made possible by the generosity of the PWPA (Professors World Peace Academy, European Branch). The editors acknowledge with deep gratitude the efforts and enthusiastic cooperation of all participants involved. Our thanks go, above all, to Dr. Heinrich Weber, the Secretary-General of the PWPA-European Branch, who not only made the entire project possible, but also watched over its development and helped it in every respect in an unbureaucratic way; and to Mr. Manfred Hauser, the Secretary-General of the PWPA-Austrian Branch, who saw to it that the participants' stay in Vienna was every bit as pleasant as one would expect. Our thanks also go to Mrs. Dorothea Hill, Professor Radnitzky's secretary, for struggling through a heavy load of secretarial responsibilities.

Gerard Radnitzky and Peter Bernholz

ABSTRACTS

M. T. GHISELIN: *PRINCIPLES AND PROSPECTS FOR GENERAL ECONOMY*

Biology and economics can be treated as two subdivisions of a single branch of knowledge called "general economy." This is defined as *the study of how the availability and utilization of resources affect the structure and activity of organized beings.* "Bioeconomics" deals with the common interests of economists and biologists. A good example is the principles of the division and combination of labor. These apply to machines, anatomical structure, the behavior of all organisms, and the organization of complex social structures, including scholarly and academic ones. The prospects for progress in general economy are hampered by traditional institutional arrangements, but could be improved by judicious investment in infrastructure.

JOHN GRAY: *THE ECONOMIC APPROACH TO HUMAN BEHAVIOR: ITS PROSPECTS AND LIMITATIONS*

In this short exploratory paper, which has four sections, I have a two-fold theoretical goal: to identify the central claims of the economic approach to "non-economic" behavior; and to specify the most important limitations of the scientific research program which this approach yields. Accordingly, in the first section I aim to state the core theses of the economic approach in an exact way. In Sections Two and Three, I assess the application of the economic approach to my own discipline, political science, and the relations of "economic" explanations with the evolutionary and functionalist explanations found in Hayekian theory and sociobiology. In the fourth section, I consider some of the principal difficulties of the economic approach which might compromise its aspiration to become the unifying theory of the social sciences. In the conclusion, I make some remarks as to the comparative prospects of the economic approach in its competition with its main theoretical rivals. I conclude that, if the economic approach fails completely to explain the behavior of individuals, this is a limitation of all social-scientific explanations, and not just of the economic approach.

LOUIS DE ALESSI: *NATURE AND METHODOLOGICAL FOUNDATIONS OF SOME RECENT EXTENSIONS OF ECONOMIC THEORY*

Recent advances in economic theory, stimulated by serious limitations of the neoclassical framework, have greatly extended the theory's range of application, not only to a broader range of phenomena within the traditional domain of economics, but also to new and important fields previously dominated by other disciplines. From a methodological perspective, these advances are particularly promising because they stem from the reduction of economic theory to a simpler, more general construct that enhances the substantive content of the theory and establishes a more powerful base for further generalizations.

The paper contains five sections. Section I develops the methodological approach used, which may be described as Popperian positivism, within the context of economic theory and practice. Section II opens with a brief discussion of neoclassical economic theory, defined as the conjunction of the utility maximization theory of consumer choice and the profit maximization theory of the firm. Some of the theory's limitations are then noted, focusing on the failure to predict accurately and consistently the production and pricing choices of privately-owned firms and to even address the increasingly important sector of the economy encompassing nonproprietary business organizations (e.g., firms owned or regulated by government, mutuals, and all other nonprofits). The analysis then establishes the methodological foundations for neoclassical theory's current reformulation, which is simply the generalization of the utility maximization hypothesis to all (individual) choices under constraints, taking explicit account of the constraints imposed by the structure of property rights and the nature of transaction costs.

Section III presents a detailed analysis of the nature and significance of the structure of property rights and of positive transaction (including information) costs. In particular, it explores the consequences of private, usufruct, and common ownership rights and develops the view that business firms arise to solve the shirking-information problem of team production. The analysis is then used to examine the effect of transaction costs on the choice of organizational form, contractual

3

arrangements, and business practices, highlighting the simplification and increased substantive content of the theory.

Section IV employs this reformulation of neoclassical theory to investigate the nature and economic consequences of recent trends in the legal rules of products liability. The analysis suggests that, in order to predict the range of activities brought within a firm (that is, the degree of vertical integration), the concept of shirking must be expanded to include behavior that results in injury to other members of the team, consumers-users, and third parties.

Section V contains a few concluding remarks.

R. E. MEINERS: *ECONOMIC CONSIDERATIONS IN HISTORY: THEORY AND A LITTLE PRACTICE*

Economic history, the application of economic analysis to historical events, has undergone substantial change in the last two to three decades, as the accepted methodology has shifted to an emphasis on the proper application of neoclassical economic theory. Prior to this change, economic historians were largely indistinguishable from other historians except in subject-matter specialization. Commentary about economic phenomena was mostly detached from formal economic analysis, as economic historians failed to share in the more powerful modes of economic analysis that developed in the twentieth century. The two "new schools" of economic history, that often share the rubric of the cliometrics school, emphasize econometrics, that is, empirical investigations of historical events subjected to economic analysis, and property-rights analysis, which emphasizes the identification of the institutional constraints needed to apply economic analysis successfully to understand historical phenomena. This paper discusses these developments and the criticisms levied by traditional economic historians against their techniques.

The second major portion of this paper is an application of the new property-rights analysis to a specific historical phenomenon, the explosive growth of the federal government in the United States in the twentieth century. The primary hypothesis posited is that the adoption of the Sixteenth and Seventeenth amendments to the federal constitution, allowing the imposition of federal income taxes and providing for the direct election of United States senators, were important institutional changes that helped trigger the growth of the federal government after 1913. The effects of the institutional constraints are discussed and some evidence of the impact of the change in constraints is presented.

A. F. HEATH: *THE ECONOMIC THEORY OF DEMOC-*
RACY: THE RISE OF LIBERALS IN BRITAIN

The major development in British politics in the postwar period has been the rise of the centrist Liberal party and the transformation from a two-party to a three-party system. This poses a major challenge to the economic theory of democracy, as most commentators have attributed the Liberal revival either to ideological shifts in the position of the Conservative and Labor parties or to an increasing volume of protest-voting, expressing dissatisfaction with government performance. If true, these explanations refute the fundamental axioms of the economic approach, namely, rational vote-maximizing political parties and rational utility-maximizing voters.

The paper begins by outlining the standard economic theory of democracy as developed by Anthony Downs, and by showing that an exogenous shift in voters' preferences from a bimodal to a trimodal distribution could account for the changes, while still retaining the axioms of the standard economic approach. Data from the series of British Election Studies is then used to test this economic theory of change, the ideological theory, and the protest theory.

The protest theory is found to be the most plausible of the three, since the data show little change either in voters' preferences or in the perceived positions of the parties. However, it is by no means clear that Liberal voting is correctly characterized as an irrational protest. A two-dimensional analysis of policy preferences shows that there is indeed a rational basis for Liberal voting, the main paradox being that so few of the people who agree with the Liberal party's position on the issues actually vote Liberal.

It is finally suggested that the diverse empirical results reported in the paper can be integrated if the economic approach is extended to include uncertainty. Thus, preferences for the Liberal position may be discounted because of the uncertainty of their likely performance in office, but the poor performance of the Conservative and Labor parties in office means that their relative advantage over the Liberals, on the grounds of experience, has been gradually eroded. The protest theory is therefore correct in attributing the rise of the Liberals to the increasing dissatisfaction with Labor and Conservative governments, but this can be easily accommodated within a rational-choice theory of political behavior.

6

J. S. COLEMAN: *NORMS AS SOCIAL CAPITAL*

Social norms are a staple of functionalist social theory rather than of rational-choice theory. However, their importance to the functioning of social systems means that unless rational-choice theory is to be blind to certain social phenomena, it should attempt to account for their existence and adherence to them. The former task especially is one largely unexamined.

The paper argues that social norms arise when an actor's action imposes externalities, positive or negative, on others, but markets in rights to control the action are impeded, making Coase's solution feasible. This premise is used to account for the extent of a norm's legitimacy, including legitimacy from the point of view of the actor in question, and for normative conflicts.

This premise, together with some results from work on agency, is used to predict what norms will be internalized rather than enforced by external sanctions. Finally, the paper argues that because actions with externalities are not governed by their consequences, barriers to social norms reduce social efficiency, and leave the system at a lower level of social efficiency than when norms are fully developed.

WALTER BLOCK: *TRADING MONEY FOR SILENCE*

There have been many attempts in the literature of legal philosophy to justify the prohibition against blackmail, and there have been numerous court cases, in widely disparate countries, which have found such activities illegal. But there exists no theoretical or judicial argument in support of the prohibition of blackmail which can satisfactorily be reconciled with the "rule of law" concerning individual freedoms and property rights.

In the classical understanding of rights and liberties, an individual may legitimately threaten to do that which he has an actual right to do. But blackmail is no more than the threat to exercise one's rights of free speech, to publicize, for example, information which might be harmful to the holder of a secret. In the absence of any demand for money to guarantee silence, there is no question but that such statements would be licit. Even when coupled with such a demand, it is argued below that the threat to expose a secret cannot be legitimately interpreted as illegal.

As well, this paper sharply distinguishes legitimate blackmail from illegitimate extortion, which is the demand for money based on the threat of carrying out an activity (arson, kidnapping, mayhem) which is clearly in *violation* of person or property. An historical analysis indicates that common-law prohibitions were originally focused on extortion alone, and that by an unwarranted extension, these laws came to be interpreted by the judiciary so as to forbid blackmail also; it is claimed, however, that no justification for this extension has been put forth.

8

H. G. MANNE: *INTELLECTUAL STYLES AND THE EVOLUTION OF AMERICAN CORPORATION LAW*

This paper is presented as a case study in the evolution of legal doctrine, with special emphasis to the field of corporation law in the United States. This field is especially interesting, because it incorporates important segments of three principal variants of legal rules used in the United States, common law, statutory enactments (both at the federal and state levels), and administrative regulation. In addition, it is a field that has been peculiarly influenced by both political and economic scholarship.

The earliest large American corporations, in the modern sense of having dispersed ownership, were the railroads. English common law was of little value in developing appropriate laws for this new challenge. As a result there evolved a series of rules adopted by state legislators that were in essence privately negotiated, so-called "special charters." Eventually this system became too cumbersome and too unrewarding for the legislators, and a general statutory system of semi-automatic corporate formation became universal in the United States. These statutes, which are still the basis of much American corporation law, were permissive in nature, requiring a minimum of disclosure in corporate Articles of Incorporation and few mandatory rules. Provisions could be "contracted out of," though generally the system functioned effectively as specified for larger corporations.

Academic and ideological complaint about the system as not being sufficiently democratic reached its height with the publication of the classic work by Berle and Means, *The Modern Corporation and Private Property* in 1932. This work was extremely timely, since political circumstances were correct for a major regulatory move on corporations, and in 1933 and 1934, the federal government adopted the first significant federal regulation of corporate financial activities.

The Berle and Means work dominated academic thinking for the next thirty years, and it supported the regulatory view that corporate managers, presumably including directors, could not be left to their own unregulated interests. Courts proved susceptible to this intellectual pressure and to the political developments. It is not surprising, therefore, that during the 30s, 40s and 50s, more rigorous legal standards for the duty owed by corporate managers to shareholders evolved.

9

Beginning in the early 1960s, however, these developments began to be examined from the perspective of modern economic theory. Much of this economics, crucial to an understanding of the operation of large corporations, was not available at the time Berle and Means wrote, and therefore much of the modern criticism of their work is misdirected. A combination of public choice theory, property-rights economics, transactions cost economics, and the modern theory of the firm all contributed significantly to the new economic paradigm of the corporation, now generally accepted by serious scholars of the field.

The economic view is that a variety of market constraints operate to make the system function efficiently without regulation and without significant judicial oversight. Careful empirical work strongly supports this view. Intellectual lag, especially among lawyers and law professors, however, has caused the distinguished American Law Institute recently to seek a further strengthening of the law in the direction implied by the old Berle and Means thesis. It is now an open question whether the emerging evolutionary-economic view of corporation law will be popularly understood quickly enough to prevent the adoption of an intellectual anachronism as the standard for the field.

ISAAC EHRLICH AND HIROYUKI CHUMA: *THE DEMAND FOR LIFE: THEORY AND APPLICATION*

While the desire to live may be unlimited, the demand for both quality and quantity of life must be limited by the finiteness of human resources. Economic theory has traditionally emphasized this conclusion in connection with the demand for conventional goods and services, or life's "quality." This discussion extends the scope of the economic methodology to apply to the choice of quantity or length of life as well. We view the determination of length of life as a choice variable which is affected, at least on the margin, not just by what nature or exogenous biological processes dictate, but also by what people do to maintain and preserve their health, or to protect themselves against a myriad of biological, environmental, and work-related hazards to their health and life.

Akin to the concept of demand in modern economic theory is the concept of "value." Indeed, we derive in this analysis qualitative and quantitative measures of the marginal value of life or the value of life-saving as shadow prices of optimal longevity or life-expectancy, depending upon whether we treat length of life as a certain or a stochastic variable (we do both).

The thrust of the paper is devoted to the discussion of the effects of variations in economic and demographic variables such as endowed wealth, health, innate ability or market-earning potential, and age on both the extent to which people will devote resources to increase their longevity or odds of survival, and on the "risk premium" they will place on exposing their lives and limbs to detrimental risks. We conclude with a few illustrations of the power of the analysis to explain actual variations in human longevity as well as specific aspects of occupational choices in which risk of injury and death are important factors.

11

M. T. GHISELIN: *THE ECONOMICS OF SCIENTIFIC DISCOVERY*

Disputes over the rationality of science may be resolved by substituting economic critieria of rationality for philosophical ones. Scientists are explorers, not prophets: they maximize discovery, not certitude. As producers and consumers of intellectual capital goods, it is not unreasonable for them to embrace an hypothesis before it has been fully tested. Departures from ideals may reflect time constraints and the needs for cheap and effective marketing. Authority is a cheap substitute for firsthand experience, not evidence for a social criterion of what is true. The broadly economic behavior of scientists provides criteria for deciding who should receive credit for a contribution. The reward system provides incentives for effectual communication and disincentives for cheating. The interests of science, academia, and government do not necessarily coincide, especially in the short term. Uncertainty, especially in the long term, provides a strong motive for objectivity.

GERARD RADNITZKY: *COST-BENEFIT THINKING IN THE METHODOLOGY OF RESEARCH*

What benefits may be gained from applying the CBA-frame, suitably generalized, in methodology? While CBA does not solve any methodological problems, it provides an organizing schema that helps the researcher to see which sorts of questions should be taken into account in a particular problem situation. Popperian methodology is viewed as an application of CBA to epistemic situations.

The paper has three introductory sections. Section I develops the theme that the principle of economy operates in all rational problem solving, and that all practical problems contain knowledge problems. Section II provides an explicatum of the concept of rational action. Section III deals with the general problem of when it is rational to tentatively "adopt" a particular position (hypothesis, theory, viewpoint, criterion, etc.) and when rational to put it into question. In dealing with cognitive problems, the context in which the problem is placed plays a decisive role. Methodological problems can be solved only if they are moved out of the justificationist context (the context of true belief), in which they have been placed by logical positivists and others, and placed in a non-justificationist or criticist context.

The main part of the paper is devoted to the problem of the rational handling of two sorts of positions: statements describing a single event (observation reports, so-called "basic statements") and universal statements or theories. This corresponds to two key problems of methodology: the "problem of the empirical base" and the problem of rational theory preference. With respect to the problem of the empirical "basis," CBA helps us to recognize that it is not a major problem of methodology, but a problem of epistemology; with respect to the problem of theory preference, CBA shows what exactly the problem consists of and legitimizes certain methodological rules for theory choice.

Section IV addresses itself to the problem of when it is rational to "adopt" a particular basic statement in the sense of regarding it as unproblematic at the moment, and when rational to put it into question. How can a particular basic statement be criticized? In the practice of research, the handling of basic statements does not involve any decision. In the methodological reconstruction it is advisable to reconstruct this handling as hinging upon an investment decision: when testing a theory T, whether or not to invest in processing a particular basic statement (potential falsifier of T) into a statement describing a reproducible event (falsifying hypothesis for T). CBA provides guidelines for this decision. The valuation of the costs of defending a basic statement that is problematic is objective. The various theses of Section IV are illustrated by examples.

Section V concerns itself with the problem of when it is rational to prefer a particular theory to its rival(s). Comparison of past performance in explaining and predicting enables us to make a conjecture about the problem-solving capabilities of the competitors. It is assumed that differences in this capability are due to differences in the ability to describe, to differences in comparative truthlikeness. The problem of rational theory preference includes part of the problem of rational problem preference (through the appraisal *ex post* of the relative "scientific importance" of the problems which one of the competing theories solves while its rivals do not), and it leads to the problem of allocation of resources to projects (through problem preference *ex ante*, which is the key issue of a research policy that is internal to science). The researcher as a "discovery-maximizing producer" orients himself on the estimated returns in new knowledge of different projects that compete for scarce resources of time and effort. The rational option for one of two competing theories is based upon a CBA where the valuation of benefits and costs is objective. Theory change is an objective process, at least in those fields of study where theorizing is closely controlled by empirical testing. In such basic science, a better theory drives out a less good theory. These theses and the usefulness of CBA are illustrated by examples culled from the history of science. The rational response to falsification is guided by CBA-considerations. The costs of defending a falsified theory or a theory that is less good than its competitor(s) are evaluated objectively. These costs are opportunity costs, epistemic resources forgone. The cost of immunizing strategies is loss of empirical content of the theory that is being tested. Opting for the less good theory forces one to reject the explanations that can be constructed with the help of the better theory and eventually to reject also that theory, which is tantamount to the loss of a valuable epistemic resource.

The researcher as an entrepreneur in discoveries has continuously to make methodological decisions, including risky investment decisions; he operates as a methodologist, whether he is aware of this or not. The CBA-frame helps him to articulate the various steps in the decision-making processes and, hence, makes them more criticizable. Therefore, the CBA-frame constitutes an epistemic resource for the researcher as well as for the professional methodologist.

JACK HIRSHLEIFER: *THE ECONOMIC APPROACH TO CONFLICT*

As defined here, conflict ensues when one or more competitors in life's contests adopt strategies of interfering with rivals—most obviously, by direct violence. Since under certain circumstances, strategies leading to conflict will rationally be chosen as ways of acquiring resources, conflict can be analyzed as an economic activity.

In general, there will be a greater likelihood of conflict, due to a smaller "potential settlement region" (PSR), when the parties have malevolent (rather than benevolent or merely neutral) *preferences*, when the respective *productive opportunities* are competitive (rather than complementary), and when *perceptions* of likelihood of victory are optimistic. While conflict is in part an educational process, forcing perceptions to converge over time toward more correct evaluations, this does not necessarily lead to settlement, owing to the asymmetrical effects upon the contending parties.

Different payoff environments, which can be pictured as game-theory matrices, lead to quite different solutions in terms of the balance of conflictual versus cooperative strategies. Three such environments are of great interest: Battle of the Sexes (BOS), Chicken or Hawk-Dove (HD), and Prisoner's Dilemma (PD).

Assuming unsophisticated play, the respective *evolutionary equilibria*—i.e., the population proportions that represent stable Nash equilibria—are as follows: (1) With BOS as payoff environment, depending upon the starting-point, the population will evolve toward coordinated choice of one or the other of the mutually (though unequally) beneficial outcome-pairs. (2) Under HD, the population evolves toward a mixed solution, in which costly conflict encounters occur a percentage of the time. (3) Under PD, the population evolves toward entirely uncooperative behavior. More sophisticated play leads to a variety of partial or total escapes from these different "cooperation traps," depending upon the payoff environment involved and also upon the details of the interaction protocol. (E.g., how often will the game be repeated? Can one or more parties adopt contingent or commitment strategies? Are the moves chosen simultaneously or sequentially?)

Viewed as an "industry," military conflict for resources is characterized by a balance of increasing versus decreasing returns. There tend to be *increasing returns* within any sufficiently limited geographical

15

area, since victory and defeat feed on themselves. On the other hand, there tend to be *decreasing returns* to the projection of military power over distance. The balance of these two forces explains the system of nation-states, in which one authority has overwhelmingly dominant power in a home domain, but frontiers persist along which competing powers are more or less equal. The potential for achieving power by violent struggle also helps explain the internal structure of organizations, e.g., when hierarchical versus egalitarian systems can be expected to emerge.

GORDON TULLOCK: *AUTOCRACY*

Most governments in the world today, and in most times in history, have been dictatorships or monarchies, both of which are covered by the word "autocracy." Social scientists have done very little in studying these very common forms of government. The author of this paper is currently working on a book dealing with this subject and this paper is part of the preliminary work. This paper deals with only one problem which faces an autocrat, the problem of remaining in power in spite of the fact that he is surrounded by high-ranking officials who would be delighted to replace him as dictator.

No formal theory is developed because, unfortunately, the author is unable to think of a complete theory. A consistent approach drawn from *Public Choice* is implemented, however, and the problems facing the autocrat, together with various techniques which have been traditionally used by dictators, are examined.

PETER BERNHOLZ: *A GENERAL CONSTITUTIONAL POSSIBILITY THEOREM*

Given any non-oligarchic assignment of rights to decide among all pairs of outcomes to any subsets of society, and given corresponding non-stochastic decision rules for these subsets, it is known following Arrow and Sen, respectively, that there exists at least one profile of individual preferences such that 1) intransitive and cyclical social preferences are present, and 2) Pareto-optimal outcomes are dominated by non-Pareto-optimal outcomes in these cycles. The present paper, by contrast, takes any profile of individual preferences as given and the assignment of rights to subsets of society (the non-oligarchic constitution) as variable. It is shown that 1) there always exists an assignment such that cyclical and intransitive social preferences are not present, 2) there is always a purely liberal constitution (which may, however, be oligarchic) but not a constitution with total direct democracy of this kind, and 3) any Pareto-optimal outcome can be most preferred by society.

Part I

PRINCIPLES AND PROSPECTS FOR GENERAL ECONOMY

MICHAEL T. GHISELIN

Perhaps the most significant act of synthesis in the history of the human intellect occurred in September of 1838, when Charles Darwin read a book on political economy by Thomas Malthus, and consequently laid the foundation for modern evolutionary biology. In retrospect this makes a certain amount of sense. That biology and economics deal with similar problems, using comparable principles, has not escaped the attention of perceptive intellects, including Karl Marx and Alfred Marshall. Resources, scarcity, and competition, together with the laws of nature that govern them, apply to all organisms everywhere, not just to ourselves. "Ecology" and "economics" are words that derive from the same root. Marshall affirmed that economics is a branch of biology in the broadest sense. The fact that economic laws and principles apply to solitary organisms implies that economics is not a social science. That they also apply to machines suggests that biology is a branch of economics. Given such considerations I have proposed (Ghiselin, 1978) that we recognize a branch of learning called "general economy." As two, coequal subunits it would have traditional economics, or political economy, on the one hand, and biology, or natural economy, on the other (see Hirshleifer, 1978a).

Scholarly disciplines have the character they do partly because of the history of investigation, and this may ill-reflect the actual and possible subject-matter. Economics has largely been the province of those interested in commerce and politics, and has been associated with the business schools. Biology, on the other hand, has been connected with natural history and medicine. Only in a few areas, such as agricultural economics and fisheries biology, have the two had obvious linkages, and even these have been rather tenuous. Although a few people, such as the physicist Alfred Lotka, have contributed to both, communication

21

between the two grand areas of investigation has been remarkably infrequent, and superficial at that. A substantial amount of jargon has been transferred, but real advances in ecology have largely resulted from the independent discovery of what had long been available in the standard works and even elementary textbooks on economics (see, for example, Tullock, 1971). Only in the last few years has there been an attempt on the part of biologists to apply, deliberately and on a whole-sale basis, the principles of economics to their science (Ghiselin, 1974a). In my own case it was only after having worked on certain recondite problems in anatomy and ecology that it dawned upon me that *The Wealth of Nations* had something to offer. Within economics, Alchian's (1950) inspired notion that a kind of natural selection affects the firm was likewise only intended as a refinement of traditional theory. Even now, the fine contribution of Nelson and Winter (1980) to evolutionary economics owes little to biology proper. It was largely the work of Hirshleifer (1978) that brought the opportunities for synthesis to the attention of economists.

A similar development occurred when Rubin (1971) and others applied evolutionary and economic thinking to the common law. Once more it began as an effort to solve a technical problem, but grew and developed into a major effort to expand the horizons of economics. At a meeting in Miami in 1980, these separate enterprises were brought together (see the proceedings in *Research in Law and Economics, Volume 4, 1982*). But this is only the beginning. Economic laws apply to everything that is subject to natural selection in the broadest sense. This includes cultural entities of every sort. Thus, the splitting of languages into dialects and then into new languages has numerous parallels with the process we biologists call "speciation" (Ghiselin, 1974b). Indeed, it is a most instructive exercise to see how far one can apply economic ways of thinking to every organized object in the world—to every living creature, to every group of them, to all of their parts, productions, and activities.

The possibility of such an expanded enterprise suggests that we may even have to redefine "economics," though one would hope without doing violence to the original meaning of that term. It seems to me that defining economics in terms of choice (see the article by Manne in the present volume) is too restrictive. Even traditional economics considers situations in which no choice has been exercised. Therefore we might consider the following: *General economy is the study of how the availability and utilization of resources affect the structure and activity of organized beings.* The definitions of such terms as "resource" and "organized" had best be left unspecified here. It is worth pointing out, however, that the various branches can be defined merely by specifying the kind of organized entities one has in mind. Perhaps we will need special terms for economic approaches to such areas as linguistics and the law. For my own area of greatest interest, the term "'bioeconomics" is already in use. It has good parallels in "biochemistry" and "biomechanics." Although bioeconomics is often confused with sociobiology, the two are by no means the same. It is possible to study societies without considering economic aspects. Of greater significance, bioeconomics is more general than sociobiology, as it deals with solitary organisms in addition to social ones, and with parts such as organs and cells. The notion that sociobiology will somehow preempt the rest of biology and economics as well is utterly illogical. The more general is not to be subsumed under the more particular. Furthermore, contemporary sociobiology generally emphasizes a certain kind of genetics, and sometimes has an ideological or even quasi-religious aspect that many find objectionable. Some people find bioeconomics attractive because it provides an alternative. One can study it without reference to genetics, especially with respect to learned behavior. To bioeconomics, genes are just one of many resources and constraints.

The parallels among the various branches of general economy are not metaphorical or merely analogical. Were that the case, then the study of different kinds of objects from the economic point of view would be no more than heuristical. Of course the heuristical value exists, and justifies the approach. The fundamental point here is that the different kinds of objects studied are all subject to the same basic laws of nature, and differ only with respect to particulars and special conditions. By expanding the scope of economics we attain arguments grounded upon coherence and consilience. The laws can be tested by reference to a broader range of materials. Insofar as the different kinds of evidence point to the same conclusions, we vastly benefit from their joint and independent implication. To put this in more concrete terms, we gain the sort of benefit that physics did when its laws were made to apply to all matter, whether earthly or terrestrial, and that biology did, when taxonomy and biogeography were brought together by the principle of common ancestry. "One universe, one economy, one economics" (Ghiselin, 1974a).

The dissolution of artificial disciplinary boundaries suggests the possibility of solving problems of the highest interest. Biology and economics each have a body of theory and technique, built up for the most part independently. Theories developed in the one area may be applied, developed, or tested in the other. We biologists, for example, tend to think on a much longer time scale than economists do—often literally hundreds of millions of years—and we have a great deal of experience with selective mechanisms. Economists on the other hand have a vastly superior understanding of competition in all of its ramifications. The empirical data are equally intriguing. Human culture, behavior and economic activity are far more complicated in most respects than are their counterparts in other species. Because plants and animals are simpleminded at best, we can leave foresight largely out of consideration when studying them. Likewise, the very sophistication of human behavior opens up a whole range of possibilities that do not exist elsewhere.

Let us now consider a concrete example, namely, how we can apply the principle of the division of labor to bioeconomics and political economy alike. As in my essay,"The Economy of the Body" (Ghiselin, 1978), things will be kept simple and nontechnical for the sake of the exposition. It is remarkable how little economists have done with the division of labor, in spite of the fact that it was fundamental to the work of Adam Smith. He gives only three advantages to the division of labor. In the first place, it increases dexterity through practice. Second, it saves on the time necessary for switching tasks. Third, the resulting attention to detail leads to invention. Little has been added in the subsequent economic literature. We should mention, however, that social scientists have given us some dubious possibilities. Durkheim (1933) thought that the division of labor exists in order to bring the members of society together. Marxists have treated it as a means of keeping them apart. One may observe a division of labor among such objects as the blades of a pocketknife. Clearly that kind of social function fails here, though one might want to dispute what to make of it. The neglect of the division of labor by economists is evident from the fact that they generally assumed that the more minutely labor is divided the better. Herbert Spencer made this assumption one basis for his theory of necessary progress. Biologists likewise have used it as a criterion for what is a "higher" organism.

Again, remarkably little has been done with the principle of the division of labor by biologists since it was introduced into the literature by the Belgian physiologist Henri Milne-Edwards (1851 and other works). It is frequently remarked upon in passing, and, especially in works on social insects, treated descriptively. However, there seems to have been no serious effort to develop the principle before my own (Ghiselin, 1974a). I pointed out that it is advantageous to divide labor or to combine it according to the particular situation. Activities that interfere with each other should be divided, those that complement each other should be combined. This insight arose out of my research on the evolution of hermaphroditism. In separate-sexed animals like ourselves (gonochorists), labor is divided. In hermaphrodites, including many flowers and snails, it is combined. In my early research on hermaphroditic snails (Ghiselin, 1966), I noted that the primitive ones were equipped with a single genital duct, so that the male and female functions occurred in the same organ and eggs and sperm tended to get misdirected. At a later evolutionary stage the single duct divided into two separate ones serving male and female functions. At that time I was studying the division of labor but was blissfully unaware of it. In this case it was what I later called the "spatial division of labor": different tasks in different places. The other kind, the temporal division of labor, was developed much later, in the form of the "size-advantage model" for organisms that change sex (Ghiselin, 1969). Once again, I did not realize that this was economics at the time. Be this as it may, we can treat it graphically in a manner familiar to economics (Figure1.1). Here reproductive success (RS) on the vertical axis is plotted against body-size on the horizontal axis. Giving different values to RS for males and females, we hypothesize a condition in which the

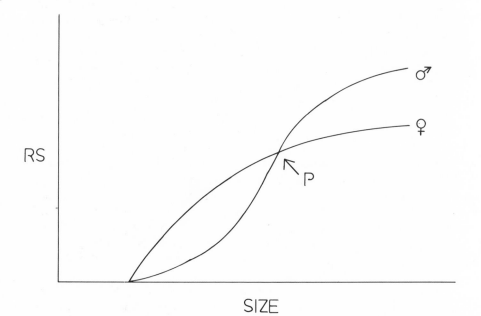

FIG. 1.1: **The size-advantage model for sex-changes in fish and other organisms. Reproductive success (RS) is a function of body size. Change from female to male occurs at P.**

relative ability to reproduce changes with growth. In many cases this happens because the large males are more effective at fighting, and monopolize the females. Changing at P (the indifference point) gives maximal RS over the life of the animal. Note that many refinements are called for here. For one thing, there may be a cost of retooling, or downtime, while the animals are changing sex. This model has been remarkably successful, and is the paradigm (in the sense of a starting-point and an exemplar) for much work on sex-allocation theory (see Charnov, 1982). It applies to a remarkably wide diversity of organisms, and has led to the discovery that sex-switches are far more common than anybody had suspected. But more importantly it has been varied, refined, and supplemented. It covers both female-male and male-female switches (respectively, protogyny as is common in coral reef fishes, and protandry, known among others in shrimp and snails). In a manuscript delayed in press for several years (Ghiselin, 1986), I vary it to explain alternating hermaphroditism, switching repeatedly back from one sex to the other as in certain oysters. Here the analogy is with someone who alternates between two jobs that tire two sets of muscles, for example, reading and gardening. Scale effects are known to biologists and economists alike. Very small animals can get along without a circulatory system. Firms experience economies and diseconomies of scale.

Combining labor allows simultaneous hermaphrodites to mate with any fertile conspecific organism. But it also imposes higher fixed costs, insofar as they have to possess the organs of both sexes. There is also the possibility of mating with one's self—something that organisms generally avoid except as a last resort. When we start dealing with more than one organism, the situation gets more complicated because we have to deal with both the competitive and the cooperative division of labor. The latter maximizes the output of a whole organism, and also of an entire firm, even when it means reducing the output of some part, such as an organ or an employee. The competitive division of labor leads to diverse firms in a free-enterprise economy or to a diversity of niches being occupied in a natural economy. Different principles have to be invoked to deal with them, and serious misunderstandings result if one confuses the two.

Let us consider how the same general principles apply to our own species, using academic man for an example, as will be done in a later chapter in this book. Scholars tend to specialize as knowledge accumulates, with ever minuter subdividing and multiplying of fields. It is generally assumed that this is a good thing, if perhaps not an unmixed blessing. There is a serious question as to whether it raises output by lowering quality. The most obvious drawback to specialization is that it may militate against creativity. Results in one discipline may be applicable to another one, but they must be known to be used. Academics give lip service to this notion, and generally try to impose breadth upon their students. To some extent, however, this may be an excuse for getting certain subjects taught, perhaps as a kind of make-work arrangement for researchers. Be this as it may, it is clear that we can apply Adam Smith's principle that the division of labor is limited by the extent of the market to how narrowly one can specialize. The larger the university, the greater the potential for concentration upon narrow areas of study, and the less the number of contacts outside one's area that he needs in order to keep from getting bored. An optimal range of scholarly activity from this point of view would be the maximum at which one could deal with the "important" literature and have it available for one's students. One needs only one kind of equipment, can readily tap into the grapevine, and is in a good position to find jobs for one's graduate students, to sabotage grant-proposals, and otherwise to control the sources of power. On the other hand, a specialist may not find an extensive enough market for the products of his teaching, if he floods it with an excessively homogeneous group of students. Indeed, he is apt to create competitors for himself and for one another. As the market becomes increasingly saturated, it pays to diversify, and this may mean becoming more of a generalist.

Adam Smith also adumbrated what I have said about the combination of labor. His example was the familiar matter of teaching and research. Someone who combines these two activities can read one book and apply the knowledge gained to both. Teaching is also a good learning experience, and a way to keep up with one's field and get paid for it. And it can bring in a certain amount of psychic income. On the other hand, the kind of teaching one does may, or may not, combine well with one's research. Scientists tend to do a more conscientious job at teaching graduate students than do their colleagues in the humanities. The reason has nothing to do with personality, but only means that in the sciences graduate students form a part of the research team. A condition of reciprocity is set up, and teachers have a vested interest in the quality of the students' education.

The structure of academic organizations militates against flexibility. The problem is particularly difficult for those who want to do something out of the ordinary. One might think, for example, that studying a science and its history would provide an effective combination, and to some extent it does. A scientist or teacher benefits from knowing the literature of his field, and in areas like anatomy this includes the older literature. So long as history remains an avocation, it is encouraged by academic scientists. But a serious research effort means crossing departmental boundaries, with all the disadvantages that entails. One is expected to teach, do research, and train graduate students in the same department. As a Berkeley zoologist, I was able to get a grant to study the history of comparative anatomy, but it was of no use for my zoologist graduate students, and did little for my department. To a certain extent, one can specialize in being a generalist. At one time that was what philosophers were expected to do. But as philosophy has become increasingly academic, it has largely abandoned that role. Either one philosophizes about philosophy, or one philosophizes about, say, science. In the latter case one either has to expend a great deal of effort finding out about science, or deal with a version of science that is merely a product of the creative imagination. A compromise between breadth and depth is apt to lead to superficiality. One solution here is to be narrow in several different fields. Another is to serve as a kind of intellectual middleman, but that can mean being content with evaluating and communicating the work of others, when what one really wants is the stimulus to creativity that comes with breadth. In my experience, evolutionary biology provides a very good base of operations for a generalist. All sorts of things evolve, and one has an excuse for devoting one's attention to any of them. General economy could function in much the same way.

Figure 1.1 can be adapted to the academic life, if, as was proposed in the original publication, we make the horizontal axis represent age rather than size. Different kinds of activities become relatively profitable as organisms get older. Consider teaching and research. Sometimes one gains more if one concentrates on research until one gains a certain amount of knowledge and experience. At a certain point it should become appropriate to switch from one role to the other. However, as teaching and research combine very well, we should expect a switch to the analogue of a simultaneous hermaphrodite! Such an arrangement occurs in a few sea-anemones, but the analogies are, to put it mildly, forced. All this really shows is that there are good economic reasons for changing activities in the course of one's career. Doing this effectually requires that one combine activities in an appropriate manner. One obvious strategem is to use one kind of experience as a resource when doing something else. This has been noteworthy in the founding of some new disciplines, such as molecular biology.

These considerations apply directly to our planning for the future development of general economy. Institutional structure constrains the flow of epistemic resources. For example, biology is vertically integrated with chemistry. Biologists have to know a lot of chemistry, but the relationship here is asymmetrical. Chemists do not have to know much biology. Hence the flow of epistemic resources tends to be upward toward higher integrational levels, and rarely downward. Nonetheless, a few chemists are interested in collaborating with biologists, for example, those who work on "natural products" (Faulkner and Ghiselin, 1983). A lack of horizontal integration is evident in systematic biology. Botanists and zoologists tend not to read each other's journals. One result is frictional forces that retard the flow of epistemic resources in much the same way that the language barriers do. Work on sex-switches in plants, for example, lagged considerably behind that on animals. The delay would have been considerably greater had not evolutionary ecology provided a stimulus for integrating horizontally.

As the situation currently exists, the various branches of general economy remain poorly integrated. The cost of integrating them may seem prohibitive. Most specialists are ill-disposed to learn a whole new discipline. They have enough work to do just keeping up with their own. However, costs might be kept down, if the fundamentals were emphasized rather than the details, and might be paid, if the prospects for a return upon the investment looked good enough. The opportunities should be made generally known to those who are most apt to sieze upon them. Some new institutional arrangements would seem to be called for. It may mean a series of interdisciplinary conferences or sessions at meetings of various professional societies. It may mean new courses and other academic amenities. A common language would help, as would a group of exemplary problems that could serve as a focus of attention for those with diverse backgrounds. Above all else, however, the opportunities for research should be identified and exploited, and the results communicated to those who will find them useful. Once the opportunities become generally known, it should be relatively easy to attract intellectual capital to the enterprise.

NOTES

I thank the John D. and Catherine T. MacArthur Foundation for support, and Gordon Tullock and Jack Hirshleifer for advice on the manuscript.

REFERENCES

Alchian, Armen A., "Uncertainty, Evolution and Economic Theory," *The Journal of Political Economy*, 58 (1950) 211–221.

Charnov, Eric L., *The Theory of Sex-Allocation*. Princeton: University Press (1982).

Durkheim, Emile, *The Division of Labor in Society*. New York: Macmillan (1933).

Faulkner, D. John, and Michael T. Ghiselin, "Chemical Defense and the Evolutionary Ecology of Dorid Nudibranchs and Some Other Opisthobranch Gastropods," *Marine Ecology Progress Series*, 13 (1983) 295–301.

Ghiselin, Michael T., "Reproductive Function and the Evolution of Opisthobranch Gastropods," *Malacologia*, 3 (1966) 327–378.

———— "The Evolution of Hermaphroditism among Animals," *The Quarterly Review of Biology*, 44 (1969) 189–208.

———— *The Economy of Nature and the Evolution of Sex*, Berkeley: University of California Press (1974a).

———— "A Radical Solution to the Species Problem," *Systematic Zoology*, 23 (1974b) 536–544.

———— "The Economy of the Body," *American Economic Review*, 68 (1978) 233–237.

———— (1986). "Evolutionary Aspects of Marine Invertebrate Reproduction," Arthur C. Giese and John S. Pearse, Eds., *Reproduction of Marine Invertebrates*, Vol. 9., Palo Alto: Blackwell.

Hirshleifer, Jack, "Natural Economy Versus Political Economy," *Journal of Social Biological Structures*, 1 (1978a) 319–337.

———— "Economics from a Biological Viewpoint," *Journal of Law and Economics*, 20 (1978b) 1–53.

Nelson, Richard R., and Sidney B. Winter, *An Evolutionary Theory of Economic Change.* Cambridge: Harvard University Press (1982).

Rubin, Paul H, "Why is the Common Law Efficient?" *Journal of Legal Studies,* 6 (1977) 51-65.

Tullock, Gordon, "The Coal Tit as a Careful Shopper," *American Naturalist,* 105 (1971) 77–80.

THE ECONOMIC APPROACH TO HUMAN BEHAVIOR: ITS PROSPECTS AND LIMITATIONS

JOHN GRAY

INTRODUCTORY REMARKS

In this short exploratory paper, which has four sections, I have a two-fold theoretical goal: to identify the central claims of the economic approach to "non-economic" behavior; and to specify the most important limitations of the scientific research program, which this approach yields. Accordingly, in the first section I aim to state the core theses of the economic approach in an exact way. In Sections Two and Three, I assess the application of the economic approach to my own discipline, political science, and the relations of "economic" explanations with the evolutionary and functionalist explanations found in Hayekian theory and sociobiology. In the fourth section, I consider some of the principal difficulties of the economic approach which might compromise its aspiration to become the unifying theory of the social sciences. In the Conclusion, I make some remarks as to the comparative prospects of the economic approach in its competition with its main theoretical rivals.

I THE ECONOMIC APPROACH DEFINED

"The Value, or Worth of man, is as of all other things, his Price; that is to say, so much as would be given for the use of his Power: and therefore is not absolute; but a thing dependent on the need and judgement

33

of another . . . . And as in other things, so in men, not the seller but the buyer determines the Price. For let a man (as most men do) rate themselves as the highest Value they can; yet their true Value is no more than it is esteemed by others." (Thomas Hobbes, *Leviathan,* Ch. 10)

Gary Becker, the preeminent contemporary theorist of the economic approach, has defined its central content in a clear statement: "The combined assumptions of maximizing behavior, market equilibrium and stable preferences, used relentlessly and unflinchingly, form the heart of the economic approach as I see it."[1] Elsewhere, Becker has asserted that " . . . everyone more or less agrees that rational behavior simply implies consistent maximization of a well-ordered function, such as a utility or profit function."[2] There seem to be several distinct elements in Becker's characterization of the economic approach. There is, first of all, *a postulate of maximization:* human behavior is understood to be the outcome of a maximizing strategy, that is to say, it expresses the attempt to achieve the greatest satisfaction of preferences with a *given* expenditure of resources or to achieve a given level of satisfaction of preferences with the least expenditure of resources. Note that this is a stronger postulate than many that are often made about human behavior. It is far stronger than the "rationality principle" invoked by Popper in his advocacy of the method of situational analysis: this method, which Popper asserts "is the method of economic analysis," though it has applications to "the 'logic of power',"[3] seeks to understand human conduct as a response to the situation in which the agent conceives himself to be. This agent has goals as well as beliefs about his situation, but his behavior is not here theorized as emerging from any maximizing strategy: the agent's goals or preferences may, indeed, not even be consistently ordered and they often fail to square with his beliefs about available options. Popper's postulate of rationality is far weaker than Becker's postulate of maximization, then, but it is not for that reason weak in the sense of being empty or trivial: for it suggests at least that human behavior is not adequately captured as a conditioned reflex or as a programmed response to mechanical stimuli, and it invites the effort to grasp how the agent conceives his predicament. Beyond that, of course, Popper's method looks to the unintended consequences of human actions, but that is a different matter.

It is, perhaps, worth noting that many economists are closer to Popper in their account of rationality than they are to Becker. The economists of the Austrian School, in particular, have contested the restriction of economic rationality to *homo economicus* imposed by Becker and other economists in the Chicago tradition. Allocating resources or economizing on means to ends is, the Austrians insist, only one aspect of action itself: action is, for these economists, necessarily or definitionally purposeful or goal-oriented, but it is a fiction to suppose that the agent has anything resembling a complete ordering of his preferences, or a complete knowledge of the options available to him. Indeed, von Mises goes so far as to argue against transitivity (consistency) of preferences being made a necessary element of rational choice.[4] The central contention of the Austrians against the Chicago School, that assumptions about maximization and consistency or completeness of preference orderings are contrary to fact, and unnecessary to the project of theorizing behavior as rational, raises questions about the role of realism in social and economic theory to which I shall return later. At this stage, I wish to observe that, even if Becker's postulate of maximization be abandoned and a weaker requirement of rationality adopted as part of the economic approach, it is still at once substantive and controversial: for it proposes applying the same postulate of rationality, maximizing or otherwise, to all human behavior, whether or not it is ordinarily viewed as akin to behavior in the marketplace. It proposes to extend the economic theories of consumer choice, capital formation and trade, that is to say, into areas (such as marriage, fertility, crime, and politics) which have traditionally been conceived as intelligible only by reference to rationality principles distinct from those invoked to theorize the marketplace. This remains a rich and important claim even if Becker's maximizing assumption is dropped.

The extension of the rationality principles underlying the orthodox theory of the market to other areas of social interaction involves using a second distinct element in the economic approach, namely, that of *the implicit market*. It is proposed that social exchanges of a sort not categorially different from those that occur in a conventional market may occur outside it—in criminal behavior or sexual relations, for example—in the absence of many features (money prices, for example, or legal property rights) which structure market behaviors of the ordinary sort. Of course, conventional markets may come in many shapes and forms, and so may implicit markets, but the idea of social interactions as being theorizable across the board as exchanges involving implicit prices for goods or services is what distinguishes this second element in the economic approach. In Becker's account, again, there is a stronger contention, that of market equilibrium, which many other economists, especially Austrians and Keynesians, would wish to question in its uses in macroeconomic theory and whose translation into a microeconomic theory of "non-economic" behavior they would seek to resist. But we need not accept Becker's assumption that implicit markets tend to equilibrium to acknowledge the usefulness and illuminating power of the idea of an implicit market itself. In Becker's own work, it has shown itself to have an extraordinary predictive and explanatory power in the theory of marriage and fertility. As Becker's work in this area has been summarized:

> One of the great recent contributions to economic analysis has been a full application to the domestic sector of the analytic framework traditionally reserved for the firm and the consumer. In making the household a unit of production in the same right as the classical firm, its analytical bases are revealed to be identical to those of the firm. As in the firm, the two parties to a household (bound together for long periods by contract) avoid transaction costs and the risk of being deprived at any moment of the inputs of the other partner, or, for that matter, of the common output of the household. What *is* the household, if not the contractual engagement of two parties to furnish specific "inputs" and to share, in given proportions, the benefits of the combined "output"? Rather than incessantly and expensively renegotiating and supervising the innumerable contracts inherent in the exchanges of everyday domestic life, the two parties settle the general terms of the exchange in a longterm contract. It is a partnership of mutual control, that is, altogether like the classical firm. Owing to the small size of a family "firm" and the intimate knowledge which each partner possesses of the other's characteristics, the organization of a production team inside the household costs less (under this regime of mutual control) than it does under a regime of commercial tariffs in the market. The only element which distinguishes the classical firm analytically from the household is that, inside the household, the relationship between the partners can be desired for its own sake.

The third element in Becker's conception of economic approach, *the postulate of stable preferences*, seems again unnecessarily demanding. Clearly, any social or economic theory must—if it is not to belong entirely to what Hayek has called the "pure logic of choice"[6]—work with some general suppositions as to the content of human desires and their relative stability. If by stability of preferences Becker intends to postulate their fixity, however, it is unclear that this is any necessary part of economic approach. Consumer choice theory seems to get along without such a strong postulate, and all that seems to be needed is the assumption that human beings have goals and preferences incompletely ordered and far from perfectly mapped even onto their patchy knowledge of their own circumstances—which they have a strong tendency to try to satisfy. In this effort to satisfy their preferences, the economic approach contends, they are as likely to make assessments of the costs and benefits to themselves of various social states in making decisions about which acquaintances to cultivate or which partner to marry as they are when buying a car or choosing a career. This seems to be the central content of the economic approach, and its empirical testability seems to be unaffected by whether it can be theorized in terms of the notion of human capital which Becker himself often employs. I will discuss the question of the predictive power of the economic approach in the last section of this paper.

II THE ECONOMIC APPROACH AS APPLIED TO POLITICAL BEHAVIOR: A REVOLUTIONARY PARADIGM?

" . . . in the first place, I put for a generall inclination of all mankind, a perpetuall and restlesse desire of Power after power, that ceaseth only in death. And the cause of this, is not always that a man hopes for a more intensive delight, than he has already attained to; or that he cannot be content with a moderate power; but because he cannot assume the power and means to live well, which he hath present, without the acquisition of more." (Thomas Hobbes, *Leviathan*, Ch. 10)

The theory of collective action developed independently of the economic approach and it contains distinct theoretical claims of its own. At the same time, it shares with the economic approach that conception of social explanation which invokes what Hardin has called "narrow rationality." As he puts it:

" . . . all too often we are less helped by the benevolent invisible hand than we are injured by the malevolent back of the hand; that is, in seeking private interests, we fail to secure greater collective interests. The narrow rationality of self-interest that can benefit us all in market exchange can also prevent us from succeeding in collective endeavours . . . . The argument of the logic of collective action is based on the strong assumption that individual actions are motivated by self-interest—or on the assumption of what I will commonly call narrow rationality or, more briefly, rationality."[7]

As it stands, this statement seems to me to be an exaggeration, and not to pick out the theoretical claims which distinguish collective action theory from the broader economic approach. For the propositions of collective action theory to hold, it is not necessary for agents to be moved solely or even mainly by self-interest: as Derek Parfit has shown in detail in the most notable contribution to moral philosophy of our century,[8] the logic of the Prisoner's Dilemma (which I take to be a central element in collective action theory) is present even where agents are all altruistic. What seems essential to this logic is only that, because the actions of many individuals are not so coordinated as to produce reliable expectations among them, each individual will have reason to act in a way which injures all. A pure form of the Prisoner's Dilemma is Hobbes's state of nature, in which each man must seek power over other men because he has no certainty that agreements will be kept and he needs power to protect his most basic interests. In Hobbes, the war of all against all results, not from natural aggression, but rather from the condition of uncertainty in which men find themselves without a sovereign power.

The rationality presupposed by collective action theory is not, then, the narrow rationality of self-interest or egoism. What, then, is it? It can best be called *calculational rationality* and may be contrasted with the rationality captured by Kantian universalizability or regularian behavior. The individual agent of collective action theory will not act, Kant-fashion, according to principles he can universalize, because he has no security that others will do likewise and, if he proceeds to govern his conduct by a Kantian ideal of rationality in defiance of this uncertainty, he will simply be destroyed, or at any rate, he is likely to be injured and even his moral goals thwarted. Nor, on the other hand, does the individual of collective action theory subscribe unreflectively to any code of conduct or moral convention. If he did, and his adherence to this code was highly resistant to erosion by the delinquencies of others, then many at least of the classical Prisoner's Dilemmas could not arise. (If the two criminals in the standard model belong to a criminal culture in which certain conventions of loyalty are given unquestioning support, it is hard to see how any Prisoner's Dilemma could arise—though it might, to be sure, arise in the relations of the criminal community with other communities). The individual of collective action theory, then, must be a calculator (even if he is not a maximizer) rather than a rule-follower.

There is much in collective action theory besides the game-theoretic exploration of Prisoner's Dilemmas. As Gordon Tullock's *The Social Dilemma*[9] shows, the analysis of the demand and supply of public goods, the tendency of small concentrated groups to collude against large dispersed groups and the problems associated with the emergence of stable conventions have thrown a good deal of light on political behavior. Much conventional political theory has been dominated by an ignorant contempt for market processes and an absurdly voluntaristic estimate of the possibilities of political action. One of the abiding achievements of the Virginia School, in which the research program of collective choice theory has been most fruitfully pursued, is to reveal political behavior as dominated by the same logic (though in a very different institutional context) as market behavior. Thus, we have seen a most interesting series of studies of the economics of bureaucracies, of policy-formation, of wars and revolutions, of charities and so on.[10] Again, as Robert Nozick has noted,[11] the application of an "economic" (or public choice) approach to voting behavior explains why the logic of political competition in democratic elections typically yields redistributional programs of which the middle classes are the greatest net beneficiaries. Finally, there is in the public choice version of the economic approach a potentially very powerful explanation of the stability of totalitarian regimes which has as yet been little developed. There have been several accounts of the process whereby the competition for votes in an unlimited democracy tends inexorably to destroy limited government and expand the sphere of state intervention. Much less explored are the dynamics of political and social interaction in totalitarian orders whereby a *political state of nature* is created with many of the properties of the Hobbesian war of all against all. In a circumstance of ubiquitous state power uncontrolled by the rule of law, where both the necessities of life and valued privileges are instantly revocable by political fiat, every agent is constrained as a matter of survival to collaborate with institutions and to sustain practices which harm him as well as everyone else. Thus, informing on neighbors may be preemptive[12] and part of a strategy for achieving or maintaining the supremely positional good of power without which all other goods are in a totalitarian order or insecure, while corruption and the ubiquitous black economy serve as indispensable guarantors of the stability of that order.[13] The atomization of social life in totalitarian states is often remarked upon, but the character of social life in such states as a vast, generalized Prisoner's Dilemma whose outcome is a stable political state of nature is less often observed and would greatly repay empirical investigation and theoretical study.

What are the limitations of the economic approach to political life, given that it is the most successful attempt thus far at a genuine science of politics? The economic approach has well-known difficulties in accounting for the decision to vote. Since the marginality of seats is rarely, if ever, extreme enough for a single vote to make a crucial difference to the outcome of an election, it is always, or almost always, a better use of time and resources for individuals if they chose not to vote and to attain their goals (egoistic or altruistic) by other means. Explaining the decision to vote, then, usually involves drawing on conceptions of expressive rationality rather than the sort of calculational reasoning I have identified as central to the economic approach. There is, however, a more general limitation of the economic approach worth mentioning, namely its relative neglect of conventions as means of coordinating individual behavior. The element of convention which is so signally missing from Hobbes's political thought was introduced, within a framework of thought in most other respects essentially Hobbesian, by David Hume, when he argued that "common interest and utility beget infallibly a standard of right and wrong." Hume illustrates the principle by what has sometimes been called the Wagoner's Dilemma, whereby rules of the road emerge from repeated interactions of individual wagoners with each other that are in the common interest of all wagoners. As he puts it: "They cannot even pass one another on the road without rules. Wagoners, coachmen, and postilions have principles, by which they give way; and these are chiefly founded on mutual ease and convenience. . . . That the lighter machine yield to the heavier, and, in machines of the same kind, that the empty yield to the loaded; this rule is founded on convenience."[14] This Humean account of the spontaneous development of conventions, and of the vital role of conventions in circumventing Prisoner's Dilemmas and coordinating social activity without constant recourse to coercion, has been given a recent statement by Ullman-Margalit in her neglected study *The Emergence of Norms*.[15] Does this phenomenon embody a serious challenge to the economic approach? Advocates of the economic approach to social and political life often deny that the emergence of conventions constitutes any important limitation to their framework. They do so by explaining the process of norm-generation as the outcome of a many-person iterated Prisoner's Dilemma—as the result, in other words, of a super-game in which it is calculational rationality itself that circumvents the recurrence of the Prisoner's Dilemma. Such explanations take us at once into areas of technical controversy in game theory which I am neither willing nor competent to arbitrate. At the same time, they bring us closer to the more fundamental challenge to the economic approach given by the emergence of conventions—namely, the invisible-hand explanation of these and other social formations as the results, not of human design, but of human actions filtered by an evolutionary process. How does the economic approach stand, then, as compared with an evolutionary scheme of social explanation? And what are the distinctive theoretical claims made by exponents of the evolutionary approach? Let us see.

III THE ECONOMIC APPROACH, EVOLUTIONARY SOCIAL THEORY AND THE CLAIMS OF SOCIOBIOLOGY

It is true, that certain living creatures, as Bees, and Ants, live sociably one with another, (which are therefore by Aristotle numbred amongst Politicall creatures;) and yet have no other direction, than their particular judgements and appetites; not speech, whereby one of them can signifie to another, what he thinks expedient for the common benefit: and there-fore some man may perhaps desire to know, why Mankind cannot do the same. To which I answer,

First, that men are continually in competition for Honour and Dignity, which these creatures are not; and consequently amongst men there ari-seth on that ground, Envy and Hatred, and finally Warre; but amongst these not so.

Secondly, that amongst these creatures, the Common good differeth not from the Private; and being by nature enclined to their private, they procure thereby the common benefit. But man, whose Joy consisteth in comparing himselfe with other men, can relish nothing but what is eminent.

Thirdly, that these creatures, having not (as man) the use of reason, do not see, not think they see any fault, in the administration of their com-mon businesse: whereas amongst men, there are very many, that thinke themselves wiser, and abler to govern the Publique, better than the rest; and these strive to reforme and innovate, one this way, another that way; and thereby bring it into Distraction and Civill warre.

Fourthly, that these creatures, though they have some use of voice, in making knowne to one another their desires, and other affections; yet they want that art of words, by which some men can represent to others, that which is Good, in the likenesse of Evill; and Evill, in the likeness of Good; and augment, or diminish the apparent greatnesse of Good and Evill; discontenting men, and troubling their Peace at their pleasure.

Fifthly, irrationall creatures cannot distinguish betweene *Injury* and *Dammage;* and therefore as long as they be at ease, they are not offended with their fellowes: whereas Man is then most trouble-some, when he is most at ease: for then it is that he loves to shew his Wis-dome, and controule the Actions of them that governe the Common-wealth.

Lastly, the agreement of these creatures is Naturall; that of men, is by Covenant only, which is Artificiall: and therefore it is no wonder if there be somwhat else required (besides Covenant) to make their Agreement constant and lasting; which is a Common Power, to keep them in awe, and to direct their actions to the Common Benefit. (Thomas Hobbes, *Leviathan*, Ch. 17)

How might the economic approach conflict with an evolutionary approach to the understanding of human behavior? It might do so, in the first place, in virtue of the methodologically individualist character of economic explanations and because there is a possibility that evolutionary explanations cannot be given a methodologically individualist form. Nozick has noted[16] that invisible-hand explanations are hard to cast in such a form and there seems to be a real tension in Hayek's version of evolutionary social theory with his own methodological individualist commitments. Stated at its crudest, the difficulty is that evolutionary explanations have as their primitive unit, not the acting individual of the economic approach, but either the genetic lineage or the population. Certainly in the work of the later Hayek,[17] social evolution proceeds by the natural selection, not of individuals, but of social groups or populations via the practical competition of their codes of conduct. I do not want here to inquire whether a conception of social or cultural evolution in terms of the natural selection of groups or populations can be squared with the dominant neo-Darwinian orthodoxy in philosophical biology or, if not, whether that matters. My point is rather that there seems to be a definite divergence between a form of methodological individualism—the contemporary variant of Hobbes's resolutive-compositive method—which takes human actions as being the terminal level of explanation of social events (even if it is alert to the generation of social order by the unintended consequences of human actions) and an evolutionary approach which accounts for the human subject itself, its preferences and choices, in terms which appeal to theoretical entities "smaller" (the gene) or "greater" (the population) than the individual. The research program of the evolutionary approach deconstructs the human individual, so to speak, in a way that disqualifies treating individual actions, choices, preferences, etc., as termini in social explanation.

There is another side to the problem. An evolutionary approach, such as Hayek's, which treats social institutions as emergent properties of human actions tends almost inevitably to yield forms of holistic explanation which again displace human agency from explanatory primacy. The problem is deepened when, as in Hayek, there is a strong emphasis on the rationality of purposeless rule-following. Hayek's idea here is that social institutions may be regarded as vehicles or embodiments of tacit knowledge about society: moral and practical traditions, customs and conventions are not intelligible as means or instruments adopted to achieve known ends, but rather embody knowledge available in articulate or explicit form to none of the individuals who participate in them. The tension with the economic approach is here two-fold. On the one hand, in suggesting not only that men do, but that they are rational to, follow inherited social rules blindly, because of the theoretically irretrievable knowledge stored in such rules, the Hayekian schema disfavors the conception of practical rationality as instrumental calculation which is at the heart of the economic approach. On the other hand, in holding that individual behavior is always mostly behavior in accordance with inherited rules, and in conceiving social evolution in terms of a natural selection of such rules, Hayek's approach seems to inhibit any explanation of the rules themselves that is couched in straightforwardly economic terms.

We ought not to conclude from this, however, that Hayek's approach necessarily prevails over the economic approach, nor even that the two are unavoidably divergent at all important points. It may be, as Gary Becker has suggested to me, that the evolutionary approach is fruitful only over very long stretches of historical time, whereas the economic approach can illuminate social changes spanning decades and centuries. In addition, Hayek's approach has difficulties of its own, which are not found in the economic approach. It has, to begin with, all the difficulties of functionalism in social explanation. Functionalist explanation, whether it be found in the writings of Parsons, Hayek or in a Marxist such as G. A. Cohen,[18] is a species of teleological explanation which has been successfully expelled from the natural and the life sciences: why should we suppose it to be appropriate in the human sciences? Despite efforts to rebut their argument, I cannot but think that the devastating criticisms of functionalism in biology and in social theory by Monod[19] and Elster,[20] respectively, are entirely conclusive. As I have myself argued elsewhere,[21] Cohen's effort to recast Marxian historical materialism in Darwinian functionalist form founders on the fact that it seeks to explain transitions from one productive mode to another by a principle—the filtering out of inefficient productive arrangements—which has an institutional mechanism in only one mode of production, that of the capitalist market economy. Functionalist social theory neither provides any general account of the mechanisms of social adaptation nor even any clear criterion of what "equilibrium" or "adaptation" amount to in social systems.

A different problem with Hayekian evolutionist social theory is that the presumption that long-standing social practices have important utilities or social functions is sometimes defeated. Olson, in his account of the causes of contemporary stagnation, identifies a crucial difficulty in the Hayekian conservative argument to the utility of ancient traditions when he observes that " . . . there is an 'internal contradiction' in the development of stable societies. This is not the contradiction that

Marx claimed to have found, but rather an inherent conflict between the colossal economic and political advantages of peace and the longer-term losses that come from the accumulating networks of distributional coalitions that can survive only in stable environments."[22] Olson's insight is that a stable framework of legal rules, though it is a necessary condition of economic growth, at the same time permits the formation of collusive interest groups whose activities inhibit growth. Occasional catastrophes—defeat in war, or revolutionary upheavals—are then necessary to disrupt the coalitions of interest groups which have slowly formed in periods of stability. If economic growth be adopted as a test of social utility, at any rate, then the stability conferred by an inheritance of slowly changing and stable rules may be far from optimistic. It seems to me that this problem, which may be only an instance of Elster's problem of the irrationality of evolution,[23] is one that the public choice variant of the economic approach is better fitted than Hayekian evolutionism to solve inasmuch as the public choice approach acknowledges explicitly the dependency of "efficient" social outcomes of an institutional framework which guarantee the conditions of voluntary exchange. A rationalist criticism of the evolutionary inheritance of rules and practices of the public choice school's neo-Hobbesian kind seems unavoidable and desirable, once we recognize that social evolution has no inherent tendency to throw up outcomes that are optimistic on any plausible criterion.

The predictive and explanatory power of the economic approach to political behavior seems great, then, especially as it has been theorized in the Virginia School, and to have important advantages over the Hayekian evolutionary schema. At the same time, this does not entail that the economic approach might not someday be unified with an evolutionary perspective. Becker has himself in a seminal paper[24] made fascinating suggestions as to how the economic approach might be linked with, and even embedded in socio-biological explanations of altruism, rule-following and so on. His proposal is that we treat kinship altruism, broadly egoistic preferences and time preferences as having evolved on account of their value as survival traits. The calculational mentality itself, when qualified by important rule-following behaviors, would seem ideally suited for this sort of evolutionary explanation. Much remains to be done in the area of overlap between the economic approach and sociobiology. Becker's own work, and that of such as Epstein in the theory of law,[25] suggest that it is not unreasonable to have high hopes of a science of human behavior in which the economic approach and sociobiology are seen as complementary rather than competitive. But could even such an integrated research program hope to yield a comprehensive theory of human behavior? Is such a comprehensive human science even possible? It is to this question that I now turn.

IV INHERENT LIMITATIONS OF THE ECONOMIC APPROACH

" . . . words are wise mens counters, they do but reckon by them; but they are the mony of fooles, that value them by the authority of an Aristotle, a Cicero, or a Thomas, or any other Doctor whatsoever, if but a man." (Thomas Hobbes, *Leviathan*, Ch. 4)

One very fundamental objection to the economic approach is an objection which applies to any project of a "naturalistic" science of society. I refer to the argument of Peter Winch,[26] and others who hold to a certain (contested[27]) interpretation of Wittgenstein's later philosophy, that there is a categorical gulf between causal and rational explanations such that only the latter are ever appropriate to intelligent human conduct. For these critics, Becker's project, like that of Pareto before him, founders on a positivistic conflation of the two orders of explanation, and so cannot even begin to progress. This attempt to disqualify a priori the Becker research program seems to me to be open to very serious objections. Explanatory categories are not given to us as Platonistic objects, fixed and immutable, but rather emerge from the practice of research itself. If, as the predictive success of Becker's approach in at least some areas of "non-economic" social life suggests, his research program is capable of yielding surprising and sometimes counter-intuitive results, this should give us a reason for jettisoning or substantially revising the causal-rational dichotomy invoked uncritically by these objections. If, as I think we must agree, *having a reason for what we do* is the primordial notion at the bottom of all discourse about practical rationality, still it does not follow from this that the reasons that move men to act cannot be captured in a causal theory. Indeed, the project of developing explanations of human behavior which, because they account for systematic distortion and collective self-deception in social belief systems, have a critical or deflationary effect on how men see themselves and their social world, is an entirely legitimate one which this Wittgensteinian argument would tend to inhibit. Even if Marxian and Paretian theories of ideology and rationalization have often been regrettably crude and mechanistic, this should not be taken as a reason against fashioning better theories of belief-formation which deploy the Becker scheme. In fact, the application of the economic approach to questions of cognitive psychology would seem to be one of its most promising research prospects.

This radical apriorist criticism of Becker's research program, then, must fail. A more serious challenge, to which I alluded briefly when I mentioned the apparent impossibility of finding an "economic" explanation of the decision to vote, is given by the theory of expressive rationality. According to this view, which has sources in the philosophy of Hegel and in much Romantic writing, a great deal of human behavior is not purposeful or calculational at all, but rather self-expressive or self-disclosing. We vote, or go to church, sing, pray or make love, meet our friends or go on long voyages, not always in order to achieve any further end or to implement any rational plan of life, but simply to express our sense of ourselves as being the kind of people we are. It seems hard, if not impossible, to account for the phenomena of patriotism and nationalism, of deep attachment to linguistic traditions and of many sorts of military and political struggle, in terms which appeal primarily to calculational rationality. (How might calculational rationality encompass the Polish watchword, invoked in several hopeless risings during Polish history, "We fight to die"?) Admittedly, an explanation of the psychological and cultural role of identification with continuing social structures in building a dependable personal identity might someday be developed in sociobiological terms, on the lines of sociobiological explanations of altruism and religious faith;[28] but at present, such explanations would be extremely speculative. If there is in human behavior an autonomous realm of expressive behavior in which calculational rationality is largely absent, this must present an insuperable obstacle to the ambition that the economic approach develop into a master science of human affairs.

At a still deeper level, the economic approach would seem to presuppose the truth of determinism in the human world. (It need not presuppose physical determinism.) Especially when it is conjoined with a sociobiological perspective, the economic approach tends to picture human beings as survival mechanisms, gene-machines programmed to persist and reproduce themselves whose intellectual and creative activities all subserve the basic goals. The reductionist implication of such a view of human beings may someday be irresistible, but it cannot yet be judged to have the empirical content which compels assent. Even in the hard-core of economic theory of the standard sort, G. L. S. Shackle[29] has advanced powerful criticisms of any approach which neglects the subjective and creative character of expectations or which invokes the spurious objectivity of conventional probability theory, and he has subjected game theory to a no less powerful criticism—that it neglects "the logic of surprise"—on similar lines. If there is in human choice a surd element, unsusceptible of prediction or further explanation, then once again the larger ambition of the eonomic approach must founder. Not that I wish to suggest that no theory could ever encompass all such singularities—some recent economic theory, such as Alchian's,[30] has been notably successful in incorporating stochastic processes in its account of business success and failure. Alchian's applications of an evolutionary model to market process have in fact several advantages, not least of which is that they meet the criticism that rational choice theory is unrealistic by treating rationality, not as an attribute of the agent, but rather as an emergent property of the interactions of many agents in a definite institutional context. The rationality of agents is then theorized in ways which embody methodological realism at the macro-level, so that the economic approach need not resort to the desperate device of treating its models as ideal-typical. I do not, then, argue that the economic approach is fatally flawed inasmuch as it cannot theorize satisfactorily microsocial exchanges and the individual choices that constitute them. The implication of any criticism is rather that, even if the economic approach achieved good results at the macro-level, the presence of creative origination at the micro–or individual–level must limit its prospects as a complete and comprehensive theory of social behavior. Perhaps this is only to say that, where there is real freedom of choice in the metaphysical sense, there must also be ignorance, or at least (in Shackle's expression) unknowledge.

CONCLUDING REMARKS

Despite its inherent limitations, the economic approach has clear advantages over its principal rival in social theory, functionalism. As a predictor of political behavior, it does far better than Marxian or cultural theories of political life and has in the Virginia School produced the closest approximation to a science of politics we are likely to see. If, in virtue of an irreducible element of creative originality in human thought and action, it cannot theorize completely successfully the behavior of individuals, this is a fate that has befallen all other social theories with which we are acquainted. It is not a special defect of the economic approach, nor is it a failure that all of us will wholly regret.

NOTES

1. Gary S. Becker, *The Economic Approach to Human Behaviour,* University of Chicago Press, (1976) p. 5.

2. ———— "Irrational Behaviour and Economic Theory," *Journal of Political Economy,* (1962).

3. Karl R. Popper, *The Open Society and Its Enemies,* Vol. 2, Routledge and Kegan Paul, (1973) p. 97.

4. Ludwig von Mises, *Human Action,* Contemporary Books Inc., Chicago (1963) p. 103: "Constancy and rationality are entirely different notions."

5. Jean-Luc Migré, "Methodologie économique et économie non-marchande," *Revue d' économie politique,* (1977) p. 44.

6. F. A. Hayek, *Individualism and Economic Order,* Routledge and Kegan Paul (1976) Chapter 2.

7. Russell Hardin, *Collective Action,* Johns Hopkins University Press, (1982) p. 6.

8. Derek Parfit, *Reasons and Persons,* Oxford University Press, (1984) Chapters 2 and 4.

9. Gordon Tullock, *The Social Dilemma: the Economics of War and Revolution,* University Publications, (1974).

10. See Roger LeRoy Miller, *The Economics of Macro Issues,* Canfield Press, San Francisco, (1976).

11. Robert Nozick, *Anarchy, State and Utopia,* Basil Blackwell, Oxford (1974) pp. 274–5.

12. See Konstantin Simis, *USSR: Secrets of a Corrupt Society,* J. M. Dent, London, (1982) Chapters 5–6, 8–9.

13. See Paul Craig Roberts, *Alienation and the Soviet Economy,* University of New Mexico Press, Albuquerque, (1971).

14. David Hume, *Enquiry Concerning the Principles of Morals in Essential Works of David Hume,* Bantam Books, New York, (1965) p. 211.

15. Edna Ullmann-Margalit, *The Emergence of Norms,* Oxford University Press (1977).

16. See R. Nozick, *Anarchy, State and Utopia*, pp. 18–22; and, for a more extended discussion, Nozick's "On Austrian Methodology," *Synthese* 36 (19–7), pp. 353–361.

17. I refer particularly to the first volume of Hayek's work in progress, *The Fatal Conceit*, which I have been privileged to read. See also John Gray, *Hayek on Liberty*, Basil Blackwell, (1984).

18. See G. A. Cohen, *Karl Marx's Theory of History: a Defence*, Clarendon Press: Oxford, (1978) Chaps. 9 and 10.

19. See J. Monod, *Chance and Necessity*.

20. See J. Elster, *Logic and Society*, Wiley, (1978) pp. 121–2, 144–5; *Ulysses and the Sirens*, Cambridge University Press, (1979) pp. 28–35.

21. John Gray, "Philosophy, Science and Myth in Marxism," in *Marx and Marxism*, Royal Institute of Philosophy Lectures, Vol. 14, Cambridge University Press, pp. 82–90.

22. Mancur Olson, *The Rise and Decline of Nations: Economic Growth, Stagflation and Social Rigidities*, Yale University Press, (1982).

23. J. Elster, *Ulysses and the Sirens*, pp. 4–8.

24. Gary Becker, "Altruism, Egoism and Genetic Fitness," *The Economic Approach to Human Behaviour*, p. 294 et seq.

25. See for example, Richard Epstein "A Taste for Privacy? Evolution and the Emergence of a Naturalistic Ethic," *The Journal of Legal Studies*, Vol. IX (December 1980), pp. 665–668.

26. Peter Winch, *The Idea of a Social Science*, Routledge and Kegan Paul, (1958).

27. Some aspects of Winch's interpretation of Wittgenstein are criticized in David Bloor's *Wittgenstein: a Social Theory of Knowledge*, Macmillan, (1983) pp. 168–181.

28. For a sociobiological account of religious faith, see E. O. Wilson's brilliant *Human Nature*, Bantam, (1979) Chapter 8.

29. See G. L. S. Shackle, *Epistemics and Economics*, Cambridge University Press, (1972) Chapter 36. But for a Beckerite theorist who uses probability theory imaginatively in many areas of social life, see Reuven Brenner's fascinating *History: the Human Gamble*, University of Chicago Press, (1983) especially Chapter 1.

30. See especially Armen A. Alchian, "Uncertainty, Evolution and Economic Theory," in *Economic Forces at Work*, Liberty Press, Indianapolis, (1977) pp. 15–35.

NATURE AND METHODOLOGICAL FOUNDATIONS OF SOME RECENT EXTENSIONS OF ECONOMIC THEORY

LOUIS DE ALESSI

Recent advances in economic theory, stimulated by serious limitations of the neoclassical framework, have greatly extended the theory's range of application not only to a broader range of phenomena within the traditional domain of economics, but also to new and important fields previously monopolized by other disciplines. From a methodological perspective, these advances are particularly promising because they stem from the reduction of economic theory to a simpler, more general framework that enhances the substantive content of the theory and establishes a more powerful base for further generalizations.

Section I provides a summary of the methodological approach. Section II contains a brief discussion of neoclassical economic theory, its limitations, and the methodological foundations of its current reformulation with special emphasis, developed in Section III, on the role of transaction costs and property rights. Section IV employs this reformulation of the theory to analyze the nature and economic consequences of recent trends in the legal rules of liability. Section V contains a few concluding remarks.

I METHODOLOGICAL APPROACH

Much of the early criticism of neoclassical economic theory focused on its alleged lack of realism and reflected, at least in part, a failure to understand the nature of scientific inquiry. The various controversies eventually polarized around Friedman's essay (1953) on positive economics and resulted in general acceptance of the proposition that the validity of economic theory must be judged by the agreement of the theory's implications with observation.

This positivist methodology traces its philosophical roots to the work of Rudolf Carnap, Herbert Feigl, Philip Frank, Kurt Gödel, and other members of the Vienna Circle in the 1920s and 1930s (Caldwell, 1982, Ch. 2). Developed further by A. J. Ayer, Richard Braithwaite, Carl Hempel, Ernest Nagel, and others (Caldwell, 1982, Ch. 3) and modified by Karl Popper's powerful argument for using empirical falsifiability as the criterion of testability in science (Popper, 1959), this approach provided a rigorous benchmark for economists' growing interest in empirical research.

Positivism continues to receive broad acceptance within the economics profession (Blaug, 1980), although it no longer wholly reflects current thinking among philosophers of science (Caldwell, 1982). Nevertheless, as sketched below, it still provides a unifying theme for examining the methodology of economics.

Economics, like any other science, is concerned with the establishment of general laws covering the behavior of the empirical events within its domain of inquiry. General laws are simply hypotheses unrestricted in time and space; they indicate how economic variables are related and allow statements regarding the consequences of a change in circumstances. Because the question of why a particular event occurs asks for the general law covering that class of events, theory provides an explanation of the events being investigated (Braithwaite, 1960, p. 2).

Scientific laws typically are organized into a complex hierarchical system (theory) in which the fundamental hypotheses or axioms logically imply all other hypotheses. Thus, the theory must be properly axiomatized according to the rules of logic and mathematics. Because the theory deals with empirical events, however, it cannot be tautological—Friedman's (1959) and Samuelson's (1963) comments to the contrary notwithstanding (De Alessi, 1965, 1971). That is, a scientific theory must contain at least some contingent propositions, propositions whose truth or falsity can only be determined empirically. Indeed, empirical falsifiability of at least some implications has been taken as the criterion of demarcation between applied (scientific) and pure (e.g., mathematics) systems (Popper, 1959).

On this view, economic theory is an applied deductive system in which observable consequences (implications) logically follow from the conjunction of empirical events (the antecedent conditions) with the axioms of the theory. It follows that economic theory yields conditional (if . . ., then . . .) hypotheses, in which the realization of the consequences depends upon both the realization of the empirical conditions specified in the antecedent clause and the validity of the theory.

In order to test the validity of the theory, both the antecedent conditions and the consequences must be related to empirical events. Unless such a relationship can be established, either directly or through more detailed laws, the theory is simply inapplicable in that domain. Note, however, that not all terms in the theory must have an empirical counterpart.[1] Moreover, those terms that must have an empirical counterpart need not be fully described. Because no finite set of statements can ever fully describe an event, no description can ever be fully realistic (Nagel, 1963). Accordingly, the completeness of the description is itself an economic decision, being determined by the expected cost of adding more details and the usefulness of the expected increase in the accuracy of the predictions.

Economic theory, like any other theory, is subject to continuous evaluation. The theoretical structure is scrutinized to eliminate flaws in logic and to ensure that the axioms are independent, free from contradiction, and both sufficient and necessary (by the rule of Ockham's razor) for deducing all statements belonging to the theory. At the same time, a theory's implications are tested empirically to determine their predictive power and range of application as well as to indicate the nature and direction of further modifications designed to increase the theory's predictive and explanatory powers.

The process of testing and revising a theory is complex and slow. Casual empiricism frequently yields belief in extensions or limitations which, in fact, do not exist (e.g., Cheung, 1973). More important, seemingly rigorous tests may use data or statistical techniques that are inappropriate, fail to include all the relevant variables, or suffer from outright errors in computation or logic. Repeated scrutiny and tests under varying circumstances, therefore, are necessary to establish confidence in the validity of the findings. Moreover, economic theory and evidence suggest that a theory is seldom, if ever, rejected in the face of acknowledged limitations until a more complete theory becomes available to replace it.

Because a theory is never complete, there are always areas in which it is (or appears to be) inapplicable or falsified by experience, or in which it competes with alternative theoretical constructs, including *ad hoc* hypotheses. Accordingly, accepted theory is continuously being revised to provide a more rigorous framework capable of yielding more accurate predictions over a wider range of phenomena. In the process, its axioms typically become simpler and more general (Schlegel, 1967).

The methodological approach just described explicitly rejects instrumentalism, the view that the truth status of theories, hypotheses, or assumptions is irrelevant as long as the conclusions logically derived from them are consistent with observation (Boland, 1979, p. 509). Thus, as an extreme example, a statistical relationship among variables could simply be postulated, and accepted without further explanation, as long as the resulting predictions were consistent with observation (Wong, 1973, p. 315). Friedman's methodology has been described as instrumentalist (Boland, 1973; Wong, 1973), a characterization that recently—and, perhaps, mistakenly—he seems to have accepted (Wible, 1982, p. 358).

The actual process of a theory's evolution, of course, is far from orderly. Researchers differ in their training, interests, and intellectual honesty as well as in the constraints under which they work. Individual researchers' pursuit of their own self-interest yields a cacophony of frequently discordant notes over a broad spectrum of quality, with variations in melody and lyrics often arranged by politicians and other special interest groups. Nevertheless, those contributions that advance knowledge provide some individuals with better tools with which to promote their interests, whether through further scientific advances (which yield prestige and income) or through business activities (which also yield prestige and income via such things as the production of new, cheaper, or more durable commodities). Accordingly, substantive advances are more likely to survive in the marketplace of ideas, enriching the theory as well as those that use it and making it a more powerful engine of analysis.

II RECENT ADVANCES IN ECONOMIC THEORY

Adam Smith's Wealth of Nations (1776, 1937) presented the first coherent statement of modern economics. As subsequent generations of economists sought to develop a more rigorous and complete statement of the theory, they progressively abstracted from the complexities of the real world to focus on the behavior of idealized variables under highly purified conditions. Among other simplifications, such as the characterization of both inputs and outputs as perfectly homogeneous and divisible, economists gradually eliminated all institutional arrangements from consideration. In particular, they assumed—either explicitly or implicitly—that all rights to the use of resources were fully allocated, privately held, and exchanged at zero transaction costs, broadly interpreted to mean zero information, negotiation, and enforcement costs (Bator, 1957).

Simplifications of this nature are necessary if the theory is to be sufficiently general to deal with the full range of events within its domain. When the theory is applied to particular circumstances, however, the variables describing those circumstances must be related to empirical entities and taken into account. This requirement was seldom observed, perhaps because economists confused the assumptions (antecedent conditions) that define a particular spatiotemporal domain of the theory with the assumptions (axioms) that define the theory's initial hypotheses (Nagel, 1963).

By the 1950s, neoclassical economics, defined as the conjunction of the utility maximization theory of consumer choice and the profit maximization theory of the firm, was under intense attack on both theoretical and empirical grounds (e.g., Simon, 1959). Some economists rejected the theory's maximization postulates as too limiting, while others showed that at least some of the theory's implications were inconsistent with experience.

In particular, there was growing evidence that the profit maximization hypothesis was incapable of predicting accurately and consistently the production and pricing choices of business firms. Moreover, there was belated appreciation that the profit maximization hypothesis did not even apply to an increasingly important economic sector. This is the sector encompassing business firms owned or regulated by government, cooperatives, nonprofits, and all other nonproprietary forms of business organization. Indeed, economic theory did not even provide a full explanation of why business firms exist, let alone why particular forms of business organization evolve and survive.

To correct at least some of the perceived shortcomings of neoclassical theory, economists offered a broad spectrum of alternatives. These varied from *ad hoc* models, such as the maximization of sales (Baumol, 1959) and satisfying behavior (Simon, 1962), to various modifications of received theory, including the substitution of wealth for profit maximization (Alchian, 1965a).

In time, the most promising line of revision took the form of generalizing the utility maximization hypothesis to all choices under constraints (Alchian and Kessel, 1962; Williamson, 1963; Furubotn and Pejovich, 1972; De Alessi, 1980), taking explicit account of the institutional setting and transaction costs. Although this reformulation has not and will not solve all problems, it is a logical step in the development of the theory, as well as a necessary condition for assessing the theory's usefulness relative to other alternatives, providing a more solid foundation for future revisions.

Beginning in the late 1950s, Alchian (1959, 1961, 1965b, 1967), Demsetz (1964, 1967), and others (e.g., De Alessi, 1967) showed that different institutions typically embody different structures of individual rights to the use of resources. These property rights determine, via actual or imputed prices, how the benefits and the harms emanating from a decision are allocated between the decision-maker and other individuals. If different structures of property rights provide individual decision-makers—whether within household, business, or government—with different structures of costs and rewards, then their choices are affected systematically and result in different consequences.

Concurrently, Coase (1960), Stigler (1961), Williamson (1967), and others (e.g., Demsetz, 1969) began exploring the consequences of positive transaction costs. Their research showed that transaction costs not only affect the extent to which resources are realigned in response to a change in circumstances, but also exert a powerful influence on the evolution and survival of institutional arrangements designed to facilitate the flow of resources to their highest-valued use.

The methodological advantages of reformulating neoclassical economics to take account of property rights and transaction costs are becoming increasingly obvious. First, the theory is simpler. Business choices are explicitly derived from the hypothesis that individual decision-makers within the firm maximize their own utility, thus ending the apparent dichotomy between the theory of consumer choice and the theory of the firm. This simplification has been abetted by the introduction of the household's production function (Lancaster, 1966) and the continuing generalization of the consumer's utility function (Ehrlich, infra). Second, the theory is more general. Focusing on the individual decision-maker necessarily focuses on the characteristics of the particular system used for arriving at group decisions, thus fostering the analysis of a broader range of organizational forms. As a result, the theory's implications have been extended to encompass not only those phenomena covered by neoclassical economics but also many of those addressed by existing *ad hoc* models. Third, the theory's implications are receiving growing empirical support (De Alessi, 1980).

Neoclassical economic theory, even granting its failures and limitations, has been sufficiently powerful, relative to other theoretical constructs in the social sciences, to encourage its extension to a broad range of events outside its traditional domain (Gray, infra.) Thus, for example, economics has been applied with success to issues in political science (e.g., Buchanan and Tullock, 1962; Bernholz, infra; Hirshleifer, infra; Tullock, infra), sociology (e.g., Becker 1957; Coleman, infra), jurisprudence (e.g., Posner, 1972; Manne, infra), history (Meiners, infra), philosophy (Radnitzky, infra), and biology (Ghiselin, infra).

Recent advances, however, promise to support even greater incursions into other fields. The increased simplicity and generality of economic theory have greatly extended its range of application and, perhaps even more important, have provided a stronger base for further revisions and extensions.

III PROPERTY RIGHTS AND TRANSACTION COSTS

Property rights are the rights of individuals to the use of resources. For example, an individual may be allowed to harm (reduce the wealth of) competitors by producing a superior product but not by setting fire to their factories, while the same individual may be allowed to shoot an intruder but not to sell certain goods below a price floor or above a price ceiling.

The system of property rights that characterizes a society provides a mechanism for assigning to particular individuals the authority to select how specific resources may be used, given a set of nonprohibited uses (Alchian, 1965b). In particular, it specifies the nature of the rights that an individual may hold to the use, income, and transferability of resources. Note that property rights are enforced not only by formal legal rules and the power of the state, but also by social conventions (Coleman, infra).

To explore the concept of property rights more precisely, consider private, usufruct, and common ownership arrangements. Private property means that an individual's rights to the use of resources are exclusive and voluntarily transferable. That is, individuals have the exclusive authority to choose the use and receive the income of the resources they own. Moreover, they can sell these ownership rights to others at mutually agreed prices, thereby fully capitalizing future consequences into current transfer prices. Usufruct ownership, on the other hand, typically confers exclusive rights to the use of specific resources as well as exclusive and transferable rights to any output they might yield, but prohibits any temporary or permanent transfer of the resource rights to others. As a result, individuals are able to capture the benefits of any investment they might make only as long as they continue using the resource. Common ownership typically means that an individual's rights to the use of resources are acquired on a first-come first-served basis (or some other non-price rationing scheme) and are neither exclusive nor transferable, although the rights to any output they might yield may be both exclusive and transferable. The system of property rights thus determines how prices, including income, are set (Alchian, 1965b).

Note that the bundle of rights to the use of a particular resource may be partitioned, so that some rights may be held in private, others in usufruct, and still others in common. For example, the lessor of a house typically retains exclusive, transferable rights to the stream of rental income and to the house itself, subject to the terms of the lease. The lessee has the right to use the house in ways prescribed by the lease. And different groups of individuals may hold in common the right to fly over the house, dump smoke on it, or make noise near it.

The use of private property in a society depends in part on the costs of transacting and the benefits generated. Lower transaction costs or higher benefits, other things being the same, imply that private property rights are more carefully defined, more fully allocated, and better enforced. The more dominant within the bundle are private property rights, in turn, the closer is the relationship between the welfare of the individual owners and the economic (social) consequences of their decisions, and the greater is the incentive of owners to take account of the benefits and harms that their decisions visit on others. Indeed, in the limit (zero transaction costs) there are no external effects: individuals capitalize and take full account of all harms and all benefits resulting from their actions. As a result, resources are priced at their opportunity cost and flow to their highest-valued use. It follows that a reallocation of the rights to the use of resources will not affect their subsequent use except indirectly through the net effect of the change in the distribution of wealth on the demands for different commodities (Coase, 1960; De Alessi, 1978).

Transaction costs, of course, typically are positive and rise at the margin. It follows that, in some cases, the cost of defining, establishing, and enforcing some private property rights exceeds the benefits. As a result, some property rights are not fully defined, assigned (e.g., some resources are owned in common), or enforced (e.g., some trespassing is tolerated). Taking account of transaction costs, however, the allocation of resources is still efficient in the sense that a stricter definition, assignment, and enforcement of private property rights (that is, fewer usufruct and common rights in the bundle) would result in a smaller output (De Alessi, 1983b, 1983c). If individuals perceive the institution of private (common) ownership as a good in itself, of course, its benefits would be higher and more (less) of the rights would be defined, assigned, and enforced in equilibrium.

Under some systems of property rights, such as common ownership, the realignment of specific rights may be inhibited or prohibited, and therefore costlier, than under other systems, such as private property. As a result, resources are less likely to flow to those individuals with a comparative advantage in their use, and output is smaller. Taking existing institutions as a constraint, however, implies that the allocation of resources is still efficient.[2]

The question may be raised why institutions that seem to result in a smaller output become established and survive. One hypothesis is that such institutions are a source of utility and individuals are willing to forego other commodities in order to have more of them. That is, the output is larger than it appears to be. It is doubtful, however, that individuals would consider particular institutions as ends in themselves rather than as means to other goals. A much more likely explanation, and one that has a good deal of supporting evidence, is that seemingly inefficient institutions arise to mask and otherwise facilitate the transfer of wealth to groups with a comparative advantage in the use of political power (De Alessi, 1982).

Note that institutions adapt relatively slowly to changes in circumstances, and may appear to function inefficiently in the interim. Because adjustment is costly, however, it would seldom be instantaneous. To the extent that responses are systematically faster or slower than the optimal rate, in the sense that they result in a smaller apparent output, the explanation again would have to be sought in wealth redistribution. Recent work on the evolution of different systems of property rights and their consequences is casting further light on these issues (Demsetz, 1964; Libecap, 1978; Umbeck, 1981).

Transaction costs are a major determinant of the choice of contractual arrangements. Thus, for example, a strict regime of private property rights, zero transaction costs, and risk neutrality implies that firms would not exist. Owners of resources would simply function as independent contractors, buying inputs from other resource owners, adding their own contribution, and selling the output to consumers or to other independent contractors in the production-distribution chain.

The organization of economic activity through independent contractors would prevail even if the nature of the production function were such that several individuals, working together as a team, could produce more than the combined results of their separate efforts. Under the conditions specified, individuals would work as a team and the (marginal) product attributable to each member of the team would be measured continuously and costlessly. Any reduction in individual effort would be detected instantaneously at zero cost and fully reflected in reduced compensation. No shirking could exist.

Transaction costs, however, typically are positive. Accordingly, a team member who shirked would reap the full benefits from shirking (e.g., increased leisure) but bear only a proportional share of the loss in output. Then each team member would have some incentive to shirk.

Current developments in economic theory suggest that firms arise to solve the shirking-information problem of team production (Alchian and Demsetz, 1972). Thus, private enterprises are viewed as a set of voluntary contractual arrangements among owners of the rights to the use of resources. If monitoring costs are relatively low, then employer-employee contracts evolve. This solution characterizes the firm of neoclassical economic theory, wherein the owners of the assets most specific to the firm (that is, the assets with the highest quasi rents) specialize in monitoring and, to inhibit their own shirking, hold residual claim to the firm's earnings (Klein, Crawford, and Alchian, 1978).[3]

In this context, the cost of raising large sums of equity capital is a key explanatory variable in the development of the modern corporation with transferable shares (Ekelund and Tollison, 1980). Shareholders own the specialized assets and bear the value consequences of decisions made within the firm and of changes in market conditions, while managers specialize in deciding how resources are used and act as agents for the stockholders. Agency costs help to explain the appearance of organizations with autonomous profit centers and conglomerates with wholly-owned subsidiaries (Jensen and Meckling, 1976; Fama, 1980).

If shirking is relatively costly to monitor, and team size can be relatively small, then profit sharing arrangements develop. This hypothesis explains the existence of partnerships in professional and intellectual work, share contracts in mining and agriculture, and similar phenomena (Cheung, 1969; Hallagan, 1978).

Mutuals and nonprofit organizations evolve when individuals wish to blunt market incentives and encourage specific kinds of shirking. These organizational forms limit the ability of any one group within the coalition to fully capture the benefits of improved performance as judged by market standards, thus lowering the opportunity cost of desired activities (e.g., cancer research) and thereby encouraging their expansion.

Government ownership of business enterprises, in addition to facilitating wealth transfers, may also occur to solve the shirking-information problem of team production (De Alessi, 1982). Thus, for example, contracting by the United States with a private firm for the provision of defense, even if such a contract could be drawn, might be sufficiently difficult to monitor and enforce that it would encourage vertical integration within government.

Note that shirking includes a wider range of post-contractual opportunistic behavior than has been examined so far. Thus, if a party to a contract commits resources in such a way that their value in the next-best alternative is greatly reduced, it becomes open to opportunistic behavior by the other parties to the contract. As a result, the owner of the specialized assets has the incentive to allocate resources to protect itself against opportunistic behavior. Because opportunistic behavior raises the cost of contracting among business enterprises, it encourages some vertical integration (Klein, Crawford, and Alchian, 1978).

Indeed, there is increased understanding of a whole range of previously puzzling phenomena that, on closer analysis, turn out to be open market, competitive solutions designed to economize on transaction costs. Thus, some seemingly unfair agreements such as standard form contracts (Klein, 1980) and some seemingly collusive business practices such as basing-point pricing with cross hauling and freight absorption (Haddock, 1982) evolve and survive in open markets simply because they economize on information costs. Similarly, such contractual arrangements as franchises, resale price maintenance, exclusive territories, initial specific investments, right of first refusal, termination clauses, and exclusive dealing provisions typically are designed to economize on transaction costs by providing market-enforced guarantees against post-contractual opportunistic behavior (Klein, 1980; Williamson, 1975, 1979, 1983). Economizing on transaction costs leads to lower prices and a more competitive environment, suggesting that antitrust activity aimed for decades at the phenomena just discussed has been misplaced (Baumol, 1982; Demsetz, 1982).

Whether certain transactions take place within a coalition or among coalitions is determined by transaction costs and by the extent to which individuals bear the value consequences of their decisions (the system of property rights). Thus, for example, the incentive to economize on monitoring costs leads firms to adopt production processes which, although costlier in other dimensions, result in lower overall production costs. Similarly, the weakening of private property rights—perhaps due to government regulation—blunts the incentive to adopt lower-cost production techniques and encourages bringing within the firm too few or too many activities as judged by open market standards. Indeed, differences in transaction costs and in ownership arrangements imply systematic differences in such things as the size, technology used, range and quality of output, and pricing behavior of enterprises (De Alessi, 1980).

Focusing on the behavior of individual decision-makers within economic organizations, and taking transaction costs and property rights into account, has permitted some major extensions of economic theory. These include the analysis of a broad spectrum of business organizations at both the firm (e.g., private unregulated, private regulated, mutual, cooperative, worker-managed, government-owned) and the industry level (monopolistic competition, oligopoly, monopoly) as well as the analysis of government bureaucracies (e.g., independent regulatory commissions, bureaus, departments), of alternative ownership arrangements in land, labor, and capital over time and across countries (e.g., socialist and communist regimes, Indian tribes), of the full range of legal issues (e.g., tort, antitrust), and of broader sociological phenomena (e.g., marriage, family).

IV AGENCY LAW, PRODUCTS LIABILITY LAW, AND THE ORGANIZATION OF ECONOMIC ACTIVITY

Within the last century, liability law in the United States has undergone a revolution. Thus, products liability law has moved from a rule of *caveat emptor* to a rule of *caveat venditor* (McKean, 1970). Although the causes and consequences of this shift are not yet fully understood, taking account of property rights and transaction costs is offering some important insights, and suggests that the effects of the change may be far more pervasive than initially perceived (De Alessi and Staaf, 1984).

If transaction costs were zero, the rule of liability would not affect the organization of economic activity (Coase, 1960). Given the rule of liability, recontracting would take place until each party—whether manufacturer, wholesaler, retailer, or consumer—performed each activity to the extent to which it had a comparative advantage (i.e., it was the least-cost avoider of harm). Under zero transaction costs, the rule of liability does not affect comparative advantage and therefore does not affect who performs each activity.

In the real world, of course, transaction costs typically are positive and rise at the margin. Moreover, property rights are not fully allocated and privately held. As a result, both the opportunity and the incentive to reallocate resources to the least-cost avoider of harm are reduced (Coase, 1960; Demsetz, 1972; De Alessi, 1978). The rule of liability, therefore, matters.

Individuals typically are liable for their own tortious acts. Liability for the actions of individuals engaged in team (joint) production, however, may be extended to other members of the team under two separate and independent sets of legal principles, agency law and products liability law (De Alessi and Staaf, 1984).

Both agency and products liability law are intended, in part, to protect third parties. Agency law covers those relations in which the individual acts on behalf of someone else. For present purposes, the essence of agency law lies in the doctrine of *respondeat superior*, which is designed to protect innocent bystanders (Seavy, 1964). Products liability, on the other hand, is intended to protect third-parties who do not have a contractual relationship (privity) with the manufacturer-seller (Prosser, 1971). Note that transactions under products liability law are voluntary (e.g., a consumer is injured while using a product that the consumer had purchased from a retailer). In the absence of fraud or misrepresentation, whether a transaction is voluntary or involuntary is a matter of degree and depends on the level of transaction costs.

AGENCY LAW

Agency law's *respondeat superior* rests on the legal fiction that principal (master) and agent (servant) are one. If the agent is negligent, the principal is held strictly liable even if wholly without fault. The principal, however, typically has the right of indemnification against the agent. As applied under *respondeat superior*, the term "principal" means the firm's residual claimants. Directors, officers, managers, and foremen who have no property interest in the firm generally are not held liable (Restatement of Agency, 1958). Thus, agency law can be interpreted as placing liability on those who monitor or control a team's production process.

The relevance of control is emphasized by the absence of liability under agency law for the actions of an independent contractor when the hiring firm does not have the right to monitor the inputs used by the latter. Moreover, the exceptions to this rule, such as negligent selection of the independent contractor and undertaking activities that are ultrahazardous, also appear to be related to the issue of control. Thus, agency law allows entrepreneurs to specialize in certain risks associated with the production and distribution process and to avoid other risks by hiring independent contractors.

Liability under agency law partially offsets the reduction in transaction costs obtained by organizing activities within a firm. Such activities entail additional monitoring costs resulting from liability for the negligent acts of employees, liability that would not exist if independent contractors were used.

PRODUCTS LIABILITY LAW

Caveat Emptor. Products liability law initially paralleled agency principles. Under *caveat emptor*, which received its classic statement in *Winterbottom v. Wright* (1842), a user could not sue anyone for injuries or damages resulting from the use of a defective product unless there was a contractual relation (privity) that specified the rights and duties between the parties. In *Winterbottom* the injured driver of the defective mailcoach, unable to sue the employer postmaster who enjoyed government immunity, sued the person who had contracted with the employer to maintain the coach. The court barred the action because of lack of privity.

The rule of *caveat emptor*, as laid down in *Winterbottom*, had numerous exceptions relating to particular products such as food, drugs, firearms, and dynamite. In part, these exceptions seem to have been developed to protect innocent third-party bystanders who did not voluntarily accept the risk.

The essential feature of *caveat emptor* was the ability of a firm to subcontract to others some phase of the production or distribution process and thereby obtain immunity from liability for product injuries, except for any contractual liability that might ultimately link the consumer with the firm through a series of warranty or contract actions. Although the firm presumably monitored the output of the subcontractor, it was not held liable for failing to inspect the output of a negligent subcontractor. Thus, processes that did not involve advantages of monitoring joint inputs would be contracted out to other firms, coincidentally reducing the exposure of liability to third parties.

Caveat emptor is the implicit legal setting of the neoclassical theory of the firm as well as of its current reformulation by Alchian and Demsetz (1972) and others.

Negligence. The next watershed in case law was *Macpherson v. Buick Motor Co.* (1916), which involved a fact pattern strikingly similar to *Winterbottom* and marked the change to a rule of negligence. Here, Buick was held liable for injuries resulting from a defective wheel manufactured by an independent contractor.

Macpherson extended the concept of jointness in the production process by holding the manufacturer liable for failure to monitor (inspect) the output of a negligent independent contractor, a firm separately monitored and controlled. This rule provided additional incentive to integrate vertically as long as the costs of joining and monitoring the separable stages of production (inputs) were less than the costs of monitoring the outputs of independent contractors.

The negligence rule can be interpreted as a warranty implied by law. To the extent that the courts implicitly or explicitly used the Learned Hand formula,[4] the standard of quality could not fall below the point where the expected loss arising from a defective product equalled or exceeded the cost of avoiding that loss through such measures as quality control, design, and warning. For many buyers, especially those who are risk averse, this is the standard of quality demanded. For buyers who are risk preferrers, a standard of care below the Learned Hand formula would be desirable provided that there is a corresponding decrease in price.

In some jurisdictions, consumers who prefer more risk in return for a lower price could make the substitution through disclaimer or exculpatory clauses in the purchase agreement. Because of the lack of privity, however, such clauses would be ineffective against innocent third parties injured by the product. Thus, under the negligence rule, firms have an incentive to increase product quality above that demanded by some consumers.

One interesting feature of the negligence rule is that it permits a defense of contributory negligence. This doctrine can be explained on the basis of the control argument, in that consumers are held negligent for failing to monitor activities in which they have a comparative advantage relative to the firms in the production-distribution chain.

Strict Liability. The decision in *Greenman v. Yuba Power Products, Inc.* (1962) shifted the rule to strict liability, under which no attribution of negligence is necessary, further extending the concept of jointness. Strict liability means that business enterprises in the same production-distribution chain may be held jointly and severally liable for any injury resulting from a product defect originating at any stage of the production-distribution chain.

Under strict liability, firms are required to sell a limited insurance policy jointly with the good, the limits of the liability varying across jurisdictions. If transaction costs were zero, the firm would sell the insurance to each consumer at its actuarial cost, taking account of the specific consumer's characteristics. Given these conditions, the results would be the same as those under *caveat emptor* assuming that consumers were averse or neutral to risk.

Because transaction costs are positive, however, the firm can only sell the insurance at the (average) premium covering the average expected loss of all consumers. It follows that higher-income consumers whose expected loss is sufficiently greater than the average would find it cheaper to switch from higher-cost, safer products to lower-cost, less safe products sold jointly with an insurance policy that fully covers all losses (Oi, 1973). Partially offsetting this shift, some lower-income consumers would also find it cheaper to switch from particularly unsafe products, with a higher expected loss, toward safer products. On net balance, strict liability may result in riskier products and the redistribution of wealth from lower to higher income consumers.

The negligence standard already provided firms with the incentive to produce levels of quality and design that were cost effective as measured by the market. Accordingly, strict liability was not likely to have much effect on quality or design—except possibly through a shift in demand toward riskier products or a decrease in consumption due to a lack of information by consumers-users (Shavell, 1980).

The decision in *Greenman* was based primarily on the court's desire to spread the risk of product defects. Not surprisingly, jurisdictions adopting *Greenman* have sought to purge considerations of culpability or fault, concepts associated with negligence. Other jurisdictions, however, have adopted Section 402A of the Restatement of Torts (1965). The Restatement allows culpability or fault to be taken into account through the unreasonably dangerous requirement of Section 402A, where the balancing of risk and utility appears to be a variation of the Learned Hand formula. The evolution of strict products liability has not been consistent, and jurisdictions differ considerably regarding who is protected and who is liable as well as regarding the damages and the defenses allowed.

Regardless of the court's intentions, the effectiveness of strict liability in achieving the objective of risk spreading depends upon the extent to which the harms from defective products in fact can be anticipated. In principle, a clear distinction exists between risk, which is associated with events whose probability distribution is known, and uncertainty, which, by definition, is associated with events whose probability distribution does not exist.

If the liability imposed on the firm is associated with risky events, then it will result in self-insurance or market-insurance. The premiums become part of the cost of doing business, and will be passed on to consumers-users. The unreasonably dangerous requirement of Section 402A suggests that a firm would be held liable only if it could have anticipated the loss, and the risks are then spread among all consumers-users.

If the liability of the firm is associated with uncertain events, however, it cannot be anticipated and, therefore, is not insurable. Accordingly, it must be borne *ex post facto* by the owners (residual claimants) of the firm.

The *Greenman* standard and, to a lesser degree, the Section 402A standard, tend to blur the distinction between risk and uncertainty. Accordingly, they result in economic consequences that go well beyond risk spreading and create considerable confusion over the extent and limits of liability.

The change in the rule of liability from *caveat emptor* to strict liability, given positive transaction costs, has shifted some risk from users, including consumers, to producers, broadly defined to include manufacturers, distributors, and retailers (McKean, 1970; Calabresi and Melamed, 1972; Epstein, 1973; Posner, 1979). This shift implies that producers have the incentive to lower their risk by acquiring insurance, by changing the type, design, method of manufacture, and method of distribution of their products, and by revising contractual agreements to legally limit liability or permit increased monitoring.

For example, a manufacturer liable under strict liability for the failure of its distributors and retailers to maintain quality has more incentive to monitor the latter. If such monitoring can be handled more cheaply within the firm, there will be more incentive to integrate vertically.

Industry Wide Liability. More recently, court decisions in *Sindell v. Abbott Laboratories* (1980) and other pharmaceutical cases have tentatively introduced the concept of enterprise or industry-wide liability. Under this doctrine, a firm would be held liable in proportion to its market share unless it could prove that it was not at fault (Sheiner, 1978).

In the case of some products, such as generic drugs, a firm would find it impossible to prove that it was not at fault. Then each firm would have the incentive to shirk, and produce a lower quality product, because each firm could capture the full gains from shirking while bearing liability only to the extent of its market share. Indeed, to the extent that the courts sought to tap the deep pocket of the larger firms and disregarded those firms that accounted for a relatively small share of the market, smaller firms would have a significant incentive to shirk because they would escape liability entirely.

Shirking by everyone usually is unprofitable, and some firms would have the incentive to seek alternative solutions. One possible outcome would be that larger firms would produce brand-name drugs, with heavy investment on advertising and product recognition, while generic and lower-quality brand-name drugs would be produced by firms that essentially would be judgment proof, that is, firms whose net wealth is maintained so low that the firms simply go bankrupt when exposed to nontrivial liability. This bifurcation of the market would result in a higher full price of drugs to consumers.

Another possible outcome would be the evolution of contractual arrangements, such as industry-wide mergers, that would provide a framework for monitoring the industry as a whole. Government anti-trust policies, however, limit the extent of such contractual strategies and encourage other solutions. The latter would include government supervision or outright manufacture of the product, imposing a system of property rights that would give rise to its own, perhaps more serious, limitations (De Alessi, 1974, 1980).

The trend in products liability law suggested by enterprise liability ignores not only the issue of control but also the distinction between risk and uncertainty. Thus, there appears to be a general trend towards the atrophy of the control test for the imposition of liability.

V CONCLUSION

This paper has examined the nature and methodological foundations of the current reformulation of neoclassical economic theory. Taking account of institutional constraints and transaction costs has allowed some major extensions of the theory, making possible a more rigorous and complete analysis of the evolution, survival, and consequences of alternative social systems.

To date, much of the research has focused on the narrower problem of the nature and evolution of business organizations viewed as con-tractual coalitions designed to solve the shirking-information problem of team production. Within this context, shirking has been interpreted almost exclusively as a phenomenon that yields a reduction in physical output. The analysis of agency law and products liability law, however, suggests that the concept of shirking must be expanded to include behavior that results in injuries to other team members, consumers-users, or third parties.

To explain the conditions that determine the structure of the firm and the industry, and whether the gains from specialization and coop-erative production can best be obtained within an organization like the firm, or among firms, requires more than a simple examination of the costs of monitoring and the gains from team production. The extent of liability must also be considered. Indeed, extending liability beyond the "natural" team production process creates a legal jointness that is an important, independent factor in determining whether given activities are organized within a firm or not.

NOTES

Part of the discussion presented in this paper is drawn from the author's earlier work (De Alessi, 1983a; De Alessi and Staaf, 1984). The author is indebted to Robert J. Staaf for helpful comments.

1. Some of the axioms may assert the existence of properties that serve as links between the set of fundamental hypotheses and derived, falsifiable implications. Such theoretical terms obtain meaning from the role they play in the calculus representing the theory, and their validity is determined by the validity of the implications they help generate (Braithwaite, 1960, Ch. 3).

2. Efficiency is defined simply as the solution of a constrained maximization problem (De Alessi, 1983b). Thus, given the constraints that characterize a particular spatiotemporal domain, the associated equilibrium solution is efficient. The judgment whether the solution associated with one set of constraints is more or less "efficient" than the solution associated with an alternative set of constraints typically entails criteria (for example, Pareto conditions) that are not value-free or are inapplicable in practice, and thus falls within the scope of normative rather than positive economics.

3. Competitive forces further inhibit shirking. Competition from other enterprises provides a check on performance, encourages the evolution of internal control devices for monitoring the performance of the team as well as of individual team members, and ultimately eliminates higher-cost producers (Fama, 1980). Competition in the capital market transfers ownership and control of specialized assets to those coalitions better able to use them (Manne, 1965). Finally, competition for managerial and other team positions from candidates within and without the coalition discourages shirking by team members.

4. In *United States v. Carroll Towing Company* (1947), Judge Learned Hand stated:
   "Since there are occasions when every vessel will break away from her moorings, and since, if she does, she becomes a menace to those about her, the owner's duty, as in other similar situations, to provide against resulting injuries is a function of three variables: (1) the probability that she will break away; (2) the gravity of the resulting injury, if she does; (3) the burden of adequate precautions. Possibly it serves to bring this notion into relief to state it in algebraic terms: if the probability be called P; the injury L; and the burden B; liability depends on whether B is less than L multiplied by P; i.e., whether B is less than PL." (p. 173).

REFERENCES

Alchian, Armen A., "The Basis of Some Recent Advances in the Theory of Management of the Firm," *Journal of Industrial Economics* (December, 1965) XIV, pp. 30–41. (a)

————— "How Should Prices Be Set?" *Il Politico* (June, 1967) XXXII, pp. 369–382.

—————, "Private Property and the Relative Cost of Tenure," in Philip D. Bradley (ed.), *The Public Stake in Union Power*, University Press of Virginia, Charlottesville, (1959).

—————, "Some Economics of Property," Rand Corporation, Santa Monica (1961).

—————, "Some Economics of Property Rights," *Il Politico* (December, 1965) XXX, pp. 816–829 (b).

—————, and Demsetz, Harold, "Production, Information Costs, and Economic Organization," *American Economic Review* (December, 1972) LXII, pp. 777–795.

————— and Kessel, Reuben A., "Competition, Monopoly, and the Pursuit of Money," in National Bureau of Economic Research, *Aspects of Labor Economics*, Princeton University Press, Princeton (1962).

Bator, Francis M., "The Simple Analytics of Welfare Maximization," *American Economic Review* (March, 1957) XLVII, pp. 22–29.

Baumol, William J., *Business Behavior, Value and Growth*, Harcourt Brace & World, New York (1959).

—————, "Contestable Markets: An Uprising in Industry Structure," *American Economic Review* (March, 1982) LXXII, pp. 1–15.

Becker, Gary S., *The Economics of Discrimination*, University of Chicago Press, Chicago (1957).

Bernholz, Peter, "A General Constitutional Possibility Theorem," infra.

Blaug, Mark, *The Methodology of Economics*, Cambridge University Press, Cambridge, England (1980).

Boland, Laurence A., "A Critique of Friedman's Critics," *Journal of Economic Literature* (June, 1979) XVII, pp. 503–522.

Braithwaite, Richard B., *Scientific Explanation*, Harper Torchbooks, New York (1960).

71

Buchanan, James M. and Gordon Tullock, *The Calculus of Consent*, University of Michigan Press, Ann Arbor (1962).

Calabresi, Guido and Douglas A. Melamed, "Property Rules, Liability Rules, and Inalienability: One View of the Cathedral," *Harvard Law Review* (April, 1972) LXXXV, pp. 1089–1128.

Caldwell, Bruce, *Beyond Positivism*, George Allen & Unwin, London (1982).

Cheung, Steven N. S., "The Fable of the Bees: An Economic Investigation," *Journal of Law and Economics* (April, 1973) XVI, pp. 11–34.

———, "Transaction Costs, Risk Aversion, and the Choice of Contractual Arrangements," *Journal of Law and Economics* (April, 1969) XII, pp. 23–42.

Coase, Ronald H, "The Problem of Social Cost," *Journal of Law and Economics* (October, 1960) III, pp. 1–44.

Coleman, James S., "Norms as Social Capital," infra.

De Alessi, Louis, "Economic Theory as a Language," *Quarterly Journal of Economics* (August, 1965) LXXIX, pp. 472–477.

———, "The Economics of Property Rights: A Review of the Evidence," *Research in Law and Economics* (1980) II, pp. 1–47.

———, "Implications of Property Rights for Government Investment Choices," *American Economic Review* (March, 1969) LIX, pp. 13–24.

———, "On the Nature and Consequences of Private and Public Enterprises," *Minnesota Law Review* (October, 1982) LXVII, pp. 201–219.

———, "Property Rights and Transaction Costs: A New Perspective in Economic Theory," *Social Science Journal* (July, 1983) XX, pp. 59–69 (a).

———, "Property Rights, Transaction Costs, and X-Efficiency: An Essay in Economic Theory," *American Economic Review* (March, 1983) LXXIII, pp. 64–81 (b).

———, "Property Rights, Transaction Costs and X-Efficiency: Reply," *American Economic Review* (September, 1983) LXXIII, pp. 843–845 (c).

———, "Reversals of Assumptions and Implications," *Journal of Political Economy* (July/August, 1971) LXXIX, pp. 867–877.

———, "The Role of Liability for Loss of Use When Property Is Totally Destroyed: Some Economic Considerations," *University of Miami Law Review* (March, 1978) XIII, pp. 255–266.

——— and Robert J. Staaf, "Liability, Control, and the Organization of Economic Activity," unpublished manuscript, (1984).

Demsetz, Harold, "Barriers to Entry," *American Economic Review* (March, 1982) LXXII, pp. 47–57.

———, "The Exchange and Enforcement of Property Rights," *Journal of Law and Economics* (October, 1964) VII, pp. 11–26.

———, "Information and Efficiency: Another Viewpoint," *Journal of Law and Economics* (April, 1969) XII, pp. 1–22.

———, "Toward a Theory of Property Rights," *American Economic Review, Proceedings* (May, 1967) LVII, pp. 347–359.

———, "When Does the Rule of Liability Matter?" *Journal of Legal Studies* (January, 1972) I, pp. 13–28.

Ehrlich, Isaac, "The Demand for Life: Theory and Application," infra.

Ekelund, B. Robert, Jr., and Robert D. Tollison, "Mercantilist Origins of the Corporation," *Bell Journal of Economics* (Autumn, 1980) XI, pp. 715–720.

Epstein, Richard A., "A Theory of Strict Liability," *Journal of Legal Studies* (January, 1973) II, pp. 151–204.

Fama, Eugene F., "Agency Problems and the Theory of the Firm," *Journal of Political Economy* (April, 1980) LXXXVIII, pp. 288–307.

Friedman, Milton, "The Methodology of Positive Economics," in M. Friedman (ed.), *Essays In Positive Economics*, University of Chicago Press, Chicago (1953).

Furubotn, Eirik G. and Svetozar Pejovich, "Property Rights and Economic Theory: A Survey of Recent Literature," *Journal of Economic Literature* (December, 1972) X, pp. 1137–1162.

Ghiselin, Michael T., "The Economics of Scientific Discovery," infra.

———, *The Economy of Nature and The Evolution of Sex*, University of California Press, Berkeley-Los Angeles-London (1974).

Gray, John, "The Economic Approach to Human Behavior: Its Prospects and Limitations," infra.

Haddock, David D., "Basing-Point Pricing: Competitive vs. Collusive Theories," *American Economic Review* (June, 1982) LXXII, pp. 289–306.

Hallagan, William, "Self-Selection by Contractual Choice and the Theory of Sharecropping," *Bell Journal of Economics* (Autumn, 1978) IX, pp. 344–354.

Hirshleifer, Jack, "The Economic Approach to Conflict," infra.

Jensen, Michael C. and William H. Meckling, "Theory of the Firm: Managerial Behavior, Agency Costs, and Ownership Structure," *Journal of Financial Economics* (October, 1976) III, pp. 305–360.

Klein, Benjamin, "Transaction Costs Determinants of 'Unfair' Contractual Arrangements," *American Economic Review, Proceedings* (May, 1980), LXX, pp. 356–362.

———, Crawford, G. Robert and Armen A. Alchian, "Vertical Integration, Appropriable Rents, and the Competitive Contracting Process," *Journal of Law and Economics* (October, 1978) XXI, pp. 297–326.

Lancaster, Kelvin, "A New Approach to Consumer Theory," *Journal of Political Economy* (April, 1966) LXXIV, pp. 132–157.

Libecap, Gary D, "Economic Variables and the Development of Law: The Case of Western Mineral Rights," *Journal of Economic History* (June, 1978) XXXVIII, pp. 338–362.

Manne, Henry G., "Intellectual Styles and the Evolution of American Corporation Law," infra.

———, "Mergers and the Market for Corporate Control," *Journal of Political Economy* (April, 1965) LXXIII, pp. 753–761.

McKean, Roland, "Products Liability: Implications of Some Changing Property Rights," *Quarterly Journal of Economics* (November, 1970) LXXXIV, pp. 611–626.

Meiners, Roger E., "Economic Considerations in History: Theory and a Little Practice," infra.

Nagel, Ernest, "Assumptions in Economic Theory," *American Economic Review, Proceedings* (May, 1963) LIII, pp. 211–219.

Oi, Walter Y., "The Economics of Product Safety," *Bell Journal of Economics and Management Science* (Spring, 1973) IV, pp. 3–28.

Popper, Karl, *The Logic of Scientific Discovery*, Basic Books, New York (1959).

Posner, Richard A., *Economic Analysis of Law*, Little, Brown & Co., Boston and Toronto (1972).

———, "Epstein's Tort Theory: A Critique," *Journal of Legal Studies* (June, 1979) VIII, pp. 457–475.

Prosser, William L., *Handbook of the Law of Torts*, 4th ed., West Publishing, St. Paul (1971).

Radnitzky, Gerard, "The Role of Cost-Benefit Analysis in the Methodology of Research," infra.

Samuelson, Paul A., "Problems in Methodology: Discussion," *American Economic Review, Proceedings* (May, 1963) LIII, pp. 211–219.

Schlegel, R., *Completeness In Science*, Appleton-Century-Crofts, New York (1967).

Seavy, Warren A., *Handbook of the Law of Agency*, West Publishing, St. Paul (1964).

Shavell, Steven, "Strict Liability vs. Negligence," *Journal of Legal Studies* (January, 1980) XIX, pp. 1–26.

Sheiner, Naomi, "DES and a Proposed Theory of Enterprise Liability," *Fordham Law Review* (April, 1978) XLVI, pp. 963–1007.

Simon, Herbert A., "New Developments in the Theory of the Firm," *American Economic Review, Proceedings* (May, 1962) LII, pp. 1–15.

————, "Theories of Decision Making in Economics and Behavioral Science," *American Economic Review* (June, 1959) XLIX, pp. 253–283.

Smith, Adam, *An Inquiry into the Nature and Causes of the Wealth of Nations (1776)*, Edwin Cannan (ed.), Modern Library, New York (1937).

Stigler, George J., "The Economics of Information," *Journal of Political Economy* (June, 1961) LXIX, pp. 213–225.

Tullock, Gordon, "Autocracy," infra.

Umbeck, John, "Might Makes Right: A Theory of the Foundation and Initial Distribution of Property Rights," *Economic Inquiry* (January, 1981) XIX, pp. 38–59.

Wible, James R., "Friedman's Positive Economics and Philosophy of Science," *Southern Economic Journal* (October, 1982) XLIX, pp. 350–360.

Williamson, Oliver E., "Credible Commitments: Using Hostages to Support Exchange," *American Economic Review* (September, 1983) LXXIII, pp. 519–540.

————, "Hierarchical Control and Optimum Firm Size," *Journal of Political Economy* (April, 1967) LXXV, pp. 123–138.

————, "Managerial Discretion and Business Behavior," *American Economic Review* (December, 1963) LIII, pp. 1032–1057.

————, *Markets and Hierarchies: Analysis and Antitrust Implications*, Free Press, New York (1975).

————, "Transaction Cost Economics: The Governance of Contractual Relations," *Journal of Law and Economics* (October, 1979) XXII, pp. 233–261.

Wong, Stanley, "The 'F-Twist' and the Methodology of Paul Samuelson," *American Economic Review* (June, 1973) LXIII, pp. 313–325.

Restatement (Second) of Torts, American Law Institute Publishers, St. Paul (1965).

Listing of Legal Cases

Greenman v. Yuba Power Products, Inc., 59 Cal. 2d 57, 377 P. 2d 897, 27 Cal. Reptr. 697 (1962).

MacPherson v. Buick Motor Co., 217 N.Y. 382, 111 N.E. 1050 (1916).

Sindell v. Abbott Laboratories, 26 Cal. 3d 588, 607 P. 2d 924, 163 Cal. Rptr. 132 (1980).

United States v. Carroll Towing Co., 159 F. 2d 169 (1947).

Winterbottom v. Wright, 152 Eng. Rep. 402 (1842).

Part II

ECONOMIC CONSIDERATIONS IN HISTORY: THEORY AND A LITTLE PRACTICE

ROGER E. MEINERS

I INTRODUCTION

The intellectual origins of the development of a discipline or of major changes in the methodology of a discipline are worth recounting not only for posterity, but because they may help us understand the nature of the evolution of inquiry. This paper provides an overview of the evolution of the method of inquiry in economic history (the application of economic theory to historical events). Specifically, the paper concerns the "new economic history" that has emerged in the last few decades. This field was first branded "cliometrics," to distinguish it from traditional inquiry in economic history, but today is the essence of economic history.

According to one study,[1] the cliometric revolution can be traced to 1957 when A. H. Conrad and J. R. Meyer presented papers entitled "Economic Theory, Statistical Inference, and Economic History," and "The Economics of Slavery in the Ante-Bellum South" at the annual Economic History Association meetings. William Parker, a distinguished cliometrician, identified other originating sources of cliometric techniques during the early 1960s.[2] These include Gerschenkron's seminars at Harvard, Douglass North's circle at the University of Washington, studies by the Purdue faculty, and the various connections and researches of Robert Fogel. By the early 1970s, cliometrics and economic history were considered as virtual synonyms at Harvard, Washington (Seattle), Wisconsin, Pennsylvania, Berkeley, Stanford, Yale and Chicago.

The explosive growth of cliometrics was largely due to the interaction of two intellectual trends, one in economic history and one in economics. Under the influence of the American Institutional School of Richard Ely (a founder of the American Economic Association in the late 1800s) and Wesley Clair Mitchell (popularizer of economic data gathering, but not of econometric analysis, in the early 1900s), U.S. economic historians (and to an extent those in Britain, as well) had become generally indistinguishable from other historians in everything but subject-matter specialization. An economic historian studied "economic phenomena," often with some reference to "economic data." Depressions, inflations, the expansion or decline of various industries were grist for his mill. Commentary about these phenomena was, however, almost entirely detached from formal economic analysis, and shared in misconceptions similar to those contained in the "ersatz economics" of political speech writers.

During this century economics was developing an ever wider scope of inquiry and progressively more subtle and powerful modes of analysis.[3] At the same time, "economic historians" were becoming progressively less sophisticated in economics. When contemporary economists focused their attention on historical issues, the results were startling. Conventional economic historians could not respond to the "new school" because they had little training in deductive inference and little understanding of statistical method or the application of microeconomic reasoning to historical phenomena.

Although cliometricians invariably describe themselves as economic historians,[4] such a description may be as misleading as the popular belief that economics is concerned solely with money prices and financial strategies. In fact, cliometrics is no more confined to strictly "economic phenomena" than economics is to what is more properly termed "business finance." Virtually all issues in the "performance and structure" of "social institutions" is subject to cliometric analysis. The dividing line between cliometrics and other historical research is *not* found in the nature of the subject matter being studied. Cliometrics is, rather, distinguished from ordinary history by the explicit application of economic theory to historical phenomena (as opposed to the implicit application of theories from other disciplines common in traditional "economic history" to historical phenomena).

The basic distinction between an economic explanation of historical events and explanations based on psychology, sociology, or various forms of eclecticism and historicism, lies in the "methodology" or the underlying premises of the competing theories about human behavior.

Economic studies of large-scale historical phenomena assume that human tastes, wants, or desires are "constant."[5] This does not mean that individuals lack uniqueness or that people do not change their minds. Nor does it deny the existence of what James Coleman calls "norms" in his contribution to this volume. It means simply that all persons seek certain basic "commodities"—food, shelter, entertainment, etc.—and that differences in the various goods that different people use to satisfy these desires are the results of varying relative costs and differences in the knowledge endowments of differently situated individuals. Particular persons within a society constantly experiment with new alternatives to satisfy basic desires; successful experiments are quickly incorporated into social consumption patterns.

An economic explanation of historical events and large-scale changes in behavior thus reduces to an examination and explanation of the changes in relative costs and information that have caused individuals to alter the means used in their quest for utility maximization. That we do things differently than our forebearers, or from persons in "less developed countries," is the result of alternatives being available to us that are not open to them. Whenever an "historical explanation" must resort to the incantation of differences in "attitudes," "cultures," or "tastes" among peoples in order to complete its task, it has sunk below the level of economic history as conceived by the cliometrician.

Although it is not clear that all cliometricians would articulate the nature of their research program in quite these terms,[6] it is apparent that the different types of problems they have addressed and the different camps into which they have formed themselves fit into this framework. It also seems that the major criticisms leveled by conventional historians against cliometrics evaporate when viewed from this perspective.

The first half of this paper is devoted to a discussion of the origins and development of the new schools of economic history. The methodological bases of the cliometric school and of the property rights school, and their criticisms by traditional economic historians, are discussed in turn. The second half of the paper then turns to the application of the methodology of the new economic history, particularly from a property rights approach, to a specific issue, the growth of the federal government in the United States. The hypothesis is posited, the issues discussed, the constraints identified and their effects discussed, and some evidence is examined. The paper concludes with a summary of the major points addressed in the section on the growth of government and suggests directions for further inquiry.

II SCHOOLS OF CLIOMETRIC INQUIRY

Cliometric studies may be broadly grouped into one of two categories: those that are technical analyses of data (mainly applications of econometrics) and those that are speculative or theoretical (e.g., "property rights") inquiries. These categories are not *necessarily* exclusive, but most papers and most researchers emphasize one or the other of these approaches.

A THE ECONOMETRIC EMPHASIS

The first of these categories is probably the most widely known and has been the domain of some of the more prestigious cliometric scholars (e.g., Robert Fogel, Stanley Engermann, Milton Friedman and Anna Schwartz, Donald McCloskey and Max Hartwell, as well as most of the researchers publishing in *Research in Economic History*).

As Donald McCloskey has noted in his evaluation of this literature,[7] the cliometricians of the empirical (number crunching) school have concerned themselves with a variety of issues, including patterns of feudal land tenure, the importance of railroads in the United States' economic development, the productivity of slave labor in the South, patterns of demographic growth and decline, shipping and maritime trade in colonial development, the effects and causes of regulation of the railroads, and the role of monetary sources in causing recessions and depressions. In addition, McCloskey has isolated three major types of studies common in this cliometric/econometric tradition.

The first, and most pedestrian, is the critical reinterpretation of simple economic arguments and correction of the misuse and misinterpretation of data by prior conventional historians.[8] As an example, much of the righteous fury expressed by chroniclers of the Industrial Revolution in England might have been quenched by the corrective of reasoning in terms of opportunity cost and by econometric analysis of the data the same researchers had so carefully collected. Such an inquiry would disclose that the lot of the poorer classes steadily improved after the 1830s and was not as wretched as it had been in rural England of previous ages. Much of what has passed as the evils of industrialization is attributable to rapid urbanization, as country dwellers sought new opportunities in the cities. While urban/industrial life of that period would be unappealing to us, it was preferable to the rural/agrarian opportunities existing at that time.

The clear preference of the technical sophisticate of the econometric branch of cliometrics is, however, to go beyond a mere "rethinking of bad economics and reshuffling of the numbers of others in the light of economic theory."[9] The next step in the cliometric program for reforming the conventional method of applying economic theory is, whenever possible, to reduce historical questions to those of "economic counting." Although, in a strictly logical sense, the econometrician/cliometrician cannot determine with certainty that X caused Y, his analysis of data can present a more refined and compact view of what is *not* true about historical facts—Z did *not* cause Y. It is a corrective for the metaphors and misleading scholarly chatter concerning "vital factors" or influences "concerning which it-is-difficult-to-exaggerate-the-importance-of."[10] While it is often possible to "lie with statistics," it is even easier to distort, exaggerate, and deceive when unconstrained by the use of any systematic analytic technique for distinguishing important from incidental facts.

As McCloskey notes, the application of econometrics to the sweeping generalizations of many studies (e.g., Rostow's theory of growth and industrialization), or to previously "well-settled" issues like the productivity of slave labor, has sparked controversies forcing both sides to reason more closely and gather more evidence. Indeed, it is probably the case that cliometrics has been the impetus behind the increase in research programs that ferret-out new bodies of "hard facts" (historical data sources) during the last two decades.[11] It is precisely this process of conjecture and refutation[12] that McCloskey maintains is the highest form of the econometrician/cliometrician's art. Only when new and bold reinterpretations of formerly settled wisdom have been advanced and defended, by the use of economic reasoning supported by econometric analysis, has the "new school" made a significant impact on the older economic history establishment.

B CRITICISMS OF ECONOMETRIC METHODS IN HISTORY

Having briefly sketched the interests and techniques of one branch of cliometrics, it is worthwhile to examine, with equal brevity, the criticisms of this methodological development by "conventional" economic historians.

One of the better accepted and least intelligible criticisms of cliometrics is that it is representative of the "counterfactual approach to history." Alternatively expressed, cliometricians consider what would have been the consequences of different configurations of historical events in explaining and justifying their hypotheses about what actually happened. (This technique is rather like a statistical *reductio ad absurdum* of opposing historical explanations.) According to traditional economic historians critical of this cliometric technique, "true" history concerns itself only with what "in fact" happened, never with what might have happened had conditions been different. That the roots of this confusion over empirical method are at least as ancient as Lord Bacon, does not make the error more palatable. Raw facts, to the extent they exist, do not "speak," and certainly have nothing to tell anyone about *causes* in history or society.

Causes are inferential attributes of hypotheses. Hypotheses are tested by reference to facts but are not "derived from" or "suggested by" facts.[13] In such tests it is the mark of good econometric technique, and of informative history, not to test one's theory against a null hypothesis or undefined alternative. For both the economic historian and the theoretical statistician, the interesting alternative to "X caused Y" is "Z caused Y," not "Y just happened" (no cause). Since the notion that history may be a unique sequence of events without interconnections has no appeal for the historian, then critical examination of *alternative* causal explanations for particular historical events must be at the core of what the historian does. As McCloskey notes, it is only when what has been universally accepted as "obviously true" is challenged, that truly scholarly discussion, debate, and research begins.[14]

Examination of two other criticisms leveled against cliometrics is useful as an introduction to the property rights emphasis in cliometric research. Critics of the cliometric approach have held that the models of its practitioners are excessively complex and intricate *and* that the cliometric approach is only suited to relatively trivial problems that can be narrowed down to isolated cases involving few variables. This combination of arguments is not unfamiliar in the history of economic controversy. It emerged during the middle classical period (mid-1800s) in Europe, England, and America, and is frequently dusted-off whenever a new area of human or social study comes under the scrutiny of economic analysis. Variants of the argument may be characterized as follows: (1) the charge of "excessive abstraction" and of "sole reliance on inferential reasoning" and (2) the charge of triviality or of one-dimensional analysis. The one view was traditionally connected with the Baconian attacks of J. K. Ingram and other British historical economists against Classicism in the mid-nineteenth century, while the Marxists and other rationalist historicists on the continent leveled the same attack in the late nineteenth and early twentieth centuries. An example of a combination of these views in an attack against cliometrics is found in McClelland's "Cliometrics versus Institutional History."[15] A more general defense of social science against these patterns of criticism is found in Popper's *Poverty of Historicism*.[16]

The first of these views emphasizes that all social inquiry, and certainly all historical writing, should "stay close to the facts" and not "engage in long chains of deductive inference" (Marshall). Insofar as this counsel is directed at the need for explicit theory formulation and tests of previous implicit assumptions, it is, of course, valid. However, the more typical interpretations entail an implicit rejection of the role of formal (testable) hypothesis formulation in history. According to this view, either it is *always* premature to construct an explanation of particular historical phenomena (since there are still facts which *could* be collected) or such explanations must *necessarily* involve an indefinitely large number of explanatory variables and principles. Because the practicing and publishing historian must *per force* ignore the former advice, the practical criticism advanced against cliometrics from this perspective reduces to the claim that the cliometrician unwisely ignores a variety of non-economic forces that are important, and that are alleged to predominate often in the phenomena being explained. While cliometrics can thus describe everything about *one* aspect of historical causation, it will, in most instances, be blinded to the "more fundamental" reasons why things happened as they did.

Although it may be conceded that the econometrically-oriented cliometrician has certain blind-spots in his approach, the criticism noted above does not correctly identify the nature of his limitations. Econometric analysis is bounded not by some imagined division between what is and what is not economically motivated behavior, but by what properties of the behavior can be and have been cardinally measured. So long as one historical situation (or explanation) is distinguishable from others in terms of cardinally measurable differences in the constraints faced by the historical actors, the situation is amenable to econometric/cliometric analysis. Ordinal measures, though less useful than cardinal measures, can be used to test hypotheses, and often are in economic history because of the nature of the data. There are non-parametric statistical techniques that allow the use of relative rankings.

There are, of course, situations in which the values of the constraints on choice cannot be measured cardinally. In such historical situations econometric analysis may not be helpful, but economic theory (especially "property rights analysis") can be useful. That certain causal factors cannot be cardinally described does not mean that they cannot be ordinally ranked and then compared with similar factors in other situations. In fact, the usual case of market decision making is that the actors only know whether A is preferable to, equally preferred to, or less preferred than, alternative B. In this context, an inability to perform cardinal operations on choice-relevant constraints was long ago considered and solved in economics.[17] Insofar as "cliometrics" is used synonymously with "the new economic history," and is not necessarily limited to the application of econometric techniques, the causal factors in a situation need not be "quantitative," in the strong sense of that term.

C PROPERTY RIGHTS AND HISTORY

The second major division in cliometric studies is that of "property rights analysis" of social phenomena. Such analyses have run the spectrum from rather narrowly focused studies, such as why labor-owned and labor-managed firms in Yugoslavia tend to invest less than "capitalistic" (stockowner-owned) corporations in the United States, to more grandiose studies concerning the rise (economic development) of the western world. The reader is referred to the De Alessi paper in this volume for a property rights discussion by a leading scholar in that field. All property rights analyses, however, share a common microeconomic perspective on the institution or institutions being examined, whether the institution is a government bureau, a capitalistic firm, a nonprofit foundation, a social club, a court, a system of land tenure, or a religious organization. In each case the analysis proceeds by identifying what the participants in the institution are "really" seeking, and thereby specifying the particular features of the institution that make it more or less costly at the margin for the participants to use one technique, over alternative techniques, in achieving their goals or ends. The property rights approach (or research program) has the advantage over conventional historical methods of forcing the historicist to adopt a unified and systematic view of his subject matter.

Although the previously mentioned criticism of excessive abstraction is correct in identifying one potential abuse of the "property rights" technique (in which an incautious or unscrupulous analyst might constrict a "social myth" or ideology by systematically distorting the evidence), this criticism fails to note the even greater dangers of uncontrolled hypothesis formation common in the older economic history. Because the conventional historian is laboring under no methodological prescriptions when he brews his visions of the "true" past, he can concoct an eclectic stew of ersatz psychology, sociology, and economics to form explanations or "hypotheses" that are empirically unfalsifiable and are often impervious to rational criticism or debate. The property rights theorist, on the other hand, is subject to stating his conclusions and reasoning in a form that renders them accessible to other practitioners of the same science. The adoption of a property-rights approach to economic history thus renders such studies subject to correction or falsification on the basis of either logical critiques or empirical counterexamples.[18]

That the study of history can be done badly by conventional methods does not imply that property rights analysis is any guarantee against intellectual superficiality. As Douglass North has noted, "From the viewpoint of the economic historian this neoclassical formulation (of perfectly specified property rights, no transactions costs, no externalities, and perfect competition in all markets) begs all of the interesting questions."[19] It is the attempt to specify these questions for particular institutional settings that initially distinguished property rights analysis from neoclassical economic model building and parameter-tweaking.

Some of the interesting questions include: (1) What is the extent to which property rights in particular types of scarce things are left unspecified (or are subject to rapid political redefinition or "redistribution")? (2) What sorts of information costs, relevant to the choices of consumers and resource suppliers, are there in a given situation, and what are the costs and benefits of investment in information? (3) Are the decision-making or production systems of certain institutions subject to free rider problems, and, if so, what are the costs and benefits to the various participants of changing these systems? (4) What sort of institutions tend to generate "simple" wealth-maximizing behavior and what sorts generate a complex mixture of goal-seeking? While the "pure theorist" is free to hypothesize any possible world with whatever imaginable (but unattainable) characteristics, the property rights theorist must first attempt to find out "where we are" before he can intelligently examine the costs and benefits of proposed changes. Similarly, the historian using property rights analysis may either:

(1) Examine why things turned out as they did, despite contrary expectations and publicly announced goals to be achieved by constructed institutions (essentially a problem in the logic of institutional statics), or

(2) Inquire why institutions changed or evolved along one path rather than another (a problem in the dynamics of institutional evolution).

The former sort of study is almost always subject to a more thorough specification of constraints, as well as more critical debate and better directed empirical research concerning the correctness of the specification. But it is usually more "narrow" than the latter, and certainly less sweeping in its generalizations and conclusions.

D CRITICISMS OF THE PROPERTY RIGHTS APPROACH TO ECONOMIC HISTORY

The central criticism of the property rights approach to economic history is simply that the property rights theorist attempts to explain too much from too little. According to this view, historical events are the consequence of complex causal factors, from the particular personalities of the actors to broad social trends. To be done properly history must account for historical phenomena in all its richness.

This criticism is but another expression of the historicist preoccupation with the complexity of phenomena and the role of "right intuition" and "aesthetic appreciation" in historical studies.[20] According to this historicist perspective, historical phenomena are impenetrably complex so far as the unaided intellect is concerned. The "essence" of history is only open to the special senses of a few gifted individuals who can intuit what is important and what is trivial in the overwhelming mass of available records. History is thus art, but it is a form of art subject to truth and falsity of a special sort. To know the truth of history is to possess what the German "rationalists" called "understanding."

Diametrically opposed to this conception is the view (of property rights analysis and, more broadly, economics) that human behavior differs according to differences in the costs of alternative actions. These differences in costs are ultimately traceable to observable differences in the particular physical or institutional constraints faced by differently situated individuals. Anyone may observe these differences, and, although they may not be "intuitively obvious" *ex ante*, they are understandable by scholars of ordinary intelligence once they have been discovered and explained.

The second major strain in the above noted criticism is the implicit belief that the property rights analyst/economist deals solely with "economic motives" to action (wealth maximization, narrowly conceived). Because there are also a host of other reasons why people do the things they do, then an economic analysis must be, at best, incomplete and, at worst, misleading. This criticism, again, fails to recognize that the linchpin of economic analysis is not nominal wealth maximization *per se* (except in the most impersonal and one-dimensional perfectly-competitive settings) but is, rather, utility maximization with "constant tastes." This framework of analysis may thus be extended to any sort of situation explainable in terms of a comparison of altered constraints on action. That men may sometimes seek only money, while in other situations they pursue a complex set of goals, has more to do with how well money exchanges (markets) are developed in such situations than it does with purported differences in tastes.

III   AN APPLICATION OF THE NEW ECONOMIC HISTORY

This part of the paper presents some initial research concerning the size and growth of the federal government in the United States. The analysis is presented both as an example of economic history utilizing the methods of the new economic history, especially the property rights approach, and as an example of how the results of this method contrast with discussions of the same topic by conventional historians.

A   THE HYPOTHESIS

The principal hypothesis here is that the federal government was larger in the nineteenth century than statistics generally relied upon would indicate, but that the growth of the federal sector was effectively blocked until there were major changes in the institutional constraints faced by participants in the political process.

There has been substantial increase in interest over the last decade in the phenomenon called "the growth of government." However, many studies have been limited to an examination of data describing that growth.[21] Public choice theory has helped to explain why politicians encourage the growth and why public resources are expended as they are.[22] Other economic studies have explored the relative efficiency of public enterprises, in their different forms, and sometimes have compared these enterprises to private enterprises.[23] Why the growth of the federal government occurred when it did and as it did, that is, what the origins of this growth are, has not been extensively explored.

There seems to be a general assumption that as countries become relatively wealthier they "must" have, or they prefer to have, relatively larger governmental sectors.[24] It is possible that this is true, but no explanation as to why it may be true has been advanced.[25] Casting doubt on that assertion is the observation that one of the wealthier European nations, Switzerland, has a relatively "small" federal government. Furthermore, we observe many low income countries with relatively large federal governments. *Ad hoc* "explanations" or rationalizations, buttressed by anecdotal evidence, are not sufficient to qualify as scientific explanations of a process such as the growth of government.

B   A DIGRESSION ON PUBLIC CHOICE

Prior to the invention of the field called public choice, neither political science or economics had developed models to provide systematic analysis of political (governmental) phenomena.[26] Economists' concerns about government tended to be limited to macroeconomic issues (growth of the economy, inflation, etc.) and to public finance, which tended to focus on methods for extracting resources for public purposes and the relative (normative) merits of alternative schemes of taxation, and to a "welfare" analysis of monopoly and regulatory policies. It has been only in the last thirty years that economics has begun to be systematically applied to matters previously left to political science. Although the antecedents of public choice are old, the application of economic methodology to political phenomena is recent. Rational, selfish, utility-maximizing individuals are now understood to participate in the political sector, just as in the private sector. This paper does not review the methods or substantial contribution of public choice scholarship, but relies upon its methods in considering the growth of government and the behavior of politicians.

C   THE ISSUE

The percentage of the nation's income devoted to public sector activity has increased considerably, by any measure, during the twentieth century.[27] Although real per capita income may be a constraint on the growth rate of government revenues at any particular time, income growth alone does not seem to explain the growth of the public sector in the United States.[28] Because economic theory hypothesizes that people are rational utility maximizers, we must look to changes in constraints, not changes in human motivation, to help explain why some things evolve and why others do not.

In studying the size and growth of the federal government there are two main areas of inquiry. One concerns how to measure the size of the government at any point in time. Whenever we examine the government at a particular time, we must establish the parameters of what is defined as governmental, and attempt to maintain those parameters for purposes of comparing governmental size at different times on a reasonably consistent basis. This objective entails both a concern about the validity and comparability of statistics over time, and also a concern about what to include in the statistical base; i.e., a definition of what is governmental activity. The other major area of inquiry concerns the measurement of governmental growth, also a statistical concern, and an identification of the *causes* of this growth; i.e., what stimulates the process by which resources are reallocated via the public sector. Although exogenous events, such as another country declaring war, could cause a change in the resources devoted to the public sector, endogenous events that change the constraints faced by politicians (including events caused by politicians) are also important in explaining why the growth of government may have occurred. This paper focuses on an identification of those endogenous political constraints that have changed and how politicians have operated before and after these changes in endogenous constraints.

D INSTITUTIONAL CONSTRAINTS

There were significant changes in the constraints facing politicians in the early part of the twentieth century. The major hypothesis here is that the existence of the earlier constraints, which were constant for over a century before that time, were instrumental in blocking an increase in the growth of the federal government before World War I. Why the changes in the constraints discussed below occurred I do not know. Nor have I found an explanation, or alleged explanation, in the economic history and traditional history. The discussions reviewed so far emphasize intuitive relationships between selected historical events, a common mistake by historians of confusing manifestations of causation with the causes themselves.

It is hypothesized here that there were two major institutional changes (changes in constraints or property rights) that fostered the expansion of the federal government. One was the Sixteenth Amendment to the Constitution, allowing the imposition of income taxes. The second change, also effected in 1913, was the Seventeenth Amendment to the Constitution, providing for the direct election of United States senators. Which of these may be more important, and if one was a contributor to the existence of the other, is not developed here.[29]

Before discussing these major institutional changes, it is worth noting the possible impact on governmental growth of two other changes that occurred about the same time. One is the development of the primary election system in the late 1800s and early 1900s. Prior to that time candidates for most offices were selected by party conventions or other methods that involved a small number of voters. The popular election of candidates for office may have changed the incentives of officeholders and would-be officeholders. The other change that may have had an effect on the growth of the federal government was the expansion of the voting franchise. Although the franchise gradually expanded among adult male citizens during the nineteenth century, the Nineteenth Amendment, effected in 1920, provided voting rights to adult female citizens. The result was a fifty percent increase in the number of voters in the 1920 presidential election over the 1916 election. That contrasts to the thirty years it took, before 1916, for a similar increase in the number of participating voters (largely due to population growth). The change in the composition of the franchise, and its subsequent continued expansion, may be related to the growth of the federal government in the twentieth century, but it is mentioned here only as a hint of lines of research needed to fully flesh-out our understanding of the political economy of this period.

Before the Sixteenth Amendment there was a constitutional constraint that effectively limited the ability of Congress to raise revenues, thereby limiting the scope of federal activities. The history subsequent to the amendment (which was accompanied the same year by the imposition of an income tax) has been studied by scholars concerned with the growth of government. Economic theory assumes that, for all intents and purposes, politicians were the same people, with the same incentives, before and after the existence of the income tax. Yet little attention has been paid to how politicians adjusted to conditions prevailing before the revenue bonanza provided by the income tax. As will be discussed below, although the income constraint was effective, politicians were creative and found alternative resources and sources of non-monetary revenue to distribute to their electors.

The structure of the Constitution before the Seventeenth Amendment also placed a constraint on the growth of the federal government, although it may have played a smaller role than the denial of income taxes in deterring the overall growth of government. Prior to the direct election of senators, they were elected by state legislatures. The hypothesis proffered here is that federal senators were agents of their state legislatures and could be expected to act in a manner consistent with the interests of those legislatures. After 1913 the interests of senators became much more like those of their colleagues in the House of Representatives, who were always elected by popular vote. (Although, as noted above, House members were often not nominated by popular vote until the twentieth century.)

A non-exhaustive survey of the history and legal history literature concerning the Sixteenth and Seventeenth Amendments, and their possible consequences, has failed to disclose any critical analyses of the interests favoring these measures. In one sense this is not surprising— many historians only attempt to be accurate reporters, providing merely a narrative of events. However, such scholarship, although incomplete, has the merit of at least providing an accurate chronicle of history. This approach is more useful than the selective reporting done by historians who have little methodological consistency to their analysis but an ideological point to advance. Both schools, however, suffer from a lack of any consistent analytic framework to guide their research and presentation of results. As a generalization, most historians report the Sixteenth and Seventeenth Amendments as foregone conclusions. These events are not worthy of much discussion beyond the passing observation that they were the product of a "reform movement." Although the hypothesis that the amendments were in fact of major importance may not be supported by the evidence, a study of the forces that produced them is important in understanding why such changes in property rights occur. It is illustrative of the state of modern historical work that these amendments have been virtually ignored. To many twentieth century liberals, history is only a story of good guys and bad guys. The vast majority of the population is regarded as too inconsequential or too stupid to be labelled good or bad; besides, ordinary people have had little to do with "making" history. The Sixteenth and Seventeenth Amendments, like many other events, are regarded only as a detail of "historical progress." They are seen as the inevitable product of the forces of good. They are steps in a beneficial process of change, not the beginning of a new institutional framework, so they are worthy of little consideration.

E   EFFECTS OF CONSTRAINTS PRIOR TO THE SIXTEENTH AND SEVENTEENTH AMENDMENTS

Before the Sixteenth Amendment, the legality of direct taxes on income was suspect. An income tax was used during the Civil War, expiring in 1872. It applied to individual incomes over $4,000 per year, although various deductions were used. Another income tax was legislated in 1894 but was struck down as unconstitutional by the Supreme Court before it took effect.[30] The Court held:

> The power to lay direct taxes apportioned among the several states in proportion to their representation in the popular branch of Congress, a representation based on population as ascertained by the census, was

plenary and absolute; but to lay direct taxes without apportionment was forbidden. The power to lay duties, imposts, and excises was subject to the qualification that the imposition must be uniform throughout the United States.*** In the light of the struggle in the convention as to whether or not the new nation should be empowered to levy taxes directly on the individual . . . it would seem beyond reasonable question that direct taxation . . . was purposely restrained to apportionment according to representation. . . .*** The founders anticipated that the expenditures of the states, their counties, cities, and towns would chiefly be met by direct taxation on accumulated property, while they expected that those of the federal government would be for the most part met by indirect taxes.*** Whatever the speculative views of political economists or revenue reformers may be. . . . There can be but one answer, unless the constitutional restriction is to be treated as utterly illusory and futile, and the object of its framers defeated.[31]

The Court went on to lecture Congress to the effect that, if it wished to collect direct taxes, it must determine the amount desired and bill each state according to its population. The states could levy any kind of direct tax they pleased to raise the revenues for the federal government.[32]

Congress enacted direct tax levies on the states five times: 1798 (to help eliminate the Revolutionary War debt); 1813, 1815, and 1816 (for the War of 1812); and 1861 (for the Civil War). These levies totaled $34 million and collected $28.1 million, of which $14.2 million (from the Civil War levy) was returned to the states in 1891. This method of financing federal expenditures accounted for a small fraction of one percent of all federal revenues during the first one hundred years of the Republic.[33] Denied the use of direct taxes by the Constitution and by the failure of Congress to levy taxes on the states, the federal government (i.e., Congress) relied upon two primary sources of income: tariffs (and other customs duties) and taxes on commodities (primarily on liquor and tobacco). Before the Civil War, customs duties consistently accounted for the large majority of federal revenues; after the war, until the introduction of the income tax, customs duties and commodity taxes usually accounted for over ninety percent of federal revenues.[34] Because international trade always accounted for a small share of gross national product in the United States, and because only so much liquor and tobacco is consumed, these income sources were clearly limited in their ability to generate revenues.[35] Congress was, however, continuously creative in looking for products to tax. For example, in 1882, federal taxes were levied on: friction matches, patent medicines, perfumes, bank checks, and bank deposits. In later years, oleomargarine, chewing gum, and other products were added. Businesses were also taxed. To help pay for the Spanish-American War (1898), Congress levied taxes on banks, pawnbrokers, theaters, circuses, museums, concert halls, bowling alleys, and poolrooms. For instance, each bank was supposed to pay $50 per year, a circus $100 per year for each state in which they performed, and bowling alleys $5 per year per alley.

There were sundry other sources Congress cleverly thought to tax, but the constitutional prohibition against a federal income tax seems to have been substantial in holding down the revenue flow Congress might have otherwise obtained. As Table 2.1 shows, by 1900 per capita federal expenditures were at least triple the 1800 level of expenditures. However, because real per capita income had also at least tripled during the century, the level of federal expenditures as a share of national income was probably no higher in 1900 than it was in 1800, and may have been lower.[36]

Based on this information about the relative stability of federal expenditures for the first 125 years of the Republic, I conclude that the lack of ability to levy direct taxes was an important constraint on federal governmental growth. The members of Congress were ingenious in exploiting the sources that were available, and constantly tinkered

Table 2.1 Federal Expenditures*

Year	Total	% GNP	Per Capita
1800	$ 10,000		$2.04
1810	8,474,000		1.17
1820	18,285,000		1.90
1830	15,141,000		1.18
1840	24,213,000		1.42
1850	40,947,000		1.76
1860	63,200,000		2.01
1870	293,656,000	.029	7.61
1880	264,847,000	.015	5.28
1890	297,736,000	.013	4.75
1900	487,713,000	.013	6.39

*Nominal dollar terms; expenditures include interest payments.

with new possible sources, but the ability to exploit the best source of revenues was largely excluded until 1913. As will be noted below, the election of senators by state legislatures probably contributed to the lack of growth in the federal government. One reason may have been that senators generally would oppose the ability of the federal government to levy income taxes. However, as is developed in the discussion about the incentives of senators, prior to the Sixteenth and Seventeenth Amendments all members of Congress had the same general incentives as do members of Congress today. The diligence with which they searched for federal revenue sources is one bit of evidence for this; another is the manner in which they treated the largest single asset of the federal government, the public lands.

Before the Seventeenth Amendment, most members of the United States Senate were picked by state legislatures.[37] Because members of the Senate relied upon members of the state legislatures for their continuance in office, they had an incentive to respond to the interests of the majority of the members of the state legislature, rather than to a majority of the voters in the state. Obviously, many of the interests of state legislators and citizens would coincide, but, compared to members of the House of Representatives, one would predict that senators would behave more as agents of the more direct interests of state legislators rather than as agents of blocks of voters within the state. The primary differences in incentives of senators and representatives would be that, other things equal, senators would oppose expanding federal jurisdiction and revenues at the expense of state jurisdiction and revenues. Senators would try to channel federal revenues into state coffers for redistribution by the state legislatures, rather than favoring direct Congressional distribution of these resources (as would be preferred by members of the House). This incentive would produce a smaller federal government than one would expect with direct popular election of senators.

Evidence that members of the Senate acted as agents of state legislatures before the Seventeenth Amendment may be observed in differences in their voting behavior on legislation, when compared to the voting behavior of members of the House. On many legislative issues both sets of representatives from any state would have similar incentives; for example, Congressmen from textile-producing states would vote for certain protective measures for textiles, whether they were in the House or Senate. However, on some bills the interests of state legislatures are not consistent with the interests of the federal legislature. A study of legislative proposals during the 1800s should provide evidence relevant to the correctness of this hypothesis.

F EVIDENCE OF THE EFFECTS OF THE CONSTRAINTS

Legislation and proposed legislation concerning one policy area was selected for study of the hypothesis that senators acted as agents of state legislatures, and of the hypothesis that Congressional politicians engaged in active redistribution before the Sixteenth Amendment (but relied on money substitutes to redistribute due to the lack of direct tax revenues). Land distribution policy in the 1800s is the area considered. Secondary sources—the major historical studies of federal land policies—have been primarily relied upon.

A digression about the origins of land policy will be helpful at this point. When the original thirteen states of the union agreed to the Articles of Confederation, the six fixed-border states insisted, before agreeing to sign, that the seven other states fix their boundaries and cede their claims to western lands. The seven states claimed title to lands west of their original boundaries that were extensive and, in some cases, indefinite. The fixed-border states were concerned that the other states would become very powerful politically and dominate the confederation as population grew in the western lands. Boundaries were agreed to for all states and the western lands were ceded to the federal government. From that point on, the federal government was to hold title to almost all lands other than the original thirteen states. Major acquisitions included the Louisiana Purchase of 1803, the purchase of Florida in 1819, the annexation of Texas in 1845 (Texas contained no federal lands), the Oregon territory in 1846, the Texas purchase of 1850, the taking of the Southwest from Mexico after the War of 1848, the Gadsden Purchase of 1853, and the Alaska purchase of 1867. In sum, the continental United States, plus Alaska, was owned by the federal government initially, with the exceptions of the east coast states (less Florida), Tennessee, Kentucky, Texas, and private land claims in other states totaling less than 2.6 percent of the land in the states not listed above. The federal government held title to over two-thirds of the land mass in the United States (including Alaska).

This land was, I contend, the primary source of redistributive wealth for federal politicians in the nineteenth century. Denied access to a large stream of current monetary revenues, the members of Congress "spent" federal lands. Beginning with the first session of Congress, there was intense legislative activity about land policy. Members of the House generally advocated the sale of land at low prices in small plots, while the Senate usually pushed for the sale of land in larger tracts at higher prices. This pattern of interest was clearly established by 1820 and can be observed in legislation at least until 1896. The Senate favored measures to increase the revenue flow from federal lands, and, at times, measures intended to benefit established financial interests and the interest of large land speculators. The House favored maximum federal control over the western lands and distribution at zero price or below market prices in small lots to as many individuals as possible. That is, both houses of Congress wished to dispose of the federal lands for the benefit of various residents of the nation, but their disposal schemes were substantively different, indicating that they were appealing to different interests.

Over an eighty year period at least thirteen major pieces of proposed legislation resulted in voting splits in the Senate and House. Because several of the bills were voted on in several sessions of Congress, there were at least twenty voting splits on land policy. In each case, the Senate favored legislation promoting western land sales. The reason for this seems to be an attempt by senators to increase the flow of revenue to the federal government for expenditures that would benefit existing states, or in order to turn the money over to the states directly. Another frequently alleged reason for the interest of the Senate was that they were responding to the "monied interests"—investors who wished to purchase large blocks of land and who supposedly controlled state legislatures. In addition, at least several senators, including Daniel Webster, were large western land-owners, and apparently profited by pre-selecting land they believed to be very desirable. The House, on the other hand, opposed measures to maximize the rate of sale of the land, or the rate of income flow from the land (over any time period). Its primary concern was the distribution of land, even at a zero price, in small plots to individuals. Like the President, the House had little interest in legislation giving federal revenues to the states; rather, they seemed interested in distributing resources to a large number of voters.[38]

The following are examples of bills on which the house split votes: 1832—Senate voted for, House against, a bill to distribute revenues from land sales directly to state treasuries; 1837—Senate voted for, House against, a bill allowing the states to tax federal lands within state boundaries; 1858-59—at least five times the House passed, Senate defeated, a bill allowing homesteading (Senate wanted sales only); 1871-72-73—House passed, Senate defeated, a bill to give (transferable rights to) land to all veterans of the Civil War; 1886—Senate voted for, House against, a bill sanctioning claims by large landholders in the West (often fraudulent claims); 1894-96—Senate voted for, House against, use of timber lands by corporations (House wanted only local, small timber users).

These bills make an arguable case that differences in the votes could be attributed to the interests of members of the Senate in pleasing state legislators. Although historians have observed the differences in House and Senate votes, none have provided a rational analysis of why these votes differ. Instead, we are provided with ideological mythology: that one political party favored the "little man"while another was owned by the railroad interests, etc.[39]

G CONCLUSION

The behavior of politicians in the nineteenth century indicates that they acted in a manner difficult to distinguish from politicians of the twentieth century (although the latter have more successfully spurred the growth of the federal government). Several conclusions may be reached after an examination of the policies adopted prior to the Sixteenth and Seventeenth Amendments. Regardless of their incentives to make the government grow, politicans were effectively blocked by the lack of an income tax and by the lack of senatorial incentives to increase the scope of federal activities at the expense of the states. Per capita federal expenditures do not appear to have grown much, if any, during the nineteenth century. However, if a value could be placed on the equivalent of the one-third of land volume of the United States that was distributed by the federal government during the nineteeth century, it can be argued that the expenditures were considerably higher than are accounted for in the federal budget figures. Because land distribution ended about the turn of this century, and real dollar expenditures were no higher than a century before, one might argue that the federal government had declined in importance during the nineteenth century. That is, because the government sold or gave away its primary asset, it was less wealthy at the end of the century than it was in prior decades.

Whatever the case, there is evidence that the *growth* of the federal government, as a source of redistributive activity, has not been a gradual process going back to the beginning of the Republic. It is something that happened only in this century. It is probably not possible to contend that it was only the Sixteenth and Seventeenth Amendments that allowed the government to grow, and that without them the federal sector would be as "small" as it was a century ago. However, the limitations imposed by the Constitution do appear to be consistent with the lack of growth prior to 1913 and the subsequent growth once these barriers were removed.

NOTES

The author would like to offer his sincere thanks to Craig Bolton of Emory University, David Haddock of Yale University, and Louis De Alessi of the University of Miami for their thoughtful assistance in the preparation of this paper.

1. Coats, p. 185.

2. *Ibid.* p. 197.

3. *Ibid.* p. 198 ff.

4. McCloskey, p. 28; North, p. 3.

5. For a more detailed explanation of the methodological dividing line between economics and the other social sciences, see Becker and Stigler, and Becker, Ch. 1.

6. Indeed certain cliometricians, such as Douglass North in his *Structure & Change in Economic History*, Chs. 1 & 5, seem to explicitly reject the notion of omnipotent economic explanations.

7. McCloskey, pp. 18-22.

8. McCloskey, p. 17.

9. *Ibid.*, p. 15.

10. *Ibid.*, p. 17.

11. *Ibid.*, p. 21.

12. The term embodies Karl Popper's description of how scientific knowledge of all sorts accumulates and is refined over time, see his "Science: Conjectures and Refutations," and his "Three Views Concerning Human Knowledge" in his *Conjectures and Refutations*.

13. Popper, *The Logic of Scientific Discovery*, Ch. 1.

14. McCloskey, p. 21 ff.

15. McClelland

16. Popper, *The Poverty of Historicism*.

17. Hicks, Ch. 1.

18. This is, according to Popper, the distinguishing characteristic of a scientific versus dogmatic approach to the study of social or physical phenomena.

See his *The Poverty of Historicism* and Chs. 1–3 of his *The Logic of Scientific Discovery.*

19. North, p. 5.

20. Popper, *The Poverty of Historicism*, Part 1.

21. See Borcherding for a good example.

22. See Mueller for an overview.

23. See De Alessi for an overview.

24. "Wagner's Law" asserts that "among progressive peoples . . . an increase regularly takes place in the activity of both the central and local governments. . . . In this way the economic needs of the people . . . are satisfied. . . . "(Bullock, p. 24)

25. This may be due to my incomplete search of the literature.

26. Homage should be paid to Gordon Tullock, a contributor here, as one of the founders of the field. A seminal work in public choice is the book by Buchanan and Tullock cited in the bibliography.

27. The percentage of GNP devoted to the federal government has increased from 2.4 percent in 1913 to about 24 percent in 1948. The percentage of GNP devoted to all governments has increased from 8.0 percent in 1913 to at least 42 percent in 1984. Unless otherwise noted, all discussion in this paper is in reference to the United States.

28. This seems to be so in the United States unless one assumes some threshold level of income was required—peculiarly to the United States—for growth in government to begin. There was substantial real economic growth in the nineteenth century but perhaps no real growth of the federal government.

29. My suspicion is that the Seventeenth Amendment may have been more likely to have helped produce the Sixteenth Amendment than the other way around. The reason for this may be evident in the subsequent discussion.

30. 157 U.S. 429 (1895) and 158 U.S. 601 (1895).

31. 158 U.S. 601 at 618, 619, 621, 627.

32. At that time about one-third of the states had an income tax, although revenues were quite small. See Bullock, p. 275.

33. Bullock, p. 299 ff.

34. Bullock, Ch. 18.

35. Imported merchandise did not total $1 billion per year until 1903. Relatively high tax rates were placed on tobacco and liquor. For example, the tax on a gallon of liquor in the 1880s was $0.90.

36. *Historical Statistics,* Series F 1–16. Extrapolation to 1800 assumes growth rate of economy no higher than the rate after 1870. Borcherding (p. 22) notes that federal expenditures, as a percent of GNP, fell from 4.5 percent in 1870 to 2.4 percent in 1890, 1902, and 1913.

37. Beginning around the turn of the century, some states allowed popular votes for Senators.

38. One might ponder the consequences if Congress had not had the incentive to work so diligently to dispose of public lands, by whatever schemes, to private hands. For a discussion of twentieth century federal land policies, and their consequences, see Libecap.

39 Such commentary is almost ubiquitous in historical writings about that period, or any other, of American history.

REFERENCES

Becker, Gary, *The Economic Approach to Human Behavior,* Chicago: University of Chicago Press, (1976).

Becker, Gary and Stigler, George, "De Gustibus Non Est Disputandum," *American Economic Review* 67 (2) (March, 1977) pp. 76–90.

Boland, Lawrence A., *The Foundations of Economic Method,* London: George Allen & Unwin (1982).

Borcherding, Thomes E., (ed.), *Budgets and Bureaucrats: The Sources of Government Growth,* Durham, N.C.: Duke University Press (1977).

Buchanan, James M. and Tullock, Gordon, *The Calculus of Consent,* Ann Arbor: University of Michigan Press (1962).

Bullock, Charles J., *Selected Readings in Public Finance,* Boston: Ginn & Co. (1906).

Coats, A.W., "The Historical Context of the New Economic History," *Journal of European Economic History* 9(1) (Spring, 1980), pp. 185–207.

De Alessi, Louis, "On The Nature and Consequences of Private and Public Enterprises," *Minnesota Law Review* 67(1) (Oct., 1982).

Donaldson, Thomas, *The Public Domain*, Washington, D.C.: Government Printing Office (1884).

Hicks, John R., *Value and Capital*, 2nd Ed., London: Oxford University Press (1967).

Hibbard, Benjamin H., *A History of the Public Land Policies*, New York: Peter Smith (1939).

Historical Statistics of the United States: Colonial Times to 1970, Washington, D.C.: Government Printing Office (1975).

Libecap, Gary D., *Locking Up the Range*, Cambridge: Ballinger Publishing Co. (1981).

McClelland, Peter D., "Cliometrics versus Institutional History," *Research in Economic History* 3 (1978) pp. 369–378.

McCloskey, Donald N., "The Achievements of the Cliometric School," *Journal of Economic History* 38(1) (March, 1978) pp. 13–28.

Mueller, Dennis C., *Public Choice*, Cambridge: Cambridge University Press (1979).

North, Douglass C., *Structure and Change in Economic History*, (New York: W. W. Norton & Co. (1981).

Popper, Karl, *Conjectures and Refutations*, New York: Basic Books (1962).

————, *The Logic of Scientific Discovery*, 2d Ed., New York: Harper & Row (1968).

————, *The Poverty of Historicism*, 3rd Ed., New York: Harper & Row (1964).

Robbins, Roy M., *Our Landed Heritage*, Lincoln: University of Nebraska Press (1942).

THE ECONOMIC THEORY OF DEMOCRACY: THE RISE OF THE LIBERALS IN BRITAIN

ANTHONY F. HEATH

The most striking feature of British politics over the last thirty years has been the rise of the Liberal party, joined recently by the Social Democratic Party to form a new, centrist Alliance. In the 1951 General Election, the Conservative and Labor parties between them secured 97 percent of the vote; as Table 2.1 shows, this had fallen by 1983 to 72 percent. The Alliance obtained almost as many votes as the Labor party, and in many parts of Britain, had become the major opposition to the Conservatives. Britain had seemingly changed from a two-party to a multiparty system.

It is far from obvious why this change has occurred. In the 1950s the two dominant parties appeared to have converged at the center of the political spectrum, just as the economic theory of democracy predicted. Both accepted the mixed economy and the welfare state. Successful economic management, rather than the advocacy of distinctive political or economic principles, seemed to be the best way to win the popular vote. On the face of it there was no incentive for either party to change its position. They had finally crushed the Liberals, who had been the governing party earlier in the century, and seemed set to alternate in government. There seemed to be no room at the time for a third major party in British politics, certainly not in competition for the center ground.

Yet in the succeeding thirty years we have witnessed a revival of ideology—an increasing polarization between the Conservatives and Labor parties as each has lurched to right and left, respectively—and a yawning gap in the center which has been gratefully filled by the Lib-

105

Table 2.1   Share of the Vote

	Conservative %	Labor %	Liberal %	Other %
1950	43	47	9	1
1951	48	49	3	0
1955	49	47	3	1
1959	49	45	6	1
1964	43	45	11	1
1966	41	49	9	1
1970	46	44	8	2
Feb., 1974	39	38	20	3
Oct., 1974	37	40	19	4
1979	45	38	14	3
1983	44	28	26	2

Note: table excludes votes cast in Northern Ireland.
1983 "Liberal" category includes Social Democratic Party votes.
Sources: 1950–1974 figures—Craig (1976), Tables 1.17–1.25 and Table 4.01.
1979 figures—Craig (1980), Tables 1 and 2.
1983 figures—Craig (unpublished figures).

erals and their new allies in the Social Democratic Party. As Ivor Crewe has suggested, in the 1970s the two dominant parties returned to the old politics of class conflict, and the electorate did not like it (Crewe et al., 1977).

This poses a serious challenge to economic theories of political behavior. The cornerstone of these theories is that parties aim to maximize votes and treat policies merely as means towards this end:

> From the self-interest axiom springs our view of what motivates the political actions of party members. We assume that they act solely in order to attain the income, prestige, and power which come from being in office. Thus politicians in our model never seek office as a means of carrying out particular policies; their only goal is to reap the rewards of holding office per se. They treat policies purely as means to the attainment of their private ends, which they can reach only by being elected. (Downs, 1957, p.28)

If Britain has shifted from being a two-party to a multiparty system as a consequence of largely ideological shifts within the two major parties, the fundamental assumption of the economic model is violated, and the model proves unable to cope with the central paradox of contemporary British politics. We suggest, then, that this is a crucial challenge to the economic theory of political behavior. Failure to withstand it must represent a major defeat for economic modeling.

What we propose to do in this paper is to consider alternative explanations for the decline of the two-party system and to subject these to empirical test. The major thrust of the paper is thus empirical rather than theoretical. As our source of data we shall be using the series of election studies which have taken place after every general election in Britain since 1964. These studies consist of detailed questionnaires administered to representative probability samples of the electorate and covering the respondents' social and demographic characteristics and their political attitudes and preferences.

We shall be testing three rival theories. The first is an economic theory in the spirit of Downs's original formulation and which asserts that the ideological movements of the two major parties have been rational, vote-maximizing strategies responding to shifts in the distribution of voters along the main left-right continuum. The second is an ideological theory which asserts that the parties have been driven by ideological considerations to which the voters have made largely rational responses. And the third is a protest theory asserting that it is the voters who have behaved irrationally, casting "negative" rather than "positive" votes for the centrist parties.

I THE THEORIES: ECONOMIC ANALYSES OF POLITICAL CHANGE

Let us begin by considering the economic theory of political behavior in more detail and considering how it might account for the rise of a center party. The classic formulation is that of Anthony Downs, and is in essence very simple. He borrows a theory developed by the economists Hotelling (1929) and Smithies (1941) to account for the spatial location of shops and uses it instead to explain the ideological location of political parties. He assumes that there are utility-maximizing voters, analogous to the utility-maximizing consumer of economic theory, and vote-maximizing political parties analogous to the profit-maximizing firm. He further assumes that the main sphere for political action, and hence for affecting voters' utility, is government intervention in the market. At one extreme a government could socialize all production and distribution; at the other, it could allow an entirely *laissez-faire* economy. This gives a one-dimensional left-right continuum, and each party will be located at different points on the continuum, some preferring complete socialism, others a mixed economy, and so on. Each voter will accordingly support the party which comes closest to his own position.

The positions which the parties will take up in their efforts to secure office will, Downs argues, depend on the distribution of voters along the continuum. If they are evenly distributed along it, then the parties must, if they are rational, converge towards the center. This can be seen from Figure 2.1

Suppose there are two parties, one at a_1 and the other at b_1. All people to the left of a_1 will vote for Party A, since it is closer to their preferred positions than is Party B. Correspondingly, all people to the right of b_1 will vote for Party B; even if they are extreme proponents of *laissez faire*, it will still be rational for them to vote for B because its policies, unpalatable though they may be, are still preferable to A's. Failure to vote, therefore, could result in the even worse disaster that Party A will be returned to power.

Turning finally to the people who take up positions between a_1 and b_1, it can be seen that these voters will divide evenly between the two parties. Party B will therefore win the election since it is closer to the center and has more voters "outside" it than has Party A. Faced with this, Party A must change its position if it is to have any hope of winning. Movement to the left will clearly be counterproductive, but movement to the right might succeed. If the party moved to a_2, it would still get the support of all the voters to its left (since it remains preferable in their eyes to Party B). and it would still divide the (reduced) middle ground evenly. But since it is now closer to the center than B, it gets more support in total and must win the election. Party B also sees this, and equilibrium is reached when both parties lie side by side at the center of the continuum.

This argument assumes that there are no "transport costs" for consumers or "relocation costs" for the firms. But of course there are likely to be such costs both in the economic and political marketplaces. For the voter, the equivalent of transport costs will be the difficulty of discerning any difference between the parties if they are a long way from him (or her) on the ideological continuum. So as the parties move

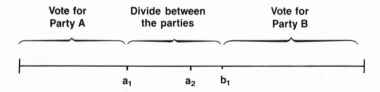

FIG. 2.1: Party positions. (Source: Heath, 1976)

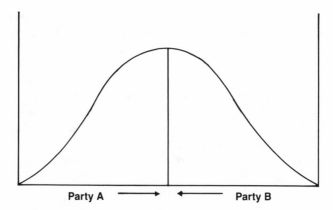

FIG. 2.2: **Political spectrum. (Source: Heath, 1976)**

closer together towards the center of the continuum, voters at the two extremes will become less inclined to vote as they find it harder to detect any difference between the parties. This may in turn provide an incentive to the parties to stay some way apart from each other.

How powerful this incentive is, will, of course, depend on the distribution of voters. Suppose they are concentrated in the center of the political spectrum, as in Figure 2.2.

In this case the incentive for a party to stay away from the center is not at all great. The possible loss of extremists will not deter the parties from converging since there are so few voters to be lost at the extremes compared with the number to be gained in the middle. Contrast this, however, with a polarized distribution of voters as in Figure 2.3.

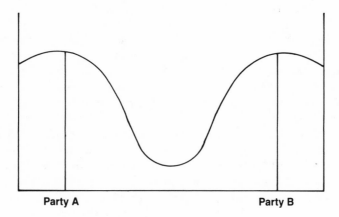

FIG. 2.3: **Polarized Distribution. (Source: Heath, 1976)**

In the polarized case the potential loss of extremist voters as the parties converge towards the center could outweigh the gains from recruits at the center. Downs therefore felt able to conclude that "If voters' preferences are distributed so that voters are massed bimodally near the extremes, the parties will remain poles apart in ideology.".[1]

This now gives us a possible explanation for political change. A shift in the distribution of voters would give rational, vote-maximizing parties an incentive to shift their positions, too, or, if relocation costs are high, might provide an opportunity for a new party to gain support. This is Downs's own explanation for the rise of the Labor party in Britain during the first half of the century:

> The crucial factor . . . was the shift of the electorate's distribution along the political scale as a result of the extension of suffrage to a vast number of new voters, many of whom were near the extreme left. Whenever such a radical change in the distribution of voters occurs, existent parties will probably be unable to adjust rapidly because they are ideologically immobile [the equivalent of relocation costs]. New parties, however, are not weighed down by this impediment. Unencumbered by ideological commitments, they can select the most opportune point on the scale at which to locate, and structure their ideologies accordingly. (Downs, 1957, p. 129)

In principle, this kind of explanation could account for the decline of the Labor party as well as for its rise. Thus the extension of the franchise might have produced, as Downs suggests, a bloc of left-wing voters and, overall, a polarized distribution like that of Figure 2.3. However, the expansion of white-collar employment (particularly in the welfare state) during the postwar period might have converted this bimodal distribution into a trimodal one, as in Figure 2.4.

The rise of the Liberal party could thus be accounted for by the rise of the "new" middle class of public-sector employees who share neither the capitalistic interests of the "old" middle class nor the socialist interests of the traditional working class. Such a model must assume that the Conservative and Labor parties had not converged quite so much in the 1950s as is usually assumed; to sustain an economic theory of political change we have to revise conventional wisdom in this one respect. (If these two parties had converged on the center of the spectrum, they would have been the beneficiaries of the "new" middle-class votes and a Liberal revival would have been most unlikely.) We should also note that the dynamic element in our model comes from exogenous shifts in voters' preferences. The economic theory on its

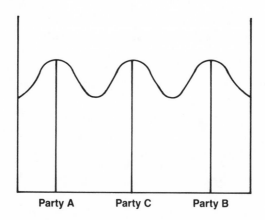

Party A   Party C   Party B

FIG. 2.4: Trimodal distribution. (Source: Heath, 1976)

own is a static one and does not explain change, but an exogenous shift such as the one suggested does allow us to keep the economic theory of vote-maximizing parties and rational, self-interested voters intact. What we must look for in our series of election studies therefore is evidence of shifting voter preferences.

IDEOLOGICAL SOURCES OF CHANGE

There are, however, alternative explanations of the changes in Britain's recent political history, explanations which are on the face of it equally plausible and which fundamentally challenge the assumptions of the economic model. Consider, first of all, the ideological model. Unlike the economic model which we have just considered, it assumes that it is the parties, not the voters, who have changed their positions on the left-right dimension spectrum, and it asserts that they have done so for ideological rather than vote-maximizing reasons.

The case for an ideological explanation has been put forward most powerfully by Ivor Crewe and his colleagues. They suggested that the centrist tendencies of both Labor and Conservative governments during the 1950s and 1960s went into reverse in the early 1970s: "Under the new Conservative administration there was a resurgence of ideological and class polarization. During its first eighteen months it attempted a switch to economic policies that were more strongly determined by market considerations than under any previous postwar Conservative government." And the Labor party too, they argued, changed direction during its spell in opposition in the early 1970s:

"Labor pledged itself to a programme of industrial and land nationalization more extensive than anything contemplated in the 1960s. The
years 1970–74 marked a period in which the Labor party reasserted the
class interests and socialist principles for which it symbolically stands
and from which it appeared to have deviated when last in office"
(Crewe et al., 1977, pp. 135–6).

The ideological theory, therefore, fundamentally modifies the
assumptions about party motivation employed in the economic model,
although it retains the assumptions of rational voters. The voters, it is
argued, did not like this return to the "old" politics of class conflict.
They had not changed their own ideological positions. Voters at the
center of the spectrum, therefore, quite rationally turned towards the
Liberal party as the Conservative and Labor parties moved away to
the right and left, respectively. These two parties paid the price for their
irrationality by losing votes, and the Liberals were the grateful
beneficiaries.

THE RISING TIDE OF PROTEST

Perhaps the most common account of the Liberal vote offered by academic political scientists is that of a protest vote. Himmelweit, for
example, argues as follows:

> The Liberal voters in one election are rarely the same people in another.
> Each election produces a new crop of Liberals thrown up by the vagaries
> of the two main parties. This makes the paradigm, appropriate for dis-
> cussing the changing fortunes of the Conservative and Labour party,
> inappropriate when discussing changes in the fortunes of the Liberal
> party. A more appropriate paradigm is one which looks, not so much at
> which attracts the voter to the Liberal party, but rather at what draws the
> voter away from the party for which he or she had previously voted. *The
> Liberal vote is a vote of disaffection; it represents movement away from a
> party rather than movement to the party; it is a vote signifying departure
> rather than arrival* (Himmelweit, 1981, p. 159. Italics in original).

The account she gives of the Liberal voter is rather difficult to fit into
the usual model of the rational consumer. She suggest that the Liberal
voter is "the comparative shopper par excellence. However, his shop-
ping is guided more by dislike for products he had bought in the past
than enthusiasm for the one he finally selects" (p. 171). But the difference is that while we all have to eat, we don't have to vote. The rational
voter who dislikes both Conservative and Labor parties but who has

no positive liking for Liberal policies either, would be expected to abstain. A protest vote under these circumstance must surely be treated as a symbolic or expressive gesture rather than an instrumental action. In the Downsian model, a vote, as opposed to an abstention, will always be either for the preferred party or for a second-best party if the preferred party has no chance of winning. Abstention and tactical voting have a place in the economic model; protest voting does not.

Himmelweit does not offer any cogent reasons why such protest voting should have increased, but others who adopt essentially the same view of the Liberal vote ascribe its rise to the failures of both Conservative and Labor governments in the 1960s and 1970s to solve Britain's economic problems. "One would expect" wrote James Alt, "years of economic failure to loosen people's ties to the political parties and the political system" (1979, p. 200). The failure of both main parties to deal with inflation in the early 1970s (and unemployment in the late 1970s), may thus have produced a sense of disillusionment with the political system and the established parties. Other writers too have claimed to see a decline or indeed a collapse in Britain's civic culture and the legitimacy of the two-party system resulting from these successive economic failures (for example, Douglas, 1976). On this view, then, the rise of the Liberals represents increasing disaffection from the two major political parties rather than a positive vote for centrist policies. To test this view we should investigate whether or not there really are stable ideological preferences, stable parties, but rising disaffection with their performance in office.

In summary, then, the economic analysis of political change assumes both rational parties and rational voters, and ascribes the change to the shifting distribution of voters' preferences. The ideological analysis assumes that the two main parties have shifted their positions away from the center despite an unchanging distribution of voters' preferences. And the protest theory leaves both parties and voters in their accustomed positions on the political spectrum but looks for rising levels of dissatisfaction with government performance.

II SOME EVIDENCE: VOTERS' CHANGING PREFERENCES?

Tables 2.3–2.7 enable us to make some preliminary assessments of the three theories. Let us begin with the distribution of voters' preferences. Table 2.3 looks at one of the key features of the left-right continuum,

Table 2.3   Attitudes Towards Nationalization

	A Lot More Industries Should Be Nationalized %	A Few More Industries Should Be Nationalized %	No More Industries Should Be Nationalized %	Some Industries Should Be Privatized %	N
1964	8	18	45	18	1818
1966	8	17	42	19	1899
Feb., 1974	9	16	40	21	2462
Oct., 1974	9	20	41	20	2365
1979	6	10	40	37	1893

Note: Percentages do not add up to 100 because of "don't knows."
Sources: British election studies, 1964–1979

namely public ownership of the means of production. Respondents were asked to choose between the following four statements:

A. A lot more industries should be nationalized.

B. Only a few more industries should be nationalized.

C. No more industries should be nationalized but the industries that are nationalized now should stay nationalized.

D. Some of the industries that are nationalized now should be denationalized.

With rather minor wording changes these statements have been put to respondents in all the election studies except that in 1970. And Table 2.3 shows that there has indeed been a marked shift of the electorate to the right over the period as a whole, only eighteen percent of electors in 1964 being in favor of privatisation, compared with thirty-seven percent in 1979.

However, a shift to the right cannot, on its own, account for the rise of a center party. The usual Downsian account would simpy predict an increase in support for the right-wing party. What we need, to sustain the economic model of political change, is a shift to a trimodal distribution. It is unfortunate that the pioneers of the election studies chose to use a four-point rather than a five-point scale for measuring attitudes towards nationalization; we need a minimum of five points in order to detect a trimodal distribution. It is quite possible that the increased proportion of electors who believed that "some industries should be denationalized" contains a new peak of free marketeers on the extreme right of the underlying continuum. The shift of the Conservative party to the right might just conceivably be explained as a rational response to the growth in the number of right-wing electors. However, the timing of this change makes the story implausible; the increased support for privatization does not come until 1979, well after the alleged shift of the Conservative party to free market policies occurred. It is much more plausible to suppose that right-wing Conservative policies and rhetoric converted Tory supporters to more right-wing views. This, if true, completely reverses the usual causal ordering of economic models. Voters' preferences are no longer autonomous "givens" but are instead responsive to political manipulation.

Nor is the evidence for the economic model of political change any more convincing when we turn to the left wing of the ideological spectrum. There is no sign at all of a new peak emerging on the far left, and the steadiness of responses over the 1964–1974 period gives us no hope that changing preferences can account for the great Liberal surge of February 1974 and the decline of the two-party system. On this evidence, and it is by far the best time-series on voters' preferences which we have, the economic model is not in good shape.

PARTIES CHANGING POSITIONS?

The ideological theory of changing party positions fares only slightly better. In each of the election studies respondents were asked:

> Considering everything the parties stand for, would you say that there is a good deal of difference between the parties, some difference, or not much difference?

From 1974 onwards, respondents were asked specifically about the differences they perceived between the Labor and Conservative parties. Remembering this change of wording, we can see from Table 2.4 that "perceived differences" between the parties actually declined substantially between 1964 and 1974, recovering in 1979 to their original level.

It is, perhaps, rather surprising that the electorate failed to notice the widening ideological gap between the two parties in the early 1970s that Crewe described. The return of class politics seems to have gone unnoticed by the voters in 1974 and we cannot therefore take the outcome of that year's two elections as evidence of any repudiation of class politics. We do not necessarily have to accuse the electorate of ignorance or unobservance, however. While the party manifestos undoubtedly changed in the way Crewe described, the voters will also

Table 2.4   Perceived Differences Between the Parties

	A Great Deal of Difference %	Some Difference %	Not Much Difference %	N
1964	45	23	26	1818
1966	42	26	28	1899
1970	32	28	37	1287
Feb., 1974	33	29	35	2462
Oct., 1974	39	30	30	2365
1979	46	29	22	1893

Note: Percentages do not add up to 100 because of "don't knows."
Sources: British election studies, 1964–79.

have noticed that the centrist Harold Wilson, who had presided over the pragmatic governments of the 1960s, remained leader of the Labor government. And while Edward Heath had initiated the Conservative party's shift to the right, he had also steered the famous U-turn as Prime Minister, moving 180 degrees from free marketeering to incomes policy and government rescues for "lame duck" industries.

The electorate, then, may have disbelieved the ideology of the party manifestos and have paid more attention to the known characteristics of the party leaders. And they were probably right. The 1974 Labor government was not noted for its radical, socialist policies, and Mr. Heath's utterances from the back benches have been markedly less radical than Mrs. Thatcher's rhetoric as leader. It is surely quite likely that the electorate only came to believe that a Labor government would really try to put some socialist principles into practice when Mr. Foot became leader, in the autumn of 1980, and that it was only the experience of Mrs. Thatcher's first term of office that convinced them that she meant it when she said "this lady's not for turning."

In any event, it is what the electorate believes about the parties, whether or not they are correct, which will influence how they vote, and it seems clear that in 1974 they did not believe Conservative and Labor parties had moved away from the center. There is also some evidence from the election study series that the parties, treated as social collectivities rather than as manifestos, had not moved apart ideologically. Table 2.5 looks at the changing attitudes of Labor and Conservative partisans, that is, of respondents who strongly identify with their respective parties and who typically adopt more ideological stances. It is striking that, while both groups have moved to the right,

Table 2.5 Labor and Conservative Partisans

		A Lot More Industries Should Be Nationalized %	A Few More Industries Should Be Nationalized %	No More Industries Should Be Nationalized %	Some Industries Should Be Privatized %	Index of Dissimilarity
1964	Labor	25	40	29	6	60
	Conservative	1	4	52	43	
1966	Labor	25	34	33	8	53
	Conservative	2	4	46	48	
Feb., 1974	Labor	28	32	34	6	53
	Conservative	3	4	50	43	
Oct., 1974	Labor	31	40	25	4	68
	Conservative	1	2	50	47	
1979	Labor	26	21	44	9	66
	Conservative	1	1	22	75	

Sources: British election studies, 1964–79

the difference between them (as measured by the index of dissimilarity) has shown no major change over the period as a whole. Relative to each other, the partisans have stayed still. There is no sign from these survey data that the Labor party had been captured by socialist activists who have pulled it to the left (although, of course, we cannot rule out a much smaller minority of activists within the larger group of partisans).

Our interpretation of Tables 2.4 and 2.5, then, is that whatever might have happened to the party manifestos in the 1970s, the electorate did not believe that the party leaderships had changed or that the policies they put into practice would be any different from before. The Liberal revival of 1974 cannot be explained by the change in manifestos. Our last hope to explain that revival now seems to lie with the protest theory.

VOTERS' CHANGING EVALUATIONS?

Unfortunately, the time-series on satisfaction with government performance is much more problematic than that on nationalization, with rather major wording changes from one election study to another. In the early election studies, respondents were asked, "Speaking generally, how satisfied are you with the Government's handling of Britain's economic affairs?" But in the later studies, respondents were asked not to speak generally but to evaluate the Government's handling of specific economic problems, namely inflation (from 1974) and unemployment (from 1979). If we assume that electors who were satisfied with the handling of *both* problems are equivalent to those who had earlier been satisfied "generally speaking," we get something approaching a time-series and this is shown in Table 2.6. It does indeed show some decline in satisfaction with government performance, although the data are not wholly compelling.

There is some further, rather more circumstantial evidence for the protest theory as well. Alt et al. (1977, p. 353) have shown that Liberals are particularly likely to be opposed both to trade unions and to big business. They are, it might be suggested, protesting against the excessive power wielded by both these institutions and the political parties associated with them. The election studies contain a good time-series on this. In every study the respondents have been asked whether "big business has too much power in this country" and, separately, whether "trade unions have too much power or not." The question wording has not changed, and we can put the two questions together to see the level of combined dissatisfaction. This is done in Table 2.7 which shows a big increase over the key years 1964–1974.

Table 2.6 Satisfaction with Government Performance

| | GENERAL SATISFACTION WITH THE GOVERNMENT'S HANDLING OF BRITAIN'S ECONOMIC AFFAIRS | | | |
	% Satisfied	% Neutral/ Don't Know	% Dissatisfied	N
1964	50	28	22	1818
1970	47	22	31	1287

| | SATISFACTION WITH THE LAST GOVERNMENT'S HANDLING OF RISING PRICES | | |
	% Satisfied	% Not Satisfied	N
Feb., 1974	33	64	2462
Oct., 1974	47	50	2365

| | SATISFACTION WITH THE LAST GOVERNMENT'S HANDLING BOTH OF PRICES AND OF UNEMPLOYMENT | | |
	% Satisfied with Both	% Mixed	% Not Satisfied with Either	N
1979	39	27	27	1893

Sources: 1964 and 1970 Data—Butler and Stokes (1974), Appendix B; 1974–1979 Data—British election studies, 1974–79

Table 2.7 Trade Unions and Business Power

	% Trade Unions Have Too Much Power	% Big Business Has Too Much Power	% Both Have Too Much Power	N
1964	54	54	28	1818
1966	64	54	35	1899
1970	65	47	29	1287
Oct., 1974	78	56	44	2365
1979	78	53	43	1893

Sources: British election studies, 1964–79

After these first three rounds, it is clear that the protest theory is well ahead on points. It must be said, however, that we do not yet have a knockout. It is one thing to show increasing levels of dissatisfaction with the major parties and their associated union and business organizations; it is another to show that the motivation for Liberal and Social Democratic party voting is largely negative and represents a symbolic protest against the established parties rather than a positive and rational preference for a new, untried but perhaps more effective team. Our original Downsian theory may not have fared too well as yet, but this by no means rules out alternative economic formulations.

III   MORE EVIDENCE: NEGATIVE VOTING?

Let us proceed, then, by looking for more direct evidence that the Liberal vote is a negative rather than positive one. Himmelweit's grounds for her disaffection account were her failure to find any distinctive set of attitudes which characterized Liberal voters. They appeared to be a transient population of electors, most of whom might be expected to return to their "natural" parties after making their brief protest, and who had less in common with each other than with the parties from whom they had defected.

The greater "softness" or fluidity of the Liberal vote is well-established, although it is perfectly explicable in Downsian terms: a centrist party is by definition "at risk" on both flanks, and it will, other things being equal, have a larger proportion of supporters vulnerable to assaults from the outer parties. Conversely, of course, it has more potential converts to gain from the inner flanks of the two other parties. "Softness" of the center vote, then, tells us no more than that most changes take place at the margins.

The heterogeneity of Liberal support seems on the face of it a more damaging finding. The most telling evidence comes from Lemieux (1977). He shows that in some cases the positions espoused by Liberal voters are not actually the policies of the Liberal party itself. For example, middle-class voters who wanted Britain to leave the Common Market were relatively likely to vote Liberal, presumably in protest against the Conservative's pro-EEC policy, despite the fact that the Liberals are the most consistently pro-Common Market political party in postwar Britain. Conversely, the working class voter who was most likely to cast a Liberal vote instead of the "natural" Labor vote was the one who wanted to stay in the Common Market, presumably protest-

Table 2.8 Liberal Defection and Issue Opinions

	PERCENTAGE VOTING LIBERAL	
	Middle Class	Working Class
Common Market:		
Should the government stay in on the present terms?	16.1 (322)	32.7 (55)
Stay in, but renegotiate?	27.0 (415)	27.9 (480)
Get out completely?	41.1 (121)	21.6 (458)

Note: Figures in parentheses give cell size.
Source: Lemieux (1977).

ing against the Labor party's anti-EEC policy. Table 2.8 gives Lemieux's results.

The asymmetry in Table 2.8 is indeed rather striking. Lemieux therefore concluded that "the simplest unifying explanation of the result is that the Liberals are receiving a negative protest vote directed against the specific policies advocated by the expected party of origin" (1977, p. 337).

However, what Lemieux fails to observe is that the proportion of Liberal voters who are protesters "out of line" with actual Liberal policy is really rather small. The potential Conservatives who wanted to get out of the Common Market completely amounted to only 121 respondents in Lemieux's sample, and were greatly outnumbered by the 737 who wished to stay in (either on the present terms or renegotiating). In absolute, although not relative, terms the Liberals made many more gains from electors who wanted to stay in the Common Market and who were thus in line with both Conservative and Liberal policy. We do not deny, then, that a proportion of Liberals may be protesters, but it is far from clear that the majority are.

POSITIVE VOTING?

The evidence that the Liberal vote is a negative, protest vote is not therefore very compelling. Is it perhaps possible after all to rescue the theory of rational voting? The first step is to see if voters do in fact cast their ballots for the party which comes closest to them on the left-right continuum, and this can be done using the 1979 election study.

As we remarked earlier, the major component of the left-right continuum is usually thought to be the extent of government intervention in the economy. Respondents in the 1979 survey were given three statements on this topic:

A. "The best way to tackle unemployment is to allow *private companies* to keep more of their profits to create more jobs."

B. "It doesn't matter much either way."

C. "It is mainly up to the *Government* to tackle unemployment by using tax money to create jobs."

They were asked which of these three statements came closest to their own view and how strongly they agreed with the statement. Their answers generate a seven-point scale ranging from "very strongly in favor of A" to "very strongly in favour of C." Respondents were also asked where they placed the Conservative and Labor parties on this scale, most of them placing the Conservatives at the extreme right and the Labor party either at the extreme left or close to it. Unfortunately, the investigators did not ask respondents where they placed the Liberal party, but from other evidence we can be fairly certain that they would be placed at, or close to, the center. Figure 2.5 shows the distribution of voters on the scale and their perception of the parties' positions.

Figure 2.5 does indeed show the trimodal distribution of voters required for the Downsian theory of politics, but it is not at all the shape that could have generated the actual distribution of the vote in 1979. In 1979 the Conservatives obtained forty-five percent of the vote, but nearly sixty percent of respondents placed themselves at the same point as, or adjacent to, the Conservatives on the left-right scale. Again, Labor won thirty-eight percent of the votes in the election, but only around twenty-five percent of respondents placed themselves at the same point on the scale or at the two adjacent points. Clearly, the elementary theory provided by Downs will not do.

Gordon Tullock, however, has suggested that a multidimensional view of politics is required in place of the one-dimensional model of Downs (Tullock, 1967). In any election there are always a number of issues, and they do not always fall neatly into the left-right continuum. In Britain in 1979, for example, government expenditure on the social services was almost as important an issue as unemployment policy, but peoples' preferences for the parties' positions were by no means identical on the two issues. This can be seen from Figure 2.6, which charts the extent to which respondents agreed with, and perceived the parties to agree with, the following statements:

A. "Taxes should be cut even if it means some reduction in government services such as health, education and welfare."

BEST WAY TO CREATE JOBS: RESPONDENTS' PREFERENCES

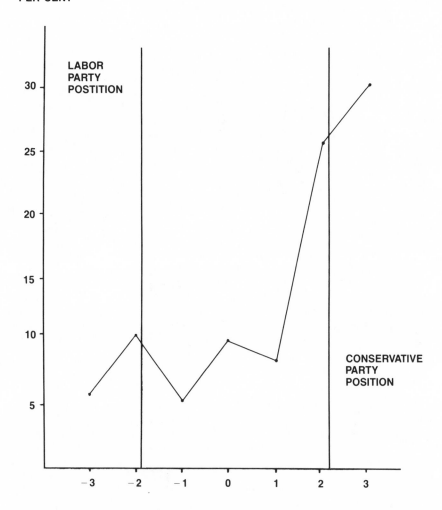

FIG. 2.5: Best way to create jobs. (Source: British Election Study, 1979)

TAXES VS. GOVERNMENT SERVICES: RESPONDENTS' PREFERENCES

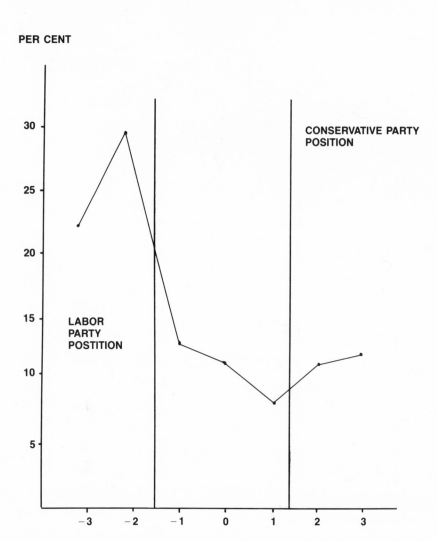

FIG. 2.6: Taxes vs. Government services. (Source: British Election Study, 1979)

B. "It doesn't matter much either way."

C. "Government services such as health, education and welfare should be kept up even if it means that taxes cannot be reduced."

This time we get a bimodal distribution of voters' preferences, and one heavily skewed towards the left and the Labor position. If people had voted solely according to their views on this issue, Labor would have won by a landslide. Perhaps, therefore, if we take a two-dimensional view and look at both issues simultaneously we might get a bit closer to the actual election result.

As a first approximation let us assume that the two axes are orthogonal to each other and that we have equal-interval scales. This gives us a straightforward two-dimensional matrix with forty-nine cells, and we can plot the distribution of voters accordingly. This is done in Figure 2.7.

We can immediately see the value of the two-dimensional approach. Respondents do not lie only along the main diagonal from bottom left to top right, as they would if there were a single underlying dimension. Instead, we see that three of the four quadrants of the diagram are relatively heavily populated. There are indeed large clusters around the Labor and Conservative positions in the bottom-left and top-right quadrants, respectively. But there is also an even larger clustering in the bottom-right quadrant, representing people who are opposed to government intervention in the economy but wish to see the maintenance of the welfare state. We have a clear trimodal distribution of voters which could equally clearly provide the basis for three political parties. The rise of the Liberals, therefore, could in principle be explained by the shift of voters away from the top-right and bottom-left quadrants in which they had previously been located and into this third, bottom-right quadrant which had been left unoccupied by the Conservative or Labor parties.

THE RATIONAL VOTER REVIVED?

Unfortunately, the rational model of voting cannot be rescued yet. It is one thing to show a trimodal distribution; it is another to show that the voters do actually cast their ballots for the party which lies closest to them. Since there are technical problems in deciding exactly how close someone is to a particular party (since our assumption of an interval scale is almost certainly false), let us simply take some illustrative cells in the matrix. To begin with, let us consider the cell (3,3) in Figure 2.7. This is the cell in the top right corner; it represents one of the three

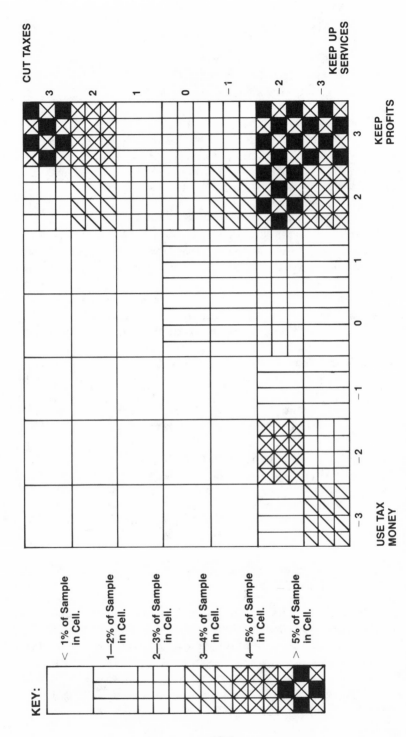

FIG. 2.7: Distribution of voters. (Source: British Election Study, 1979)

KEY:

	< 1% of Sample in Cell.
	1—2% of Sample in Cell.
	2—3% of Sample in Cell.
	3—4% of Sample in Cell.
	4—5% of Sample in Cell.
	> 5% of Sample in Cell.

126

modes and is unambiguously closer to the Conservative party's position than to any other. Of the respondents who located themselves in this cell, seventy-two percent voted Conservative, ten percent Labor, and eight percent Liberal.

Next, consider the $(-2, -2)$ cell which lies towards the bottom left-hand corner. It represents the second of the three modes and also happens to be the cell where respondents were most likely to place the Labor party. Of the respondents who located themselves in this cell, sixty-four percent voted Labor, fifteen percent Conservative, and six percent Liberal. (The remainder in both cases either abstained or voted for one of the minor parties like the Scottish National Party.)

These two findings are comforting enough, since we would not expect even the two-dimensional model to give a perfect fit. There are bound to be voters who took other issues or personalities into account, quite aside from those who changed their mind in the weeks between the election and survey, or who misremembered their vote. Rather, the fact that there is a huge Conservative lead in the $(3,3)$ cell and an almost equally huge lead for Labor in the $(-2, -2)$ cell is strong support for the rational voter theory. Unfortunately, however, there is not a single cell in the whole matrix where there is an equally substantial Liberal lead. Indeed, there is only one cell where the Liberals have a lead at all. This is the $(+1, -1)$ cell. It lies just inside the third, bottom-right quadrant and is the one where we would expect the Liberal party to be located. Thirty-one percent of the respondents who located themselves in it voted Liberal, twenty-eight percent Conservative, and nineteen percent Labor. In contrast, the $(+2, -2)$ cell, which lies immediately next to it, which represents the third of the three modes, and which appears much closer to the Liberal position than to either Conservative or Labor, shows the Liberals actually in third position behind both their rivals. Of the respondents who located themselves in this cell, forty-four percent voted Conservative, twenty-six percent Labor, and a meager fifteen percent Liberal.

What are we to make, then, of this rather puzzling finding? It does not seem to be specifically the Liberal voter who is irrational, but rather the *other* voters in the bottom-right quadrant who *fail* to vote Liberal despite their closeness to the Liberal party's position. And rather than explaining the rise of the Liberals, this finding seems to suggest that the Liberals ought to have fared a great deal better than they did. Clearly, ideological position alone (even when we take two dimensions into account) is insufficient to account for these data on voting behavior.

Neither the economic, ideological or protest theories would thus seem able, without modification, to account for our empirical findings. Of course, it is always possible to think up ancillary hypotheses after the event to account for discrepancies between the theory and the real world. We could, for example, postulate additional dimensions which might succeed in differentiating Liberal voters from the rest. It was, however, the failure to find such dimensions which led writers like Himmelweit and Lemieux to advance the protest theory. A more promising line, we think, is to introduce the notion of expectations. Voters and political parties, just like consumers and business firms, live in a world of uncertainty. Voters cannot be sure that the political parties will not be blown off course and consequently fail to implement the policies laid down in their manifestos. As in the theory of *expected* utility maximization, voters need to take into account the party's probability of success as well as its stated position.

Government effectiveness has been shown to be one of the major determinants of its chances of being reelected (see, for example, Hibbs, 1982). What we are now suggesting is that, in line with the findings presented in Table 2.6, there has been growing dissatisfaction with the performance of *both* major parties during their periods in office. The 1966 Labor government was distinctly unsuccessful in regulating strikes and managing the economy. The electorate turned to the Conservatives in 1970, but they did no better. Rather than returning to the doubtful competence of the Labor party in 1974, increasing proportions of the electorate made the by-no-means irrational decision to cast a vote for the untried Liberals instead.

The concept of expectations, therefore, seems to us one of the best hopes for integrating the diverse empirical findings which we have reported in this paper. Without postulating any irrationality or protest voting, we can in principle account for the Liberals' inability to recruit a majority of voters in the bottom-right quadrant of Figure 2.7 on the grounds that electors discount Liberal promises because of their inexperience in office. And without postulating any changes in voters' ideological positions, we could in principle account for the loss in support for Labor (and to a lesser extent in support for the Conservatives) over the last thirty years in terms of the electorate's declining confidence in their capacity to govern effectively. As their competence is increasingly called into question, their advantage as sitting incumbents over the untried and inexperienced leadership of the Liberals becomes reduced. The "economic calculus" of expected utility maximization increasingly favors the newcomers, although their inexperience remains a handicap, witness their failure to mobilize all their potential supporters in the bottom-right quadrant. The economic model can be rescued after all.

NOTES

The data utilized in this paper is taken from the series of election studies which have taken place after every General Election in Britain since 1964. These data have been reanalyzed from the tapes made available by the Economic and Social Research Council Data Archive at the University of Essex. We would like to thank them for their help, and to acknowledge the work of the original investigators who collected the material, namely David Butler and Donald Stokes (1964–1970) and Ivor Crewe, Bo Sarlvik, and David Robertson (1974–1979).

1. Downs (1957) p. 188. For a critique of this argument, however, see Barry (1970) and Heath (1976).

REFERENCES

Alt, J.; Crewe, I.; and Sarlvik, B., "Angels in Plastic: The Liberal Surge in 1974," British Journal of Political Science, 25 (1977) pp. 343–368.

Alt, J., The Politics of Economic Decline: Economic Management and Political Behaviour in Britain since 1974, Cambridge: Cambridge University Press (1979).

Barry, B., Sociologists, Economists and Democracy: Economic Management and Political Behaviour in Britain since 1974, Cambridge: Cambridge University Press (1970).

Butler, D. and Stokes, D., Political Change in Britain: The Evolution of Electoral Choice, 2d edition, London: Macmillan (1974).

Craig, F. W. S., British Electoral Facts 1885–1975, 3d edition, London: Macmillan (1976).

Craig, F. W. S., Britain Votes 2: British Parliamentary Election Results 1974–1979, 2d edition, Chichester (England): Parliamentary Research Services (1980).

Crewe, I.; Sarlvik, B.; and Alt, J., "Partisan Dealignment in Britain 1964–1974," British Journal of Political Science, 7 (1977) pp. 129–190.

Douglas, J., "The Overloaded Crown," British Journal of Political Science, 6 (1976) p. 488.

Downs, A., An Economic Theory of Democracy, New York: Harper and Row (1957).

Heath, A. F., *Rational Choice and Social Exchange*, Cambridge: Cambridge University Press (1976).

Hibbs, D. A., "Economic Outcomes and Political Support for British Governments among Occupational Classes: a Dynamic Analysis," *American Political Science Review*, 76 (1982) pp. 259–279.

Himmelweit, H. T.; Humphreys, P.; Jaeger, M.; and Katz, M., *How Voters Decide*, London: Academic Press (1981).

Hotelling, H., "Stability in Competition," *Economic Journal*, 39 (1929) pp. 41–57.

Lemieux, P. H., "Political Issues and Liberal Support in the February 1974, British General Election," *Political Studies*, 25 (1977) pp. 323–342.

Smithies, A., "Optimal Location in Spatial Competition." *Journal of Political Economy*, 49 (1941) pp. 423–39.

Tullock, G., *Toward a Mathematics of Politics*, Ann Arbor: University of Michigan Press (1967).

Part III

NORMS AS SOCIAL CAPITAL

JAMES S. COLEMAN

INTRODUCTION

Use of the concept of social norms is one of the stigmata of the sociologist. Other social sciences are either uneasy with the concept—political scientists use it as a last resort—or ignore it altogether, as do economists. A few legal theorists, like Kelsen (1945), employ the concept of norm as a grounding for law; but in general, legal theorists are unconcerned with norms which are not embodied in law.

Yet, for sociologists the concept is ubiquitous. It has not one, but *two* entries in the Encyclopedia of the Social Sciences (both written by sociologists), and one of them begins, "No concept is invoked more often by social scientists in explanations of human behavior than 'norm.'" As an example, Ralf Dahrendorf (by no means one of those sociologists most wedded to the concept) in an essay "On the Origin of Social Inequality," states:

> The origin of inequality is thus to be found in the existence in all human societies of norms of behavior to which sanctions are attached. . . . The derivation suggested here has the advantage of leading back to presuppositions (the existence of norms and the necessity of sanctions) which at least in the context of social theory may be taken as axiomatic (1968).

Though norms and sanctions may be taken as axiomatic by many sociologists, they constitute an unacceptable *deus ex machina* for most other social scientists, and for a few sociologists—a concept brought in to explain some social behavior that is otherwise difficult to explain. Especially for theories based on rational choice, invoking a norm to explain behavior constitutes an almost diametrically opposed approach. The rational choice theorist sees action as the result of choice made by a purposive actor; the social-norm theorist sees behavior as the result of conformity to norms.

133

It is clear, despite the aversion of non-sociologists to the concept of norm, that norms do exist, they are important in many areas of behavior, and that they are backed up by sanctions. It is also clear, however, that much behavior is not in conformity to norms, forcing the social-norm theorist to an *ad hoc* introduction of the concept of "deviance" to account for this lack of conformity.

My aim in this paper is to examine norms from a rational choice perspective, recognizing that norms do come into existence, that they do constrain behavior, and that they therefore cannot be ignored in social theory. In this way, I will hope to lay the basis for a different usage of the concept of norm, a usage which fits within the rational choice framework. In this usage, of course, one must forego invoking a norm as an easy explanation of behavior, or assuming that the existence of a norm will necessarily be accompanied by observance of it. What I will examine is the emergence, formation, and character of norms, as well as the sanctions that go with them. Thus, rather than taking norms as given, I will ask what accounts for their coming into being, for the character they take, and for the kinds of sanctions employed in support of a norm. I will not examine the question of obedience to a norm except to dispense with the question in the next paragraphs, for within a rational choice framework, there are few theoretical problems involved.

OBEDIENCE TO A NORM IN RATIONAL CHOICE THEORY

There is probably nothing that so sharply distinguishes rational choice theory and functionalist theory in sociology as their orientations to obedience to a norm. Functionalist theory ordinarily takes the normative structure as a starting point, and then assumes that there will be conformity to the norms. Behavior is determined by the norms. However, to cope with the empirical fact that conformity is not universal, functionalists (e.g., Parsons, 1951) then must devise a theory of deviance to account for the lack of complete conformity. In functional theory, the norms constitute that portion of social organization which tells persons what to do and not do, the social intelligence that moves the particular pieces on the chessboard.

In rational choice theory, norms constitute constraints within which choices are made, and are little different from other constraints. If there are conflicting norms which prescribe different actions, these merely change the utility function (and thus, possibly the action chosen); they do not determine action. For example, in application of rational choice theory to voting behavior, there arises a "paradox of voting" in any large electorate, because the vote will have an infinitesimal effect which cannot counterbalance the cost of casting a vote, small though it is. Rational choice theorists who have attempted to account for voting by postulating a norm that a citizen should vote, do so by adding a term to the utility function (Riker and Ordeshook, 1973).

Norms which have been internalized through socialization directly modify the utilities of certain actions, while norms that depend on external sanctions modify the utilities only to the degree that the actor believes that external sanctions will be applied. In either case, however, the modifications they bring about serve only to change the balance of costs and benefits associated with particular actions. There is not a social intelligence moving the pieces on the chessboard; they move themselves, each under its own guidance system. If there are supra-individual social intelligences, they must work in a more indirect fashion, by affecting the parameters that go into each of these individual guidance systems. Indeed, this is the way that a mature rational choice theory would treat social norms—as supra-individual entities that affect the costs and benefits which individuals take into account when exercising choice. The problem for rational choice theory is how to account for the emergence of these supra-individual entities and for their character.

THE CHARACTER OF NORMS

Norms are expectations about action—one's own action, that of others, or both—which express what action is right or what action is wrong. A norm may prescribe certain actions such as the norm that an athlete on a team should play his best. Or it may proscribe certain actions, such as the norm among observant Jews and Muslims of not eating pork, or the norm once held among observant Catholics of not eating meat on Friday.

It follows from the fact that persons express an expectation about another's actions that those who express such an expectation are expressing a right to influence the other's actions. And insofar as the latter shares the norm, he accepts this right as legitimate.

It follows also that if the person whose action is at issue acts in accord with the norm, he acts in a way that is less to his immediate interest than if he disregarded the norm. For if this were not so, then his own choice, in the absence of the norm, would lead to the same action, and the norm would be superfluous.

Norms are accompanied by sanctions, either some sort of reward for carrying out a prescribed action (for example, approval and prestige from teammates to an athlete who has played especially hard) or some sort of punishment for carrying out a proscribed action (for example, disapproval from fellow-observers for disregarding religious dietary norms). However, sanctions are sometimes internal, if a norm has been internalized through socialization. A deeply religious person who has always observed dietary proscriptions may become physically ill upon breaking the proscription. Even many persons who have internalized this norm less strongly will continue to observe it when alone or in a strange setting, unaccompanied by anyone who might disapprove of the action.

Sociologists sometimes distinguish social norms from social conventions, with the latter defined as informal rules which facilitate social interactions, but are "conventional," i.e., could as well have a different form. Driving on the right side is an example. A convention may also carry sanctions, because, once established, it creates a situation in which violation of the convention creates difficulties for others. I will not explicitly distinguish conventions from norms except at a point later in the paper.

Norms are ordinarily held, that is agreed upon, by a number of persons, although the group within which the norm is shared may be as small as two. There are, for example, many norms shared by husband and wife that are specific to that couple, such as a norm that the husband make breakfast in the morning. In some cases, norms are held by one set of persons for the actions of another set, such as the norm sometimes held by adults that dictates that "Children are to be seen and not heard," or the norm held by principal and teachers in some schools about the length of a boy's hair. Often, however, the set of persons who hold the norm (and apply sanctions to others for breaking it) is the same set of persons whose actions are subject to the norm. In this case, each person stands in two relations to the norm: as sanctioner and as sanctionee. An example is the norm that a citizen should vote. This double relation to a norm creates the apparent anomaly that a person may simultaneously be in the position of sanctioning others' actions, yet disregarding the norm in his own actions. A person may exhort others to vote or express disapproval at their failure to vote, yet not take the time to vote himself.

Norms are not all at the same level, but in some cases constitute structures or systems, with an hierarchical component.[1] In this, they can have a structure similar to that of a system expressible by use of formal logic.

These are some of the properties of norms that also give an initial sense of the phenomenon itself. These properties, however, raise a number of questions, and it is those questions which I will address in this paper.

QUESTIONS ABOUT NORMS

1. One of the first questions derives from the fact that a norm held by some persons about another's actions reflects the assumption of a right to influence the other's actions. The question is, where does this right come from? What gives a person such a right, and why is that right recognized by others (i.e., those who hold the norm)?

2. If a person, whose actions are subject to a norm, shares the norm, he accepts the legitimacy of this right of others to influence his action. Why does he accept this right as legitimate when it is disadvantageous to his immediate interests to act in accord with the norm?

3. What delineates the set of persons who share a norm, that is, the persons who assume a right to influence particular actions? For certain norms, this set may be very small, as in the case of norms held by a married couple about their actions vis-à-vis one another. In others, it is very large, as in the case of norms that a citizen should vote, or norms which impose an incest taboo.

4. Sometimes there are normative conflicts, in which two sets of persons hold opposing norms about the same actions. For example, a high school girl on a date at a beach house on the lake finds herself in a crowd in which the others, including her date, are smoking marijuana. The others encourage her to do so as well, showing disapproval and disdain at her reluctance. The reluctance, in turn, is produced by her knowledge that her parents would disapprove. The question: What is the class of situation in which such conflict of norms arises?

5. When a norm is not shared by sanctioner and sanctionee, what is the source of the disparity? For example, I go down with my cup to the hot water to get some tea. All tea bags are gone, but I express no dismay, remarking to another person standing there: "This often happens, but I have some tea bags back at my office saved for such occasions." The person responds in a disapproving way, "It's people like you, stashing tea bags away, who create the problem."

    How is it that he perceives a right to express this disapproval, while I do not share the norm? (For if I shared the norm, I would not have saved the tea bags, or if I had, I would not have commented to him about it, recognizing that to do so would invite disapproval.)

6. What is responsible for different norms in similar circumstances? For example: A child, aged three, walking with its mother on a sidewalk in Berlin, unwraps a small piece of candy and drops the cellophane on the sidewalk. An older woman, passing, scolds the child for dropping the cellophane and admonishes the mother for not disciplining the child. A child, aged three and a half, walking with its mother on a sidewalk in New York City, unwraps a piece of candy and drops the cellophane on the sidewalk. An older woman is passing by, but says nothing, not even noticing the action of the child. *Questions:* Why the difference? Is it an idiosyncratic difference between the two women, or a difference between Berlin and New York? And if it is the latter, what accounts for systematic differences of this sort?

7. Some norms are enforced primarily through external sanctions exercised at the time the action takes place, others primarily through internalization of sanctions to be exercised by the actor himself as future occasions of action arise, a process of internalization that is brought about during a period of socialization in childhood, as well as at other points later in life. What distinguishes the two sets, the one externally enforced at the time of the action, and the other enforced by an internal sanctioning structure that was created long before the action?

8. What differentiates the conditions that generate norms from the conditions that generate laws? Both laws and norms are designed to inhibit actions that impose negative externalities on others, so that they might be expected to be substitutable. In California, a recent referendum would have, if passed, resulted in a law that proscribed smoking in certain settings which are currently proscribed only by norms. In this case, a law almost came to replace a norm; but in other cases, no such correspondence exists. When norms rather than laws? When laws rather than norms?

NORMS AND EXTERNALITIES OF ACTION

Neoclassical economics, based on rational choice theory, is applied to a narrow and limited set of actions: those actions in which the consequences are limited to the actors who are parties to the action. In individual choice, such as a consumption decision, this is a single actor. In exchange, there are two parties to the exchange, and the exchange has consequences only for the two.

It is when there are consequences of action for actors who have no control over it that neoclassical economic theory bogs down. The action in such a case has externalities (positive or negative), or is a public good (or bad), with consequences that cannot be arbitrarily restricted. The central problem that arises for rational choice theory in such situations is that these consequences of the action, experienced by actors other than the actor or actors in control of the action, do not enter the latter's utility function. The action which maximizes the utility of the actor who takes the action may be far from maximizing the utilities of others who experience consequences of the action. One problem introduced is the problem of interpersonal comparison of utilities, to determine what action would maximize "social efficiency" (however ill-defined that term may be). But that is only symptomatic of the larger problem, that there is no general way in which the consequences of the action for the other affected actors can enter the utility function of the actor taking the action. Actors harmed by the action that benefits the actor in control of the action experience negative externalities, as exemplified by non-smokers sitting near a smoker. Those benefited by it experience positive externalities as exemplified by passersby who benefit from a householder's cleaning snow from his sidewalk. The social problem in the first case is how to limit the action which is harming others (and how much to limit it). The problem in the second case is how to encourage and increase the action, and to what level it should be encouraged. A special case of the latter problem is the problem of paying the cost of a public good, when each actor's action has beneficial consequences for others, but the benefits to himself are less than the costs he will incur. Only if enough actors, who bring the benefits for each above the costs that each experiences, can be induced to carry out (or contribute to) the action, will it be carried out, to the net benefit of each. A parallel problem exists for a public bad, such as in overgrazing of the commons, in which each herd-owner's increase in grazing will increase his own benefits, but at a cost to others. Only if the herd-owners can all be induced to limit their grazing will the grazing be reduced to the level at which it will produce maximum nutrition.

A solution for such problems, when it can be brought into being, stems from considerations in Coase's 1960 paper, "The Problem of Social Cost." This is to develop a market in rights of control, in which the actors who do not have control of the action may purchase rights of control from those who do, limited only by their interest in the action (i.e., the utility difference it makes for them) and their resources. It is easy to see that if there are no transaction costs in such a market, then the outcome will be a social optimum (which is defined only relative to the initial resource endowments of the various parties in the market), at which no further exchanges are mutually beneficial. Those hurt by this level of action would be even more hurt by parting with the resources that the actor controlling it would take to limit it further.

In the case of a public good, each of the actors who is benefited by the actions of others would exchange rights of partial control of his own action for rights of partial control of the actions of each of the others. This in effect would make each actor's action controlled by a collective decision made by all the affected parties.

Related markets have been developed in some regulation of environmental pollution, with the amount of total pollution allowed not set by market forces, but with marketing of rights to pollute among those who operate pollution-generating plants (see Noll, 1971). And it is likely that the process by which the provision of public goods comes under the control of a collective decision (that is, the shift of activities from individual control to governmental control) can usefully be conceptualized as exchange among those affected of rights of partial control over their actions. This will result in each having a vote in determining the actions of each.

Yet, there are many activities in society in which markets in rights of control cannot easily come into being, for one or another reason. In a social situation where one person is smoking and another finds it irritating, the second can hardly come to the first and say, "How much will you take to stop smoking?" Or a high school girl on a date in which all others present would like her to smoke marijuana, while her parents would not, can hardly ask for bids from the two parties for control of her action. In elections, markets in votes are sometimes established, as in the buying of votes of urban lower classes by party machines; however, this practice is illegal. Thus, there is a wide range of situations in which an action has extensive external effects, but in which a market in rights of control of the action is either impracticable or illegal.

The central premise of this paper is that norms arise when actions have external effects, including the extreme cases of public goods or public bads. Further, norms arise in those cases in which markets cannot easily be established, or transaction costs are high.

The externalities created by the action may be positive or negative. In high schools, for example, students in the school give deference and prestige to athletes who are members of a winning team, to the degree that the athlete contributes to the team's success, and the degree that the team's success contributes to the school's general standing in the community (and the degree to which this contributes to the other students' feelings of well-being or pride).

In contrast, students ordinarily do not give such rewards to scholars who get especially high grades, and they often impose norms to restrict the amount of effort put into schoolwork. In this case, the externalities are negative, insofar as the teacher grades on the curve. High-performing students increase for other students the effort necessary to produce the same grade, thus making matters more difficult for others.

Several points follow from the central premise stated above, that norms arise when actions have external effects. This directly answers some of the questions raised earlier. Question Three asked what delineates the set of persons who share a norm about a certain action. The implication of this premise is that the norm is shared—or potentially shared—by all those who are affected in the same direction by the action. Those persons claim a right to have partial control over the action, and they exercise the claim by attempting to impose normative sanctions upon the actor to induce the direction of action that benefits them, though often at the actor's expense.

Question Four asks about the class of situations in which there are normative conflicts, with two groups attempting to impose norms in opposite directions on the same action. The implication of the premise that I have stated is that such a situation arises when an action has positive externalities for one set of persons, and negative externalities for another. In the example of the girl whose friends' approval is contingent on her smoking marijuana, and her parents' is contingent on her not doing so (or their ignorance of her doing so), there are such opposing externalities. If she does not smoke, she dampens the party, destroys the consensus, and perhaps reminds some of those present of the normative conflicts they are under. If she does smoke (and her parents learn of it), they are made unhappy, as their hopes and aspirations for her are undercut.

WHY ACCEPT A NORM AS LEGITIMATE WHEN IT HURTS TO DO SO?

Why do persons accept the legitimacy of others' claims to a right to partially control their action, when this acceptance constitutes an immediate disadvantage? This is Question Two asked earlier. Persons do not, of course, always obey normative prescriptions or proscriptions, but they *often* do, and the question is: Why?

The question of when a person will obey the norm is different from the question of when he will regard the norm as legitimate. Obedience of the norm will occur when the sanctions (external or internal) are sufficiently great and sufficiently certain to make disobedience less immediately attractive than obedience. But acceptance of others' claims as legitimate is neither necessary nor sufficient for obedience to the norm. It may be that not all such acceptance can be accounted for by rational choice theory as currently constituted. (For example, social psychologists such as Asch (1956) and Sherif (1936) have shown that a person's very perceptions can be altered by the others' report of their perceptions.)

However, acceptance can, at least in some cases, be explicable by rational choice principles. Although a person may see acceptance of this right as being to his *immediate* disadvantage, he may well see it— quite apart from any sanctions imposed—as otherwise to his long-term advantage. This is oftentimes the case when the person may, on other occasions, be in the position of the person expressing this right, that is, in the position of a person affected by, but without control of, another's action of the same type. Accepting the legitimacy of others' rights to partially control his action aids in giving him a legitimate right to control other's similar actions. Rejecting that legitimacy constitutes an action against the legitimacy of his right on those other occasions. For example: If others in a dormitory attempt to impose a norm that one cannot use the dormitory public telephone for more than ten minutes if others are waiting, then if one member of the dormitory rejects the legitimacy of such control, he cannot claim the right to limit others' telephone calls. Thus, one circumstance in which a person may rationally accept a claim of others to partially control his action is that in which he stands potentially in the position of sanctioner of others' actions—for acceptance of others' claims aids him in controlling their actions which affect him.

Returning to the example of the dormitory and the norms governing telephone calls, it is clear that some persons, who make short calls, will often be in the position of a sanctioner, while others, who make few long calls, will often be in the position of sanctionee. Depending on how often he sees himself in these two positions, he may or may not find it to his long-term advantage to accept the legitimacy of the claim when he is making a telephone call.

Recognition of the fact that persons differ in the relative frequency that they will be in the position of sanctioner and sanctionee can give guidelines toward prediction of who will accept a claim as legitimate and who will not. A person who finds himself in the position of actor, more often constrained by the norm than protected by it, will be less likely to accept it as legitimate, because, on balance, its existence is less likely to benefit him. For example, the claim in a community of a right by the members to constrain—through expressions of disapproval—

the bathing suit styles worn at the community swimming pool will more likely be regarded as legitimate by the older and uglier members of the community, who will seldom wear bathing suits that would be challenged, than by the young and beautiful, whose bathing wear is more likely to be challenged.

There is also the apparent fact that observance of a norm itself leads a person to impose the norm on others—even when the person himself observes the norm only because of the sanctions it carries. If this is seen within a rational choice framework, it implies that the external effects of others' actions on a person depend on that person's own action. If a beautiful girl wears a conventional bathing suit, conforming to the norm, she is more likely to find another girl's revealing suit improper and harmful to her interests than if she herself wore a similar suit. If a man is among a group of other men all of whom are wearing ties, and is subject to normative expressions of approach or disapproval from these others, that man's own reaction to a newcomer's wearing or not wearing a tie will depend on whether he himself is wearing one.

In the other structural condition—when those whose action is sanctioned are not also in the position of sanctioner of that action, such as children whose actions are sanctioned by adults, or smokers whose actions are sanctioned by non-smokers—the matter is somewhat different. If the person whose actions are being sanctioned has other relations with the sanctioner, then he may obey the norm, in order to gain a credit with the sanctioner, but this can occur without accepting the norm's legitimacy. In such cases, the acceptance of legitimacy appears to arise in ways not directly explicable in terms of rational choice. What appears to most affect acceptance is the number of other persons holding the norm, and the numbers who do not accept it. This is an area in which research is necessary.

All the above is relevant to norms which have not been internalized. For a norm that has been internalized, the matter is somewhat different. If a person came to *identify with*, that is, to see his interests as identical to those of, a socializing agent, then the imagined claim of a right to control by this agent will be legitimate, because it is a claim deriving from interests he sees as his own.

WHAT CREATES DIFFERENCES IN ASSUMPTION OF THE RIGHT TO EXERCISE CONTROL?

In two settings which appear to be structurally the same, one of them will exhibit persons claiming the right to control others' actions, while the other will not, as in the Berlin versus New York example described earlier. Or in a homogeneous community, one member will regard a certain action as legitimately under some community control, while the other will not, as exemplified by the episode with the tea bags described earlier. What is responsible for these differences?

Consider first the episode with the tea bags. One member of the community will exercise sanctions, another will not. The first member regards the action of hoarding tea bags, in the case of scarcity, as harming all, thus giving him as a community member the right to exercise control through expressing disapproval. The most fundamental level of difference is that the second may not see this as a legitimate right, because he does not perceive that this action is important in bringing about scarcity.

However, even if this difference is absent, with both members regarding the community member's expression of disapproval as a legitimate right, the second may fail to act because of differences in one or more elements which enter the cost-benefit equation for expressing disapproval:

a) The psychic cost of expressing disapproval to another;

b) the perceived effect of expressing disapproval in inhibiting the hoarding action;

c) the cost of experiencing an absence of tea bags.

It is interesting to note that the last element (c) is one which both increases the likelihood of expressing disapproval of others' actions and the likelihood of violating the norm by hoarding tea bags. Thus, we would expect to find some circumstances in which the persons who would be likeliest to impose a sanction on others to uphold the norm, would also be likeliest to violate the norm—an apparent paradox which follows directly from rationality.

To return to the case of the candy wrapper, we can ask: Why the difference between two settings such as Berlin and New York, which appear structurally the same? It appears that the Berlin lady regarded the cleanliness of the public sidewalks as an outcome affecting the welfare of all (and in particular herself) and thus, properly the responsibility of all. The implications of such an assumption are that each has the right to exercise surveillance over all actions that can affect the sidewalks' cleanliness, and to impose sanctions on those who take such actions.

In New York, the comparable lady either (a) did not regard the cleanliness of the sidewalks as an outcome affecting all, or (b) held the same assumptions as the lady in Berlin, but chose not to exercise the right because the effort involved in doing so would be greater than the expected return in the form of a cleaner sidewalk. The presence or absence of cellophane from a piece of candy would make no difference to the general level of sidewalk cleanliness, because it was already so littered; or the response expected from the mother and child would less likely be acquiescence to the reprimand.

This does not, of course, explain why the norm came into being in Berlin and not in New York. An historical explanation is obviously necessary, one which could involve such elements as the levels of city sanitation services in the two cities.

The example suggests also another aspect of such norms, that is, their precarious status. The effect of exercising a sanction, as the lady did in reprimanding the child, can under the best of circumstances have only a small effect on the level of cleanliness and in turn, the level of cleanliness does not have a major impact on a person's level of satisfaction. Consequently, the benefits of exercising a sanction can never be much greater than the costs. A small decrease in the level of cleanliness, or a slightly reduced dependence of a citizen's satisfaction on sidewalk cleanliness (as might occur, for example, as a new generation replaced the old), or a minor change in the expectation of an acquiescent response could reduce the benefits of sanctioning below the costs for many citizens. This could then have a spiraling effect, as the decrease in level of sidewalk cleanliness led to a continual reduction in the number of persons who experienced a net expected benefit from exercising a sanction. The end result would be a high level of litter on the sidewalks, constrained only by the actions of the city sanitation services and some citizens' internalized norms which inhibited them from littering the sidewalks. With succeeding generations, even the internalized norms would be reduced, as fewer mothers found it worthwhile to discipline their children when they littered the sidewalks.

An increase in the level of city sanitation services would be necessary if the sidewalks were to be kept in some modicum of cleanliness, although even this increase would not be sufficient to restore the earlier level of cleanliness. Although the level of services could be increased sufficiently to restore the earlier level of cleanliness, citizens might not tax themselves to provide such a level. The cost of restoring that level through sanitation services would likely be greater than the costs of imposing informal sanctions when the norm was still in force.

WHAT GIVES THE SANCTIONER A RIGHT TO IMPOSE A SANCTION?

This is Question One posed earlier. To answer it, it is first necessary to recognize that a right of this sort, not recognized in law, is wholly subjective.[2] Some persons may recognize a legitimate right of A to sanction B, while others do not.

The first point in an answer is that C's recognition of a legitimate right of A to sanction B will depend on C's interests: If C has interests like those of A (that is, if B's actions have externalities for C in the same direction as for A), then C will be likely to recognize A as having a legitimate right to sanction B. This implies that the greater the number of people for whom B's actions have externalities, the wider will be the recognition of A's legitimate right to sanction B.

In a collectivity, all of whose members' actions have externalities for each other, each will ordinarily recognize the others as having a legitimate right to sanction each of the others, including himself—so long as the externalities taken together affect the utility of each more than does his own action. In such structures, where the similar action of each imposes externalities on the others, either positive (as in the case of a team working toward a common goal) or negative (as in the case of hoarding or littering), the action is potentially self-policing, since all have an interest in transferring some part of the right to control their action to others, in return for a partial right to control their action.[3] It may not come to be self-policing in fact, because of logistical or other barriers. But it is potentially so, if those barriers can be removed.

When interests are not homogeneous in this fashion, there may be wide variations in C's recognition of A as having a legitimate right to sanction B, the variations dependent on the degree to which C's interest is similar to A, or similar to that of B. Thus, the existence of widely-accepted legitimacy for A's sanctioning of B cannot be taken as given. Although there will be a generally-regarded legitimate right of A in certain situations such as those described above, in others there will not. With the present state of theory, empirical investigation is necessary in all situations in which interests are not homogeneous.

WHY NORMS RATHER THAN LAWS?[4]

Question Eight asked why in a particular circumstance there are norms rather than laws, while in another, there are laws. I will attempt only to give a few suggestions toward an answer. The question arises, of course, almost entirely with respect to norms that proscribe actions, since there are few laws that prescribe particular actions.

First, norms and laws are to some extent substitutable. In the early days of the West in the United States, there was no formal law in some places. Community norms substituted, with the "posse" sometimes hunting down a man believed to have committed an action that would be severely punished in the civilization from which these frontiersmen came. Between nomadic tribes in some parts of the Middle East, governed by no intertribal law, there has long prevailed a normative principle of "an eye for an eye, a tooth for a tooth," with the retaliation exercised on any member of the tribe from which the offender came. It was similar until recent years between some clans in isolated sections of Appalachia in the United States.

Law has a number of benefits, however, for constraining certain actions. They carry with them an institutional means of determining "guilt," that is the legitimate applicability of a sanction, while norms do not. Laws have themselves been instituted by a constitutionally-legitimated procedure, which gives them a universal legitimacy, while there is no such procedure to universalize the legitimacy of a norm. In addition, for those actions that are deemed sufficiently harmful to warrant coercive treatment of the actor (such as incarceration), the use of norms rather than laws would be ineffective if the actor was physically more powerful than those experiencing the externalities.

However, law has deficiencies as well. It can be excessively cumbersome if too detailed. In any given social order, there are some actions that it would be generally agreed should be individually controlled, even though they may visit some negative externalities upon others. It is more efficient, given that law is more costly to enforce than norms, to leave control of the action in the hands of the actor, except where the negative externalities are sufficiently greater than the benefits experienced by the actor to compensate for the extra costs of using the law.

There may be, in the division of labor between laws and norms, a principle similar to that proposed by Posner to account for the evolutionary pattern shown by common law. Posner argues that common law comes to place control of an action in those hands that make for greater economic efficiency, in deciding between plaintiff and defendant. It may be that, in a liberal society, there is the presumption that an actor should have the legal right to control his action unless that action always and everywhere will impose on others negative externalities that, using a utilitarian criterion, are greater in aggregate than the benefits of the action to the actor—and sufficiently so to warrant the cost of policing.

Altogether, the balance between laws and norms involves problems of political and moral philosophy, and cannot be treated here in more than this cursory way.

DO NORMS ARISE ONLY WHEN THERE ARE EXTERNALITIES OF ACTION?

There are some norms which seem not to be generated by an action's imposition of externalities on others. For example, in high schools, certain subgroups of girls or boys will have strong norms about how their members dress. (I am indebted to Henry Manne for reminding me of this widespread phenomenon. See my *Adolescent Society* (1961) for various examples among high school students.) In the 1950's "duck-tail" haircuts constituted a norm which would be observed only by certain groups of boys. Certain groups of girls might be marked by bobby sox (or even the particular color of bobby sox), certain groups of boys by white bucks, others by black leather jackets.

Do such prescriptive norms arise, as the general principle I have stated would imply, from the positive externalities that observing the dress norm has for other members of the group? I believe the answer is that they do. For a group of persons who want to show the solidarity of their group and to differentiate it from others, common dress constitutes a very efficient means of doing so. Each member's obeying the norm strengthens the expression of this common solidarity, and this differentiation from others. It is similar in observance of religious codes of dress, diet, and other differentiating characteristics (see Goode, 1960). Observance by fellow-members aids and supports each member, while failure to observe constitutes a threat to the collectivity as a collectivity.

Thus, it appears that dress norms do obey the general principle. Furthermore, once this is recognized, the strength of dress codes in a particular subgroup can show the strength of interest of the members in expressing their solidarity and their differentiation from others.

WHY ARE SOME NORMS INTERNALIZED?

To a sociologist accustomed to assuming socialized members of society, such a question appears naive in the extreme. For different reasons, the question appears naive to anyone who has had to deal, for any period of time, with a child below the age of five or six, or with an adult sociopath, a person who has failed to internalize any social norms that would constrain his self-interested actions.

Yet socialization, and internalization of norms which would constrain the employ of self-interested calculation, has no place in rational choice theory, unless it is simply assumed to enter the utility function. However, as soon as we take the perspective of the parent of a small child or a person who must cope with a sociopath, we immediately see the rationality of attempting to create an internal sanctioning system, a "conscience" or "superego" that would make unnecessary the continual external policing of action.

This does not, of course, mean that such changes within the person can be brought about, but only that *if* they can be brought about with a limited amount of effort, it may be rational for the person or persons who interact with the child or the sociopath to do this. Elementary knowledge of psychology, or even experience in social life, indicates that internalization of norms can and does take place, so its general feasibility need not be a matter of concern, although the cost of socialization might be.

Socialization is carried out not only by parents in the home, but by other agents as well. Nation-states use the schools, as well as various nationalistic events and patriotic propaganda, to socialize the child to identify with the nation, to take its interest as his own. Professional schools and graduate schools socialize a candidate into the discipline, to lead him to identify himself with the profession or the discipline, to "become a (sociologist)." Religious orders, the army, and other institutions use various techniques to socialize a novitiate into the new identity, discarding the old self.

In all these cases, the socialization attempts to create a new "self," whose actions are dictated by the imagined will of the actor with which he has identified himself: parents, nation-state, religious order, profession, or academic discipline. It is that will which generates the internal sanctions for future actions.

To decide whether internalization of a norm in another actor is rational, the cost of bringing about the internalization to given degrees of effectiveness must be balanced against the discounted future costs of policing to bring about the same degrees of compliance. Here, the degree of compliance is selected by balancing costs of non-compliance against the costs of sanctioning by the most efficient (internal or external) means.

It is relatively easy to distinguish external sanctions from the attempt to instill an internal sanctioning system. A parent who slaps a child's hand or withdraws a pleasure to punish an action, or gives the child something it likes, such as candy, to reward an action, is employing an external sanction. A parent who shows that an action of the child's has made the parent feel hurt, and who threatens to withdraw love when a child has carried out a disapproved action, or who exhibits happiness and expresses love for the child when the child has carried out an approved action, is employing an internal sanction.

Although I do not hope to make much headway in answering the question of what combination of internalization and external sanctions is efficient, and how this varies for different norms, there are certain relatively straightforward points that can be made.

A first point is that internalization becomes increasingly efficient with an increase in the number of different types of actions that the socializing actor (say, the parent) wants to control via norms. The basic process of creating identification with the parent constitutes, in effect, a capital cost, with an additional marginal cost for each different action to be made subject to normative constraint. The capital cost seems to be the much larger of these two types of cost, so that the total cost of subjecting a large number of actions to normative constraint by a sanctioning agent is not much greater than the cost of doing so for a small number of actions. Thus, once a mother has brought about a condition in which her daughter internalizes the mother's wishes, the mother can extend the number of prescriptions and proscriptions contained in her wishes without great cost.

One prediction from this is that those parents who wish to normatively constrain a wide range of their children's actions will be more likely to use internal sanctions (rather than external ones) than those parents who wish to constrain a lesser range of actions.

A second point is that parents or other actors who may be in a position to establish an internal sanctioning system do not reap all the benefits from it. Parents must pay the costs of internalization, while it is others who will experience some of the future benefits. It is true that parents will experience some benefits during the period the child is at home, but since these are only a fraction of the benefits, we would expect an underinvestment in internalization. This underinvestment should be especially great for those norms which have least to do with a child's action, but have to do primarily with actions later in life.

However, one way that parents can receive a greater return on their investment in internalization is through identifying with the child, and continuing to inform themselves about the child later in life. Such identification, together with information about the child's actions that accord with the parent's wishes and gain approval from others, can bring satisfaction to the parent, thereby making an investment in internalization profitable. This would lead to the prediction that the use of internal rather than external sanctions by the parent will be greater if the parent expects that the future associates of the child will hold the same values as the parent, e.g., in a stable society.

There is, however, a difference between families. Some families have a strong interest in their status in the community, and see their children's actions, throughout life, as affecting that status. Others have little status in the community, and thus little to lose by the deviant behavior of their children throughout life. We would expect parents in the latter families to seriously underinvest in creating internal sanctions, while parents in the former families would invest much more heavily in internal sanctions. Studies of socialization practices of different social groups are quite consistent with this, showing that the lower the social status, the less internal sanctions are used (see Kohn, 1977). Further predictions could be tested as well, for any aspect of social structure which affected the degree to which the child's later actions would harm the family's interests (such as residence in a more anonymous urban setting as compared to a small-town setting, or the degree of anticipated geographic mobility and discontinuity in the family) would strengthen or weaken the relation between the family's interest in its status and the degree to which socialization practices incorporate internal sanctions. Thus, as most of these conditions increase, we can predict that families of the same social status will less often use internal sanctions, and more often, external sanctions; persons in future generations will be decreasingly socialized.

There is a problem in the theory of the firm in economics that is relevant to the question of internalization. This is the problem of agency (see Fama and Jensen, 1983), which is the principal's problem of how to get an agent to act in the principal's interest. In this problem, one question is the role of incentives (such as stock options, stock ownership, piecework, performance bonuses, commissions, company patriotism) that make the agent's interest largely coincident with that of the principal (in that the agent's interest is satisfied through the outcome or product that also satisfies the principal's interest), *versus* the role of supervision, in which the agent's actions are policed. One rather straightforward principle that has been stated in that literature is that the efficiency of supervision, relative to incentives, decreases as the actions necessary to produce it are more costly to observe or are less easily observed, and therefore, less easily supervised. Thus, a worker in a cottage industry is more likely to be paid by the piece than a factory worker making the same product, because the factory worker is more easily supervised. Conversely, the less measurable the outcome or product of the agent's activity, the less likely that incentives rather than supervision is to be used. For example, a schoolteacher is not likely to receive incentive pay, while a salesman is often paid on commission.

Just as some agents' activities are more easily observed than are others, some norm-governed actions are more easily observed than others. Whether a person is telling the truth, for example, is in many circumstances difficult to determine; thus, the efficiency of external sanctions compared to internal ones is lower than for a more easily observed action.

Quite generally, the problem of agency in economics (that is, the principal's problem of how much to invest in getting the agent to act in the principal's interest, and what is the most efficient means) has much in common with the parents' problem of sanctioning a child, and the creating of internal sanctions *versus* external ones. There is, however, a structural difference between the problem of agency and the problem of socialization of the child. In the latter case, as stated earlier, there is no single principal who will suffer the costs of misdirected agent actions. Parents, who carry out most of the socializing activity, experience direct consequences of the child's actions only through the period of childhood and youth.

This section obviously only raises the questions of internalization of norms, leaving most of the questions unresolved. For example, nothing has been said about the conditions under which acceptance of internalization by the child will be more or less successful. (One generalization in the principal-agent problem, which may be useful here, is that the agent is more likely to accept the principal's interest as his own the more he sees his own future as contingent on the principal.) In addition, I have only touched upon the fact that internalization is to some degree a public good benefiting many who do not contribute to the costs of socialization. But as with other sections of this paper, the aim is not to solve the problems, but only to make a beginning at examining them.

SOCIAL NORMS AS SOCIAL CAPITAL

There has been for some time in sociology, certainly since George Homans published in 1958 his paper "Social Behavior as Exchange," the recognition that many social interactions can be usefully conceptualized as exchange between the parties to the interaction, with the interaction continuing if the exchange was profitable for both. The actions fit the paradigm of neoclassical economics involving exchange of divisible private goods, carried out sometimes in a market context (as in a dating market), and sometimes in a bilateral or small-numbers context. But just as neoclassical economics was slow in recognizing the fundamental differences introduced by externalities and public goods, those who use "exchange theory" in sociology have been slow in recognizing that many social actions and transactions generate externalities or have the character of public goods or bads. This has meant that exchange theory in sociology has been incorrectly individualistic, failing to recognize that externalities create an interest in exercising control over the action, an interest that may come to be regarded as a legitimate right, and thereby, failing to grasp that social norms, together with their accompanying sanctions, are expressions of that right. Where social norms can come into being to allow the actors affected by externalities to gain an appropriate level of partial control of the action, the result is a socially efficient outcome, in the sense that the level and direction of action is governed by all its consequences. If, for one reason or another, these norms fail to come into existence or are destroyed, the level and direction of action are governed only by the interests of the actor who takes the action, and the outcome is not socially efficient, because some of its consequences play no part in governing it. The social system then comes to consist of individualistic solutions to individual problems, with all suffering at the hands of each, as each carries out his actions unconstrained by their consequences for others.

It is in this sense that social norms constitute social capital. Their presence results in higher levels of satisfaction—though perhaps at the cost of reducing the satisfaction of some members whose actions are most constrained by the norms. Their absence allows individuals to realize greater satisfaction from their own actions, but leaves them with less satisfaction overall, as they suffer from the unconstrained actions of others. The system is not quite a Hobbesian "war of all against all," for there are governmental and formal institutions to sanction actions in certain areas, which insure the provision of public goods and inhibit public bads. It is, however, a system of "each for himself," with each imposing external diseconomies upon the others.

NOTES

The author expresses his gratitude to members of a seminar at Russell Sage Foundation, members of a seminar at Ohio State University, and members of the Vienna colloquium for comments helpful in the revision of this paper.

1. I am indebted to Robert Merton for clarifying this point to me.

2. Thanks go to Walter Block for raising questions on the earlier draft of this paper which helped me clarify this point.

3. I am indebted to Peter Bernholz for pointing out the self-policing potential of certain norms.

4. I thank Isaac Ehrlich for raising this question in the conference.

REFERENCES

Asch, Solomon, *Studies of Independence and Conformity*, Washington: American Psychological Association, (1956).

Coase, Ronald H., "The Problem of Social Cost," *Journal of Law and Economics*, Vol. 3 (1960) pp. 1–44.

Coleman, James S., *The Adolescent Society*, New York: Free Press (1961).

Dahrendorf, Ralph, *Essays in the Theory of Society*, Stanford: Stanford University Press (1968).

Fama, Eugene F., "Agency Problem and the Theory of the Firm," *Journal of Political Economy*, Vol. 88 (April, 1980) pp. 288–307.

Fama, E. F., and M. C. Jensen, "Agency Problems and Residual Claims," *Journal of Law and Economics*, Vol. 26 (June, 1983).

Goode, William, "Norm Commitment and Conformity to Role-Status Obligations," *American Journal of Sociology*, Vol. 66 (1960) pp. 246–258.

Homans, George, "Social Behavior As Exchange," *American Journal of Sociology*, Vol. 65 (1958) pp. 597–606.

Kelsen, Hans, *General Theory of Law and State*, Cambridge: Harvard University Press (1945).

Kohn, Melvin L., *Class and Conformity*, Second edition, Chicago: The University of Chicago Press (1977).

Lindenberg, S., "Normen und die Allokation Sozialer Wertschatzung, In Horst Todt, ed. *Schriften des Vereins fur Sozialpolitik*, Berlin (1984).

Noll, Roger, *Reforming Regulations: An Evaluation of the Asch Council Proposals*, Washington: Brookings (1971).

Noll, Roger, "The Feasibility of Marketable Emissions Permits in the United States," In J. Finsinger, ed. *Public Sector Economics*, London: MacMillan (1983).

Parsons, Talcott, *The Social System*, New York: Free Press (1951).

Riker, W. H., and P. C. Ordeshook, *An Introduction to Positive Political Theory*, Englewood Cliffs, N.J.: Prentice Hall (1973).

Sherif, Muzafer, *The Psychology of Social Norms*, New York: Harper (1936).

TRADING MONEY FOR SILENCE

DR. WALTER BLOCK

I INTRODUCTION

When the term "blackmail" was first used in 1722, it had a specific and exact meaning. Not only was its meaning precise, but it was used, in law, to prohibit actions which were clearly at variance with the most basic and cherished of all human rights—the right to remain unmolested in one's person and property.

The Act of 1722, or the Waltham Black Act of 1722, was passed as the result of the depredations of a gang of thieves called the Waltham Blacks, who were deer stealers, operating near the town of Waltham, England, with blackened faces. As well, this gang undertook the quaint practice of sending letters "demanding venison and money, and threatening some great violence, if such their unlawful demand should be refused."[1] Hence the term "blackmail." This law was clearly meant to punish demands for a victim's money or wealth, coupled with threats to inflict violence on person or property, such as to burn down the house of a non-cooperating individual.

If the law prohibiting blackmail began with a clear and limited mandate, it was soon expanded through a series of judicial determinations and new legislative enactments. So much so that the law of blackmail began proscribing threats to do that which one would otherwise have a full and complete right to do—such as exercise one's rights of free speech—were no money demanded as an alternative.[2]

That is, were no money demanded as a payment to keep silent, even money to which one is legally entitled, it would be perfectly legal for one person to gossip about another's bed-wetting, adultery, or homosexuality. The right to free speech protects such idle chatter. But were this person to approach the other and offer to remain silent in return for a payment, he would be guilty of blackmail, a punishable offence in most countries whose legal system derives from that of England.

In common parlance, the concept of blackmail has come to be used very loosely indeed, at least compared to its original meaning, and is now applied to practically any commercial transaction disapproved of by the speaker. For example, the OPEC price hike of 1973 was widely castigated as "economic blackmail." This paper shall attempt to chronicle the widening of the legal definition of blackmail. Its burden shall be to show that the ever more encompassing behavior prohibited under modern blackmail legislation has been inimical to the public good, has transgressed canons of justice, logic, and rights to free speech, and has endangered, not protected, persons and property rights. The organization is as follows: in Section II we shall trace the evolution of the concept of blackmail from its original setting in the common law to its present expanded definition. Section III shall be devoted to determining whether one can legitimately threaten to tell secrets one would otherwise have the right to reveal—unless one is paid to desist. In Section IV we comment on cases (A) where the "victim" approaches the blackmailer; (B) where the threat is to expose a victimless (homosexual, heterosexual and then gambling) crime; and (C) where the threat is to expose a real crime. Section V attempts to account for the prohibition of blackmail (given that the activity is really licit). Section VI considers several objections to our theory and we conclude with Section VII.

II THE CHANGING DEFINITION OF BLACKMAIL

Originally, as we have seen, blackmail in the common law was confined to threatening violence, or other violations of the rights of person or property. For example, according to G. L. Williams,

> As has been seen, there can in general be no stealing where the property is handed over as the result of threats, unless the threats are of force or false imprisonment ... the common-law doctrine has never been extended beyond threats of physical force or false imprisonment; thus a person who obtains goods by threats of accusation of immorality would not be guilty of larceny.[3]

And says Winder in his analysis of British Law:

> The Act of 1734 recites that "many of His Majesty's subjects have of late frequently been put in great fear and danger of their lives by wicked and ill-disposed persons assaulting and attempting to rob them" and declares

to be felony the conduct of such persons who "with any offensive weapon or instrument, unlawfully and maliciously assault, or shall by menaces, or in or by any forcible or violent manner, demand any money, goods or chattels, of or from any other person or persons with a felonious intent to rob or commit robbery." In its original context there can be no doubt that "menaces" means such menaces as, if the demand accompanying them be complied with, robbery is committed: the words "with intent to rob" make this clear and they give effect to the declared object of the Act. There can be no intent to rob unless the handing over of the property demanded amounts to robbery. Therefore, "menaces" in section I meant present threats of immediate battery if the property be not delivered up to the accused.[4]

Another historical source of this concept is derived from piracy:

Blackmail was originally the tribute exacted by free-booters in the northern border counties to secure lands and goods from despoilment or robbery.[5]

And again:

. . . in those forms which require the presence of "menaces" there had to be, originally, and until fairly recently, something like a threat of personal violence or of violence to property.[6]

Moreover, there are numerous law cases which bear out this narrow definition of blackmail. For example, in *R v. Parker,* a creditor was found guilty of criminal offense for forging a letter in an attempt to recover money owed him. This is consistent with the limited construction, since forgery is itself equivalent to an assault on property, and hence an action which is *per se* proscribed.[7]

In *Sheldon v. Lock,* a threat of a civil suit in order to facilitate the collection of a debt was ruled not actionable. The court found that: "A threat to do what one has a legal right to do is not, as a general rule, duress and will not support an action for damages." In *State v. Morgan* a threat made at gunpoint that the victim would "suffer the consequences" was deemed a violation of law. In *R v. Smith,* the defendant was found guilty of threatening to burn down the prosecutor's premises unless he paid off the accused.

So we see that blackmail was originally limited to the use of a threat of violence, or rights violations, in order to obtain valuable considerations. As well, this understanding has continued through the years, as has been indicated. However, the concept of blackmail was soon extended to include threats which did not entail physical abuse, or the violation of rights. And this broadened understanding has also been the basis of law in more recent years as well.

As early as 1776, in the Georgian Statutes (4 Geo .4, c.54) the extortion (blackmail) of money by verbal "threat to accuse a man of unnatural practices" was held to be criminal.[8] According to Winder, however, "At first, therefore, blackmail implied a threat of violent injury to property and according to the Oxford dictionary was not used, by extension, in its modern sense until the nineteenth century. The first example given of its modern use is from the year 1840."[9] In Winder's view, intimidation in the earlier court cases "was understood to mean physical intimidation."[10] But not so in later cases. In the analysis of C. R. Williams, "it was natural" for the draftsmen of the (Blackmail) Act of 1823 to extend the definitions of blackmail from "demands coupled with a threat of violence to the person or to property" to the utterance of "verbal threats to accuse another of serious crime."[11] In the modern day, the concept of blackmail has been well and truly extended from the old physical violence concept to a new one, which includes physical violence as well as the threat of anything else under the sun that might discomfort a person. So much so, that the typical legal commentator and much modern legislation fail to even make this distinction. For example, Livermore, in discussing the Arizona Revised Criminal Code, desribes it as follows: "In addition to the conventional proscription of threats of physical injury, property damage, criminal conduct, and reputational injury, a general clause forbids threatening 'any other act which would not in itself materially benefit the defendant but which is calculated to harm another person materially.'"[12] And states G. L. Williams: ". . . it is rightly treated as blackmail to attempt to obtain money . . . by the threat to accuse of discreditable conduct."[13]

As well, there are numerous legal cases which have cemented the widened comprehension of blackmail. For example, states Lord Wright in *Thorne v. Motor Trade Association*, "I think the word 'menace' is to be liberally construed and not as limited to threats of violence but as indicating threats of any action detrimental to or unpleasant to the person addressed." Stated Lord Atkin in this case:

> If the matter came to us for decision for the first time I think there would be something to be said for a construction of "menace" which connoted threats of violence and injury to person or property, and a constrast might be made between "menaces" and "threats" as used in other sections of the various statutes. But in several cases it has been decided that "menace" in this subsection and its predecessors is simply equivalent to threat: *Reg. v. Tomlinson; Rex v. Boyle and Merchant.*

In *R v. Boyle*, Lord Reading, C. J., speaking in behalf of the Court of Criminal Appeal, stated: "We do not think that the meaning of the word 'menaces', in the section is so restricted. Whatever may have been the view in earlier days under the old statutes and decisions a wider meaning has been given to the word by later decisions. . . ." *R v. Tomlinson* was considered to be the first clear-cut case to extend the concept of blackmail. States Winder: "It was not until *R v. Tomlinson* in 1895 that there was indisputable authority for interpreting 'menaces' in a wide sense."[14] In this case, defendant was convicted of demanding money under the threat of telling a man's wife and friends of his alleged immoral behavior with another woman. Lord Chief Justice Russell of Killomen, C. J. stated:

> I should have regretted if the Court had felt compelled to confine the construction of the word "menaces" in the way suggested (limited to injury to person or property), with the result of excluding such conduct as that of the prisoner from the purview of the criminal law. . . . [I]t may (also) well be held . . . to include menaces or threats of a danger by an accusation of misconduct, though of misconduct not amounting to a crime, and that it is not confined to a threat of injury to the person or property of the person threatened. (material in parentheses inserted)

Other examples include *Clayton*, where two policemen were found guilty of threatening to falsely charge a girl, unless she gave herself to one of them. *R v. Robinson* was another early case in which blackmail in the modern extended sense was punished. Here, the defendant demanded property, threatening to accuse a man of murder. In *Pacholko*, a Canadian case, the Saskatchewan Court of Appeal found that any threat of injury to character is equivalent to blackmail.

As a result of this brief glimpse into the history of blackmail, our analysis is faced with a quandary. On the one hand, we shall want to maintain that the traditional common-law, limited concept of blackmail is indeed criminal behavior, deserving the full punishment of the law. On the other hand, we shall want to maintain that the additional behavior proscribed by the modern, extended concept of blackmail, is, subject to considerations and reservations to be developed below, legitimate and non-criminal and should be legalized, however immoral it may be. But the modern conception of blackmail prohibits both threats of violence as well as other threats. We cannot, therefore, wholly condemn it. As well, there is constant confusion engendered by the use of the term "blackmail" to refer to two such very different kinds of acts.

The difficulty is, as matters stand, that there is no single word which describes only the original narrow concept of blackmail (a threat for money which violates rights) and no single word to describe what has been added to this concept (a threat for money which does not violate rights). Both blackmail and extortion are used synonymously to describe the wider, modern concept of blackmail (threat for money which either violates rights or does not.)

There is always a risk in offering a stipulative definition. "The world will little note, nor long remember," such efforts. Nevertheless, in this confused situation, this is the path we have chosen. Accordingly, we shall not in this paper use the term "blackmail" to refer to the case where a demand for money is made on the basis of a threat of the initiation of physical violence or other clearly criminal behavior. Rather, we shall reserve the word "extortion" to denote such activities.[15] We shall reserve the appellation "blackmail" for those who limit their threats to that which, in the absence of a demand for money, would be considered legal.[16]

We engage in this semantical device in the interests of clarity. For there is a sharp, deep, crucial and vitally important distinction to be drawn between those who threaten rights' violations in order to obtain money from other people, and those who only threaten to exercise their own legitimate prerogatives unless such funds are forthcoming.[17] This distinction can and must be drawn.

Now it may be, as contended by those who refuse to differentiate between these two types of behavior, that both blackmail (threatening to exercise one's own rights) and extortion (threatening to violate the rights of other people) are, or should be, criminal acts. If so, this conclusion should be the result of analysis, not assumptions, and not definition.[18] By reserving "blackmail" for one type of action, and "extortion" for the other, we are at least in a position to argue that one is legitimate, the other not. Without this device, there would not even be a word to denote the act of demanding money under threat of carrying out only that which one has a right to do.

There is another good reason for using "extortion" to denote what was originally meant by "blackmail." The two words are used synonymously,[19] and one can only protest at the use of two words to do the work of one, when the job that might be accomplished by either is left undone. With this lexicographical determination, we are now in a position to more carefully address the real issues.

First, however, we must be clear on exactly what is, and what is not, an extension of the narrow common-law concept of "blackmail." (We are now calling this extortion.) That is, we must clearly demarcate the boundaries between blackmail, threatening that which one has a right to threaten and extortion, threatening that which one does not have a right to threaten.

Originally, the law proscribed only the action of public officials. "The corrupt collection of an unlawful fee by an officer under colour of office" is how it was expressed. But this has been extended to cover private citizens as well, in the *Woodward, Southerton and Edwards* cases. In the view of Stern:

> The common law definition of extortion has been "quite commonly *extended* (by statute) to include any obtaining of property from another through a wrongful use of force or fear, thus including acts not done under color of official right." The extension of the definition of extortion to include private taking, if the private taking is attended by the use of fear, has not displaced the term "under color of official right"; it has merely added to it.[20] (emphasis added)

But this is clearly not an extension of the concept of extortion. The crime is a crime whether perpetuated by a person in his role as a public servant or in his own private role. Surely there is no case here for treating persons on the public payroll differently from those who are privately employed. Thus, this change is not really an extension, or a change in the concept. Rather, it is merely the case that an unchanged law has been applied more fully and more consistently.

Another misunderstanding occurs in the literature with regard to *Taylor*. In this case, it was determined that the threat to commit arson constituted an illegitimate menace (extortion). Well and good. But G. L. Williams erroneously considers this to be an extension of the common law doctrine.[21] It is no such thing. For arson is *per se* a criminal activity, an attack on persons and/or property. One does not at all have the right to commit arson.

Yet another difficulty arises with regard to *Knewland*, a case of physical intimidation. Not only was the victim threatened with detention in a room—this was actually carried out. And yet it is described by Winder as an "other extension"[22] of the common law proscription against threatened violence against person or property. On the contrary, it was a paradigm case of extortion. According to Ashhurst, J., who delivered the opinion of "not guilty" in *Knewland*, the terror which leads a person "to apprehend an injury to his character" such as an accusation of sodomitical practices, was lacking. This is in sharp contrast to the view of blackmail put forth here. In our view, a person has no right to molest the person of another, such as in detention in a room, and that, consequently, a threat to this effect is extortionate. The defendant in *Knew-land* should have been found guilty, based on these facts. On the other hand, one should be legally able to shout from the very rooftops about acts of sodomy committed by other people. This is merely part and parcel of the right to free speech. *R v. Harry* follows the *Knewland* example. It is another case where an extortionist was set free even though he threatened what he had no right to do. The treasurer of a college rag committee demanded money for charity from several local merchants. If they refused, he threatened not to "protect them" from "inconvenience" resulting from rag-collecting activities.[23]

Hall conforms to this *Knewland* pattern as well. Here, a gamekeeper confiscated some trapping wires and a pheasant from a poacher, who threatened to beat out the gamekeeper's brains with a stick if he did not return this paraphernalia. The court held that if the accused had *thought* his demand was lawful, he could not be convicted of robbery. In the event, this extortionist was given a sentence of one year for common assault.[24]

It is certainly a paradox that the law of blackmail deals more harshly with those who threaten no more than the exercise of their free speech rights, than with those who threaten invasions of person or property. We have contended that the latter ought to be punished, not the former. However, at the very least, if the former is punished, it ought to be less severe than the latter.

Another suspect analysis occurs in the treatment by C. R. Williams[25] of five different law cases where threats were made in order to obtain money:

1) In *R v. Boyle & Merchant* the accused threatened to publish derogatory newspaper attacks against a company unless it paid for silence.

2) In *R v. Studer* the victim, an English manufacturer of German birth, was falsely told by an employee that Scotland Yard was investigating allegations that he had been trading with the enemy. Money was demanded by the employee in order to stop the investigation.

3) In *R v. Rasmussen and Spiegelglass*, the threat was to publish newspaper articles attacking the moral character and chastity of a woman.

4) In *R v. Bernhard*, a former mistress threatened to "tell all" to the wife and the newspapers.

5) In *R v. Clear*, a lorry driver, who had been in charge of a vehicle which had been stolen, demanded money from his employers as the price of not changing his account of how the vehicle came to be

stolen in such a way as to prejudice the employer's claim against his insurance company.

Says Williams, "In none of the cases above referred to was the threat of a kind which might have rendered the accused guilty of larceny had the property demanded been given to him." Williams is correct in the first four cases. In none of these was the threat to do something criminal. All are free speech cases. But in the fifth, *R v. Clear*, this is not so. Here, the lorry driver had a contractual obligation, as an employee, not to destroy his employer's property. Had he carried out his threat, this would have been equivalent to stealing money to which his employer was entitled. It would have been equivalent to destroying property of an equal value, or burning it. It was extortion, in our terms, not mere blackmail. In *Studer*, the accused was also an employee, with a contractual relationship. But here, his threat was only to not call off the (non-existant) investigation. Had he carried out this threat it would *not* have amounted to a "taking." All he had threatened to do was to refrain from doing which could not in any case be done.

The principle in analyzing these cases is as follows: Blackmail is legitimate unless a contractual obligation exists which converts it into illegitimate extortion. For example, if a detective agrees to help a blackmail victim, and instead turns around and blackmails him, the detective is guilty of extortion, not blackmail. What of a typical employment contract, which makes no explicit reference to blackmail? In *Clear*, it was part of the lorry driver's job to fulfill his duties in a manner supportive of his employer's ends, to the best of his ability. Lying about an accident, to the detriment of his employer, was in violation of this obligation. Therefore, threatening to do so was also illicit. Had a perfect stranger, a witness to the accident, threatened to lie about it in the same way, he would have been a blackmailer, not an extortionist. In contrast, in *Studer* the threat had nothing to do with the employee's function. The employee, in this case, was as completely innocent of extortion as would have been a non-employee, making the same blackmail offer. However, had the employee in *Studer* been hired as a detective to protect the company, or had his job been in any other such way relevant to this threat, then he would have been guilty of extortion, not mere blackmail.

One final point on the distinction between extortion (threatening illegitimate force), which ought to be a crime, and blackmail (threatening no more, in effect, than to become a gossip), which should no more open the citizen to a charge of criminality than that practice itself.

If a person obtains someone else's secret improperly, through fraud or any other such criminal behavior, and then threatens to reveal it unless paid not to do so, he would be considered an extortionist, not a blackmailer. This is because the blackmailer, if he is to maintain his innocence before the law, must do so completely. Let him commit *any* infraction while pursuing his otherwise non-criminal behavior, and he is sullied with illegitimacy. This would be applicable in cases of indirect criminality as well.[26] Suppose B spies upon A through improper and invasive practices, and thereby learns of his bed-wetting deviation. Whereupon he turns over this ill-gotten information to C, who is—so far—an innocent party. But if C attempts to blackmail A with this knowledge (or worse, gossips about it without even having the decency to give A the option of purchasing his silence) then C, too, should be considered an extortionist, not a legally-benign blackmailer, and punishable by law. For even though C obtained the information honestly, he has no more right to it than B, whose claim to it, by stipulation, is flawed.[27]

III   CAN ONE THREATEN WHAT ONE HAS A RIGHT TO DO?

It is the overwhelming opinion of the legal fraternity that one has no right to threaten to do that which one has every right to do unless one is paid to forbear.

For example, consider what G. L. Williams has to say on this issue:

> Suppose that D, to whom no money is owing, writes to P, saying: "Pay me £5 or I will make it known that you have committed larceny." P has in fact committed larceny. Now, to say that a man has committed larceny, if the statement is true, is not necessarily a legal wrong. It is not the tort of defamation, and it is not a criminal libel unless (1) the defamatory statement is in writing, and (2) the publication is not in the public interest. If these two conditions are not satisfied, the threat is to do an act that in itself is lawful. Nor is there any wrong merely in demanding payment of a sum of money. A man is at perfect liberty to importune a gift. The demand made is therefore lawful in itself (in the sense that is not a legal wrong, though, of course, it could not be legally enforced), *and the threat made could in itself be both lawfully made and lawfully carried out.* Yet taking the demand and the threat together they constitute blackmail. The two things that taken separately are moral and legal whites together make a moral and legal black. *Although D has a liberty to demand money and a liberty to speak the truth concerning others, and even to threaten to speak the truth, he is not at liberty to demand money under threat*

of speaking the truth. The position would be the same even if L5 were in fact owing to D: the threat of publicity would not be a proper mode of collecting the debt.[28] (emphasis added)

Another such statement arose in the course of *Rex v. Denyer.* In this case, a trade protection association demanded 250L of a trader, threatening to put him on a stop list, thus depriving him of supplies, unless he agreed to observe list prices in the future.

According to the judgement in this case:

It has been said that because this trade protection association had the legal right to put a name on the stop list, it therefore had a legal right to demand money from him as the price of abstaining from putting the name on the stop list. That proposition is not merely untrue; it is precisely the reverse of the truth. It is an excuse which might be offered by blackmailers to an indefinite extent.

The conviction was upheld by the Court of Criminal Appeal:

The association's representative had been properly convicted, and it did not follow that because the association had the right to put a person's name on the stop list that it had a right to demand money from him as the price of abstaining from so doing.

This is a crucial point in our analysis. For if people do not have the right to threaten (in order to obtain money from other people) that which would otherwise be legal for them to do, then blackmail, as we have defined it, would be a criminal activity.[29] Although this is indeed the opinion which is prevalent today, the literature does include several instances to the contrary. That is to say, there is some limited support for the view that blackmail, but only as we have defined it, should be legalized. For example, Lord Justice Romer stated in *Rex v. Denyer:*

I cannot find that the defendants have done anything of which complaint can be made in a Court, whether of civil or criminal jurisdiction. The evidence shows at the most no more than that the defendants in good faith proposed and agreed to abstain from doing something that they could lawfully do, on the condition that the plaintiffs made a payment that they could lawfully make.

And, according to a commentator on *Denyer:*

In the present case the threat involved no legal injury to (the trader). There was nothing contrary to public policy in expelling him or abstaining from so doing on condition that he paid a sum of money. But the fact that a thing perfectly legal in itself is not consistent with legal views of morality or public policy is often the dominating factor which causes a transaction to be found illegal. The (association) merely proposed and agreed to abstain from doing something that they could lawfully do, on condition that (the trader) made a payment which he could lawfully make, and there was no illegality in making the payment the consideration for the abstention. Nor was the letter in this case a demand with menaces without reasonable and probable cause, within the meaning of sec. 29 (1), though I rest my judgement on the surer ground that it was not uttered without reasonable and probable cause.

The real principle, in my view, may be expressed thus: Anyone who, without contravening morality or public policy, offers and agrees to receive, as an alternative to an act which he may lawfully perform, money which the other party may lawfully agree to pay as a consideration for such forebearance, is not guilty of a criminal offence.[30] (Material in parentheses inserted.)

This is hardly a ringing clarion-call defence of blackmail, for "without contravening morality or public policy" is very vague and amorphous. A truck could be driven through such a loophole. Nevertheless, it is limited support for this position, and its reasoning may easily be applied, as it will be below, to cases where the threat is to expose a person as an adulterer, or a homosexual, or a criminal.

This minority position derives additional support from Livermore, who claims "that one may threaten to do what one is legally entitled to do to enforce that claim."[31] And again, the obverse, "There is no sound reason to allow lawyers to threaten what is legally unavailable to them to influence actions of others."[32] If lawyers are to be prohibited from threatening that which they cannot do, then the presumption is that they should be *allowed* to threaten that which they can legally do. And this is roughly the view arrived at by Livermore two pages later in his commentary, ". . . a lawyer could, of course, remain free to threaten legal action which is available to his client."[33]

So we have two schools of thought as to whether, to use G. L. William's felicitous phrase, two legal whites can together make a legal black. The overwhelming majority of the profession holds that it can; on the other hand, by diligent searching, some demurs can be found. There are several difficulties, however, with the majority view that do not appear in the literature of law. First, it would appear that the burden of proof should be on the side that is making a counter-intuitive claim. There can be hardly anthing more counter-intuitive than the claim that two whites can make a black. And yet the majority opinion does not explain how this can be so. It does no more than G. L. Williams, and contents itself with merely asserting this claim, as if it were the intuitively logical stance, and not its contrary. But it is an affront to common sense to claim that X(1) is legitimate, X(2) is legitimate, and yet both X(1) and X(2), when taken together, are illegitimate.[34]

There is a second difficulty with the majority position. Given that the demand is white, if the threat, another white, is prohibited as extortion, then it, the second white, can be implemented without recourse to the first white. That is, the would-be blackmailer, if he is affected by the legal proscription, still has the legal option not only of merely threatening to reveal the secret or embarrassment, but of actually doing so. Of course, he cannot also ask for money for his silence. To do that would be to enact both whites. But if he does the second (implement the threat), without the first (offering his silence in return for payment), the blackmail "victim" may be far worse off as a result of the criminalization of this act. For with blackmail legalized, he has the option of benefiting by paying money in order to avoid what for him would be a worse fate, the publicization of his secret.[35] With blackmail illegal, as it should be in the majority view, the "victim's" welfare is paradoxically diminished. Says Livermore in this regard:

> Anomalously, it would be permissible to destroy reputation by bringing suit but not to allow the defendant to avoid that destruction by paying the claim. Not only would this mean a net loss to the privacy that the extortion status is, in part, aimed at protecting, but it would also involve significantly expanded litigation costs and burdens on efficient utilization of judicial resources.[36]

Besides *Denyer*, there were two other high profile cases in the blackmail literature which turned on the question of a cartel's right to discipline a violator of price-fixing arrangements, and to fine the chiseling firm in lieu of expelling or boycotting it. In 1928, in *Hardie and Lane v. Chilton*, the opposite conclusion was reached. Here it was determined

> that where a trade association was entitled by its constitution to put on a stop list the name of a person who had infringed its rule forbidding the sale of articles at other than the fixed prices, the association might, instead, lawfully adopt the more lenient course of asking the person to make a payment of money by way of compromise, and such money could be accepted and was not recoverable as if paid under duress.

In *Thorne v. MTA*, as in *Denyer*, a price-fixing violator was offered the option of paying a fine as an alternative to being boycotted (stop-listed) by the cartel. But here, the House of Lords, overruling *Denyer*, maintained that since the trade association had a right to place the violator on the stop list, it also had a right to demand money payment as an alternative. Stated Lord Atkin:

> It appears to me that if a man may lawfully, in the furtherance of business interests, do acts which will seriously injure another in his business he may also lawfully, if he is still acting in the furtherance of his business interests, offer that other to accept a sum of money as an alternative to doing the injurious acts. He must no doubt be acting not for the mere purpose of putting money in his pocket, but for some legitimate purpose other than the mere acquisition of money.

In addition, Lords Wright, Atkin, Thankerton and Roche held that, were the fine too high or "unreasonable," then the Motor Trade Association would have been guilty of extortion.

The *Thorne* case may thus be interpreted as giving support to our contention that blackmail ought to be legalized. After all, the supposed blackmailer, the secretary of the MTA, was found innocent. But if *Thorne* supports the decriminalization of blackmail, it furnishes but the weakest of support. For one thing, the requirement that the fine be "reasonable" is certainly an infringement on the blackmailer's right to charge a market price for his services. Says G. L. Williams of this requirement:

> (It) appears to be somewhat anomalous, for in no other instance of an absolutely justifiable threat is there authority for saying that the matter is affected by the amount asked as the price for abstaining from carrying out the threat. For example, D's threat not to sell his property to P unless P pays a high price for it is absolutely justifiable whatever the sum asked.[37]

For another, the defendant was held not guilty only because the MTA was deemed to have been acting "for some legitimate (business) purpose, other than the mere acquisition of money." This, too, would appear to be an infringement on the rights of blackmailers. As well, it is nonsensical, for the very purpose of business is the "mere acquisition" of money. Certainly the MTA's objection to the price-cutter stemmed from its fear that such a practice would reduce the money that could be otherwise acquired. What else furthers business interests *apart* from the acquisition of money?[38]

Let us consider one last version of this majority view before closing this section. In Campbell's view:

If X and Y are rival candidates for an appointment and X offers to withdraw his name if Y pays him money, doubtless X is offering to surrender
a material advantage which he might legitimately enjoy. But if X threatens to reveal some secret failing of Y's to the appointing board unless Y
pays him money, is X not a blackmailer? Yet he had the right to reveal
Y's secret to the board and if the revelation resulted in the rejection of Y
and the appointment of X this would be a furthering of X's legitimate
material interests and might even be in the public interest.

The real point is not whether X had an interest which he could legitimately
enjoy but whether he had an interest which he could legitimately surrender,
or offer to surrender, in return for money. There may well be interests
which a man can legitimately enjoy himself, and rights and liberties
which he can legitimately exercise in furtherance of these interests, but
which he cannot legitimately transfer to another, *e.g.*, his interest in and
right to the consortium of his wife, and there may well be interests and
rights and liberties which he can enjoy and exercise himself but which
he cannot legitimately covenant not to enjoy or exercise, *e.g.*, he has an
interest in pursuing his trade and a liberty to pursue his trade or not as
he pleases, but he cannot validly covenant, save within certain limits, to
refrain from pursuing his trade.

And in most cases of blackmail we are dealing with interests which may
be legitimately enjoyed and liberties which may be legitimately exercised but
whose surrender, or attempted surrender, for money is not only void but is a
crime. The question we have to answer is not: Had the accused an interest
which he could legitimately enjoy? but: Had the accused an interest which
he could legitimately surrender for money?[39] (Emphasis added.)

This statement is based on the contention that one can own or enjoy
a right but cannot sell or transfer it. The view stands or falls with this
contention. But it gives rise to some difficulties. As in the case of the
statement of G. L. Williams, the burden of proof would appear to rest
at Campbell's doorstep. The commonsensical notion is that, "if you
can't sell it, you don't really own it," with the obverse, "if you really
own it, then you *can* sell it." Campbell, unfortunately, provides no reasons or justification for his bare-bones denial. He merely asserts it.

The one example he vouchsafes us, that a man cannot legitimately
transfer interest in and rights to the consortium of his wife, can be handled in several ways. If marriage is interpreted along the lines of (male)
ownership, in which case the husband literally owns the wife as a
slave, as obtained in some ancient societies, then he certainly can legitimately transfer such rights. Of course, in our present society, a husband cannot literally own a wife, and cannot, therefore, explicitly make
any such transfer—certainly not without her agreement. But he cer-

tainly can do so with her permission. That is, he can divorce her, and she can marry the "purchaser," with each of them, perhaps, sharing in the financial payment.[40]

At least the example of the consortium of the wife had a certain shock value. But what are we to make of the assertion that a person "has an interest in pursuing his trade and a liberty to pursue his trade or not, as he pleases, but he cannot validly covenant, save with certain limits, to refrain from pursuing his trade?" Again, no reasons are given to support this. Nor does the example make any sense on its own. The question which immediately arises is: If a person *really* has a right to pursue his trade, why can he not accept a payment *not* to pursue it? That is, if X really has a right to reveal a secret about Y, why can he not ask for (or acquiesce in the offer of—see below) a money payment for holding his tongue?

IV BLACKMAIL CASES

Now that we have outlined the rudiments of the case in favor of legalizing blackmail, let us apply this analysis to a series of cases, and use it to contrast our position with the more orthodox one on this subject.

A VICTIM APPROACHES BLACKMAILER

Let us first consider several cases where it is not the blackmailer who approaches the "victim," but rather the "victim" who approaches the blackmailer.

Rothbard raises this point in opposition to the outlawry of a blackmail contract. Says he:

> Suppose that, . . . instead of Smith going to Jones with an offer of silence, Jones had heard of Smith's knowledge and his intent to print it, and went to Smith to offer to purchase the latter's silence? Should that contract be illegal? And if so, why? But if Jones's offer should be legal while Smith's is illegal, should it be illegal for Smith to turn down Jones's offer, and then ask for more money as the price of his silence?[41]

People v. Dioguardi is just such a case. Here, a stationery business was struck by four unions in an attempt to organize the employees. The labor pickets made it impossible for the firm to conduct business. The owner approached one McNamara, a teamster official and later defendant in the case, and offered him money to end the labor troubles. McNamara agreed, making a proposition for payment. After he and his colleague Dioguardi were paid off, the pickets vanished and labor peace ensued.[42]

As a result, the defendants were indicted, tried and convicted of extortion under New York Penal Law #850, which defines extortion as "the obtaining of property from another, or obtaining the property of a corporation from an officer . . . thereof, with his consent, induced by a wrongful use of force or fear."

The defendents argued that their behavior did not constitute a threat to do an unlawful injury, since if their proposition were rejected they would have done absolutely nothing. But in the view of A. B., the commentator: "Clearly, defendants failed to consider #858 of the Penal Law which expressly brings a threat 'not to do something' within the scope of extortion." To defend this interpretation, A. B. goes on to say:

> Might not any refusal to act unless paid (as with doctors, lawyers and plumbers) in response to a request for help be extortion? A doctor or lawyer says simply "I will not remove your troubles unless I am paid." There is no implication of power to continue the victim's troubles and the victim knows it. But when a labor official says, "I will not remove the pickets unless I am paid," a logical inference arises (which in the instant case was encouraged by the defendant) that he has the power to maintain the picket—the very thing the victim fears. The two situations are distinguished by the presence in the latter of power and a threat, express or implied, to use it wrongfully. Therein lies the wrongful use which turns an otherwise lawful act into extortion.[43]

But this simply will not do. It is of course true that the doctor or lawyer was not the cause of the victim's troubles in the first place, and has not the power to continue them. It is also true that the union officials were the cause of the stationer-victim's difficulties in the first place, and now have the power to continue them, merely by refraining from any further activity. However, their being the cause of the stationer's labor dispute was entirely within the power given them by the various labor enactments prevailing in the United States, and their power to continue these labor problems merely by doing nothing is also lawful, based on such labor legislation. So the unionists are in exactly the same moral-legal position vis-à-vis the doctor (or lawyer) insofar as extortion is concerned.[44] The doctor and unionist are acting strictly according to law. The doctor is not required by law to "remove troubles" unless he is paid, and *neither should be the unionist!* Further proof of this contention can easily be seen by considering the following counterfactual scenario. Suppose that the unionists, when approached by the businessmen, had recoiled in horror from any suggestion that they relinquish their lawful picketing in return for anything so gross as money. Suppose, that is, they had realized that by falling in with the businessman's suggestion, they would open themselves to charges of extortion.

Under these conditions, would the position of the unionists have been illegal? Certainly not. They would have been completely within their rights to continue the picketing activities permitted them by law. Would the businessman have been better or worse off? To ask this question is to answer it. Obviously, the businessman would have been *worse* off—how else explain the fact that *he* approached the unionists, and agreed to pay for labor peace? How can this power of the unionists be used "wrongfully," as contended by A. B., if, as a result of its use, the supposed victim of extortion is made better off?

A. B. then raises a red herring. He cites the case of *People v. Weinseimer*, which "presents a situation similar to *Dioguardi,* where after a *bona fide* labor dispute had been settled the men continued to stay out. The contractor was losing money and feared further losses, and therefore quickly agreed to pay the union president, who represented that he could 'fix things' for a fee. The contractor believed that unless he paid, the men would be kept out. He paid and the men returned but, when he failed to pay the last in a series of notes, the men were pulled from the job. The circumstances indicated a preconceived plan to 'strike the job' unless defendant received payment from the contractor."[45] But Weinseimer is no more guilty of extortion than are McNamara and Dioguardi. To see this clearly, suppose that the union president was as honest as the day is long, wanting only to maximize the wealth of the membership, and not his own. That is, instead of demanding (agreeing to accept) money for himself as the price of labor peace, he demanded it in the form of higher wages for all. Under these conditions, what was implicit becomes explicit: the labor laws of the land allow unions to wrest certain advantages from their employers; but the use of laws such as the Penal Code of New York (buttressed by cases such as *Dioguardi* and *Weinseimer*) are only other legislative and judicial attempts to undo what labor legislation has wrought; they are attempts to take back from the unions with one hand what the labor codes have given to organized labor with the other. With its labor laws, society gives the union sector the right to disrupt production; but with its extortion laws (and anti-"racketeering" legislation and judicial findings), society attempts to keep the unions from cashing in on the powers granted them. If society wishes to shrink back in horror from the unseemly and improper powers it has given to unions (and it should, it should), it would be far less hypocritical to rescind both its labor and extortion legislation, rather than attempt to undo the former with the latter.[44]

Threats, as we have seen, most recently in the arena of labor relations, are either forbidden outright, or at the very least are highly suspect. Are there any cases on record in the blackmail literature where such threats are seen as unequivocally legitimate? As can be expected, not too many. Research, however, uncovers the following two examples:

Scrutton, L. J. in *Hardie & Lane v. Chilton* states: " . . . a cook may ask for a rise in wages in consideration of refraining from giving notice and seeking other and possibly more congenial employment."

And Lord Wright held (in *Thorne*): " . . . a valued servant may threaten to go to other employment unless he is paid a bonus or increased wages."

Is it possible to reconcile these two statements with the findings of extortion in *Dioguardi* and *Weinseimer*? I submit it is not.[47] The cook or the "valued servant" who threatens to leave for greener pastures does no more wrong, as far as the law should be concerned, than do the picketing unionists. If the unionists have the right to strike, but not to surrender this right for money, why should the cook or servant, who have a right to quit, be able to surrender it for money? Suppose the cook's employer approaches her and asks that she return to his employ, for money considerations. If she agrees, logic demands that she too be considered an extortionist. Of course, the quitting cook and striking union engage in vastly different behavior. But the point is, *both* their activities should be lawful.

B   VICTIMLESS CRIMES

We now turn to a consideration of several extortion cases which fall under the rubric of victimless crimes. The first grouping to be considered features a demand for money on the part of the accused blackmailer, and a threat to expose the "victim" of a contravention of heterosexual mores. In *Hamilton*, for example, the threat was to reveal that prosecutrix had visited a brothel in the company of a man; this led to a conviction. In *Miard*, a woman was found innocent of blackmail even though she threatened to reveal that a clergyman had had intercourse with her. *Tomlinson* and *Dymond* in effect reversed this finding. In *Tomlinson*, the threat was to inform a husband's wife and friends of his immoral relationship with a woman. In *Dymond*, a woman was convicted for writing to a man who had allegedly indecently assaulted her; the threat was that if he did not comply with her demand for money, she would "summons" him and "let the town knowed all about your going on. (sic)" In *Bernhard*, the former mistress of a man threatened to expose her lover to his wife and the newspapers, unless he paid her off. She was found guilty, but this verdict was quashed upon appeal. Christine Keeler serves as yet another example. "She seemed to have believed that she was morally entitled, as the price of withholding her memoirs, to a sum which included the cost of a holiday for herself and a house for her parents." She was "credited with a desire for fair recompense not with an intention to extort."[48]

And in *Lambert*, "the accused suspected his wife of having an affair with X. He informed X that L250 would buy X's rights to his (the accused's) wife, and that if X did not pay, he (the accused) would inform X's employer and X's wife of his suspicions. The accused was charged with blackmail and acquitted."[49]

The problem with these cases is that guilt or innocence of extortion turned not on the question of whether or not the accused threatened something she (he) had no right to carry out, and hence no right to threaten, but on the question of whether she (he) was entitled in law to the money demanded or at least whether she (he) thought so in good faith. For instance, in *Miard*, Tindal C. J. told the jury to ascertain whether the demand "was made at a time when the party making it really and honestly believed that she had good and probable cause for so doing." In *Dymond*, Chief Justice the Earl of Reading held:

> In our judgment the question must by determined solely by reference to the language of the statute. The words are 'without any reasonable or probable cause' and nothing. . . suggests that an honest belief by the accused in a reasonable or probable cause for the demand would negative the crime. . . . It is for the jury to decide whether there was reasonable or probable cause for making the demand and it is not for them to decide whether the accused believed that she had reasonable or probable cause for making it.

But the model developed in this paper presents a quite different view. Here, it is immaterial what the accused demanded, let alone whether the accused felt justified in making this demand. As G. L. Williams said above, " . . . the threat is to do an act that is itself lawful. Nor is there any wrong merely in demanding payment of a sum of money. A man is at perfect liberty to importune a gift. The demand made is therefore lawful in itself." In our opinion, that is definitive. Two legal whites do *not* make a legal black in this case. "Case closed," as Archie Bunker might have said.[50] As we see it, the accused in all these cases is indeed guilty of blackmail, which should be non-criminal, and innocent of extortion, which should alone be a crime.

It is the same with a series of blackmail-extortion cases related to threats concerning homosexuality and other deviant acts. *Jones* was the first case to establish that a threat to accuse of sodomy is a sufficient condition for robbery (extortion, as we have defined the word). *Donnally* followed up this finding. In that case Willes, J., held that such a threat was "equivalent to actual violence; for no violence that can be offered could excite a greater terror in the mind, or make a man sooner part with his money"; that it was "a threat of personal violence, for the prosecutor had everything to fear in being dragged through the streets as a culprit charged with an unnatural crime."[51] In *Hickman*, Ashhurst, J., commented that, "a threat to accuse a man of having committed the greatest of all crimes" was "a sufficient force to constitute the crime of robbery by putting in fear: to most men the idea of losing their fame and reputation is equally, if not more terrific than the dread of personal injury." In *Elmstead* and *Egerton*, a majority of the judges took *Hickman* as binding. In *Edwards*, the "extortionist" obtained money from a woman by threatening to expose her husband as a sodomite. The accused was found innocent, but only because the threat was not made directly to the person concerned, the husband himself. In *Pollock and Divers*, the accused was also found guilty of robbery (extortion) for threatening to accuse a man of sodomy.

And most legal writers on the subject would go along with the findings of these cases. Hogan, for example, states, "we believe that most people would say that it should be blackmail to threaten to denounce a person, however truly, as a homosexual unless he paid a debt."[52]

The decisions in these homosexual cases show the same flaws as the ones in the previous heterosexual set. Is it or is it not lawful to actually accuse someone of sodomy and other "unnatural" practices? It is lawful. If so, there is no crime, for, as we have seen, there is no reason to reject the view that what may legally be threatened may legally be kept silent about—for a fee. And certainly the "victim" is better off by having this one additional option. With blackmail, he has a choice: to allow his secret to be told, or to pay up, and be spared the embarrassment.

Hogan is a commentator who fully distinguishes between "a threat to do something detrimental to P (which) could, apart from the demand, be otherwise lawful (e.g., to expose P's sexual misconduct) or otherwise unlawful (e.g., to assault P)."[53] Yet, even he falls victim to the view that "a demand against a threat to expose of sexual deviance is every bit as bad as a demand against a threat to do bodily harm,"[54] which echoes the opinions given by Willes in *Donnally* and Ashhurst in *Hickman*. But with all respect, this reasoning is incorrect. It may be true that the fear of having one's wife run off with the milkman, or losing thousands of dollars in a card game, may be far more serious, in the minds of some people, than being the victim of minor assault and battery. But that is entirely irrelevent to law. The point is that the latter is illegal, while the former two cases in no way violate the law. In a just society, a person would be incarcerated for threatening or perpetrating the latter act, not the former, even though the latter may be far less fearful than the former. Fear, or lack of it, is irrelevant. If a victim is psychologically non-fearful, does this mean that the threat to murder him, which leaves him nonplussed, should go unpunished? Hardly. (See *McGee, Boyle*.)

Our view, here, receives at least qualified support from G. L. Williams who states:

> . . . a taking by threats of accusation of discreditable conduct is not robbery, unless (according to old cases) the threat is to accuse of sodomy or indecency between males. The exception for accusation of these two offences is anomalous; it was developed at a time when the modern offences of blackmail were not upon the statute book or were not interpreted so broadly as they are now. Quite possibly the exceptions would no longer (be?) recognized (*cf.* Norton).[55]

The argument here is sensible, but perhaps a bit too optimistic, unfortunately. *Edwards*, and especially *Pollock and Divers*, came years after *Norton*.

The orthodox theory, upon which are based the heterosexual and homosexual cases we have been discussing, comes in for some sharp criticism. In the view of C. R. Williams, relying on the belief of the perpetrator in the rightness of his act is entirely subjective in nature:

> The adoption of a wholly subjective test, making the accused's criminality depend upon his own view of the propriety of his actions, is a surprising departure from the approach taken in other offences contained in the Crimes (Theft) Act. It is a requirement of offences such as theft, obtaining property by deception and robbery, that the accused be shown to have acted "dishonestly." The standard to be taken for determining what constitutes dishonesty is objective. Whether the accused has acted dishonestly is a question to be determined by the jury, applying "the current standards of ordinary decent people." Thus, a modern Robin Hood who asserted quite sincerely that he believed he was acting honestly in robbing from the rich to give to the poor would have no defense to a charge of theft or of robbery. This is because "ordinary decent peo-

ple" do not believe it to be honest to rob from the rich to give to the poor. However, if Robin were to be charged with blackmail, it would seem that his beliefs would give him a defence. The subjective nature of the test is well illustrated by the case of *R v. Lambert.* . . . The acquittal of the accused in *R v. Lambert* because he subjectively believed he was entitled to demand money in such circumstances seems surprising and unsatisfactory. More extreme examples can easily be imagined. We live in times when members of terrorist organizations often act in the name of some higher morality which they assert, quite sincerely, justifies both their aims and any methods they choose to adopt to achieve these aims. If such people were to engage in activities which would, viewed objectively, be said to constitute blackmail, could their own beliefs, however extreme, afford them a defence? One commentator has described the view that they could as "scarcely conceivable," yet such a result seems to follow with remorseless logic from the wording of the section. In his book *The Law of Theft,* Professor J. C. Smith has suggested that such a result may be avoided by saying that a person can only believe he has reasonable grounds for making a demand when he believes that reasonable men would regard the grounds as reasonable. However attractive on policy grounds such a view may be, it is submitted that the words of the section are clear, and no objective requirement can be spelt out of them.[56]

Unfortunately, from our point of view, the author of this brilliant critique levels it against current blackmail law only insofar as its subjectivity is concerned. But he accepts the basic premise of the illegitimacy of demanding (accepting) money for silence about embarrassing secrets. Another writer who focuses on the subjectivity of blackmail law as a drawback is MacKenna;[57] in *Craig,* it was maintained that not only must the belief be genuinely held, but that it also be reasonable. (Well, every step away from subjectivity—no matter how tiny and insignificant, is a step in the right direction.) Hogan, [58] and G. L. Williams,[59] however, specifically welcome the subjectivity of blackmail law.

The final set of cases that can be grouped under the rubric of victimless crimes involve demands for the repayment of debts arising out of gambling. And here, there is happily almost a unanimous belief in the proposition that one may threaten posting at Tattersall's, or other such negative publicity, in order to recover a gambling debt—without being held guilty of extortion. Defendents were found not guilty of such charges in *Nicholson,*[60] *Hyams v. Stuart-King, Burden v. Harris, Poteliakhoff v. Teakle,* and *Norreys v. Zeffert.* As if this were not enough, several legal writers have supported this position as well. According to Tiley, for example, "A threat to post the name of a betting defaulter at Tattersall's is not blackmail—such a threat is perfectly 'proper'."[61] In the view of MacKenna, " . . . it would seem . . . reasonable to demand payment of a claim incapable in any circumstances of being enforced by action, such as the claim to be paid a winning bet."[62]

Now this is all well and good. Any time the legal fraternity is convinced that demands accompanied by menaces and threats are not indictable, that is an advance for the cause of liberty. But it will not do to make too much of this rare unanimity in celebration of the rights of free speech. For these Tattersall-type or posting-gambling cases are greatly limited in scope insofar as support for the concept of legal blackmail is concerned. The would-be blackmailer is hemmed in by a welter of restrictions. He cannot make any threats other than posting. The debt must arise "out of a merely void and not illegal transaction" (Hyams). The blackmailer can only enforce debts owed to himself; he cannot act in behalf of anyone else. No more than the amount actually owed may be demanded. As well, this threat must arise out of a "legitimate business interest" and might well not apply to "a casual bet made between two private persons."[63] All in all, this is hardly a stirring victory for the forces of reason and justice to blackmailers.[64]

While on the subject of improper restrictions on blackmailer freedom, especially arising out of "legitimate business interest," we cannot forebear to mention the strange attitude exhibited toward bluffing. For example, in the words of Campbell:

> But what shall we say of the case of Z, who in an election in which X and Y are standing in the Blue and Red interests respectively, informs X of his intention to stand as Independent Ultramarine candidate and "split the Blue vote" unless X pays him a sum of money? The parallel case in the business world would appear to be that of the powerful man who announces his intention of starting operations in a field in which he has hitherto shown no interest, unless those already established in that field pay him to stay out. The plain man whould probably feel that in a case like this a good deal depended on whether there was a genuine intention to start such operations or whether it was simply a money-making bluff. And this might also be the view of the law. In *Thorne's case* both Lord Wright and Lord Roche expressed the view that even where a demand is made for the protection of an established business interest, the extortionate amount of the sum demanded would be evidence in a civil case of an intent to injure and in a criminal case of the fact that the sum was demanded without reasonable or probable cause. Perhaps, too, evidence that there was no genuine intention to exercise the lawful liberty for the surrender of which money was demanded might serve the same purpose.

We might say that the economic value of a liberty which is not connected with an existing activity of mine, which I have no apparent present intention of exercising, and which perhaps I could not exercise without considerable inconvenience, is nil or practically nil and therefore I am acting extortionately and without reasonable or probable cause if I demand any substantial sum in consideration of its surrender.[65]

As C. R. Williams would have it:

A proposes to build a supermarket near B's small grocery shop. A is quite entitled to demand as large a sum as he wishes from B as the price of not going ahead with the building of the supermarket. In such a case, A is acting in furtherance of the legitimate business interest of making as large a profit as he can in return for refraining from the pursuit of a commercial enterprise. However, if A never intended to build the supermarket at all, but was simply out to make money from B, it is submitted that he would commit an offence under s. 100 (of the Larceny Act of 1916). In such a case the interest he would be pursuing would simply be that of attempting to obtain money from a small trader by threatening to drive him out of business.[66] (Material in parentheses inserted.)

And, in the view of Livermore, "Tacts such as bluff, stridency, bombast, designed to overreach, out to be forbidden to lawyers as harrassment. . . ."[67]

What is the world coming to? If people can no longer engage in the ancient and honorable practice of bluffing, the world as we know it will soon come to an end. Will the poker player no longer be able to raise on a busted flush? Will the fishwife no longer be able to praise her dubious product? Shall we incarcerate the homeowner for offering to sell his domicile at a price higher than the bottom price for which he would have really sold? Will it be a crime for lovers to try to make each other jealous? Will football teams be penalized for faking the run, and instead going to the pass? Can an employee no longer hint to his boss about the "tremendous job offer" which has just been made him? Can the parent no longer threaten the child who refuses to do his homework that he'll get no ice cream or TV privileges, unless the parent really intends to carry through? Nonsense. The warp and woof of our lives are made up of bluff. Yes, bluff is related to blackmail; and the specter of criminality should not be allowed to waft over either.

Let us now conclude this section on victimless crimes by reflecting on one benefit rendered society by the despised and downtrodden blackmailer. To wit, due to the ceaseless and untiring efforts of this tribe, several laws prohibiting victimless crimes have been taken off the books. Says Nadelmann in this regard:

> Primarily because of judical inability to cope with extortionist actions the legislatures of some states have limited or abolished altogether such often-abused common-law actions as those of criminal conversation, seduction, alienation of affection, and breach of promise to marry. Without going into the merits of these actions it is clear that a law which is unrealistic or out-of-date provides a fertile field for profitable blackmail operations. Constant abuse of legal process in a particular field—as, for example, bastardy proceedings—suggests that either the law or the procedures is grossly unsuitable.[68]

This phenomena was also commented upon, in the *Solicitors' Journal and Weekly Reporter:*

> The action for breach of promise is another such process which may lend itself to blackmail. The plaintiff launches her action knowing she has no chance of success on the merits, but reckoning on the fact that she can publicly smirch the defendant's character, and, probably, procure his indiscreet letters to be read in court before her case is dismissed. She plays, of course, for compromise, and if the defendant faces the court, her blackmail has failed. If she has chosen her victim cleverly, however, publicity is ruin to him, and all his adviser can do as the law stands at present is to make the best terms with her, and see that she delivers to him all the defendant's letters.[69]

C ACCUSATIONS OF REAL CRIMES

We now turn to blackmail attempts in which the "victim" is threatened with a charge of criminal behavior, unless he pays off. Now this is serious business, because if the threat is carried out, the "victim" is liable to a term in prison, in some cases for many years. But there is no difference in principle, here, between being threatened with exposure as a real criminal, and as a perpetrator of a victimless "crime." For acts such as sodomy themselves carried stiff penalties, at least in bygone eras. And in the modern day, drug-related "criminals" can receive large fines and lengthy jail sentences.

Then too there is the fact that under discussion is not probity of threatening to accuse someone of a crime. This is considered legitimate on all sides. Rather, we are analyzing the propriety of refraining from accusing someone of a crime, for a fee—which is an entirely different matter. It is completely licit to threaten to accuse someone of a crime—provided that it is not done out of the motive of forebearing to do so, and then being paid off for one's silence. If the accused is actually guilty, and the accusation is in the event made, then the accuser is considered a public benefactor, not an extortionist.[70] But if the threat is made in order to elicit a payment from the guilty party, then the preponderance of legal opinion is that the accuser is indeed guilty of extortion.

For example, consider the following cases and commentaries:

Holt, C. J., in *Woodward:* "Every extortion is an actual trespass, and an action of trespass will lie against a man for frightening another out of his money. If a man will make use of a process of law to terrify another out of his money, it is such a trespass as an indictment will lie."

Says Beech: "It appears by the weight of authority that it is a criminal offense for a creditor to obtain money or property from a debtor by means of a threat to accuse the latter of a crime, although the creditor belives that the money or property is actually due him, and although he believes the debtor guilty of the crime as to which exposure is threatened."[71] And again: "The threat of a criminal prosecution though possibly a very efficient collection tool could be misused by the unscrupulous, for under the guise of collection of a just debt such a threat could be used to fleece persons not owing debts who would rather pay than be troubled with the matter."[72]

G. L. Williams points to the following as a larcenous situation: "Suppose that D writes to P a letter demanding money under the threat that if it is not forthcoming he will accuse him of having (a) committed murder and (b) obtained property by false pretenses."[73]

In addition, the following cases have established the fact that a threat to prosecute for a crime is itself a criminal (extortionate) act: *Abgood, Gill, Studer, Robinson, Robertson, Clayton* (here, the "victim" of the blackmailer was herself innocent).

Notwithstanding this preponderance of opinion, the contrary view has some rather limited support of its own in the legal profession. That is, there is also legal precedent for the view that one may threaten to prosecute for a crime, and offer the "victim" the option of paying him off for withdrawing, without being considered guilty of menacing (extortion).

Burns, as we have seen above, is one such case, but it is subject to the stipulation that the demand not exceed the money actually owed. In *Southerton,* however, there is no such limitation. Here, in the view of Winder, "It was held to be no offence at common law to obtain money by means of a threat to bring a penal action and the *ratio decidendi* would apply also to a threat to prosecute for any crime."[74] Said Lord Ellenborough, C. J., in *Southerton,* "To obtain money under a threat of any kind, or to attempt to do it is no doubt an immoral action; but to make it indictable, the threat must be of such a nature as is calculated to overcome a firm and prudent man." But he held that the threat to prosecute for a crime was "not such a threat as a firm and prudent man might not and ought not to have resisted. . . . The law distinguishes between threats of actual violence against the person, or such other threats as a man of common firmness cannot stand against, and other sorts of threats. Money obtained in the former cases under the influence of such threats may amount to robbery, but not so in cases of threats of other kinds. . . . When the defendant threatened to prosecute the party for the penalties, a man of ordinary firmness might have well said to him that he was not guilty of the offence charged, and therefore he might prosecute him at his peril."[75]

We shall have occasion (see Section V below), to object to the psychological justification for this finding. But as for the finding itself, it is precisely in accord with the thesis put forward in the present paper: that it should not be an indictable offense to demand money under the threat of embarking on an action which would otherwise be licit—in this case, prosecuting for criminal behavior.

Much has been made in the legal literature of the distinction between the threat of a civil and a criminal suit. We have just seen the mainstream opposition to the threat of criminal prosecution. As strong as is this opposition, matters are reversed when it comes to the threat of a civil suit for recovery of owed money: most commentators advocate the legitimacy of this tactic.[76]

Of course, in our own view, this distinction should have no legal relevance whatsoever. Since it is entirely legitimate to bring suit in either criminal or civil court, it ought to be licit to threaten to do so. And if this be so, it ought to be lawful to offer the "victim" the option of payment for the dropping of a suit—of *either* variety.

Nor has this distinction gone uncriticized by other writers, although on less radical grounds. Says C. R. Williams:

> The effort upon the recipient (of a threat of civil suit) would be much the same as a threat of criminal proceedings. In such a case what the victim generally fears most is public exposure of his improper conduct, and such exposure takes place equally in civil as in criminal proceedings."[77] (Material in parentheses inserted.)

G. L. Williams notes further:

> "It may also be pointed out that the distinction between threatening civil proceedings (which is allowable) and threatening criminal proceedings

(which is not) is somewhat artificial when what the victim most dreads is exposure. Exposure follows as much from the bringing of civil proceedings as from the launching of a criminal prosection."[78] (Material in parentheses inserted.)

But one of the most infuriating cases to arise on this topic is *Cohen*. Mr. Cohen wrote the following letter:

> Dear Sir: I have ample proof that the two bales of cotton you sold me was (sic) water packed, as the bales were weighed today, and lost 100 pounds with all the cotton in them, and on opening the bales, find that several buckets of water was put in it, and have full proof to that; and as this is a criminal offense, and unless you come in at once and see to it, will take the matter before the courts, and, in order to save you any cost and trouble, it will be to your interest to come at once, and attend to it. Yours truly, (signed) M. Cohen

On the basis of this distinction, Cohen was found guilty of extortion. He threatened criminal, not civil, proceedings. If so, then so much the worse for the philosophy of extortion law. Poor Cohen. Here is a man, sinned against, not himself a sinner. He has caught a fraudulent supplier red-handed. He wants only that this man make good his losses—which is his right. If so, he will drop a suit for criminal prosecution—which is also his right.[79] And yet, since he has threatened a criminal not a civil suit, as in *Dymond*, he, not the real criminal, has run afoul of the law.

We cannot end our discussion of these cases without reflecting on the good offices of the blackmailer in reducing crime. Not, of couse, that it was ever necessarily any part of the intention of the blackmailer to play so public-spirited a role. But as we know from a study of Adam Smith, it is "not from benevolence" that many economic actors accomplish beneficial, but unintended goals. And so it is with the blackmailer. Not merely the one who only wants to have his own money returned to him, as in a debt case, or in *Cohen*, where the blackmailer is the victim of fraud. Not merely when he limits his threats to those which skirt on the correct side of our misbegotten laws on extortion. But even in the case of the mangy low-down blackmailer who has the internal subjective intent to steal money over which he has no otherwise valid claims, but who, of course, limits his threats to that which would otherwise be licit. Even this lowlife blackmailer, who may well be immoral in his practices, does the public a service by helping to rid us of true criminals.

How does this work? Consider the example offered us by C. R. Williams:

> A writes to B saying, "Pay me $100 or I will tell the police I saw you shoplifting." Assuming A saw B shoplifting he is not only legally entitled to inform the police, but he has a moral duty to do so. Nonetheless, A commits an offense because, although the action threatened is justifiable, the demand made as an alternative to it is not.[80]

Let us assume that the effect, at least marginally, of declaring A's blackmailing behavior criminal will be that he is less likely to engage in it. Certainly, this is in keeping with the economic principle of upward sloping supply curves: The lower the payoff, i.e., higher the penalty, the less likely is a person to engage in the activity, *ceterus paribus*. If so, there will be *less* pressure placed upon the real criminal, B, the shoplifter. This is so because, if such blackmail as C. R. Williams mentions is illegal, and A does not engage in it, he is less likely to act so as to oppose B. With blackmail legal, A has two motives for opposing B: financial considerations (the blackmail) and public-spiritedness (turning B over to the police purely for the emotional satisfaction of stopping crime). With blackmail illegal, and presumed an effective deterrent, as it will be in at least *some* cases, then A has only the latter motive. As against that, were blackmail to be legalized, some of the formerly public-spirited might lose their sense of civic responsibility, and take up the profession of blackmail. But this too would tend to reduce the activity of real criminals. It might be less effective, in that the blackmailer must offer the criminal a "lighter sentence," i.e., an option preferable to incarceration. On the other hand, it might be more effective in crime prevention, if the blackmailers are more efficient at ferreting out such crimes than the official police.

The point is, the blackmailer is like a parasite on the criminal. In this case, A preys on B. And the more he does so, the less shoplifting and other such crime there will be. For the law of upward sloping supply applies to shoplifters as well as blackmailers. With the latter practice legalized, and presumably thereby encouraged, there will be more blackmailers preying on, and hence reducing the scope of, real criminals.

As well, the legalization of blackmail will tend to cut down on the size of criminal gangs and thus, on the cooperation between criminals. The more co-criminals, the greater will be the chances of later intra-gang blackmail. To the extent that there are economies of scale in criminal activities, this will reduce the effectiveness of crime.

And it is the same with regard to victimless crimes. The blackmailer, unknowing, and uncaring, has played a role in the liberation of groups such as homosexuals. By preying on them, he has in effect helped bring them "out of the closet"—where they became more known to each other and are thus more able to organize pressure groups of their own.[81]

V ACCOUNTING FOR THE PROHIBITION OF BLACKMAIL

Given that blackmail is not really a crime, as we have tried to establish, it is of interest to speculate about why it is considered so in law. The most obvious, if superficial, hypothesis is that such a determination is just mistaken. The average person, and jurists as well, have merely been taken in by logical fallacy. At one time, blackmail was limited to proscribing threats to obtain money which were themselves illicit. Then, through a process of improper extensions, it came to cover licit threats as well. Part of the explanation for this process of extension may have been the failure to distinguish between violations of rights on the one hand, and inflicting harm or injury on the other.[82] Now, to be sure, blackmail harms or injures the "victim" compared to the situation in which there is no blackmail. The problem with looking at things in this way is that it is open to a *reductio ad absurdum*: one can harm or injure another person in so many ways, most of them quite lawful. For instance, a businessman can open up a store next door to a shop selling the same item; surely, the newcomer "harms" the financial prospects of the older occupant.[83] Every time a marriage takes place, those who would have wished to wed either of the spouses are "injured"; their own marriage options are reduced by one. Yes, of course, blackmail harms people in this sense. But it is crucially important that the law restricts itself only to physical injury to person or property.

Perhaps a more significant hypothesis could explain the prohibition of blackmail on psychological grounds. According to this view, much of the legal profession has unfortunately come to use psychological criteria in assessing criminality. To wit, the emotional state of the "victim" of blackmail is seen as having great relevance to the "crime," and if he is psychologically fearful or disturbed by the threat, then, and to that extent, blackmail really is a crime.

The slide down this particular slippery slope all began with Lord Ellensborough, C. J., in *Southerton*,[84] who made the criteria of an extortionate threat its ability to set the ordinary "firm and prudent man" a-quaking in his boots. But then came the reaction. Later judges began to lack the same faith and confidence in the reliability, courage and perseverance of the "common man" as did Lord Ellenborough. With the distinction between blackmail and extortion built upon such a shaky, psychological foundation, it began to melt away under their onslaught. Says Winder: " . . . fear was very narrowly defined. *McGrath* holds that a man's will may be overcome by action which would not have disturbed the firm and constant man as the older judges understood him. The case is only one of several instances in which nineteenth and twentieth century judges, reflecting the thought of their generation, have expressed a poorer opinion than their ancestors of the power of the will and thereby extended the law of blackmail."[85]

The distinction between extortion and blackmail began to blur further when it became more and more obvious that for some people, a threat to do something otherwise legal (blackmail) might be as much or even more frightening than a threat to do something illegal (extortion). Says Beech in this regard: "Such a method of collection (threatening criminal prosecution) could possibly put the threatened in as much apprehension of harm as a threat of bodily harm—a method which would surely be denounced as a collection method. Therefore, it seems that for these reasons alone such collection methods should be prohibited."[86] (Material in parentheses inserted.) In *Boyle*, the following judgment was expressed: "The degree of fear or alarm which a threat may be calculated to produce upon the mind of the person on whom it is intended to operate may vary in different cases and in different circumstances. A threat to injure a man's property may be more serious to him and have greater effect upon his mind than a threat of physical violence." In the view of Winder,

> . . . although the standard of the firm and constant man is relevant under the statute, it must not be taken to be a rigid criterion, as it is at common law, but one capable of extension. In the non-criminal law of duress, the common law laid down dogmatically that only actual personal constraint or threats of immediate violence to himself or his wife or family was sufficient to overcome *virum fortem et constatem*. . . . the standard of the firm and constant man is no more definite than that of the reasonable man or the *bonus paterfamilias*. Subsequent cases show how elastic the conception has become in relation to statutory offences.[87]

And in *Tomlinson*, Wills, J., added: "With regard to the doctrine that the threat must be of a nature to operate on a man of reasonably sound or ordinarily firm mind, I only desire to say that it ought, in my judgment, to receive a liberal construction in practice; otherwise great injustice may be done, for persons who are thus practised upon are not as a rule of average firmness."

Here and there, in the legal record, are some jurists who indicate the vulnerability of relying on the ever-changing notion of the "firm and constant man" as a way of distinguishing licit from illicit threats. For example, Wilde, C. J., in *Smith*, insisted that the common law "be understood to refer rather to the nature of the threat, than its probable consequences in any particular case. Whether a threat be criminal or not, cannot be taken to depend on the nerves of the individual threatened, but on the general nature of the evil with which he is threatened. Threats attended with duress, or threats of duress, or of other personal violence or of great injury, such as is imported by the letter (arson) will come within the rule." (Material in parentheses inserted.) But, it would appear, this was too little and too late to rescue the legal profession from the trip down the psychological garden path first blazed by Lord Ellenborough. Surely, a far better distinction for him to have made in *Southerton* would have been between the otherwise licit or illicit threat. His actual finding was highly unfortunate, for he wanted to distinguish between "threats of actual violence against the person" (illicit) and "other threats" such as the threat to bring a penal action.[88] His instincts were good, in finding the accused innocent of extortion for making this latter threat. Had he based his decision on firmer philosophical rather than psychological grounds, the course of blackmail law might have taken a different turn.

There is a third hypothesis which might shed some light on the evolution of blackmail law. It is perhaps too extreme to be taken seriously, but no attempt to account for the phenomena under discussion can be complete without at least mentioning it. Baldly stated, this view contends that blackmail law has taken its present shape because this course of action is to the financial interest of the legal profession.

The economic historian can never afford to ignore the question of *cui bono?* When it is asked, some interesting information sometimes comes to light. In *Denyer*, the question arose of a creditor attempting to collect from his debtor by threatening to publish discreditable statements about him, which is criminal under Section 31 of the Larceny Act of 1916. With regard to this, the *Recorder* stated:

> If it were not the law, there would seem to be no need for a creditor to go to a solicitor or to law. All he would need was a private inquiry agent to find out what skeleton was in his debtor's cupboard, and to threaten to expose him if he were not paid.[89]

Consider also this self-serving statement:

> Professional lawyers, a modest race, have stood aside and allowed the
> judge, the police and the press, to share between them 100 per cent of
> the credit of the recent event (dealing with a threat to accuse of a crime).
> Yet perhaps their organ, *The Solicitors Journal*, may point out that the
> doom of the blackmailers came about as the direct result of the victim
> crossing the threshold of his solicitor's office, and that, in whatever cir-
> cumstances a sensible man may dispense with legal advice, he can least
> afford to do so when a blackmailer has fastened on to him and is sucking
> at his vitals. For solicitors are bound to secrecy, can approach the police,
> with whom they are friendly, without entangling their clients, and can
> deal with blackmailers, who are usually born cowards, and in mortal ter-
> ror of those they cannot threaten, as they deserve. The victim in the case
> paid over L10,000 to the gang. Had he approached his solicitors at first,
> it may safely be surmised that he could have rid himself of his incubus
> at one percent of that sum, or less.[90] (Material in parentheses inserted.)

Is there some apprehension in the following statement, which arose
in the judgment in *Cohen*, that without blackmail legally prohibited,
creditors would short-circuit the courts, and the legal profession, and
collect debts without recourse to them?

> We do not construe this statute to mean, by the use of the term 'extorting'
> to be only applicable to cases where there is no debt existing between
> the parties. On the contrary, under this article, a party may be guilty of
> the offense of sending or delivering a letter threatening to accuse another
> of a criminal offense, with the view of extorting money, although the
> party may be justly indebted to the sender of such letter. *One object of
> the statute, as we take it is to prevent persons from sending such letters and
> using the criminal laws of this state to collect debts that might be due and
> owing them.*[91] (Emphasis added.)

VI OBJECTIONS

We shall consider several objections to the theory put forth in this
paper. The first arises from within the legal profession. This is the concern that were blackmail legalized, the negative publicity the "victim"
is threatened with, in addition to affecting him adversely, would be an
unjust attack upon his reputation.

The idea here is that a person's reputation is a possession of his, just
like money, car or house; an attack upon it thus constitutes an illicit
breach of person or property, which society has singled out as justification for laws prohibiting extortion.[92] How can we then consistently

favor the prohibition of extortion as an unlawful attack on person or property, and yet countenance the legalization of blackmail, which threatens to undermine reputations, an important aspect of personal property?

Before replying directly, let us first document this concern with the negative publicity attendant upon blackmail.

Says Nadelmann, "The extortionist generally preys on his victim's fear of publicity.[93] According to the Federal Criminal Code S.1437, 95th Cong., Second Session (1978), the offense of blackmail prohibits, among many other things, expressing "a secret with intent to impair reputation." As well, the Arizona Revised Criminal Code proscribes threats of "reputational injury." Also prohibiting libel are the Libel Act of 1843 and Section 31 of the Larceny Act of 1916. According to U. S. C. A. Title 18, Section 876, Para. 4,

> Whoever, with intent to extort from any person any money or any other thing of value, knowingly so deposits or causes to be delivered, as aforesaid, any communication, with or without a name or designating mark subscribed thereto, addressed to any other person and containing any threat to injure the property or reputation of the addressee or of another, or the reputation of a deceased person, or any threat to accuse the addressee or any other person of a crime, shall be fined no more than $500 or imprisoned not more than two years, or both.

Stated Judge Augustus Hand in *United States v. Pignatelli*, "Threats to damage another's reputation are no proper means for determining a controversy. It may be adjusted either by suit or by compromise, but settlement must not be effected by using defamation as a club." In *Rassmussen and Spiegelglass*, two journalists were found guilty of blackmail for threatening to publish articles in newspapers calling into question the moral character and chastity of a woman. Similarly, in *Boyle v. Merchant*, the accused was found guilty of threatening to publish newspaper articles attacking the viability of a company. In *Pacholko*, the Saskatchewan Court of Appeal determined that all threats of injury to character are necessarily menaces.

But mere concern with injury to reputation hardly describes the lengths to which the legal profession has gone to obviate what is considered a libelous threat. The record shows that in order to guard against such a "danger," judicial interpretations stand ready to trample on rights and to make increasingly arcane and illogical distinctions. For example, consider the following statement of C. R. Williams:

> . . . if A buys a defective car under warranty from B, he may attempt to obtain compensation by threatening to make known that B refuses to

honour his warranty, but may not threaten to publicise the fact that B is
a seller of bad cars. The distinction appears desirable on principle. To
threaten to expose another to the public for not meeting a claim believed
to be just appears to be a reasonable way of attempting to obtain payment, while to threaten to expose him for improper conduct other than
the conduct of not meeting the claim does not. . . . *This distinction may
certainly involve the courts in delicate questions of characterization.* Example: A single woman claims that A is the father of her child. She writes
to him claiming maintenance for the child and threatening to publicise
the fact that he has refused to support the child if he will not agree to
pay. In such a case the court would have to decide whether the threat
was in substance a threat to expose him as one who had fathered an
illegitimate child, or as one who, having fathered an illegitimate child,
refused to support it. A similar question would be involved in the example of the purchaser of a defective car given above. *Such difficult questions
of characterization appear to be inherent in the law of blackmail.*[94] (Emphasis
added.)

Now Williams may think this distinction "appears desirable on principle," but it also, not to put too fine a point on it, does indeed "involve
the courts in delicate questions of characterization," in the solution of
which they would appear to enjoy no particular comparative advantage. But more important, this distinction has nothing to do with the
question of whether it is *just* for A to exercise his rights of free speech
in the denunciation of B as a seller of bad cars—or anything else; or
whether the single mother has a right of free speech to denounce the
father of her illegitimate child on whatever ground she wishes. No reasons are given by Williams in support of his rather tenuous
distinctions.

Another such tenuous distinction arises with regard to the Tattersall's posting cases, such as *Burden v. Harris.* In the view of G. L.
Williams,

. . . if D threatens to post P as a defaulter at Tattersall's in the payment
of his gaming debts, the threat is not blackmail, because no one who
frequents Tattersall's would think any the worse of P for gambling. The
threat is merely to publicise the fact that P has not paid his debt of honour; and this is a legitimate way of securing payment. But if D threatens
P that if he does not pay his gaming debts, he will tell P's grandmother
that he bets, this is blackmail, for this time the threat is to accuse P of
conduct that, as D knows, will be regarded by the person to whom the
accusation is made as immoral and is not merely an accusation of non-
payment of a debt. To bring one's debtor before the bar of public opinion
for not paying his debt is a reasonable way of getting payment; but not

to threaten to accuse him of disgraceful conduct other than the conduct
of not paying the debt.[95]

But several questions arise, in addition to the problem of rights to
free speech mentioned above. True, no other gambler would think any
the worse of P for gambling, but they would indeed see something
"disgraceful . . . in the failure to pay."[96] Why should this ruination of
reputation be allowed, but not that which would ensue from telling P's
grandmother?

One last example of this spurious distinction-mongering. This one
has to do with divorce:

> Any husband may bring a petition for divorce against his wife, and may
> cite any other man as co-respondent. If this is done, the latter's name
> comes into the published list of pending cases, and, if he is a doctor or
> schoolmaster, or other person depending on his moral character for his
> living, even this may do him grievous harm.[97]

The difficulty here arises with regard to the

> threat of publicity incident to the filing of (such) a lawsuit. If publicity is
> inevitable when filing takes place, how can it be wrong to tell an adver-
> sary of that consequence and allow it to be avoided. It would appear
> anomalous to argue that (one) could say "divorce will be sought on
> grounds of adultery," but could not say "your adultery, of course, will
> become public." Nonetheless, because extortion has traditionally focused
> on means, *that may well be the distinction that must be drawn.* Results may
> not change because threats are not uttered. The adulterous defendant
> would almost certainly conclude, on his own, that privacy could be pre-
> served and embarrassment avoided by settling in advance of litigation.
> But that is a conclusion for him to reach, not one we should say can be
> legally urged upon him. The fact that one may decide to pay a claim,
> fearing an assault by the claimant if payment is not made, would not
> justify a rule permitting collection by threatening assault.[98] (Material in
> parentheses inserted, emphasis added.)

As a result of such difficulties, some commentators have even gone
as far as to suggest a pre-screening process, whereby lawsuits which
threaten "the personal or business reputation of the defendant"[99]
would be so subjected, but have hastily pulled back before the preci-
pice of constitutional guarantees of trial in open court.

Having thus set the stage, we are now ready to directly confront the
charge that adverse publicity is akin to theft, in that it is like stealing a

person's private property. If this claim fails, all the agonizing about publicity related above will be seen for the exercise in futility that it is.

And the charge does fail. For a person's reputation, by its very nature, is *not* something that can be owned by the person to whom it refers. On the contrary, reputations consist of the thoughts of *other* people about us. The reputation of A consists of the thoughts of B thru Z about A. Thus, the *last* person who can be said to own the reputation of A is A himself. If blackmail threatens the reputation of its "victims," it threatens the loss of something they themselves do not own, and cannot own, in the nature of things. This will appear counter-intuitive to most people upon first considering such a claim. After all, do we not speak of "his reputation" in the possessive sense? Do not people work for years to enhance "their" reputation? And cannot people even sell their reputations, or that of their businesses, in the form of "good will"? Notwithstanding the truth of this, we still insist on the correctness of our view. Paradox though it may be, reputations consist of the very thoughts (anticipations, expectations) of other people. Even though we can capitalize on our own reputations, we do not own them, and cannot literally sell them, any more than we can own or sell other people or their thoughts (in a non-slave society). So this first objection to our theory of blackmail must be rejected.[100]

A second objection charges that the analogy of blackmail to an ordinary trade fails, because in the usual case "positive information" is traded, while in the latter what is being purchased is only "negative information." Were it not for the unfortunate prior position in which the blackmailee finds himself, he would not agree to purchase anything of the sort.

There are difficulties with this view. While it is indeed true that information (and goods and services) purchases can be looked upon as "positive" they can also be looked upon as "negative."[101] For example, unless you pay, your piano teacher will withhold her piano lessons. A neighboring property owner may have the right to build a spite fence, or a non-aesthetic building, or to paint his house in a polka-dot pattern. He may refrain from exercising this right, for a fee.[102] Moreover, the reason people demand most goods and services, e.g., food, is because of an unfortunate prior position they find themselves embroiled in, i.e., hunger.

In any case, this objection is somewhat beside the point. For what is of relevance for the criminal law is not whether information can be viewed as "positive" or "negative." Rather, it depends on whether an act threatens or commits force or fraud against innocent parties. If not, there is no case for criminalization, however "negative" the information in question. If it does, it should be legally proscribed, no matter how "positive."

According to a third objection, the blackmail contract is unenforceable; hence, blackmail should be prohibited.

We may first question whether or not the consequence of this claim is implied by its antecedent. Suppose, that is, that the blackmail contract is assumed to be unenforceable. Why does it follow that blackmail must be prohibited? For example, verbal contracts signed by no more than a handshake may be unenforceable in some jurisdictions, especially in the absence of witnesses. Should all such contracts be prohibited? Hardly.

As well, we may question the claim that a blackmail contract is necessarily unenforceable, even though, strictly speaking, this question is irrelevent to the legal status of blackmail. A type of contract may be unenforceable for no better reason than that the courts simply refuse to enforce it. If so, it is "unenforced," not "unenforceable." But there is no reason to believe that the judiciary could not, in the very nature of things, enforce a blackmail contract, if it were so-minded. To wit, if it were proven that the blackmailer "spilled the beans," even though he was contractually obligated not to do so, he could be made to pay damages.

A blackmail contract might be practically unenforceable because it might be awkward or thought to be to negotiate a lump sum payment. Under such an agreement, the blackmailee would always be at the mercy of the blackmailer. (It would be easy to leak the secret without being caught in the act of doing it.) But there are numerous cases in the world of commerce where lump sums are not the typical mode of payment. For example, most people receive weekly wages in return for their labor efforts, not a single lump sum payment for their entire life's work. So the necessity for periodic payments is certainly no barrier to enforceability.

A fourth objection argues as follows: If blackmail were legalized, there would be more ligitation. There would be squabbles concerning the blackmail contract, the legitimacy of the means used to unearth deep dark hidden secrets, etc., that could not arise under the *status quo*. While more litigation might be good for attorneys, what is good for lawyers is not necessarily what is best for society as a whole. On the contrary, in this view, the general public would bear the cost of the additional litigation.

To be sure, there would be extra litigation costs with blackmail legalized. But under such a regime of enhanced free speech rights, there would be benefits which would need to be set against these costs, in order to make a cost-benefit analysis. Apart form the additional liberty created, legalized blackmail would, as we have seen, tend to reduce crime. As well, as with all consensual trades, there is a gain in utility. There is also the fact that with at least some part of the legal fraternity involved in blackmail litigation, there would be less manpower remaining to concoct new and ingenious economic regulation. When these benefits are set against the costs of additional litigation, it is not at all clear that legalized blackmail would lead to a diminution in utility. It would be impossible to prove such an allegation in any case, given the theoretical difficulties involved with such interpersonal comparisons of utility.

However, blackmail legalization will almost certainly lead to additional litigation costs. Is this a sufficient reason for prohibiting blackmail? Not at all. For there are numerous other activities presently prohibited which would bring costly litigation in their wake were they legalized. These, too, would have to remain prohibited, based on this line of reasoning. Consider marijuana, for example. It, too, is now illegal. Were it legalized, costly litigation might well ensue. This argument, moreover, could have been used against the rescinding of (alcohol) Prohibition in the 1930s. But there is a strong case for legalizing the use of marijuana, and for maintaining the present legality of alcohol consumption. It is thus by no means clear that an activity should be prohibited merely because its legalization would lead to additional litigation.

Let us consider one last objection to our account of blackmail legislation. In this view, it is tantamount to accepting the propriety of the following scenario: A millionaire is drowning in a lake. On the shore are a lifeguard and the dying millionaire's heir. The lifeguard turns to the heir, and threatens him as follows: "Unless you give me $X, I'll rescue the drowning millionaire."

Is this a fair analogy? Well, there certainly are some marked similarities. Both are examples of decidedly nasty goings on. Both the blackmailee, and the heir, would be financially better off if the blackmailer and the lifeguard, respectively, were suddenly to disappear. One difference is that the lifeguard is honor- and duty-bound to save the swimmer (presumably he is under contract to do just that), while the blackmailer has no such obligation to remain silent. But the analogy can easily be preserved by converting the third person from a lifeguard under contract, to an uninvolved third party, a "samaritan"—who just happens to be a very good swimmer. Then both would threaten to do what they have every right to do. The fact that the swimmer-Samaritan threatens an omission, while the blackmailer threatens a commission, is of no real importance.

What is of interest is that at present there are laws prohibiting black-mail, while there is no legislation compelling good-Samaritan behav-ior. The point of the scenario, of course, is to shock us into seeing how horrible blackmail legalization would be—why it would be as bad, pre-sumably, as is the present situation where there are no compulsory good-Samaritan laws, and swimmers can threaten to rescue drowners.

Let us take the bull by the horns. Would we really be so much better off—morally, spirtually, economically—under a regime of compulsory good-Samaritanism? Perhaps in this way we can take the measure of the evils which would befall us were we to legalize blackmail.

First of all, there is always some real risk in attempting to rescue a drowning man, even for experienced lifeguards. This, of course, could be turned aside by supposing that the good Samaritan can rescue the drowner without even going into the water, perhaps by throwing him a life jacket or, in the extreme case, merely by pressing a button.

But this brings us to the crux of compulsory good-Samaritan laws. They are like a blank check on the time and effort of all people. For there are always "drowning" people somewhere in the world—victims of drought, starvation, motor vehicle accidents, sicknesses, war, phys-ical deformities. Nor is lack of knowledge a legitimate excuse with a serious good-Samaritan law. In any case, due to the information and transportation revolutions, we live in a shrinking world. Anyone really interested in finding suffering on our troubled globe will face no great task.

Moreover, if carried to its logical conclusion, and that seems to be the spirit of this exercise, compulsory good-Samaritanism would appear to imply absolute income and wealth equality. For while there is any inequality at all, there are still "sufferers" upon whom Samari-tans can vent their goodness. And more. Not only is money income egalitarianism required, but people would have to be leveled down to a common denominator in terms of intelligence, music appreciation, beauty, deposition, etc., if only we could.[103] We must conclude from this little foray that if avoidance of compulsory good-Samaritanism is the price we must pay to achieve legalized blackmail, it is hardly too formidable.

VII CONCLUSION

Let nothing said above be interpreted as affirming the propriety or morality of blackmail.[104] This practice has not been claimed to be eth-ical. Our only claim is that blackmail is not akin to theft, not an inva-sive act, nor threat thereof, nor an initiation of violence, nor a violation of rights—and that therefore it should not be prohibited through force of law.

Our present blackmail statutes are violations of the free speech rights of blackmailers. They do not protect the persons or property of the so-called victims of blackmail. Society would be better off, and human rights more secure, if our blackmail legislation were terminated.[105]

NOTES

The author wishes to thank for helpful comments and criticisms Walter Boytinck, David Gordon, Michael Walker, Mary Beth Zimmer, and participants in the Colloquium, "The Economic Approach Applied Outside the Traditional Areas of Economics", held in Vienna in June, 1984. However, all errors, of course, are the responsibility of the author alone.

(Numbered citations refer to listing in References)

1. 23, pages 34, 35; see also in this regard 21, pp. 122,123.

2. For example, the Criminal Law Revision Committee held that "there are some threats which should make the demand amount to blackmail even if there is a valid claim to the thing demanded. For example, we believe that most people would say that it should be blackmail to threaten to denounce a person, however truly, as a homosexual unless he paid a debt. It does not seem to follow from the existence of a debt that the creditor should be entitled to resort to any method, *otherwise non-criminal*, to obtain payment." (Emphasis added) (21, p. 140).

3. 22, p. 87.

4. 23, p. 42.

5. *Ibid*, p. 24.

6. *Ibid*, p. 21.

7. In the narrow definition of blackmail, threats of force against persons or property are the *only* proscribed threats. But are such threats *always* illegitimate? Surely not. Suppose, for example, that the father of a kidnap victim threatens the kidnapper with personal physical violence unless he releases his child. As long as the threatened violence is not out of proportion compared to the original crime (the kidnap), there would appear nothing untoward in such an extortionate demand. (On the question of proportion in punishment and retaliation, see 17, pp. 85–95). For the remainder of this paper, however, unless otherwise indicated, we shall assume that threatened (or carried out) acts of physical violence are all initiatory and hence unjustified, not retaliatory, or in response, and hence possibly justified.

8. 7, pp. 382, 383.

9. 23, p. 24.

10. *Ibid.*, p. 46.

11. 21, p. 135.

12. 13, p. 403, footnote 2.

13. 22, p. 168.

14. 23, pp. 37, 38.

15. Extortion is derived from the Latin word "extortus," which means to twist or wrench out. See *In re Sherin*, (cited in 2, p. 386).

16. For example, according to the Model Penal Code adapted by the American Law Institute, a person is guilty of theft by extortion if he obtains the property of another person by threatening to:
   (a) inflict bodily injury on anyone or commit any criminal offense; or
   (b) accuse anyone of a criminal offense; or
   (c) expose any secret tending to subject any person to hatred, contempt or ridicule, or to impair his credit or business repute; or
   (d) take or withhold action as an official, or cause an official to take or withhold action; or
   (e) bring about or continue a strike, boycott, or other collective unofficial action, if the property is not demanded or received for the benefit of the group in whose interest the actor purports to act; or
   (f) testify or provide information or withhold testimony or information with respect to another's legal claim or defense; or
   (g) inflict any other harm which would not benefit the actor.
   Based on our stipulative definitions, and subject to considerations as discussed below, only (a) is extortion. Points (b) through (g) shall be considered as merely blackmail.

17. Says Murray N. Rothbard in this regard: " . . . blackmail would not be illegal in the free society. For blackmail is the receipt of money in exchange for the service of not publicizing certain information about the other person. No violence or threat of violence to person or property is involved." (18, p. 443). See also 6, pp. 53–58. Says Lawrence H. White: "These threats presumably take the form: extend me further subsidized credit or outright aid, or I'll default on my debt obligations to your banks. (Technically, one should consider this extortion rather than blackmail, the difference being that a blackmailer is entitled to do that which he threatens.)" ("In Defense of Bank Failures," *Policy Report*, Vol. VI, No. 4, Apr., 1984, p. 9.)

18. In the view of the editors of the *United States Law Review*, "the phrase 'Legal Blackmail' . . . involves . . . a contradiction in terms." This would appear to be a purely definitional claim on their part. See 11, p. 474.

19. See 22, pp. 79, 81; G. L. Williams considers blackmail as "one of the most serious crimes," as akin to "moral murder." Also see the *Oxford Dictionary* definition, cited in 7, p. 382; as well, see 4, p.25; 10, p.461; and 2, p.383. Clark, 8, p. 1341, cites the equation of extortion with kidnapping and ransom demands.

20. 19, p. 16.

21. See 22, p. 87. Winder also sees the threat of arson as an extension of the common law. 23, p. 29.

22. 23, p. 29. In *McGrath* a similar situation occurred. The accused threatened and then physically prevented a woman from leaving an auction room until she paid for a contested bid. Only here, the accused was found guilty and this verdict was upheld on appeal.

23. See discussion in 21, p. 26.

24. See discussion 22, p. 90. Another paradox. Due to an anomaly of blackmail law, had defendant written this threat instead of making it orally on the scene, he would have been liable to a maximum sentence of life imprisonment under Section 29(1)(i) of the Larceny Act of 1916. This punishment of one year is in sharp contrast indeed with the penalty of imprisonment for life which was able to be imposed on a person who demanded money as an alternative for not accusing someone of a crime with a death sentence—something the accuser would have every right to do if he did not demand a payment for forebearing.

25. 21, p. 133.

26. I owe this point to Michael Walker.

27. Murray Rothbard makes this same point in a different context, copyright:

> There is . . . an exception to the right to use and disseminate the knowledge within one's head: namely, if it was procured from someone else as a conditional rather than absolute ownership. Thus, suppose that Brown allows Green into his home and shows him an invention of Brown's hitherto kept secret, but only on the condition that Green keeps this information private. In that case, Brown has granted to Green not absolute ownership of the knowledge of his invention, but conditional ownership, with Brown retaining the ownership power to disseminate the knowledge of the invention. If Green discloses the invention anyway, he is violating the residual property right of Brown to disseminate knowledge of the invention, and is therefore to that extent a thief.
>
> Violation of (common law) copyright is an equivalent violation of contract and theft of property. For suppose that Brown builds a better mousetrap and sells it widely, but stamps each mousetrap "copyright Mr. Brown". What he is then doing is selling not the entire property right in each mousetrap, but the right to do anything with the mousetrap except to sell it or an identical copy to someone else. The right to sell the Brown mousetrap is retained in perpetuity by Brown. Hence, for a mousetrap buyer, Green, to go ahead and sell identical mousetraps is a violation of his contract and of the property right of Brown, and therefore prosecutable as theft. Hence, our theory of property rights includes the inviolability of contractual copyright.
>
> A common objective runs as follows: all right, it would be criminal for Green to produce and sell the Brown mousetrap; *but suppose that*

someone else, Black, who had not made a contract with Brown, happens to see Green's mousetrap and then goes ahead and produces and sells the replica? Why should he be prosecuted? The answer is that, as in the case of our critique of negotiable instruments, no one can acquire a greater property title in something than has already been given away or sold. Green did not own the total property right in his mousetrap, in accordance with his contract with Brown—but only all rights except to sell it or a replica. But therefore Black's title in the mousetrap, the ownership of the ideas in Blacks's head, can be no greater than Green's, and therefore he too would be a violator of Brown's property even though he himself had not made the actual contract. (17, pp. 123, 124) (Emphasis added by present author.)

28. 22, p. 163.

29. Says Campbell: Insofar as it is suggested "that wherever a man has a right, that is, a legal liberty, to do something he has reasonable and probable cause to demand money as the price of not doing it, are too wide and might cover an undoubted blackmailer." (7, p. 388).

30. 3, p. 225.

31. 13, p. 406.

32. *Ibid.*, p. 409.

33. *Ibid.*, p. 411.

34. In the legal sphere, $X(1)$ is a demand (request) for money, $X(2)$ is a threat to exercise one's rights of free speech. But suppose $X(3)$ is lighting a match (which a person has a right to do) and $X(4)$ is filling one's gas tank (ditto). Here, $X(3)$ and $X(4)$ are each legitimate, when carried on in isolation, or separate from each other. When juxtaposed, however $((X(3), X(4))$, there may be problems. So perhaps it makes more "common sense" to assert that two whites can make a black? There are difficulties with this view. $X(3)X(4)$ is completely legitimate, based on the common-law tradition of property rights, *if*, that is, the act of touching a match to the gas tank occurs on one's own property, and the physical damages can be confined to one's own person and property. If there is a spill-over, and the rights of other people are violated, then this, of course, would not apply. But, by stipulation, no rights were violated in the $X(1)X(2)$ example. Hence, a disanalogy.

It will not do to make this claim that two whites cannot make a black into a general principle. After all, $X(3)$ can be marrying one woman, and $X(4)$ marrying another. Or $X(3)$ can be making out a check of one's entire check balance to one person, and $X(4)$ can be doing this for another person. Each $X(3)$ and $X(4)$ in isolation is legitimate; both juxtapositions are not. There is also the phenomena of recessive genes, and chemical reactions where two white or colorless liquids can turn black when mixed. The point is, the burden of proof must surely rest with those judicial authorities who claim that two legal whites can make a legal black. Their case cannot be proved by mere assertion. (I owe this point to David Gordon.)

35. For a ringing affirmation of this principle, consider the following statement by Murray N. Rothbard:

> If . . . Smith has the absolute right to disseminate knowledge about
> Jones (we are still assuming that the knowledge is correct) and has the
> corollary right to keep silent about that knowledge, then, *a fortiori*,
> surely he *also* has the right to go to Jones and receive payment in
> exchange for not disseminating such information. *In short, Smith has the
> right to "blackmail" Jones.* As in all voluntary exchanges, both parties
> benefit from such an exchange: Smith receives money, and Jones
> obtains the service of Smith's not disseminating information about him
> which Jones does not wish to see others possess. The right to blackmail
> is deducible from the general property right in one's person and knowl-
> edge and the right to disseminate or not disseminate that knowledge.
> How can the right to blackmail be denied? (17, p. 127) (Emphasis
> added.) Also see 6, pp 53, 54.

36. 13, p. 406.

37. 22, p. 171.

38. To the extent that the businessman acts in any other way, for example by
renting a more plush office than strict considerations for bottom-line
profit-maximizing would require, to that degree he is acting as a consumer
and not as a businessman.

39. 7, pp. 388-9.

40. Suppose marriage were interpreted as an agreement between consenting
adults, in the same way as is a business partnership. Then the husband,
with the agreement of his wife, could sell (or rent) this right, just as business partners may strike any mutually agreeable financial bargain.

41. 17, p. 125. Stern 19, p. 7, is also concerned with the businessman ("victim") who "himself makes the solicitation" (for blackmail).

42. See the discussion of this case in 1, pp. 346–351.

43. 1, p. 3.

44. It may be true that the power given them by labor legislation is improper,
and that these enactments are themselves problematical, but this is completely irrelevent to the question of blackmail. If one calls into question
this legislation, then, of course, the unionists were guilty of extortion,
since not only did they threaten invasive violence, implicit in picketing,
they actually implemented it. But the courts and our commentator, A. B.,
make no such stipulation. Not for them does practically the entire corpus
of labor legislation in the United States give illegitimate permission for
physically violent attacks on person or property (picketing). In our analysis, we shall adopt this stance. We, too, then, for purposes of analyzing
extortion, henceforth adopt the fiction that picketing and other such legal
union activities are legitimate and noninvasive.

45. 1, p. 349.

46. This phenomena is reminiscent of rent control legislation. There, too, one group of citizens, tenants, is given an unfair advantage over another, land-lords. Just as in the case of unions, these advantages are worth a lot of money to recipients. It is just as hypocritical to prohibit unions from cash-ing in on their privileges (and employers from purchasing from the unions their "right" to disrupt commerce) as it would be to prohibit tenants from being bought out by landlords (or landlords from buying out tenants), however much such voluntary transactions would make explicit the income transfer aspects of rent control which would otherwise be only implicit. For a full analysis of this legislation, see *Rent Control: Myths and Realities*, Walter Block and Edgar Olsen, eds., Vancouver: The Fraser-Institute (1981).

47. That is, it is not possible for those who maintain the legitimacy of labor legislation which allows picketing and other forcible violations of human and property rights.

48. 12, p. 479.

49. 21, p. 142.

50. Numerous legal commentators and jurists have objected to demanding property to which one is not entitled, or to demanding property over and above that to which one is entitled. For example states Hogan:

> There seems to me to be a very sharp distinction between the man who threateningly demands property to which he is not entitled and the man who threateningly demands property to which he is entitled; it seems to me to be a mistake to lump the latter with the former. I acknowledge that, in some cases, there may be grounds for making con-duct of the latter kind of offence, but such offences should not be of the same order as blackmail. (12, p. 475)

In *State v. Burns* the court held that,

> If A steals money from B, B may demand its return, and, if restitution be refused, B may threaten criminal prosecution, and, if he limits his demand to the specific amount embezzled, do no violence to the penal code. However, B may not demand of A more than is due him, and, if B by threats and duress obtains more than rightly belongs to him, he violates the statute.

In the case of *In re Sherin*, the court held as follows:

> It might be claimed that the term "extort" in itself implies the getting of something to which a party is not entitled as distinguished from get-ting that to which a party is entitled, and that therefore, by the use of that word, it clearly appears that in order to constitute "extortion" the

property obtained must be that to which the taker is not honestly and legally entitled. This is certainly a mistaken idea of the meaning of the word. . . . one can extort that to which he is rightfully entitled, as well as that to which he is not entitled. . . .

See also *Harris v. Harrison*. However, the statement in the text of G. L. Williams, together with the lack of proof that two legal whites can make a legal black, would appear to be the definitive reply to all such statements.

51. In this regard, we must also part company with Willis, J., and *Donnally*. The threat may have been "equivalent" to actual violence, but it was not a threat *of* physical violence. And it is only "equivalent" to actual violence by stretching that term beyond reasonableness. Yes, the accusation of sodomy may have led to violence. If so, it would have been the violence of *other* people, not that of the blackmailer. There is all the world of difference between initiating violence on innocent parties (which should of course be prohibited to the fullest extent of the law) and doing something which is itself completely licit, and yet encourages or leads other people to violate the law against assault. The two may be "equivalent" by some stretch of the imagination, but should not be considered equivalent in law. In the just society, the forces of law and order would protect the accused sodomite against mob violence; it would also protect the right of a person to publicly accuse another of sodomy—as well as to threaten to do so unless he is paid.

This distinction has been forcibly made by Murray Rothbard:

> Should it be illegal, we may next inquire, to "incite to riot"? Suppose that Green exhorts a crowd: "Go! Burn! Loot! Kill!" and the mob proceeds to do just that, with Green having nothing further to do with these criminal activities. Since every man is free to adopt or not adopt any course of action he wishes, we cannot say that in some way Green determined the members of the mob to their criminal activities; we cannot make him, because of his exhortation, at all responsible for their crimes. "Inciting to riot," therefore, is a pure exercise of a man's right to speak without being thereby implicated in crime. On the other hand, it is obvious that if Green happened to be involved in a plan or conspiracy with others to commit various crimes, and that then Green told them to proceed, he would then be just as implicated in the crimes as are the others—more so, if he were the mastermind who headed the criminal gang. This is a seemingly subtle distinction between the head of a criminal gang and a soapbox orator during a riot; the former is not, properly, to be charged simply with "incitement." (17, p. 80)

Applying Rothbard's terminology to *Donnally*, we may say that the accused blackmailer did not himself (threaten to) perpetrate violence on the sodomite. Rather, at the worst, he did something innocent in itself (like Rothbard's riot-inciter) which *other* people seized upon, and used as an excuse to commit violence against innocent parties. They, the mob, but *not* the blackmailer, should be seen as the initiators of the unjustified violence.

52. 12, p. 476.

53. *Ibid.*, p. 475.

54. *Ibid.*, p. 474.

55. 22, p. 80.

56. 21, pp. 141-3.

57. 14, pp. 468, 469.

58. 12, pp. 477–478.

59. 22, p. 244.

60. In this case the accused was found innocent of extortion, even though, believing he had been cheated at dice, he sent a letter demanding the money owed, and threatening to prosecute for fraud.

61. 20, p. 284.

62. 14, p. 469.

63. 7, pp. 392-395.

64. On the subject of suing for the collection of debts, here is a dunning letter which was ruled incompatible with the ABA Code of Professional Responsibility in *State v. Zeigler:*

"OH! THE JOY

How do you explain to the neighbors and the kids when the Sheriff's car pulls up front and an officer hands you the summons?

"OR, how do you explain a garnishment to the boss, and the other fellows at work???

"I don't know, but I guess you do; at least you didn't bother to answer my letter. You do not need to send me your check immediately to pay your account, because I am not going to bother you any more . . . but the Sheriff will. Oh yes, I will see you in court.

"You owe_____$_____

PAY ME NOW!!"

65. 7, pp. 389–390.

66. 21, p. 131.

67. 13, p. 411.

68. 15, pp. 360–361.

69. 5, p. 440. Says Murray Rothbard:

> But we must not be lead into the trap of holding that all contracts, what-
> ever their nature, must be enforceable (i.e., that violence may properly
> be used in their enforcement). The only reason the above contracts are
> enforceable is that breaking such contracts involves an implicit theft of
> property. Those contracts which do not involve implicit theft should not
> be enforceable in a libertarian society. Suppose, for example, that A and
> B make an agreement, a "contract," to get married in six months; or that
> A promises that, in six month's time, A will give B a certain sum of
> money. If A breaks these agreements, he may perhaps be morally rep-
> rehensible; but he has not implicitly stolen the other person's property,
> and therefore such a contract cannot be enforced. To use violence in
> order to force A to carry out such contract would be just as much a crim-
> inal invasion of A's rights as it would be if Smith decided to use violence
> against the men who boycotted his store. *Simple promises, therefore, are*
> *not properly enforceable contracts, because breaking them does not involve*
> *invasion of property or implicit theft.* (Emphasis added) (17, p. 79) (For a
> further critique of promises as the basis of contract law, see 17, pp. 133–
> 148).

70. Says Campbell, for instance, " . . . but surely my liberty to inform the police
that I know or suspect a crime to have been committed is a moral liberty—
what is immoral, and what I have no liberty to do, is to sell or attempt to
sell it for money." (7, p. 388; see also *McDonald and Vanderberg.*)

71. 2, p. 384.

72. *Ibid.,* p. 388.

73. 22, p. 88.

74. 23, p. 31.

75. The peril, one assumes is that by so doing one would open oneself up to
the risk of a suit for malicious prosecution. See also 15, p. 360.

76. For example, *William, Flower;* and the discussion of C. R. Williams on
Dymond (21, p. 128).

77. 21, p. 128.

78. 22, p. 166.

79. Says Rothbard:

> We have advanced the view that the criminal loses his rights to the
> extent that he deprives another of his rights: the theory of "proportion-

ality" . . . (But) the proportionate principle is a maximum, rather than a mandatory, punishment for the criminal. In the libertarian society, there are, as we have said, only two parties to a dispute or action at law: the victim, or plaintiff, and the alleged criminal, or defendant. It is the plaintiff that presses charges in the courts against the wrong-doer. In a libertarian world, there would be no crimes against an ill-defined "society", and therefore no such person as a "district attorney" who decides on a charge and then presses those charges against an alleged criminal. . . . there would be no compulsion on the plaintiff, or his heirs, to exact this maximum penalty. If the plaintiff or his heirs, for example, did not believe in capital punishment, for whatever reason, he could voluntarily forgive the victim of part or all of his penalty. If he were a Tolstoyan, and was opposed to punishment altogether, he could simply forgive the criminal, and that would be that. Or—and this has a long and honorable tradition in older Western law—the victim or his heir could allow the criminal to buy his way out of part or all of his punishment. Thus, if proportionality allowed the victim to send the criminal to jail for ten years, the criminal could, if the victim wished, pay the victim to reduce or eliminate his sentence. The proportionality theory only supplies the upper bound to punishment—since it tells us how much punishment a victim may rightfully impose. (Material in parentheses inserted) (17, pp. 85–86).

While on the subject of *Cohen*, consider the following outlandish scenario. Suppose that an innocent victim of a blackmailer threatens him not with a civil suit merely for recovery of damages, but threatens to prosecute him in criminal court as well. Then, under *Cohen*, this victim of blackmail will himself be held guilty of blackmail (for threatening to prosecute) along with his original blackmailer (for the original blackmail)—a sort of legal infinite regress. (I owe this example to David Gordon.)

80. 21, p. 127.

81. For further discussion on the liberating effects of blackmail, see 6, pp. 56–58.

82. For example, Section 29(4) of the Larceny Act of 1916 states: "For the purposes of this Act, it is immaterial whether any menaces or threats be of violence, injury, or accusation to be caused or made by the offender or by any other person". Willis, J., relied on this in *Tomlinson* when he stated that "that which will do a person harm comes, in my opinion, within the meaning of 'injury'."

83. If such a businessman were to announce the opening of a store under such conditions, he might be considered extortionate. According to *State v. Stockford* "any words calculated and intended to cause an ordinary person to fear an injury to his person, business, or property are sufficient to constitute a punishable threat."

84. *Supra*, p. 31. Other cases which followed upon this psychological criteria include *Boyle and Merchant*, where a threat was held to be an unlawful

menace if it was "calculated to operate upon the mind of a person or ordinarily firm mind". In *Clear* it was determined that, in the words of Sellers, L. J.:

> Words or conduct which would not intimidate or influence anyone to respond to the demand would not be menaces . . . but threats and conducts of such a nature and extent that the mind of an ordinary person of normal stability and courage might be influenced or made apprehensive so as to accede unwillingly to the demand would be sufficient for a jury's consideration.

In *McGee* it was argued that an illicit threat

> "should be calculated to intimate or put fear in an ordinarily prudent man, and that it makes no difference whether the person so threatened was actually intimidated, so long as a reasonable prudent man would have been."

In *Wyatt*, it was found that

> "in order to constitute an offence against the statute it must be shown that the appellant made such a threat as would affect the mind of a reasonable man and deprive him of his free volition, ..."

In *Edwards*, Littledale, J., stated:

> "The principle is that the person threatened is thrown off his guard, and has not the firmness to resist the extortion."

85. 23, p. 33.

86. 2, p. 388.

87. 23, pp. 36, 37.

88. *Supra*, p. 31.

89. *The Times*, Dec. 19, 1931, cited in 4, p. 25, which goes on to say: "To seek to recover a debt by threat of exposure is clearly a form of intimidation and is therefore an extorting. If it were the law that creditors could oust the jurisdiction of the Courts by threatening to rake up disreputable incidents in their debtors' past, such a state of affairs would clearly call for amending legislation"

90. 5, p. 439.

91. Cohen, 38 s.w. at 1005, p. 1006; or 37 Texas Criminal Reporter 118.

92. Nadelmann, for example, refers to "the individual's right to his reputation." (15, p. 363).

93. *Ibid.,* p. 362.

94. 21, pp. 129–30. Tiley also utilizes the case of the single women who demands money of the father of her child based on threats to reputation. (See 20, p. 384).

95. 22, pp. 169–170.

96. 7, p. 395.

97. 5, p. 439.

98. 13, p. 407.

99. 15, p. 362.

100. See 6, pp. 59–62.

101. This point was made by Nozick (16, pp. 82–86). For an extensive discussion see Walter Block and David Gordon, "Blackmail, Extortion and Free Speech: A Reply to Posner, Epstein, Nozick, and Lindgren, " *Loyola of Los Angeles Law Review,* Vol. 19, (1) (November, 1985) See especially Section IV, pp. 47–50.

102. Restrictive covenants may be the market's response, but they have been severely limited by the courts. See Bernard Siegan "Non Zoning in Houston," *Journal of Law and Economics,* Vol. XIII (1) (April, 1970) pp. 71–147.

103. Where oh where are Robert Nozick's splendid machines in this hour of greatest need? See 16, pp. 42–45 in this regard.

104. Says Rothbard, "When I first briefly adumbrated the right to blackmail, in *Man, Economy and State,* I, p. 443 n. 49, I was met with a storm of abuse by critics who apparently believed that I was advocating the morality of blackmail. Again—a failure to make the crucial distinction between the legitimacy of a right and the morality or esthetics of exercising that right!" (17, p. 127) Also see 6, pp. 53, 54.

105. For an abbreviated version of this essay, see Walter Block, "Trading Money for Silence," *University of Hawaii Law Review,* Vol. 8 (1) (Spring, 1986) pp. 57–73.

LISTING OF LEGAL CASES

Abgood (1826) 2 C. & P. 436

United States v. Addonizio (1971) F. 2d Nos. 19, 295, 19, 391, 19, 393 (3d Cir)

People v. Beggs (1918) 178 Cal. 79, 172

R v. Bernhard (1938) 2 K.B. 264 (C.C.A.)

People v. Bernoff (1944) 292 N.Y. 230, 54 N.E. 2d 376

Bianchi v. United States (1955) 219 F. 2d 182, 193, (8th Cir) 349 U.S. 915

R v. Boyle & Merchant (1914) 3 K.B. 339; 10 Cr. App. R. 180 (C.C.A.)

State v. Brown (1938) 203 Minn. 505, 282 N.W. 131

State v. Brownlee (1892) 84 Iowa 473, 51 N.W. 25

Brundage v. Blakemore (1923) 209 Ill. 311, 141 N.E. 138

State v. Brunswick (1949) 69 Ohio App. 407, 91, N.E. 2d 553

Burden v. Harris (1937) 4 All E.R. 559

State v. Burns (1931) 161 Wash. 362

Callanan v. United States (1955) 223 F. 2d 171, 174 (8th Cir.)

Campbell v. New York Evening Post (1927) 245 N.Y. 320, 157 N.E. 153

R v. Cannon & Coddington (1809) Russ & Ry 146, 168 E.R. 730

In re Chadsey (1910) 141 App. Div. 458, 462, 126 N.Y.S. 456, 459

Choquetter (1947) 89 Can. C.C. 207

R v. Clear (1968) 1 Q.B. 670

Reg v. Coghlan (1865) 4 F. & F. 316

Cohen v. State (1897) 37 Tex. Crim. Rep. 118, 38 S.W. 1005

R v. Collister & Warhurst (1955) 33 Cr. App. R. 100

Cooper (1849) 3 Cox C.C. 547

Cooper v. Phibbs (1867) L.R. 2 H.L. 149

211

Craig (1903) 29 V.L.R. 28

Rex v. Denyer (1926) 2 K.B. 258, 95 L.J., K.B. 699

People v. Dioguardi (1960) 8 N.Y. 2d 260, 273, 168 N.E. 2d 683, 692, 203 N.Y.S. 2d 870, 881

R v. Donnally (1774) 1 Leach 193

R v. Dymond (1920) 2 K.B. 260; 15 Cr. App. R. 1 (C.C.A.)

R v. Edwards (1833) IM & Rob. 257

R v. Egerton (1819) Russ & Ry. 375

R v. Elmstead (1802) 2 *Russell on Crimes*, 795

People v. Eichler (1894) 75 Hunt 26, 26 N.Y.S. 998, 9 N.Y. Crim Rep. 168

R v. Feely (1973) 1 All E.R. 341, 345; 2 W.L.R. 201, 204

People v. Fichtner (1952) 281 App. Div. 159, 118 N.Y.S. 2d 392 (2d Dept.)

Flower v. Sadler (1882) 10 Q.B.D. 572 C.A.

R v. Gardner (1824) IC. & P. 479, 171 E.R. 1282

Gibbons (1898) 12 Man. L.R. 154 (C.A.)

Gill (1827) 1 Lew. C.C. 305

People v. Griffen (1848) 2 Barb. N.Y. 427

Hall (1828) 3 C. & P. 409

R v. Hamilton (1843) 1 C. & K. 212, 1 74 E.R. 779

Hardie & Lane v. Chilton (1928) 2 K.B. 306; 97 L.J., K.B. 539

State v. Harrington (1969) 128 V.T. 242, 260 A. 2d 692

Harris v. Harrison (1963) Crim. L.R. 497

R v. Harry (1974) C.L.R. 32

Hatch (1911) 18 Can. C.C. 125 (B.C.)

R v. Hazell (1870) 23 L.T. 562

R v. Hickman (1784) 1 Leach 278

Hill v. William Hill (Park Lane) (1949) A.C. 530 (H.L.)

Hopkins (1924) V.L.R. 484

Hornstein v. Paramount Pictures (1942) 37 N.Y.S. 2d 404 (Sup. Ct.)

Hyams v. Stuart-King (1908) 2 K.B. 696

R v. Jackson (1802) 1 East P.C.

R v. Jones (1776) 1 Leach 139

Kain (1837) 8 C. & P. 187

People v. Kaplan (1934) 240 App. Div. 72, 269 N.Y.S. 161

People v. Kaye (1945) 295 N.Y. 9, 64 N.E. 2d 268

R v. Kendrick (1931) 23 Cr. App. R. 1

Kentucky State Bar Ass'n v. Taylor (1972) 482 S.W. 2d 574 Ky

R v. Knewland & Wood (1796) 2 Leach 721, 731

United States v. Kubacki (1965) 237 F. Supp. 638, 641 (E.D. Pa.)

R v. Lambert (1972) C.L.R. 422

People v. Lamm (1944) 292 N.Y. 224, 54 N.E. 2d 374

R v. Lawrence & Pomeroy (1973) 57 Cr. App. Rep. 64

People v. Lee (1950) 300 N.Y. 422, 91 N.E. 2d 870

United States v. Local 807 (1942) 315 U.S. 521

R v. Lovell (1881) 8 Q.B.D. 185

Mann v. State (1922) 47 Ohio St. 556

McDonald & Vanderberg (1892) 8 Man. L.R. 491 (C.A.)

State v. McGee (1908) 80 Conn. 614, 69 A. 1059

McGrath (1869) L.R. 1 C.C.R. 205

Mengel v. Reading Eagle Co. (1913) 241 Pa. 367, 88 All. 660

Miard (1844) 1 Cox C.C. 22

R v. Moran (1952) 36 Cr. App. R. 10; 1 All E.R. 803

State v. Morgan (1866) 50 Tenn. 262

Morris (1951) 1 K.B. 394

United States v. Nardello (1969) 393 U.S. 286, 289

United States v. Nedley (1958) 255 F. 2d 350, 355 (3d Cir.)

Nicholson (1868) 7 N.S. W.S.C.R. 155

Nick v. United States (1941) 122 F. 2d 660, 671 (8th Cir.)

Norreys v. Zeffert (1939) 2 All E.R. 187

Norton (1838) 8 C. & P. 671

Pacholko (1941) 2 D.L.R. 444

R v. Paddle (1822) Russ & Ry. 484, 168 E.R. 910

R v. Parker (1910) 74 J.P. 208

R v. Parker (1919) N.Z.L.R. 365

R v. Parkes (1973) C.L.R. 358

People v. Percin (1951) 330 Mich. 94, 47 N.W. 2d 29

Pickford (1830) 4 C. & P. 227 (C.C.R.)

United States v. Pignatelli (1942) 12SF. 2d 643 (2d Cir.), 316 U.S. 680

R v. Pollock & Divers (1966) 50 Crim. App. Rep. 149

Poteliakhoff v. Teakle (1938) 2K.B. 816

State v. Pritchard (1890) 107 N.C. 921, 12 S.E. 50

United States v. Provenzano (1964) 334 F. 2d 678, 685-6 (3d Cir.)

Rasmussen & Spiegelglass (1928) 28 S.R. (N.S.W.) 349

R v. Reane (1794) 2 Leach 616

R v. Redman (1865) L.R. 1 C.C.R. 12

In re Rempfer (1927) 51 S.D. 393, 216 N.W. 355

State v. Richards (1917) 97 Wash. 587, 167

Robertson (1864) Le. & Ca. 483, 487 (C.C.R.)

Robinson (1796) 2 Leach 749

People v. Rudolph (1950) 277 App. Div. 195, 98 N.Y.S. 2d 466

Scholey v. Mumford (1875) 60 N.Y. 498, 501

In re Sherin (1911) 27 S.D. 232, 130 N.W. 761, 40 L.R.A. (N.S.) 801

Smith (1850) 1 Den. 510 (C.C.R.)

United States v. Sopher (1966) 362 F. 2d 523, 527 (7th Cir.) 385 U.S. 928

State Stockford (1904) 77 Conn. 227, 58 A. 769

R v. Southerton (1805) 6 East 126.

Stuart (1927) 20 Cr. App. R. 74; 73 T.L.R. 715

Studer (1915) 11 Cr. App. R. 307, 85 L.J.K.B. 1017

Taylor (1859) 1 F. & F. 511

People v. Thompson (1884) 97 N.Y. 313, 318

Thorne v. Motor Trade Association (1937) A.C. 797

Tomlinson (1895) 1 Q.B. 706 (C.C.R.)

Treacy v. D.P.P. (1971) A.C. 537

Tripler v. Mayor (1891) 125 N.Y. 617, 625, 26 N.E. 721, 723

Tucker (1826) 1 Mood. C.C. 134

United States v. Varlack (1955) 225 F. 2d 665 (2d Cir.)

People v. Vitusky (1913) 155 App. Div. 139, 140 N.Y. Supp. 19 (1st Dept.)

R v. Wagstaff (1819) Russ & Ry. 398

Walton (1863) Le & Ca. 288

R v. Walton and Ogden (1863) 9 Cox C.C. 268

People v. Warden of City Prison (1912) 145 App. Div. 861, 130 N.Y. Supp 698 (1st Dept.), aff'd, 206 N.Y. 632, 99 N.E. 1116

Ware & De Freville, Ltd. v. Motor Trade Association (1921) 3 K.B. 40 C.A.

People v. Weinseimer (1907) 117 App. Div. 613, 102 N.Y. Supp. 579 (1st Dept.)

State v. Wilbourn (1934) 219 Iowa 120, 257 N.W. 571

People v. Wicks (1906) 112 app. Div. 39, 98 N.Y.S. 163

People v. Wightman (1887) 104 N.Y. 598, 11 N.E. 135

Williams v. Bayley (1866) L.R. 1 H.L. 200

R v. Woodward (1707) 11 Mod. 137; 6 East 133

Rex v. Wyatt (1922) 91L.J. K.B. 402

State v. Young (1868) 26 Iowa 122

State v. Zeigler (1975) 217 Kan. 748, 749, 538 P. 2d 643, 644

REFERENCES

1. B. A., "Criminal Law—Extortion," *Brooklyn Law Review* 27 (April, 1961) pp. 346–351.

2. Beech, Jack, "Extortion-Collection of Debts by Threats of Criminal Prosecution," *Baylor Law Review* Vol. XIII (Fall, 1961) pp. 383–389.

3. "Blackmail & Innocent Pressure," *The Law Journal* Vol. LXXIII (March 26, 1932) pp. 224–225.

4. "Blackmail & Recovery of Debts," *The Law Journal* Vol. LXXIII (January 9, 1932) pp. 25–26.

5. "Blackmailers & the Law," *Solicitors Journal & Weekly Reporter* Vol. 71 (June, 1927) pp. 439–440.

6. Block, Walter, *Defending the Undefendable*, N.Y.: Fleet (1976).

7. Campbell, A. H., "The Anomalies of Blackmail," *The Law Quarterly Review* No. CCXIX (July, 1939) pp. 382–399.

8. Clark, James E., "Extortion Cases and Coverages," *Forum* Vol. 10 (Summer, 1975) pp. 1341–1353.

9. "Demanding Money with Menaces," *Solicitors Journal & Weekly Reporter* 70 (March 27, 1926) p. 495.

10. Griep, A. K., "Criminal Law—A Study of Statutory Blackmail and Extortion in Several States," *Michigan Law Review* 44 (1945) pp. 461–468.

11. Hibschmann, Harry, "Can 'Legal Blackmail' be Legally Outlawed?" *U.S. Law Review* 69 (May, 1935) pp. 474–487.

12. Hogan, Brian, "The Theft Bill-II, Blackmail: Another View," *Criminal Law Review* (Summer, 1966) pp. 474–480.

13. Joseph M. Livermore, "Lawyer Extortion," *Arizona Law Review*, 20 (1978) pp. 403–412.

14. MacKenna, B., "The Theft Bill-II, Blackmail: A Criticism," *Criminal Law Review* (Summer, 1966) pp. 467–474.

15. Nadelmann, Kurt H., "The Newspaper Privilege and Extortion by Abuse of Legal Privilege," *Columbia Law Review* 54 (Spring, 1962) pp. 359–374.

16. Nozick, Robert, *Anarchy, State & Utopia*, N.Y.: Basic Books (1974).

17. Rothbard, Murray N., *The Ethics of Liberty*, Atlantic Highlands, N.J.: Humanities Press (1982).

18. ————, *Man, Economy & State*, Los Angeles: Nash (1970).

19. Stern, H. J., "Prosecutions of Local Political Corruption under the Hobbs Act: the Unnecessary Distinctions between Bribery and Extortion," *Seton Hall Law Review* 3(1) (Fall, 1971) pp. 1–17.

20. Tilley, John, "Reform of the Law of Blackmail," *Solicitors Journal* Vol. III (April 14, 1967) pp. 282–284.

21. Williams, C. R., "Demanding with Menaces: A Survey of the Australian Law of Blackmail," *Melbourne University Law Review* 10 (May, 1975) pp. 118–144.

22. Williams, Glanville L., "Blackmail," *Modern Law Review* 5 (July, 1941) pp. 21–49.

23. Winder, W. H., "The Development of Blackmail," *Modern Law Review* 5 (July, 1941) pp. 21–49.

24. W., S. M., "Criminal Law—Threats and Extortion," *Tennessee Law Review* 29 (Spring, 1962) pp. 462–464.

INTELLECTUAL STYLES AND THE EVOLUTION OF AMERICAN CORPORATION LAW

HENRY G. MANNE

As the field of Law and Economics has developed in recent years, we have gained significant insights both into the process of law development as well as into the real impact of various rules of law. Of course, the process of law reform may be peculiar in common-law jurisdictions, but we can be sure that the economic forces at work both to enhance and restrain private cooperative arrangements are fairly universal. A brief intellectual history of the economics of American corporation law can generate fairly important insights into the impact of corporation law as such, but it will also provide insights into how law itself develops, at least in a political-legal system similar to that of the United States.

Nineteenth century development of corporation law in the United States in some respects had no direct antecedents, though similar developments must have occurred along with industialization in other countries. We had inherited as part of the English common law bits and pieces of what is variously called company law or corporation law. But much of that English law had been devoted to the law of guilds, the church, or municipal towns.[1] Very little of this inherited corporation law addressed modern-type legal issues. It would probably not have been terribly influential in any event, since during the critical period in the United States' development of corporation law (early 1800s) we were no longer receptive to English law. This is ironic because the English had experienced their industrial revolution probably fifty years earlier than the United States and, undoubtedly, some legal precedent from England would have been useful to Americans. The English did, however, have a somewhat special problem because of the so-called

"Bubble Act" that nominally outlawed corporations.[2] For whatever reason, however, there is no evidence that the "free good" of the English precedent was availed of in the United States.

Significant development begins in the United States in the main with the spread of railroads in the early to middle nineteenth century.[3] The impact of these organizations on our statutory law is apparent. Though no direct evidence on the point is available, our state corporation statutory law was clearly appropriate only for sizeable, publicly-held institutions, and the only ones around in any number at the time were the railroads.[4] Unlike European civil codes, our written laws of that period seemed not even to contemplate the formation of small business entities with only a few owners. By and large such units were left to the field of private contracts and the common law of partnership until well into the present century.

While it is true in a very technical sense that American corporation law was at all times a creature of statute, in fact, its development bore more similarity to common-law fields, and that is how lawyers think of it.[5] By and large, with some notable exceptions to be discussed, from the early 1800s on, American corporation law has been dominated by litigated cases and case law development, not legislative change.

Early American corporation law supports Richard Posner's theory that the common law usually developed so as to reflect economic efficiency[6] and Paul Rubin's addendum to that, that legislation may also develop in a way that is not totally inefficient.[7] The two forms of law development are closely intertwined in the corporate field, since the statutes were originally quasi-codifications of case law and customary practices which evolved in private agreements without judicial sanction.

The most famous political aspect of nineteenth-century American corporation law related to the forming of corporations, early done through narrowly focused legislative acts called "special charters."[8] These were on their face legislative in character, but it is most likely that those charters were originally drafted like private contracts, after negotiations between individuals with a variety of interests. Their statutory character was largely a formality, though unfortunately we have no direct evidence about how these documents were actually drafted. We may surmise, however, that privately drafted provisions were submitted to a "friendly" legislator who, through a process now at least theoretically clear to us, caused the incorporation by a special act. In truth there was little "public interest" in these things, though the fiction was long maintained and is even advanced by corporate critics today.[9]

Very likely, competition for this "legislative" service drove the price down to a point where individual legislators could no longer profit from it.[10] Thus, by 1875, every state in the United States had a general, or automatic, incorporation act, thus effectively changing the task of incorporation from a legislative act to a non-discretionary, administrative one. There was still some lingering, optional special chartering in the 1880s, but, for all practical purposes, by the 1890s at the latest, special chartering disappeared.

The succeeding general incorporation acts seemed comprehensive on their face, but in fact they were not universally available to create limited liability companies. As we have noted, they seem almost specifically designed for large, publicly-held companies, and their general tone was permissive and facilitative, not regulatory.[11] These later general incorporation acts—the best known is that of New Jersey in 1875[12]—did little more than codify what had already become the norms in special charter agreements. The reform that did take place was merely change in an administrative process but not in the generally *laissez-faire* substantive law. This is why I say that we can support Paul Rubin's point that there is a kind of evolutionary or economic equilibrium aspect to the statutory law in this field, as well as to the common law. Both in a real sense reflected the demands of the direct users of the law. Nothing drastic changed for the "consumers" of corporation law by the switch from special chartering to a system of general legislation for incorporation. The process simply became cheaper.

The statutes generally provided for certain conditions to be met before incorporation. Most of these conditions could be met by a statement to the required effect in the articles of incorporation. Thus the amount of capital, the number and features of shares, the names of incorporators, an address where process could be served, the purpose of the business, any limitation on duration of existence, and other such basic matters were to be stated in the articles. If every kind of provision that the statute required did in fact appear, then, without further ado, a certificate of incorporation would be issued. No government official had discretion to disapprove any of the details stated in the articles; it was sufficient that they were published. Bylaws, which contained many rules critical for the company's governance, such as voting rules, powers of officers, meeting procedures, etc., were not required to be filed as were the articles of incorporation, since their content was thought to relate to internal matters, whereas the articles dealt with issues of third-party concern.

The norms of corporate organization, then as now, comprehended freely transferable voting shares; a board of directors elected by shareholders and who in turn selected the operating officers of the company; annual meetings of shareholders to elect directors but to do little else in connection with the running of the business; broad managerial powers to the officers, particularly the president; dividends paid to the shareholders at the board's discretion; and a turnover of control to creditors if debts or interest were not paid on time. The relationship between these various real-world practices and the law was little understood—or even studied—at the time.

Much of the period from 1875 to about 1930 was a period of consolidation of these statutes by case law development or by private or contractual adjustments to new financial and industrial circumstances. These statutes were, at least by the standards of the time, fairly lengthy, so there was a lot of detail that had to be hammered out in cases. Some of this litigation was more than statutory clarification, however. There was an inordinate amount of litigation on the doctrine of *ultra vires*, that is, whether a corporation was actually empowered by its charter and the statute to engage in certain behavior. It is difficult to know what the parties in these cases were really fighting about, since the judicial style of the period did not allow for a "realistic" peek behind the veil of legal obfuscation. It is plausible to assume, however, that these were control fights of a type that eventually proved to be inefficient compared to other legal techniques. In any event, for statutory and other reasons the *ultra vires* issue is all but unknown today in the American law of publicly-held companies.

There was also a lot of legal concern in this period with non-voting shares. Investment bankers, who were increasingly being used to disseminate shares, were actually fearful that if the public held a majority of a voting issue of shares, they might "misuse" it. So, typically, the investment bankers would keep control through a small issue of voting shares, and nothing but non-voting shares would be sold to the public. A "voting trust" often served the same purpose. There were heated arguments about this practice with neither side really understanding what was at issue. The argument that something was wrong related to the idea that corporate elections should be "democratic." William Z. Ripley at the Harvard Business School, Louis D. Brandeis, and the young Adolph A. Berle, Jr. all saw the central problem of corporations as their not being sufficiently democratic. J. P. Morgan, though on the other side of the issue, apparently agreed with their analysis if not their preference. He believed that if all those voting shares were in the public's hands, we would soon suffer from the excesses of democracy, i.e., uninformed, emotional, and disruptive rule. He was not about to let the "establishment" be voted out of office by mere public shareholders.

Actually, however, voting directors out of office by shareholders, though possible, is an extremely rare event in American corporate life.

One aspect of corporation law transcended nearly everything else that happened, even though it was so clearly a product of the *Zeitgeist* that it was little noticed. This was the somewhat ambiguous case law doctrine known as the "business judgment rule." Briefly, this rule stated that if the directors—and by derivation, the officers—could show that any course of action they set the corporation on grew out of their *bona fide* belief that they had exercised honest "business judgment," then no matter how stupid or costly their acts, the courts would not even hear further evidence in a damage suit brought against them by a shareholder. The significance of this doctrine was to ensure that only impersonal market forces and not judges could evaluate business decisions *ex post*. In other words we never developed a significant body of case law determining what managers could or could not do by way of running a company. Probably no doctrine was so perfectly consonant with the laissez-faire tradition of America as this one, and none was so completely at odds with what came to seem wrong about the corporate system.

Positive economic theory really had no influence on any of these legal developments. Applied economic analysis at that time was still in its infancy. There was no sense of the economist's role as a "diagnostic" scientist, and, *a fortiori*, as having anything relevant to prescribe. There was no sophisticated econometrics and, in any event, no economic model or theory of corporations that could be tested or measured. Further, the view of American law still dominant prior to 1932 was that it was produced from a benign "black box" whose results in some sense it was improper to analyze or question. It was no longer a strict natural law view, but the relationship was not too distant.[13] All of that was about to change for corporation law in 1932.

For many devotees of the intellectual issues in corporate law, the world began in 1932 with the publication of Berle and Means's *Modern Corporation and Private Property*. Here we really do move into a fascinating area of the interrelationship between intellectually presented notions and the development of law itself. No field of American law has ever been so totally dominated by one work as the corporation law area has been by the Berle and Means classic. One would probably have to go back to Blackstone's work on the English common law to see anything comparable to this amazing phenomenon. And while the substance of the Berle and Means work has been about as thoroughly discredited as a scholarly work can be,[14] its popular influence is still very much with us and, through lawyers and law professors unskilled or uneducated in economics, a live part of contemporary intellectual conflict.

Economics, in modern terms, was in its infancy at the time Berle and Means wrote, and this is important for understanding their conclusions and their influence. In all fairness, we must at the outset acknowledge that there was no economic theory in 1932 capable of explaining the modern corporate system. For an honest scholar who sought to understand how this enormous system functioned, economic models of the time provided little help.

The model used by Berle and Means was, not surprisingly, a political one. In American political and economic ideology, at least circa 1932, there were only two things that could really legitimate the assumed great political and economic power of large corporations. One was a democratic constitutional framework, and the other the constraint of a competitive market. If one or the other of these rationalizations was believed available, an institution could pass the popular test of legitimacy. The large corporation in 1932 in retrospect was an institution waiting for tragedy to befall it; it was intellectually indefensible against an attack that was probably inevitable. No one then could understand it, and therefore no one could explain and defend it.

With this background we see that Berle's approach to the large corporation was not surprising. He looked for the various political trappings that he believed would indicate democracy and found they were missing. Therefore, only economic forces could save the day. But, he concluded, markets exercised little constraint on managers' use (or abuse) of power, and the shareholders were, therefore, at the managers' not too tender mercy. Berle had only the most primitive concept of how market forces might play a role in the corporate process. He recognized that capital markets were some kind of a measure of managers' performance; thus, if they performed well, their company could get new equity capital more cheaply than if they performed badly.[15] But he was not about to build this small point into a general theory. For he was sure that if capital markets impinged seriously on managers, they could and would avoid the constraint by having more debt capital than was optimal or efficient from the shareholders' point of view. Thus managerial self-interest would dictate a systematic bias in favor of debt rather than equity capital. The managers would also pay smaller dividends than shareholders would like so they could build up internal sources of investment capital in order to avoid the capital market. Like most of his predictions, this one too has today fallen victim to careful modern empirical work.[16]

One other notion that Berle discussed did show a "hunch" that economics was in some mysterious way relevant to what he was discussing. Berle talked about the "legitimacy" of private property as if we had learned nothing on the subject since St. Thomas.[17] He tried to make sense of the metaphysical notion that private property is an extension of the physical individual. Not surprisingly, this is closely related to the concept of "title" that dominates the English common-law notion of rights in property. The idea of "title" has often been viewed as reflecting a metaphysical connection between an object and a person. But Berle found even this notion to be inconsistent with the idea of property in a modern corporation. The necessary connection between the ownership rights and the personal use of property that he thought legitimated ownership was absent in the modern corporation. The people who allegedly held the title, i.e., the legal property right, were not even the same ones who had actual control of the property. Indeed he thought that the people who were in control were not even subject to any significant constraints from the legal owners. Therefore, control and ownership were separated in the large, publicly-owned corporation, and we had no philosophy to legitimate that arrangement.

Near the end of the book Berle did suggest one new justification,[18] one that has proved very popular with high-level corporate managers. He said that, while these managers do not really have a legitimate claim to the authority they were exercising, they were nonetheless doing a socially acceptable job. This was the first modern reference to what has come now to be known as "Corporate Social Responsibility." Berle then catalogued various other alternative industrial management arrangements, including socialism, without clearly opting for any of them. For all the complaining about individual rules of corporation law in this book, it was not a diatribe against large capitalist corporations.

Where did all of this lead—and continues even now to lead—in terms of the impact that it had on corporation law, scholarship about corporations, and proper public policy towards them? The most important single influence was to offer pseudo-intellectual underpinnings for today's general mistrust of large corporate enterprise and of corporate managers.[19] Managers had occasionally been vilified in the earlier American media, but only after Berle (perhaps with a bit of help from Karl Marx) did such attitudes strongly influence sociology, literature, the general news media, television shows, movies, and much of the political debate. Now there seemed to be respectable academic justification for converting top executives into a pariah class that needed to be controlled. This probably would have occurred without Berle, but certainly corporate antagonists welcomed his assist, and certainly some intellectual justification has to exist for any political move.

This change in popular attitude in turn had a great impact on both the amount and the subject matter of corporate litigation. Starting in the 1930s, but not directly related to the new federal securities laws of the period, there was a substantial increase in the amount of litigation in the field of corporation law, particularly in cases dealing with fiduciary duty questions of officers and directors, such as conflicts of interest. This was, of course, consistent with the Berle notion that the law would have to be used to control managers' proclivities for self-interested behavior. There is no direct evidence linking this legal development to Berle's work, but neither is there any other convincing explanation for the change.

At the same time serious attention was given in the cases to sales of corporate control at a premium over the prevailing per-share market price, a special *bete noire* of Berle. A few courts suggested that the premium might, under certain circumstances, have to be shared with the non-selling shareholders or paid to the corporation. Those cases are, of course, the precursors of much of the complex modern law on corporate takeovers. Other cases suggesting an inherent conflict between shareholders and managers or between non-controlling and controlling shareholders also were brought—and, in some cases, won. These cases put great pressure on the "Business Judgment Rule," though, by and large, courts continued to use that rule to avoid having to second-guess managerial decisions where there was no clear conflict of interests. This was, however, a period in which managerial discretion was severely restrained through various forms of government regulations, most notably in the labor field.

Because of the new tone about the whole system of corporate enterprise, which, to some degree at least, reflected Berle's mistrust of that system, the possibility of plaintiffs' winning litigation against officers and directors seemed much more likely. And as a result, by a well-known hypothesis,[20] we see a great many more cases being brought. Stated differently, a new set of ideas had appeared, causing what might be termed a "legal disequilibrium." These ideas were bound to have legal consequences. So it is not surprising that litigation expanded in an effort to form a new equilibrium legal result that would somehow be adjusted to the new thinking about the role of corporate executives, the rights of shareholders, and so forth. To the extent that a body of known law is consistent with some exogenous intellectual or economic equilibrium, there will be little pressure on the law, and we won't have a great deal of litigation.[21] But either side of the equation can change and upset the equilibrium. We can change the law and thereby indirectly affect behavior and attitudes, or we can change attitudes or behavior, thus influencing the amount of litigation.

I believe the latter happened in the late 1930s, several years after Berle and Means's book. Berle popularized the notion that the law gave too much opportunity for corporate executives to misbehave and to flaunt the interests of the true owners, the shareholders.[22] This in turn brought into play another great American belief, perhaps first identified by de Tocqueville, that if something is amiss in American society, the legal system will be used to set it straight. Thus, there is a logical and an historical consistency between the "bad-man" theory of corporations—still a dominant view—and an increased utilization of litigation and the courts to police the behavior of the errant individuals.[23]

We have noted that the basic model Berle and his predecessors used to analyze the corporation was a political model, not an economic one, and that the idea of shareholder democracy loomed very large. All the legal literature on federal securities legislation until at least the late 1950s reflected that notion.[24] The whole concept of "full disclosure," the alleged central philosophy of federal securities regulation, was not until many years after the fact related to the goal of making the market function efficiently in the modern economic sense of that term. No one even thought of market efficiency as a goal, or formulated it as an original purpose of the federal regulation.[25] Defenders of regulation wanted full disclosure to make the corporate *political* system work more democratically by guaranteeing a fully informed electorate. Today no spokesman for the Securities and Exchange Commission would make that claim except in jest. Clearly the law has survived its own original *raison d'être* because something else gave it survival strength, though this could be no more than protection of the incomes of lawyers and others who sprang up to specialize in the field of securities regulation.

Another idea began to appear in the early postwar period that flows directly from the Berle and Means work, the idea of corporate social responsibility, a notion very much still with us today.[26] Social responsibility could perhaps be seen by a corporate theologian as a way of saving a corporation's soul by doing good works; certainly a corporation couldn't do it through faith. To carry the metaphor further, probably a lot of the apparent altruism engaged in by corporations is "guilt money" of a special kind. Business executives are terribly sensitive about their image. They don't relish the fact that most intellectuals believe in a "bad man" theory of corporate management.

It is not too surprising then that Berle's view on corporate social responsibility became a dominant theme at the Harvard Business

School in the twenty years or so after World War II. This had an enormous impact on corporate behavior (and law),[27] helping to influence companies to become substantial patrons of education and the arts. However, academic defense of this behavior has been minimal for at least the past fifteen years, since economists began giving serious attention to the corporation.[28] In fact few economists can be found today to take the notion seriously at all,[29] though as yet this seems to have had little influence on levels of corporate giving. Perhaps again we see a phenomenon surviving its own original causes, though in this case the rhetoric of corporate social responsibility also survives in its original form. Let there be no mistake, however; it is merely rhetoric.[30]

For nearly fifty years lawyers in the United States, both in their student days and as practitioners, were subjected exclusively to the Berle and Means view of the corporate world. Berle was a law professor, and most of the people who wrote on this subject until well into the late 1960s were law professors and not economists. Small wonder then that Berle's views have proved dominant in legal circles, since there was precious little alternative that lawyers could comprehend. As George Stigler has said, "no idea is so strong as one that has no opposition." And that was precisely the position of Berle's view of corporations in American law schools until the early 1960s.

George Stigler recently discussed the contemporary reviews by economists of the Berle and Means work.[31] One would have to characterize those reviews collectively as a verbal shrug of the shoulders. That is, nobody at the time took it seriously. The economists who read that book sensed that it was all wrong, but that's as far as they went. Their problem was indeed serious, however, for economics in the 1930s did not provide the tools necessary for analyzing the institution of the large corporation. Perhaps some economists did give thought to the problem, but they could not make any headway.[32] As we shall see, 1962 marks the first crack in the seemingly unassailable wall of Berlean theory.

Basically we see the same lack of intellectual resistance in the 1950s and 60s to the disclosure philosophy of federal securities legislation. No one could be found to oppose it either on theoretical economic grounds or because the idea was inherently impracticable. There seemed to be no doubt in anyone's mind in the 1930s, 40s, and 50s that any industry could be successfully regulated.[33] It seemed to be just a matter of getting experts into the offices to adopt and administer the right rules. By the early 1960s, however, some of the seminal work had started on what eventually evolved into the modern economics of regulation[34] and public choice theory.[35] But no economist in the United

States by this time had critically examined the field of securities regulation. Questions that we think of today as part and parcel of the field were for all practical purposes nonexistent until the early 1960s.

There were some good reasons why economists did not concern themselves with some of this financial regulation material. First, it was arcane. One had to be an expert in accounting, corporation law, and in the regulatory apparatus even to begin such work. That was a substantial investment that promised little payoff. There's no question that economists were intimidated by the field; it looked complicated, and it was. There may also have been a bias in favor of this regulation that influenced scholars not to examine it critically. Finally, both the techniques[36] and the data base[37] necessary to do careful work in the field had not yet appeared.

My own work in this field began in 1962[38] and was given added importance by Berle's reply in the same issue of the *Columbia Law Review*. Additional academic writing on this topic by me appeared in the next few years[39] and began to receive the interested notice of economists. However, it was received with cold disdain or worse by most law professors of the period.[40] A breakthrough occurred in 1967 when the American Enterprise Institute held a conference, the proceedings of which were published in a book called *Economic Policy and the Regulation of Corporate Securities*.[41] Some distinguished economists presented excellent papers, though not one of them had ever examined the field before. That collection probably did more than anything else to open the subject to serious consideration by economists, several of whom have made seminal contributions in the general field since.[42]

Even sympathetic law professors entered the SEC (Securities and Exchange Commission) field gingerly. A standard corporation law casebook of the 50s may have contained two-and-a-half pages in an eight-hundred-page book dealing with securities regulation.[43] As late as 1958 probably no more than six law schools of about 150 in the country offered a course in securities regulation. Ten years later, it would have been hard to find a significant law school that did not have such a course. By then the whole structure and organization of corporation law books had changed as federal securities regulation either replaced or supplemented traditional areas of state law.[44]

This process was not a simple forcing out of the older law; indeed, to this day, only one narrow area of SEC regulation has been found by a court to preempt state law on the same subject. But the growth shows certain evolutionary characteristics that are not immediately evident. For instance, we began after 1933 for the first time to get significant litigation or administrative proceedings involving accounting issues, typically as part of SEC fraud charges. Prior to this, there is almost a total absence of any law in the United States relating to accounting.[45] The anticipated rewards in the earlier period would not have justified a lawyer's getting heavily involved in one case with little carry-over value to other cases. Start-up costs were high, and everyone else would have a free ride on the information thus produced. Consequently, in one sense there was under-investment of lawyers' time in finance law until the SEC offered information to lawyers as a public good. The SEC trained its own legal staff, at the taxpayers' expense, but later as private practitioners these same attorneys were willing and eager to litigate in these same areas. Without the SEC, probably few private lawyers would ever have invested in this area of litigation.

Thus, a whole new area of litigation was opened up because the start-up costs were assumed in the regulatory process. And of course, a large number of legal issues simply had not existed prior to the SEC. Questions about the sufficiency of disclosures, proxy regulation, shareholder proposals, registration of shares with the SEC, for example, all became part of the standard thinking about corporation law. This in turn created an important interest on the part of specialized lawyers in continuing this system of regulation.

The most important development in this field, and also the most unorthodox, was the evolution of the SEC's Rule 10b-5, a vague statement suggesting that any form of fraud would henceforth be actionable by the agency. The rule was promulgated, just this innocuously, in 1942, to assert the Commission's jurisdictions over certain recognized fraudulent behavior.[46] But while corporation law had had a fairly orderly, and, in the main, business-sensible development prior to this rule, this rule may more properly be analogized to a cancer that has grown rapidly, unexpectedly, and with no reflection of healthy business concerns.

In this 1942 rulemaking, the SEC was merely going through appropriate formal measures to establish its jurisdiction over a certain kind of case that it could have, but had not, previously claimed power over. What developed, however, was the (alleged) belief that the SEC had power to *define* fraud in any way they saw fit. What had started out as a pure jurisdictional claim proved to be a radical alteration in the substance of the federal role in American corporation law. Unfortunately the nature of American administrative law is such that this kind of regulatory bootstrapping can go on without response from Congress. In time, when no Congressional concern is voiced, the rule as interpreted by the interested agency becomes an established part of the law with little chance of reversal.

The SEC's almost uncontrolled extension of the concept of fraud greatly influenced certain critical thinking about corporation law. It changed the traditional notion of contractual relationships in the corporation from one of arm's-length dealing between the various parties to one now covered by the common-law concept of fiduciary duty. This concept was originally designed to describe that special care the law required to be shown, for example, to a minor by a trustee holding the minor's property. This proved to be a potent concept in connection with the "bad man" view described earlier, since it too is based on the notion that courts must closely supervise the behavior of those with fiduciary duties.

It is not surprising then that Rule 10b-5 served the same kind of law-expanding function that was described above for the SEC and accounting. As with accounting, lawyers both in the SEC and outside were bound to get new ideas from the fiduciary notion and thus new theories for bringing and winning cases. Out of this, for example, came the SEC's view that insider trading represented fraud, as might a broker's overeagerness to generate stock trades or an acquiring company's offer of two different prices for shares in a control fight, to mention but a few. The resulting increase in the amount of corporate litigation was striking, and lawyers became the most powerful political group interested in the preservation of the securities regulation system.

As stated earlier, I began my own writing in this area in 1962 with what was probably the first critical look at the corporate democracy idea.[47] The academic legal community was incensed, especially when, in 1965, I explained how a functioning market for corporate control actually destroyed the logical foundations of prevailing corporate theory,[48] including the notion of the separation of ownership from control. Academic moral outrage peaked in 1966 when I argued in my book, *Insider Trading and the Stock Market*, that trading on undisclosed information by corporate officials was probably a good thing.

The major importance of this work was probably not to show the undesirability of a rule against insider trading. The greater significance, and the reason it hit the SEC and its defenders so hard, was that it introduced to the securities field for the first time the notion that later came to be known as the "efficient market."[49] The implication was clear: we did not need a regulatory system requiring full disclosure; exactly the right amount of disclosure was already being reflected in changing stock prices.[50] In addition, those price changes reflected the use of information that had not yet been disclosed to the public. We were apparently getting enough information imported into stock prices to make the market as efficient as anyone could fathom it being. Such a notion could not possibly be popular with the SEC or their dependent securities lawyers.[51] Yet the ideas of this book, and a growing progeny following it,[52] have found favorable response from the United States Supreme Court.[53] The idea of the efficient market is still mainly a concern of academic lawyers conversant with economics,[54] but its judicial recognition may not be far away. Few economic concepts as thoroughly tested and accepted as this one have failed for long to have such an influence.

Thus, the 1960s start the latest and most dramatic period in the development of modern corporation law, one in which we witness the total crumbling of Berle's intellectual influence and its political transcendence. It is also, not coincidentally, the period marking the emergence of the new integrated academic field of law and economics. In fact, to clearly understand what is happening today in corporation law, it is necessary to back up a bit and tie the corporate field in with the broader intellectual history of law and economics.

If one examines corporation law cases and treatises of the early 1900s, one sees exactly what the American Legal Realists were upset about. Judges may have had some idea of the business world, or even, as Judge Posner once said, an idea of economic theory.[55] But if so, they hid it well, since judicial writing of that period is commonly abstract, unrealistic, and totally lacking in scientific rigor. Of course, logical rigor never was the essence of common-law reasoning,[56] and in this sense the legal realists were more revolutionary than merely iconoclastic, as is usually claimed. There is more demand for logical rigor in law now than was true seventy-five years ago, and, of the various subjects that have been tried, economics has proved the most potent substitute for the older "black box" jurisprudence.

The law and economics "revolution" started with the antitrust field at the University of Chicago in the early 1950s.[57] While antitrust is not our topic here, it is crucial to understand that this was the first field of law to be systematically examined from a neoclassical economics perspective. In the early 1960s, my own work was an effort to extend this antitrust approach to the corporation law area. But the law school world was not yet prepared for such a radical approach to a traditional area of law, especially since the professors in the corporate law field were quite conservative towards the newer law and economics approach.

Some development, however, made the effort to intellectualize corporation law easier—certainly for me. In 1958, Armen Alchian and I were discussing Berle and Means and shareholder voting. Law professors at the Harvard and Yale law schools had recently proposed abolishing the vote as a useless anachronism.[58] This was their cynical reaction to the earlier shareholder democracy ideal. I didn't think that was right, but I couldn't explain why their "solution" had so little appeal for me. Alchian recommended a book that he thought might be relevant, Anthony Downs's *Economic Theory of Democracy*, the first of the two bibles of the field of public choice theory.[59] Downs noted that votes, if enough of them are assembled, carry power that people want like any economic good. Therefore, a vote too can be viewed as an economic good, deriving its value from the value of winning an election. The market for this good is peculiar to be sure, but nonetheless, there is such a market, and it is closely related to a market for information, which was intensively addressed in the same book. My own notion of a market for share votes and with it corporate control grew directly out of that work. In fact, I believe the applicability of these economic notions is clearer for corporate behavior than for political activities.

I realized in turn that a market for corporate control would have (and always had had) a significant impact on the behavior of managers. This in turn allowed a useful definition of control, a notion that Berle tried to define but never could because of the confusion in his mind between the notion of management and the notion of control.[60] Berle argued that there was an identity of the two, but there were really two separate ideas there—the fundamental issue of control being the right to select the individuals who would in fact determine managerial policy. This distinction had not theretofore appeared in cases or statutory provisions; indeed, it had not yet been discovered. And when it was, change was bound to occur.

Other intellectual developments of the late 50s and early 60s moved us closer to a comprehensive theory of corporate enterprise. One was Armen Alchian's work on property-rights economics and his notion that the legal system, which is largely what property-rights means to him, would help determine individuals' behavior in different circumstances. Thus, in a profit-making, proprietary organization, people were going to behave quite differently than they would where profitability is constrained, as in regulated utilities.[61] *A fortiori*, the same thing was true in a non-profit organization like a church or a university.[62] These notions too were essential to the development and proof of the modern economic theory of corporations.

In a 1964 article[63] I was able to put into a phrase, to which economists could immediately relate, the idea of market harmonization of management and shareholder interests. The phrase "market for corporate control" summed up the dynamic forces that allowed a system of diffused ownership of large corporations to control natural managerial incentives to take advantage of shareholders' apparent impotence. The phrase likewise pointed up the fundamental error of Berle's great work. Market forces, properly understood, were working all the time to generate a system of corporate law and practices that did conform to a new-classical equilibrium solution. The impotence of shareholders that Berle imagined was, like so many externality problems, cured by the internalization of certain costs in private, non-coordinated transactions. Here, as managers engaged in any self-serving, contra-shareholder activity, the price of shares (through the efficient market) declines to the appropriate level. Thus the cost of "buying" control by buying shares also declines. This attracts the interest of individuals and corporations who see a possibility for realizing gains on the shares they acquire in order to capture control, and who then manage the company more efficiently.

Once this basic model for publicly-held corporations was understood, work on many of the details could proceed apace. From the late 60s forward, the literature burgeoned into an enormous corpus of scholarship, both theoretical and empirical, elaborating a basic, market-oriented, contractual theory of the corporation. I will just briefly catalog a few of the more important inventions that figure in the modern scholarship on corporation law and economics. Little of it could even be imagined at the time Berle and Means wrote.

Not the least was the revolution that has occurred in econometrics and statistical techniques. Regression analysis, after all, only came into its own when the computer made it more practicable, and using it to test causal patterns in a field like this one is certainly a modern technique. Today a notion like "the market for corporate control" may not only be stated as a plausible economic theory, but it may be carefully tested empirically.[64] Here the empirical work has overwhelmingly supported the theory.

With the newer, economics-oriented view of the corporation, we begin to lose the idea of the corporation as an entity to be explored like a single, unbreakable, sovereign atom, as in Berle's approach. Now we see each company as one part of a dynamic market system in which capital funds are easily moved from one investment vehicle to another, where individuals are in constant, competitive motion, and corporate control shifts like iron filings in a magnetic field. But, within that system, as in theoretical physics, we keep breaking the things down and finding smaller and more essential particles. That's fundamentally what has happened in corporation law as we've come to see the corporation as a sort of organizing nexus for a large number of individual contracts.[65]

Along with this contractual-nexus approach has come a realization of the importance of agency costs,[66] a specialized version of Coase's transactions costs[67] out of Alchian's shirking and monitoring.[68] We can begin to understand the behavior of the individual actors in corporations in terms of the property-rights structure around them.[69] We can begin to make a more sophisticated analysis of the market for control,[70] why it functions as it does, what gives rise to transaction costs,[71] and what their significance is. With modern public choice tools, we can begin to understand why Congress tries to protect incumbent managers against competition for their jobs.[72]

Risk analysis comes into the picture. All of a sudden, it becomes possible to say intelligent things about optimal capital structures for corporations,[73] and why common shares carry votes but bonds do not.[74] That most powerful invention of modern econometrics, efficient market theory, allows us to explore numerous questions empirically that only a few years ago, seemed intractable. That theory also goes to the very heart of the SEC mandated disclosure, since it shows that we were and are getting correct signals from the stock market without any regulation.

Finally, there is a whole congeries of topics addressed by public choice specialists and related economists, under such headings as public goods, free-rider problems, prisoner's dilemmas, voting paradoxes, coordination costs, externalities and internalization.[75] It would have been just the grossest kind of mystery ten years ago why we get some of the forms of resistance we do to takeover attempts and how they should be analyzed. Now, however, we can explain in very sophisticated—and testable—terms the costs and benefits of different legal policies about these forms of behavior.[76]

These new ideas have come so rapidly that they have not yet reached all the important avenues for legal change. Senior practicing lawyers have not yet mastered the new scholarship and, for reasons explained earlier, are loath to offer a public good to their profession. This time the Securities and Exchange Commission is not so likely to provide the public good because the anticipated results are contrary to the interests that control the agency. A distinguished and influential private organization, the American Law Institute (ALI), has recently proposed a new scheme of corporation law that is almost a codification of Berle's view of large companies.[77] This ironic timing—just as the best scholarship has reached consensus on the opposite view—could not have been predicted. It can only be attributed to a lag in the dissemination of the new learning, the pervasive influence of the older views, the ideological bias of certain academic lawyers who pushed the ALI proposals, and accident.

It would be nice to predict confidently that American law will in time reflect the new view of corporations. But the course of this legal evolution is not that predictable. We would usually assume, for instance, that in time attorneys would make the newer arguments to sympathetic and comprehending judges who might then resist efforts to enmesh the courts in internal corporate decision-making. But if legislation is adopted, abandoning such keystones of traditional doctrine as the Business Judgment Rule, as the ALI proposes, there is little judges can do about it. Clearly, had the American Law Institute not made its proposals when it did, there would today be no pressure to change the law in the corporate field.

Today we understand why the legal doctrines that developed in the late nineteenth and early twentieth centuries are still appropriate and in fact optimal. It would be truly ironic if the incorrect theories of an intermediate stage now prevailed to alter the older doctrine. In a pure system of common law, with its evolutionary character and consistency with economically efficient solutions, there would be no change at this time. However, the dynamics of a political system generating legislation are so different that there is simply no way to predict at this juncture what may happen.

NOTES

1. Shepheard, *Of Corporations, Fraternities and Guilds,* London (1659).

2. Cooke, *Corporation, Trust and Company,* Cambridge, Mass. (1951).

3. See, e.g., Cadman, *The Corporation in New Jersey: Business and Politics 1791–1875,* Cambridge, Mass. (1949).

4. Manne, "Our Two Corporation Systems: Law and Economics," *Virginia Law Review,* Vol. 53 (1967) p. 259.

5. Katz, "The Philosophy of Midcentury Corporation Statutes," *Law and Contemporary Problems,* Vol. 23 (1958) p. 177.

6. Posner, *Economic Analysis of Law,* Boston (1972).

7. Rubin, "Common Law and Statute Law," *Journal of Legal Studies,* Vol. 11 (1982) p. 24.

8. Cadman, *op. cit.,* n. 3.

9. Hurst, *The Legitimacy of the Business Corporation in the Law of the United States 1780–1970,* Charlottesville (1970) p. 38.

10. Anderson and Tollison, "The Myth of the Corporation as a Creation of the State," *International Review of Law and Economics,* vol. 3 (1983) p. 107.

11. Katz, *op. cit.,* n. 5.

12. Cadman, *op. cit.,* n. 3.

13. Llewellyn, *The Common Law Tradition: Deciding Appeals,* New York (1953).

14. See generally, *Journal of Law and Economics,* vol. 26 (1983).

15. Berle and Means, *The Modern Corporation and Private Property,* New York (1932) p. 280.

16. Fischel, "The Law and Economics of Dividend Policy," *Virginia Law Review,* vol. 67 (1981) p. 699.

17. Berle and Means, *op. cit.,* n. 15, pp. 338, 346.

18. *Ibid.,* p. 356.

19. Nader, Green & Seligman, *Taming the Giant Corporation,* New York (1976).

20. Gould, "The Economics of Legal Conflicts?" *Journal of Legal Studies*, vol. 2 (1973) p. 279.

21. Rubin, "Why is the Common Law Efficient?" *Journal of Legal Studies*, vol. 6 (1977) p. 7.

22. Nader, Green & Seligman, *op. cit.*, n. 19.

23. See American Law Institute, *Principles of Corporate Governance: Analysis and Recommendations*, Tentative Draft No. 3, Philadelphia (1984).

24. Emerson and Latcham, *Shareholder Democracy*, Cleveland (1954).

25. See generally, Seligman, *The Transformation of Wall Street*, Boston (1982).

26. Manne, "The Myth of Corporate Responsibility—or—Will the Real Ralph Nader Please Stand Up?" *Business Lawyer*, vol. 26 (1970) p. 533.

27. *A. P. Smith Manufacturing Co. v. Barlow*, 13 N.J. 145, 98 A.2d 581 (1953).

28. Manne and Wallich, *The Modern Corporation and Social Responsibility* American Enterprise Institute, Washington, D.C. (1972).

29. But see, Wallich, "The Case for Social Responsibility of Corporations," in *ibid.*, p. 37; and see Manne, "The Limits and Rationale of Corporate Altruism; an Individualistic Model," *Virginia Law Review*, vol. 59 (1973) p. 708.

30. Manne, C. S. R.: Wrong Pew, Wrong Church, Wrong Doctrine, *The Alternative: An American Spectator* (Dec., 1975).

31. Stigler and Friedland, "The Literature of Economics: The Case of Berle and Means," *Journal of Law and Economics*, vol. 26 (1983) p. 237.

32. See, e.g., R. A. Gordon, *Business Leadership in the Large Corporation*, Washington, D.C. (1945).

33. Simons, *A Positive Program for Laissez-Faire*, Chicago (1934).

34. Coase, The Federal Communications Commission, *Journal of Law and Economics*, vol. 2 (1959) p. 1.

35. Buchanan and Tullock, *The Calculus of Consent*, Ann Arbor (1962).

36. Sharpe, "A Simplified Model for Portfolio Analysis," *Management Science*, (Jan., 1963) p. 277; and Fama, Fisher, Roll and Jensen, "The Adjustment of Stock Prices to New Information," *International Economics Review*, vol. 10 (1969) p. 1.

37. See Fisher and Lorie, "Rates of Return on Investments in Common Stocks," *Journal of Business*, vol. 37 (1964) p. 1.

38. Manne, "The 'Higher Criticism' of the Modern Corporation," *Columbia Law Review*, vol. 62 (1962) p. 339.

39. Manne, "Some Theoretical Aspects of Share Voting," *Columbia Law Review*, vol. 64 (1964) p. 1427; "Mergers and The Market for Corporate Control," *Journal of Political Economy*, vol. 53 (1967) p. 259.

40. See Manne, "Insider Trading and the Law Professor," *Vanderbilt Law Review*, vol. 23 (1970) p. 547.

41. Washington, D.C., 1969.

42. See especially the works of Professors George Benston, Harold Demsetz, Michael C. Jensen, and William H. Meckling.

43. See, e.g., Dodd and Baker, *Cases and Materials on Corporation Law*, 2d ed., Mineola, L.I. (1951).

44. See, e.g., Ribstein, *Business Associations*, San Francisco (1983).

45. Benston, *Corporate Financial Disclosure in the UK and the USA*, London (1976) p.7.

46. Manne, "Insider Trading and the Administrative Process," *George Washington Law Review*, vol. 35 (1967) p. 473.

47. Manne, *op. cit.*, n. 38, pp. 407–413.

48. Manne, *op. cit.*, n. 39.

49. Fama, "Efficient Captital Markets: A Review of Theory and Empirical Work," *Journal of Finance*, vol. 25 (1970) p. 383.

50. Manne and Solomon, *Wall Street in Transition*, New York (1974).

51. Manne, *op. cit.*, n. 40.

52. Fischel, "Insider Trading and Investment Analysts: An Economic Analysis of Dirks v. SEC," *Supreme Court Economic Review*, vol. 3 (1984).

53. *Dirks v. Securities and Exchange Commission*, 51 USLW 5123 (1983).

54. Fischel, *op. cit.*, n. 52.; and Banoff, "Regulatory Subsidies, Efficient Markets, and Shelf Registration: An Analysis of Rule 415," *Virginia Law Review*, vol. 70 (1984) p. 135.

55. Posner, *op. cit.*, n. 6.

56. Levi, *An Introduction to Legal Reasoning*, Chicago (1949).

57. Kitch, "The Fire of Truth: A Remembrance of Law and Economics at Chicago 1932–1970," *Journal of Law and Economics*, vol. 26 (1983) p. 163.

58. See in particular, Chayes, "The Modern Corporation and the Rule of Law," in *The Corporation in Modern Society*, (Mayson, ed.) (1959) p.25.

59. The other is Buchanan and Tullock, *op. cit.*, n. 35.

60. Berle and Means, *op. cit.*, n. 15, pp. 84–90.

61. De Alessi, "Managerial Tenure Under Private and Government Ownership in the Electric Power Industry," *Journal of Political Economy*, vol. 82 (1974) p. 645.

62. Manne, "The Political Economy of Modern Universities," in *Education in a Free Society* (Husted, ed.), Indianapolis (1973).

63. Manne, "Mergers and The Market for Corporate Control," *Journal of Political Economy*, vol. 73 (1965) p. 110.

64. See the remarkable series of studies in "A Symposium on The Market for Corporate Control: The Scientific Evidence," *Journal of Financial Economics*, vol. 11 (1983).

65. Jensen and Meckling, "Theory of the Firm: Managerial Behavior, Agency Costs and Ownership Structure," *Journal of Financial Analysis*, vol. 3 (1976) p. 305; Alchian and Demsetz, "Production, Information Costs and Economic Organization," *American Economic Review*, vol. 62 (1972) p. 777; and Williamson, "Organizational Form, Residual Claimants and Corporate Control," *Journal of Law and Economics*, vol. 26 (1983) p. 351.

66. Jensen and Meckling, *op. cit.*, n. 66.

67. Coase, "The Problem of Social Cost," *Journal of Law and Economics*, vol. 3 (1960) p. 1.

68. Alchian, "The Bases of Some Recent Advances in the Theory of the Firm," *Journal of Industrial Economics*, vol. 14 (1969) p. 30.

69. Jensen and Meckling, *op. cit.*, n. 66.

70. *Op. cit.*, n. 65.

71. Carney, "Shareholder Coordination Costs, Shark Repellents, and Takeout Mergers: The Case Against Fiduciary Duties," *American Bar Foundation Research Journal* (1983) p. 341.

72. Manne, "Cash Tender Offers for Shares—A Reply to Chairman Cohen," *Duke Law Journal* (1967) p. 231.

73. Jensen and Meckling, *op. cit.*, n. 66.

74. *Ibid.*

75. Carney, *op. cit.*, n. 72.

76. Symposium, *op. cit.*, n. 65.

77. *Op. cit.*, n. 23.

THE DEMAND FOR LIFE: THEORY AND APPLICATIONS

ISAAC EHRLICH
AND
HIROYUKI CHUMA

I INTRODUCTION

The thrust of conventional demand theory to date can be summarized as focusing on one pivotal, and seemingly all-encompassing commodity called "quality of life": Food, clothing, shelter and travel—the conventional goods and services of economic textbooks—are but specific "inputs" into, or "characteristics" of, that general commodity. Little systematic attention, by comparison, has been devoted so far to that commodity's distinct logical complement—"quantity," or "length of life." There can be little doubt that a greater amount of the latter commodity, given the former, significantly enhances human welfare, and that a choice between the two must be confined by the scarcity of real resources. A growing volume of empirical evidence indicates, furthermore, that actual human longevity, or life expectancy, has increased rather dramatically over the last two centuries, and has varied systematically and often pronouncedly by economic and demographic variables such as income, education, professional and marital status, and, of course, age. (Tables 3.1 and 3.2 below document some of these variations.) The only assumption needed for treating quantity-of-life as an "economic" decision variable is that a technology or technologies exist through which it is possible to convert basic economic resources into marginal increments in factors and conditions that actually bring about, or raise the odds of, longer life. The steady and dramatic

243

Table 3.1   Changes in Expected Life Span in the United States, 1850–1980

	1850	1901	1950	1980	Change 1850–1980	Change 1901–1980	Change 1950–1980
A. White Population							
1. At Birth							
Males	38.3	48.2	66.3	70.5	32.2	22.3	4.2
Females	40.5	51.1	72.0	78.1	37.6	27.0	6.1
2. At Age 20							
Males	60.1	62.2	69.5	72.2	12.1	10.0	2.7
Females	60.2	63.8	74.6	79.4	19.2	15.6	4.8
B. All Others							
1. At Birth							
Males		32.5	58.9	65.3		32.8	6.4
Females		35.0	62.7	74.0		39.0	11.3
2. At Age 20							
Males		55.1	63.7	67.6		12.5	3.9
Females		56.9	66.8	75.9		19.0	9.1

Source: Historical Statistics of the U.S. and Statistical Abstracts of the U.S.

advance of medical technology in this century alone would seem to confirm this assumption.

This condensed paper, which summarizes and builds on our recent paper referenced below, is devoted to a discussion of the demand for quantity-of-life in economic terms. In particular, we have proposed that economic theory can be applied systematically to derive a "demand-function for quantity-of-life" with the latter concept operationalized as either "actual longevity" or "life expectancy" of specific individual groupings, depending upon whether we treat length of life as a certain or a stochastic variable (we do both). Put differently, we view the determination of life as a voluntary choice variable which is affected, at least on the margin, not just by what nature or exogenous biological processes dictate, but also by what people do to maintain and preserve their health, or to protect themselves against a myriad of biological, environmental, and work-related hazards to their health and life.

Of course, one cannot talk about the demand for length of life independently of the demand for quality of life: to have an economic problem by Frank Knight's definition we must have a limited choice between at least two competing commodities. In our study we have defined quality itself by a pair of distinct characteristics: a general (dated) consumption good (including leisure), and healthy time avail-

Table 3.2 Selected Life
Expectancies for the White
Population by Sex and Years of
Schooling Completed, 1960

Sex and Years of School Completed	AVERAGE YEARS OF LIFE REMAINING AT AGE		
	25	45	65
White Males			
0–4	43.9	26.2	12.7
5–7	43.6	26.7	12.9
8	44.8	27.1	13.0
9–11	45.6	27.6	13.5
12	46.0	27.5	12.9
13+	47.1	28.4	13.1
White Females			
0–4	46.8	30.0	14.8
5–7	50.5	32.1	16.0
8	51.1	32.4	16.2
9–11	53.4	34.8	18.0
12	52.2	33.2	16.3
13+	56.4	37.7	20.8

Source: Kitagawa and Houser (1973),
p. 17, Table 2.4.

able per period. We thus wind up with a simultaneous consideration
and derivation of the demand for three basic commodities: (a) longevity, or life expectancy, (b) healthy time, and (c) a general consumption
good. Although the first two choice variables are largely functionally
dependent by virtue of their direct dependence on "good health" (an
objective index of healthiness), at least under one version of our analysis they are not strictly "joint product." In general, individuals can
choose to substitute or trade some of each of these commodities for the
other two in order to reach a maximum of life time satisfaction, given
the limited life time consumption opportunities.

Akin to the concept of "demand" in modern economic theory is the
concept of "value" or "shadow price," since optimizing behavior produces a unique relationship between the two. Thus, if the consumption
of bread (x) is at an optimum, the quantity demanded would be that
quantity (x*) which equates the market price of bread (P_x) with the ratio

of the marginal utility of bread to the marginal utility of income $(U_x(x^* . .)/\lambda)$. The latter ratio is the value, or shadow price of bread. This illustration indicates that a systematic derivation of the concept or measure of (private) "value of life," as perceived by individuals, is but a by-product of the systematic derivation of the optimal quantity, or demand for life, and our analysis addresses the formulation of such a measure both under conditions of certainty and uncertainty in connection with the arrival time of death. Since there are no complete markets for life or limb, there is no unique explicit market price for longevity or life expectancy. However, we can still derive, using our theoretical analysis, a measure of the shadow price or value of life from the optimality conditions governing the demand for life-extending measures such as investment in health or in personal safety (self-protection).

The basic advantage of developing a theory of the demand for life in economic terms lies not just in the systematic tracing of the fundamental factors which control the demand for life and the value of life, but, more importantly, in predicting the way in which the demand and value functions are affected when these factors vary in the cross section, across different persons, or over the life cycle of any one person. Indeed, the thrust of the theoretical analysis here will be devoted to the discussion of the effects of variations in economic and demographic variables such as endowed wealth, education, market-earning potential, and age, on both the extent to which people will devote resources to increase their longevity or odds of survival, and on the "risk premium" they will place on exposing their lives and limbs to detrimental risks.

Some of the highlights of our results are not surprising: we provide an economic rationale for why life must be finite, even for economists. We also show that the demand for longevity or life expectancy is an increasing function of initial wealth (i.e., the quantity of life is a "superior good") and a decreasing function of the cost of health investment or self-protection; that value of life is an increasing function of wealth and ultimately a decreasing function of age; that those with higher values of life will generally (but not always) have longer lives; and that a strong preference for bequest will, *ceteris paribus*, decrease the value of life-saving and the demand for life expectancy. Under some simplifying assumptions we further show that the discounted value of expected future labor income, which had served traditionally as a conventional measure of value of life in the early literature on human capital, is in fact a lower-bound measure of the value of life-saving and that in general the true value of life will be significantly higher.

The discussion will conclude with a few illustrations of the power of this analysis to explain *actual* variations in human longevity and life expectancy, as well as specific aspects of labor and nonmarket choices in which risk of injury and death are important factors. And it will address the impact of the rapid recent development of direct "markets for life" on variations in the demand for life and the value of life across different persons and different societies.

II METHODOLOGY

To deal adequately with the problem of determining optimal longevity or life expectancy it is necessary to formulate a life-cycle model and apply a dynamic optimization method to solve for the relevant "control" and "state" variables of the model, including the actual life-time horizon. There is also the issue of whether to address the problem in question within a certainty or an uncertainty framework. Michael Grossman, who was the first to formulate a systematic model of the demand for health with an open life-time horizon, chose a certainty framework, undoubtedly due to its mathematical simplicity. However, there are fundamental shortcomings in Grossman's (1972) paper which do not permit a systematic resolution of the choice of longevity and a health-investment path along his proposed approach.[1] Since we started our analysis of the demand for life by modifying and reworking Grossman's original formulation, using the relevant dynamic optimization technique, we retained the certainty framework of his model in the first part of our work (see Part IIIA). We felt, however, that treating the choice of an optimal length of life as if it could be known with certainty to the decision-maker was sufficiently unrealistic so as to cause concern regarding the usefulness of the analysis in terms of its behavioral implications. We have consequently developed an alternative model of the demand for length of life in which actual longevity is treated as a stochastic variable, and where investment in health is treated not as a gross addition to a deteriorating stock of endowed health capital (as in Grossman's analysis) but as investment in self-protection (i.e., protection of one's health and life) intended to control the odds of mortality and morbidity at any period of life, given one's survival to that period (see Part IIIB). We thus attempt to tie more closely in this paper the analysis of health investment with both the analysis of investment in human capital and that of the economics of safety.

III   SPECIFIC FORMULATION AND MAJOR RESULTS

IIIA   THE MODEL UNDER CERTAINTY

The point of reference here (following Grossman) is that a person's health is dictated by a special type of human asset called health capital, (H(t) at time t), which renders two different benefits: (a) it increases the amount of healthy time available per "period," i.e., h(t) $\equiv$ ϕ(H(t)) out of Ω "hours"; (b) it delays the approach of death, since the latter is assumed to occur automatically once H(t) drops to a minimum critical level consistent with life, called H_{min}. These services, in turn, confer both monetary and psychic benefits in the form of enhanced earning capacity w(E(t))·h(t), with w(E(t)) denoting the wage rate or rental value of a unit stock of education capital, E(t), and an independent increase in one's utility from healthy time, h(t), and longer life, T. The stock of health capital (H(o) at birth) is subject to a biological deterioration represented by an instantaneous rate of depreciation δ(t) which intensifies in magnitude as the person's age advances. The health stock can be maintained or augmented, however, by purposive investments in health I(t) through exercise and rest (involving a time input m(t)), and medical care (involving a money input M(t)), but the cost of health investment is an increasing function of the *scale* of investment (i.e., the implicit production function underlying health investment exhibits decreasing returns to scale). The equation of motion in health capital, representing the instantaneous health constraint, is given in Equation (1.2) in the Appendix, with the boundary constraint for the terminal stock of health given in Equation (1.7).

Individual choices are also limited, of course, by a conventional non-human (financial) asset constraint, and the equation of motion in that state variable, defining the magnitude of savings at any time period, is given in Equation (1.3) or (1.3a), with the boundary condition specified in Equation (1.8).

The horizon itself, T, is taken to be free in this formulation, i.e., it is determined as an outcome of the optimal policy of health maintenance. The person's objective, then, is to maximize Equation (1.1) in the Appendix, subject to Equations (1.2), through (1.8). We have resolved this maximization problem on the assumption that the horizon, T, is finite.

IIIA.a.   Why Must Life Be Finite?

One intriguing, albeit dismal, implication of the model is that it helps identify the reasons why the quantity of human life must be finite, even when longevity is assumed to be subject to choice. The fundamental reason, in the final analysis, is not different from the reason why *quality* of human life is also finite: why, that is, the actual consumption of every known goods and service is constrained for every known individual. The comparison with "mundane" goods and services may be thought inappropriate by many who would argue that the intensity of the desire for longer life far exceeds the desire for any other known commodity, at least beyond a minimal level of consumption necessary for subsistence. However, Economics as the "dismal science" insists relentlessly on the proposition that real-life choices are limited by the scarcity of *means* rather than by the intensity of the desire for the *ends* they serve.

Insofar as the possibility of life in perpetuity is concerned, one verifiable constraint is the continuous biological process of aging which, in terms of the economic model we have discussed in section IIIA, means that in the absence of any investment of resources to secure health maintenance, the person's stock of health will necessarily deteriorate to its minimal level ($H_{min} > 0$) within a *finite* interval of time. It turns out, however, that continuous health depreciation ($\delta(t) > 0$) by itself is not a sufficient condition for ruling out the possibility of infinite life. That condition is the requirement that the depreciation rate of health assets will be continuously increasing ($\dot{\delta}(t) > 0$), i.e., that the pace of aging will grow faster with age so as to rule out convergence to a steady pace of aging. Given this condition, it is then the scarcity, or finiteness, of human resources which will defeat any plan for perpetual health maintenance. Indeed, human resources must be finite even when one's work horizon is assumed to be potentially infinite: even when a person's market earning capacity itself is unaffected by the passage of time, *maximum* borrowing capacity, given an infinite horizon, must equal the present value of all future earnings which is *finite* as long as the rate of interest is positive.[2] Thus, because the monotonic increase in the rate of depreciation of health must ultimately require an infinite expenditure of resources on health maintenance, there is no way a person could afford an infinite horizon, given the limited amount of "human wealth."[3] Moreover, because the user cost of health capital, which include the rate of depreciation of the health stock, rises relative to the cost of consumption in any period of life, people will have an incentive to trade some of the former for the latter, thus settling for a finite combination of both quantity and quality of life. Ergo, the constrained optimum length of life, as opposed to the desired one, must be less than even the maximum feasible length, given the biological and "human wealth" constraint.

There is another way of presenting the last argument. The analysis of the transversality condition given in Equation (1.10) in the appendix suggests that if the horizon T approaches an infinite value, and there is a positive time preference for consumption, the "shadow price" of health capital (the marginal value of life) becomes sufficiently close to zero to make considerable investment in health capital, thus in prolonging longevity, suboptimal. It is the ultimate fall in the "value" of the quantity of life, relative to its quality, that decreases the demand for health maintenance as the contemplated horizon becomes sufficiently long.

IIIA.b. The Demand for Longevity and the Related Variables of the Model

The preceding analysis establishes not merely the finiteness of life as a consequence of optimizing behavior, but the existence of a well-defined demand function for longevity as well. This commodity, measured by T, competes with the two determinants of quality of life—a stream of the composite consumption activity $Z(t)$ and a stream of health services $h(t) = \phi(H(t))$—over the allocation of scarce life-time resources. The relevant lifetime wealth, or "budget," constraint for this choice, is an *endogenous* variable, however: a potential wealth constraint. It must be distinguished from both the conventional, Fisherian concept of wealth or Gary Becker's modification of that concept ("full wealth") in that it depends on the desired longevity itself: $w(T^*) = A(0) + \int_0^T e^{-rt} w\phi(H(t))dt$, with W and T being jointly determined.

"Potential wealth," in turn, supports the desired spending on both quality and quantity of life, as determined by the direct demand for the aggregate consumption activity, $Z^*(t)$, and the derived demand for the health investment path, $I^*(t)$. All of these direct and derived-demand functions can be stated as functions of the basic parameters of the model: endowed wealth, $A(0)$, endowed health, $H(0)$, the biologically determined rate of health depreciation, $\delta(t)$, the market and psychological time discount rates, r and ρ, the price index of health-care services, $P(t)$, and the individual's wage rate and attained level of education, $w(t)$ and $E(t)$, respectively.[4] While the demand for planned longevity, T^*, is independent of time (age), however, the demand and derived demand for (planned) consumption, health and health maintenance, are expected to vary at alternative time periods (ages), and the model can thus provide insights into what determines observed changes in these choice variables both in the cross section and over the life-cycle.

One other key variable of interest is the ratio of the two co-state variables of the model: the marginal utilities of current health and wealth, respectively [see Appendix Equations (1.9) and (1.10)], which represents the shadow price, or value, of health capital. The shadow price of health, in turn, can be thought of as the "marginal value of life," since any marginal increase in H(T) above H_{min} will delay marginally the approach of death. The significance of this variable in terms of the preceding analysis is that it influences the derived demand for health maintenance since the latter, I*(t), is determined at a level where the shadow price of health g(t) just equals the marginal cost of investment in health, $\alpha\pi I^{\alpha-1}$, or $2\pi I$ if $\alpha = 2$, (see Figure 3.1). Like the demand and derived-demand relationships of the model, the shadow price of health capital or "marginal value of life," g(t), is expected to *vary* both over the life-cycle and in the cross section as a function of the set of basic parameters which also influences the demand for consumption, health, health maintenance, and longevity.

IIIA.c.   Behavioral Implications

Starting with the key life-cycle implications of the model, two competing forces are shown to affect the dynamic path of the shadow price of health capital, g(t), and consequently the dynamic paths of health investment and health capital (the quantity of healthy time demanded) as well.[5] On the one hand, the contracting length of one's remaining life-span reduces the incentive to invest in health because the benefits accruing to such investment at older ages are expected to last over a shorter span of time. This, indeed, is the general prediction of human capital theory regarding the incentive to invest in any "conventional" human assets such as education, job training, and job mobility. On the other hand, as time moves on, the discounted value of the benefit from delaying time of death through health maintenance also increases, or, put differently, the user-cost of health investment falls, due to the saving of interest and depreciation charges achieved by delaying investment in health from younger to older ages. By this effect, the incentive to invest in health maintenance rises with age. While the theoretical analysis predicts that the decreasing marginal incentive to invest in health due to the diminished horizon is ultimately likely to overtake the increasing marginal incentive to invest due to the decreasing user-cost of investment, the force of the latter incentive is likely to have a dominating influence on individual behavior over the bulk of one's life-cycle. This analysis thus has the somewhat surprising implication that it is perfectly rational for young persons to be less concerned about eschewing consumption activities that may in the long-run be harmful

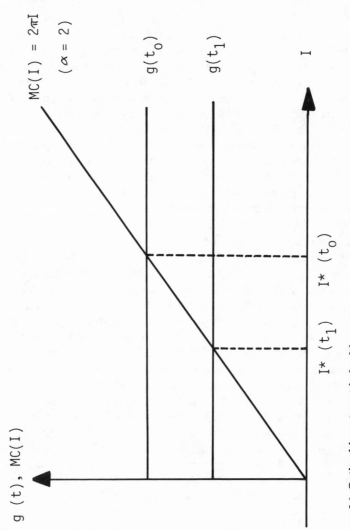

FIG. 3.1: Optimal investment in health.

to their health, like smoking, drinking, and using drugs, relative to individuals in their "prime of life." In other words, the observed tendency of middle-aged and older persons to "grow out" of harmful consumption activities, and thus invest more in health preservation, can be explained not necessarily as a consequence of changing time preferences with age or the spurious influence of a natural "selection bias" in older age cohorts, but rather as a result of the growing shadow price (value) of health capital and the correspondent rising incentive to maintain health, especially if the main benefit of such health maintenance efforts were in terms of their impact on longevity. Only at very old ages would this tendency reverse as the value of health capital falls in anticipation of life's end. Another related, and somewhat surprising implication of the model is that the level of consumption expenditure (net of health maintenance) may also fall, or increase at a much slower rate, in the last phase of life: To the extent that consumption and health are *complements* in utility, the declining stock of health capital, which inevitably takes place during the last phase of life, would offset the tendency for consumption expenditures to grow with age as a result of the force of the positive rate of interest, whenever the latter exceeds the rate of time preference (the conventional Fisherian result). This analysis thus adds an important health-dimension to life-cycle consumption theory, which has been absent in the conventional literature concerning life-cycle optimization, and which can better explain the pattern of individual consumption spending in the more advanced stages of life.

The analysis also has important implications concerning systematic cross-sectional variations in longevity and in the shadow price of health capital across persons or individual groupings of equal age. The complex analysis of comparative dynamics shows that, *ceteris paribus,* a higher level of endowed wealth, $A(0)$, will unambiguously increase both the demand for longevity and health, and the shadow price of health capital. Put differently, the analysis establishes that quantity, like quality of life, is a superior good. Similarly, higher levels of endowed health ($H(0)$) or innate earning ability (E) are expected to lead to a higher demand for health and longevity, essentially because the rise in the value of one's human assets increases one's incentive to protect and maintain such assets. Education (E) may further increase the demand for health because it may improve the productivity of one's efforts at health maintenance, thus reducing the unit investment costs. It should be noted, however, that an increase in special knowledge or productivity regarding health investment may lower one's shadow price of health capital if the demand for health investment were price-inelastic. Physicians, therefore, may invest more in their health in real terms and thus live longer than other persons, while at the same time appear to expose themselves to greater health hazards (i.e., behave as if the marginal value of their health capital is lower) essentially because their costs of maintaining or rebuilding health in the event of encountering acute medical problems would be lower than those of the general population. On some simplifying assumptions the model further implies that the demand for longevity will rise with a secular rise in market wages, or labor productivity, and with a secular improvement in effort-saving technologies, and will fall with an increase in the biological rate of health depreciation, the rate of time preference, and the prices of health care services. Not surprisingly, a reduction in the real price of medical and related health care services, P, is expected by economic theory to increase the demand for health investment and longevity.

IIIB   THE MODEL UNDER UNCERTAINTY

The least realistic aspect of the analysis thus far has been the assumption that the actual length of life is known with certainty. In practice, the arrival time of death is uncertain, as is one's health status at any given moment of life. In this second, more original part of our analysis we view the incidence of both mortality and morbidity as stochastic processes, and assume that the conditional probabilities of both can be modified or controlled through a variety of life and health protective activities. Put differently, we consider investment in health in this section to be a form of self-protection against the risks of mortality and other health hazards which systematically increase with age. Indeed, the theory of health and life protection turns out to be a generalization of the theory of self-protection which Ehrlich and Becker have applied originally (see their 1972 paper) in the case of more conventional personal hazards, using a single-period analytical setting.

For the sake of a simple continuous-time formulation, we view the incidence of mortality as a continuous independent Poisson process and assume that the arrival frequency of death, or "force of mortality" $\mu(t)$, which defines the conditional probability of the occurrence of death at age t given its non-occurrence to that age, can be controlled via self-protective expenditures I(t), as specified in Equation (2.2) in the Appendix. By this equation, the survival probability, while being a monotonically decreasing function of age, is assumed to be partially controlled by investments in health and life-protection measures through inputs of individual time and medical care much the same as investment in health capital in Section 3A. The difference here is that we choose as index of health the conditional probability of mortality at age t, $\mu(t)$, and assume that that index is controlled exclusively by *current* investments in health-protection. While, for mathematical simplicity, we therefore ignore the possible effects of past outlays on self-protection on the *conditional* risk of mortality at time t, $\mu(t)$, the Poisson process underlying the movement in mortality risk implies that the *probability of survival* to any time period t will in fact be controlled by all the accumulated past investments in health and life-protection to that date, since the latter probability is defined as an integral (in exponential form) of past conditional probabilities of mortality.[6]

Although the conditional probabilities of mortality and morbidity can in principle be controlled by separate inputs, we view them in this analysis to be monotonically related. Consequently $\mu(t)$ can be treated as a *general* index of health, as is indeed a common practice in many empirical studies which seek to use mortality risks as, at the very least, *objective* measures of individuals' health status. And since morbidity risk, in turn, is inversely related to the amount of healthy time available, the latter can be expressed as a decreasing and concave function of $\mu(t)$, as described in Equation (2.3) in the appendix.[7]

While the appropriate planning horizon in this stochastic control formulation may itself be a choice variable, analytically the problem of determining an optimal horizon may be simplified by assuming that the individual behaves as though survival beyond a maximal date D $<$ ∞ is not feasible—an assumption justified by the analysis in Section IIIA.a. In this case, the objective function at any period becomes one of maximizing the expected utility of lifetime consumption and health as specified in Equation (2.1) in the Appendix, on the assumption that there is no bequest motive. This equation, in turn, must be maximized subject to the relevant production functions, boundary conditions and the appropriate financial-assets constraint introduced in Part III of the Appendix.

The problem of optimization is quite complicated, of course, not just by virtue of the stochastic relationships analyzed, but partly because the relevant financial-assets constraint for this problem (the equation of motion in nonhuman assets $\dot{A}(t)$) depends on the "completeness" of capital markets for lending and borrowing when length of life is formally recognized to be an uncertain variable. Completeness is meant here to reflect whether the market allows for transactions in actuarial notes or annuities, in addition to transactions in regular saving notes which, in turn, depends on whether insurance or annuities companies exist in the market. Following Yaari (1965), we have analyzed two versions of the model which differ in this one assumption. In the first version we have assumed that no insurance (annuities) is available, in which case net accumulated assets in each period A(t) must be restricted to be non-negative to avoid the possibility that a person can die with a negative net worth. In the second version we allow for the existence of perfect (actuarially fair) insurance markets so that the individual is allowed to both buy or sell actuarial notes (annuities) in an amount equal to his accumulated savings or his discounted expected future savings. While the different versions yield somewhat different optimal consumption and investment paths, and a somewhat different measure of "value of life-saving," they share the same set of qualitative comparative statics predictions concerning the effects of changes in the exogenous variables of the model on the optimal demand for self-protection and life expectancy, and on the value of life saving as privately conceived.

IIIB.a.   The Demand for Life Expectancy and the Value of Life-Saving

Similarly to the analysis in Section IIIA, the life-time optimization analysis yields a set of simultaneous demand functions for both quality and quantity of life. Again, quality of life is reflected by the path of the consumption good $Z^*(t)$ and healthy time $h^*(\mu(t))$, and quantity is now reflected by the magnitude of life expectancy $T^*(t)$.

Desired life expectancy is not determined directly in this analysis, however, but as a derivative of the optimal path of health $\{\mu^*(t)\}$ which, in turn, is dictated by the path of optimal expenditure on self (life and health)-protection, $\{I^*(t)\}$. An optimal solution for $\{I^*(t)\}$ determines life expectancy since the latter is defined by the integral function $T^*(t) \equiv \int_t^D \exp\left(-\int_t^u \mu(s)ds\right) \cdot \mu(u) \cdot u\,du$, where $\exp\left(-\int_t^u \mu(s)ds\right)\mu(u)$ is the unconditional probability that a person of age t will die at age u. The optimization analysis thus produces a set of closely dependent demand functions for health investment, $I^*(t)$, health, $\mu^*(t)$, and life expectancy, $T^*(t)$, and identifies their major theoretical determinants as the model's set of basic parameters.

A distinct "demand function" of interest in this analysis is the value of a marginal reduction in the conditional probability of mortality or the shadow price of mortality risk as specified in Equations (2.9) or (2.9a) in the Appendix. This variable denotes the "value of life-saving," as originally defined by Schelling (1968) and Mishan (1971). It generalizes both the concept of "value of self-protection" implicit in Ehrlich and Becker's (1972) paper (which is the inverse of the marginal product of self-protection as defined by $p'(r)$ in Equation (28) of that paper) and the comparable measure of value of life-saving introduced by Brian Conley. The generalization concerns three distinct analytical aspects: (a) Our measure of value of life is derived from a continuous time framework of optimization that recognizes the correspondence between the demand for self-protection and value of life functions; (b) It is related directly to the "optimal value function" $J(t)/J_A(t)$, which is the monetary equivalent of the expected utility of the *remaining* life span, rather than the value of the utility derived from living with certainty (a common deficiency of value of life-saving measures derived through one-period optimization frameworks, first recognized by Gary Fromm); (c) It incorporates in the conventional value of life-saving measure the value of a reduction in the probability of morbidity, which is the additional earning and consumption benefits achieved from a greater amount of healthy time (e.g., lower physical or mental disability caused by a chronic health condition). Value-of-life measures typically have focused exclusively on the value of a higher survival probability and often ignored the value of improved quality-of-life which results from a marginal reduction in the highly correlated risk of morbidity.

IIIB.b. Behavioral Implications

The set of behavioral implications of the present model are by-and-large the same as those developed in section IIIA.c. for the key demand relationships of longevity (and health), consumption, and the marginal value of life, and therefore would not be elaborated upon. Again, we find that both life expectancy and generally (but not always) also the value of life-saving function are increasing functions of initial wealth $A(t)$, education or innate ability E, market wages, effort-saving technological innovations, and the rate of interest, and decreasing functions of the price of health care services and the rate of time preference. Again, value of life and optimal investment in health-protection can be expected to first rise and ultimately fall over the life-cycle. The existence of markets for annuities, furthermore, unambiguously raises individuals' welfare, although it has an ambiguous effect on the magnitude of the value of life-saving per se, as indicated by Equation (2.9a) in the Appendix. The reason is that while the higher return on actuarial notes increases potential wealth, a marginal reduction in the probability of mortality reduces the compensating risk premium to be paid annuity holders and thus causes a capital loss for those with positive annuity assets.

IIIB.c.   An Exact Measure of Value of Life-Saving

In a third version of our model under uncertainty, of which I shall forego any formal discussion due to its computational complexity, we set out to construct an exact measure of value of life-saving linking the latter directly to the basic human and nonhuman assets possessed by individuals. The derivation of such measure is done at the cost of invoking two simplifying assumptions: self-protection expenditures are taken to be predetermined, and the analysis ignores any functional dependence between the probabilities of mortality and morbidity and focuses exclusively on the former. At the same time, the life-cycle utility function is generalized to include a specific utility of bequest function, and both the utilities of own consumption and bequest are assumed to exhibit constant relative risk aversion, as in Richard (1977).

Under these simplifying assumptions, the modified value of life function $v(t)$ is shown to exceed, generally, a linear combination of one's net discounted labor income $L(t)$ (net of expenditures on self-protection) and accumulated nonhuman assets $A(t)$, depending upon one's bequest motive. In the extreme case where one's intensity of utility from bequest equals that of the utility from one's total (human and nonhuman) wealth, $v(t)$ is found to be exactly equal to *net labor income* $L(t)$. In all other cases involving a bequest motive and positive net savings, the value of life-saving must exceed $L(t)$—a result which confirms a similar prediction by Conley. And in the extreme case where one's bequest preference approaches zero, the value of life-saving may be expected to exceed the sum of both nonhuman and (net) human wealth $L(t) + A(t)$.[8] It is intriguing, of course, that value of life-saving will, *ceteris paribus*, fall as the strength of one's bequest preference increases: A high bequest preference simply reduces the difference in utility from being alive or dead so that the value of protecting one's life narrows just to the difference in wealth between the two states of nature—i.e., the loss of future net labor income (or human wealth). In contrast, where a bequest motive is negligible, as might be the case for heirless individuals, the loss of consumption opportunities will be a function of accumulated nonhuman assets as well, since the deceased foregoes any benefits from his (her) accumulated nonhuman assets upon death. Whether a stronger bequest motive leads unconditionally to a lower value of life-saving cannot be determined unambiguously, however, since such motive may also lead to a greater incentive to accumulate human as well as nonhuman assets.

IV   SOME ADDITIONAL APPLICATIONS AND CONCLUDING REMARKS

By establishing the "optimality" of finite life, and the existence of demand functions for quantity and quality of life, we have been able to investigate the role of personal characteristics and environmental or market conditions in determining both individuals' life expectancy and their private perceptions of the value of their life. The implied systematic dependency of actual length of life on variables such as inherited nonhuman wealth, endowed health, market earning power, or the cost of self-protection, in turn, can provide new insights into human behavior concerning intertemporal consumption and investment decisions, or the choice among activities that expose participants to varying degrees of risk to life and limb.

One obvious illustration concerns investment in education and job training. The literature on investment in these components of human capital has treated life expectancy, by and large, as being invariant to the basic determinants of the optimal investment paths. Our analysis shows, however, that a higher "endowment" of education-capital will cause an increase in the expected life span essentially because the increment in the value of human assets raises the incentive to maintain and protect these assets by protecting health and life. The extent of investment in schooling and job-training, in turn, will be encouraged, *ceteris paribus*, by an expectation of a longer productive life span. Since a higher endowment of nonhuman wealth is found in this analysis to lead to greater health and higher life expectancy, this leads to the inference that nonhuman and human wealth would be associated positively, not just because the former facilitates better access to capital markets, but also because it increases the demand for longevity. The observed positive association between education and life expectancy as seen in Table 3.2 therefore reflects the "causal" effect of the former on the latter, as well as vice versa. Also, the "return" to investment in education, as measured empirically by estimating earning-generating functions, must generally be ascribed to, and reflect the full "user cost" of, the complementary investment in health assets, rather than the investment in schooling and training alone.

Differences in life expectancy among individuals, furthermore, have a bearing on observed variations in the pattern of consumption of durable goods, as well as labor career choices. Persons with a smaller endowment of nonhuman wealth, and consequently a shorter productive life expectancy, will not only have an incentive to enter the labor market sooner than those who continue to invest in their formal schooling and training, but will also have an incentive to marry and reproduce at an earlier age than wealthier individuals, on the assumption that the utility one derives from having children is monotonically related to one's span of interacting with them over the life-cycle.[9]

Another illustration concerns individuals' participation in activities which involve exposure to risk of life and health. Our theoretical concepts of "marginal value of life" or "value of life-saving" represent, in essence, the magnitude of the financial *risk premium* required by individuals for exposing themselves to the risks of injury and death. It implies, therefore, that wealthier individuals and those with higher earning potentials will generally have a higher risk premium, and thus a higher reservation wage for participating in such risky activities. *Ceteris paribus*, one would expect that the composition of all-volunteer armies will be biased in the direction of people with less income or wealth as well as relatively low civilian market-earning opportunities in comparable but less risky endeavors.

This latter observation sheds some new light on the observed association between measures of relative poverty in the population and the frequency of crimes against persons (see Ehrlich 1973, 1977). Because of our predicted positive association between peoples' wealth and their "risk-premium" for exposure to life and health-threatening circumstances, those with lower income will be both more inclined to participate in, and less inclined to protect themselves from, criminal activities such as murder, aggravated assault, rape and mugging. Put differently, a lower value of life-saving or health-protection will contribute to both a higher incentive to commit violent crimes or self-protect against such crimes, which generally expose both offender and victim to bodily harm or the risk of fatal injury. This provides a more complete explanation for the fact that crimes against the person occur at a differentially high frequency in lower income areas, and typically involve people who are well known to each other, and who, therefore, come from the same income bracket.

Our analysis thus far is abstracted, by and large, from consideration of *organized* markets for life or limb: we have viewed investment in health primarily as *individual* endeavor. The emergence of organized markets for body organs and related means of *direct* life-extending activities such as open-heart surgery as well as heart transplants, generally implies the *flattening* of individual cost of investment schedules MC(I), since they introduce *constant* supply-prices (to individuals) for incremental additions to their stock of health or the probability of survival. The direct implications of these developments on the supply side of the market for life-saving would be to make differences in individuals' value of life-saving, or risk premiums for exposure to detrimental risks, less pronounced, while making systematic variations in their expected life spans more pronounced. Put differently, differences in the demand for life among individuals would result in greater variations in their optimal lengths of life and a lesser variation in the values they place on life-saving. This may explain, perhaps, why in more developed economies, especially in the course of the twentieth century, differences in life expectancies between males and females have become more *pronounced* than in earlier periods, assuming that all groups have been constrained by a similar supply schedule for investment in life and health protection.

NOTES

This chapter follows the presentation made by Isaac Ehrlich at the Vienna conference on applications of economic theory outside the traditional areas of economics, and is based on the joint paper cited in the references section by Ehrlich and Hiroyuki Chuma.

1. Although Grossman's (1972) model is a deterministic formulation in which the certain horizon is subject to choice, he has not imposed any terminal (or "transversality") conditions that can insure the consistency of the solutions for optimal health stock and the horizon, and permit a systematic treatment of the latter. Furthermore, unlike conventional human capital models, his analysis assumes that health investment is produced via a constant-returns-to-scale technology. However, such technology introduces, even in the context of the discreet time optimization framework he pursued, a type of "bang-bang," or indeterminancy problem in connection with the investment in health decision. This problem invalidates his formal analysis of the "demand for health" decision, and does not permit a systematic development of a demand for health or a demand for life function.

2. In terms of our model, maximum borrowing capacity in any given period, or the value of "human wealth," using Arrow and Kurz's (1970) terminology is given by $G(t) \leq \dfrac{w \cdot \Omega}{r}$, where r is a positive rate of discount.

3. The three technical conditions which are sufficient to assure a finite life are then. (a) $H_{min} > 0$, owing to the assumed exponential depreciation scheme; (b) $\dot{\delta}(t) \equiv \partial\delta(t)/\partial t > 0$; and (c) the finiteness of "human wealth," thus $G(t)$ in Footnote 2. We have termed all three as the "Man-is-no-god" hypothesis. (Mingh)

4. To simplify an already highly complex problem of optimization, education capital is taken to be an exogenous variable in this analysis, representing essentially a person's innate ability. A fuller analysis will consider both $H(t)$ and $E(t)$ to be jointly determined components of human capital.

5. Given the optimality condition for health investment $2\pi I(t) = g(t)$, the dynamic path of health investment is given by $\dot{I}(t) = \dfrac{1}{2\pi}\,\dot{g}(t)$, where $\dot{I}(t) \equiv \dfrac{dI(t)}{dt}$. The dynamic path of $g(t)$, the shadow price of health capital, in turn, is given by

$$\dot{g}(t) = [\delta(t) + r]g(t) - \left[\frac{U_h(t)}{\lambda_A(0)}\,e^{(r-\rho)} + w\right]\phi'(H(t)), \text{ where}$$
$$U_h(t) \equiv \frac{\partial U(t)}{\partial h(t)}, \; \lambda_A(0) \equiv \frac{\partial\lambda(0)}{\partial A}, \text{ and } \phi'(H(t)) \equiv \frac{d\phi(H(t))}{dH}$$

6. By the Poisson process, the probability of survival between any period i and a later period j is expressed by the exponential distribution law $p(i,j) =$

$\exp\left(-\int_i^j \mu(t)dt\right)$.

7. The concavity of this function, $\phi(\mu(t))$, as well as that of the utility function $U(Z(t), \phi(\mu(t)))$ are required to assure the sufficient conditions for an interior optimum solution in $Z(t)$ and $I(t)$.

8. This is necessarily the case if the magnitude of the relative risk aversion parameter is greater than or equal to $1/2$.

9. I owe this point to Roger E. Meiners.

APPENDIX

I TABLE 3.3: KEY VARIABLE NAMES

T, D	The actual, or maximal length of life
H(t)	The stock of health at chronological time t
H_{min}	The stock of health at the time of death
h(t)	Amount or fraction of healthy time in t; $h(t) = \phi(H(t))$
Z(t)	Flow of consumption activity
I(t)	Flow of gross investment in H(t) or $(1 - \mu(t))$
δ(t)	The rate of depreciation of H(t)
M(t)	Flow of medical service inputs in the production of I(t)
m(t)	Personal time inputs in the production of I(t)
X(t)	Flow of a composite market good in the production of Z(t)
c(t)	Personal time inputs in the production of Z(t)
E(t)	Stock of education capital
w(t)	Market wage rate; $w(t) = wE(t)$
ℓ(t)	Labor time or time at work
s(t)	Sick time in t
Ω	Total time available in t
P(t)	Unit price of medical care services, M(t)
K(t)	Unit price of all other market goods, X(t)
π(t)	(Shadow) one-unit price of I(t)
ψ(t)	(shadow) unit price of Z(t)
A(t)	Accumulated stock of nonhuman assets
β	A shift parameter representing effort-saving technological changes
r	Market rate of interest
ρ	Rate of time preference for early consumption
(1/α)	The degree of homogeneity of the production function of I(t)
B(t), V(t)	Total bequest and its utility, respectively
U(t)	Utility of "quality of life"
g(t), v(t), ν(t)	Alternative definitions of "value of life"
μ(t)	The conditional probability of mortality in t given survival to t

II THE MODEL UNDER CERTAINTY

The person's objective is to maximize the lifetime utility function

(1.1)
$$\int_0^T e^{-\rho t} U(Z(t), h(t))dt,$$

with U(t) and h(t) = ϕ(H(t)) assumed to be increasing, strictly concave and continuously differentiable in their arguments. This equation is maximized subject to equations of motion in health (H(t)) and nonhuman assets (A(t)) as follows:

(1.2) $\mathring{H}$(t) $\equiv$ I(t) − δ(t)H(t), and
(1.3) $\mathring{A}$(t) = rA(t) + w(t)ℓ(t) − P(t)M(t) − K(t)X(t)

with $\mathring{H}$(t) and $\mathring{A}$(t) denoting time derivatives, and with $\mathring{\delta}$(t) $\equiv$ $\partial\delta$(t)/∂t > 0, all t. The relevant time constraint is given by

(1.4) Ω = ℓ(t) + s(t) + m(t) + c(t), Ω − s(t) $\equiv$ h(t).

For convenience, the production function for health I(t) = I(M(t),m(t)) is assumed to be homogeneous of degree $(1/\alpha)$ < 1, and the production function of the general consumption commodity Z(t) = Z(X(t),c(t)) is assumed to be homogeneous of degree 1. The corresponding cost-of-health investment, and the cost of consumption functions are thus given by

(1.5)   C(I(t)) = $\pi \cdot$I(t)$^\alpha$, α > 1, and
(1.6)   C(Z(t)) = $\psi \cdot$Z(t), with ψ assumed to be invariant to time.

Substituting equations (1.4), (1.5) and (1.6) directly in equation (1.3) the latter becomes

(1.3a) $\mathring{A}$(t) = rA(t) + wϕ(H(t)) − πI(t)$^\alpha$ − ψZ(t)

Finally, the boundary constraints for the terminal stocks of health and wealth (nonhuman assets), if T is finite, are given by

(1.7)   H(t) > H$_{min}$ for all t other than T, and
               H(T) = H$_{min}$, with H(0) > H$_{min}$ > 0.
(1.8)   A(T) = 0,
               with A(0) $\geq$ 0,

and with no bequest motive being recognized formally.

   The objective of maximizing Equation (1.1) subject to the constraints given in Equations (1.2), (1.3a), (1.4), (1.7) and (1.8) can be pursued analytically by applying the maximum principle of optimal control theory. The decision rule becomes that of maximizing the Hamiltonian function:

(1.9) $v(t) \equiv e^{-\rho t} U(Z(t), \phi H(t)) + \lambda_H(t)[I(t) - \delta(t)H(t)]$
             $+ \lambda_A(t)[rA(t) + w\phi(H(t)) - \pi I(t)^\alpha - \psi Z(t)],$

if $I^*(t) > 0$. The transversality condition for an interior optimum in T is

(1.10) $e^{-\rho t} U(Z(t), \phi(H(T)) + \lambda_H(T)\dot{H}(T) + \lambda_A(T)\dot{A}(T) = 0,$

with $\lambda_H(T) = \lambda_H \geq 0$ ($H(T) = H_{min}$), and

$$\lambda_A(T) = \lambda_A > 0 \; (A(T) = 0).$$

In Equations (1.9) and (1.10) the co-state variables $\lambda_H(t)$ and $\lambda_A(t)$ define the marginal *utilities* of health capital H(t) and nonhuman capital A(t), respectively. Their ratio $g(t) \equiv \lambda_H(t)/\lambda_A(t)$ defines the marginal *value* of health capital (life).

III THE MODEL UNDER UNCERTAINTY

The person's objective here is to maximize the lifetime expected utlity function at time t

(2.1) $J(A(t), t; \alpha) = \underset{Z,I}{\text{Max}} \; E \left\{ \int_t^{\tilde{D}} e^{-\rho(s-t)} U(Z(s), h(\mu(s)))ds \right\},$

where $t \leq \tilde{D} \leq D$, α denotes a vector of exogenous parameters and E denotes an expected utility operator. Desired bequest is zero in this formulation. Equation (2.1) is maximized subject to the following constraints:

(2.2) $\mu(t) = \bar{\mu}(t) - I(t),$

with $I(t) = I(m(t), M(t))$ still assumed to be homogeneous of degree 1/2; $\mu(t) > 0$; and both $\bar{\mu}(t)$ and $d\bar{\mu}(t)/dt \equiv \overset{\circ}{\bar{\mu}}(t) > 0$;

(2.3) $h(t) = \phi(\mu(t))$, with $\phi'(\cdot) < 0$ and $\phi''(\cdot) < 0$.

The financial-assets constraint depends on whether there exist transactions in acturial notes (annuities). Where no such transactions are allowed, the wealth constraint can be specified as

(2.4) $\dot{A}(t) = rA(t) + w\phi(\mu(t)) - \pi I^2(t) - \psi Z(t),$

where A(t) is known with certainty given survival to t. A(t) is restricted, however, to be strictly positive at all times (cf. Yaari, 1965). If there are perfect insurance markets which allow trade in annuities at actuarially fair risk premiums, the financial constraint becomes

(2.4a) $\dot{A}(t) = [r + \mu(t)]A(t) + w\phi(\mu(t)) - \pi I^2(t) - \psi Z(t),$

where A(t) now represents the current value of all past savings, accumulated at the relevant rate of return on actuarial notes. The time constraint and the production function of Z(t) are the same as those given in Equations (1.4) and (1.6). The boundary conditions are

(2.5) $J(A(D), D; \alpha) = 0,$ and
(2.6) $A(D) \geq 0;$ with $A(0) \geq 0.$

Following the stochastic dynamic programming approach in Merton (1971), the optimal solution for Z*(t) and I*(t) must satisfy the Bellman-Jacobi partial differential equation obeyed by the optimal value function J(t). If no insurance markets are available, the latter is given by

(2.7) $-J_t = - (\rho + \mu^*) J + U(Z^*, \phi(\mu^*))$
$$+ J_A [rA + w\phi(\mu^*) - \pi I^{*2} - \psi Z^*],$$

where $J_t \equiv \partial J(A(t), t; \alpha)/\partial t$, and Z* and I* satisfy the optimality conditions

(2.8) $U_Z(Z^*, \phi(\mu^*)) = \psi J_A,$
(2.9) $2\pi I^* = J/J_A + [w + (1/J_A)U_h(Z^*, \phi(\mu^*))][-\phi'(\mu^*)] \equiv v^*$

If perfect markets for insurance are available, Equation (2.7) becomes

(2.7a) $-J_t = - (\rho + \mu^*)J + U(Z^*, \phi(\mu^*))$
$$+ J_A[(r + \mu^*)A + w\phi(\mu^*) - \pi I^{*2} - \psi Z^*],$$

where A(t) has the interpretation given to it in Equation (2.4a). Equation (2.9) becomes

(2.9a) $2 \pi I^* = [J/J_A] + [w + (1/J_A)U_h(Z^*, \phi(\mu^*))][- \phi'(\mu^*)] \equiv v_1^*$

where J, J_a and A have the interpretation given them in Equation (2.7a). The terms v* and v_1^* in equations (2.9) and (2.9a) represent the value of life-saving.

REFERENCES

Arrow, Kenneth J. and M. Kurz, *Public Investment, the Rate of Return and Optimal Fiscal Policy*, Johns Hopkins Press (1970).

Becker, Gary S., "A Theory of the Allocation of Time," *Economic Journal* 75 (1965) pp. 493–517.

Conley, Brian C., "The Value of Life in the Demand for Safety," *American Economic Review* 66 (1976) pp. 45–55.

Ehrlich, Isaac, "Participation in Illegitimate Activities: A Theoretical and Empirical Investigation," *Journal of Political Economy* 81(3), (1973) pp. 521–65.

————, "Capital Punishment and Deterrence: Some Further Thoughts and Additional Evidence," *Journal of Political Economy* 85 (4), (1977) pp. 741–88.

Ehrlich, Isaac, and Gary S. Becker, "Market Insurance, Self-Insurance and Self-Protection," *Journal of Political Economy* 80 (4), (1972) pp. 623–48.

———— and Hiroyuki Chuma, "The Demand for Longevity and the Value of Life: An Economic Analysis," Draft manuscript (March, 1986).

Fisher, Irving, *The Theory of Interest*, London: Macmillan (1930).

Fromm, Gary, Comment on T. C. Schelling's "The Life You Save May Be Your Own," in *Problems in Public Expenditure Analysis*, S. B. Chase, editor, Washington, D.C.: The Brookings Institution (1968) pp. 166–76.

Grossman, Michael, *The Demand for Health: A Theoretical and Empirical Investigation*, New York, National Bureau of Economic Research (1973).

Kitagawa, E., and P. Hauser, *Differential Mortality in the United States*, Cambridge: Harvard University Press (1973).

Merton, Robert C., "Optimum Consumption and Portfolio Rules in a Continuous-Time Model," *Journal of Economic Theory* 3 (1971) pp. 373–413.

Mishan, E. J., "Evaluation of Life and Limb: A Theoretical Approach," *Journal of Political Economy* 79 (1971) pp. 687–705.

Richard, Scott F., "Optimal Consumption, Portfolio, and Life-Insurance Rules for Uncertain Lived Individual in a Continuous Time Model," *Journal of Financial Economics* 2 (1975) pp. 187–203.

Schelling, T. C., "The Life You Save May Be Your Own," in *Problems in Public Expenditure Analysis*, S. B. Chase, editor, Washington, D.C.: Brookings Institution (1968).

Yaari, M. E., "Uncertain Lifetime, Life Insurance and the Theory of the Consumer," *Review of Economics Studies* (1965) pp. 137–150.

Part IV

THE ECONOMICS OF SCIENTIFIC DISCOVERY

MICHAEL T. GHISELIN

In an earlier chapter of this book, I explored the thesis that biology and economics are subdivisions of a single branch of knowledge called "general economy." This suggests that we may treat all aspects of human behavior from a bioeconomic point of view. Sociology would then be viewed as analogous to evolutionary statics, and history to paleontology and kindred disciplines. We could then envision intellectual history within a broad evolutionary perspective, and a new philosophy of science might emerge. This would have many advantages, not the least of which would be that we could quantify the study of scientific investigation.[1] I intend to explore such possibilities in later works. The present essay merely illustrates the approach, by showing how economic thinking can be used to explain some aspects of the behavior of scientists that have seemed problematic to our predecessors. It should be remarked that economic studies of science do exist, but thus far they have all but ignored the non-pecuniary aspects. An important exception is a book by Tullock (1966). This neglect is symptomatic of the narrow manner in which economics has traditionally been conceived.

Historians and philosophers are now deeply divided over the issue of what is called "rationality" in science (see Newton-Smith, 1978). At the risk of gross oversimplification, let us divide those who have discussed such matters into "rationalists" and "irrationalists." Rationalists claim that science is, or at least ought to be, rational. Good examples are Popper (1962) and Lakatos (1978), the former a philosopher, the latter originally a mathematician. They generally advocate the sort of theory of scientific method that has been developed by modern logicians. Among irrationalists, we have Kuhn (1970), who claims that science is not, in point of fact, rational, and Feyerabend (1975), who argues that it should not be rational. Kuhn at least has been profoundly influenced by the work of sociologists, who have documented a great

271

deal of what seems to be irrational behavior on the part of scientists. Much is attributed to social forces and group-thinking. In the present volume, Radnitzky has traced much of this irrationalism to the later works of Wittgenstein. Perhaps the failure of a rationalist research program led to an overreaction.

Rationalists and irrationalists alike have a basically non-evolutionary outlook. This in spite of the fact that Popperian theory has fostered evolutionary epistomology. According to this view, there is blind variation and selective retention (Campbell, 1974). As Radnitzky (1980, 1982) points out, Popper has rejected the "foundationalist quest for certainty." That this amounts to rediscovery of pragmatism is clear from the title of a book by Dewey (1929). Both Popper and Dewey of course went a long way in the direction of an evolutionary approach, and both were impressed by Darwin's accomplishment. But just as Dewey's work contains unfortunate vestiges of Hegelianism, so Popper never fully transcended the influence of the Vienna Circle. Both had to treat creativity as a peripheral issue rather than a central one. Just as many theorists have viewed natural selection as a merely negative culling out of the unfit, refutationists tend to overemphasize the elimination of error. Fitness means taking advantage of "business opportunities," not just avoiding competition. Popper's frequent, and misguided, attacks on the theory of natural selection are symptomatic. It has been left to some of his admirers, including myself, to show how beautifully natural selection exemplifies what is true in Popper's epistemology (Ghiselin, 1969).

To a biologist it seems inevitable that, just as species evolve from other species, theories have to come from one source or another. The Kuhnian approach is antithetical to this view. It treats the history of science as if it were a succession of special creations, with paradigms merely replacing one another in temporal sequence—much as the geological record was envisioned by Baron Cuvier. My work on Darwin (Ghiselin, 1969), like that of Cohen (1980) on Newton, treats scientific change as more evolutionary than revolutionary. My version of paradigm theory (Ghiselin, 1971) is individualistic, rather than group-oriented. Instead of the paradigm being the possession of a school or group of scientists, I have treated it as the property of individual scientists. In other words, it is a private, rather than a social, affair. This view is not to be confused with that of those who like to make science "personal" in the sense of "subjective," but rather takes a neurophysiologically realistic view of what kind of entity can reason. For both classical economics and modern evolutionary biology, the fundamental mechanism is individualistic competition. Supraorganismal entities, including those which qualify as individuals, possess nothing analogous to a nervous system. And species possess nothing that can render them adapted. Any "invisible hand" that optimizes a free-enterprise economy has to be the fortuitous by-product of self-interest. It is not to be denied, of course, that scientific communities, firms, and species play an important role in the world (Ghiselin, 1974a). Indeed, it has long seemed likely to me that one important role of science and art is the amelioration of interpersonal relationships (Ghiselin, 1974b). The point is only that biological and economic theory rule out "organicist" views.

The dispute over rationalism presupposes a philosophical, rather than an economic or biological, concept of appropriate conduct. Formal logic is taken as the ideal for right thinking. From this point of view, "rational" is equated with "ratiocinative,"with judgment that is explicit, conscious, and deliberate. "Economic" rationalism is not the same thing, but is more akin to what biologists have in mind when they speak of adaptation. It makes the weaker claim that economic behavior tends to be reasonable, irrespective of what makes it so. We must not confuse the non-rational with the irrational. From the point of view of evolutionary theory, the mind is the slave of the gonads. We repeat what worked for achieving our ancestors' reproductive success, and rarely give it much thought. Economically this is a good thing: thinking is costly, and we do it where it gives a good return. In both biology and economics, optimality theory has been adversely affected by teleology. We need to stop thinking about what things are "for" and consider instead what has happened (Ghiselin, 1974b). This point is not adequately appreciated, even by many who consider themselves evolutionary biologists. The theory of evolution predicts, and the data of biology bear it out, that there will be instances of adaptation, maladaptation, and adaptive neutrality. Not the least reason for this is that populations lack the kind of foresight that sometimes allows human beings to avoid getting into suboptimal conditions. To deal effectively with its materials, general economy has to be an "historical science" in a sense radically different from one frequently used in philosophy. By an historical science I mean something like a combination of physics and astronomy. According to the new evolutionary philosophy there is no fundamental difference between the sciences that deal with living and non-living objects. Nomothetic physics and nomothetic biology alike establish laws of nature about classes of individuals, such as classes of planets, and classes of species. Laws of nature make no reference to the individuals that instantiate those classes. A combination of laws and history suffices to explain and predict the properties of the objects under study, without having to presuppose that anything has to be optimal.

If we view the behavior of scientists as rational in the economic sense, we part company with the expectations of some theorists. Like entrepreneurs, scientists optimize one thing or another. But we should not expect them to follow the inclinations of those philosophers who believe that they ought to be maximizing certitude. Scientists are explorers, not prophets. They maximize discovery, not Truth. But this fact in no way implies that the truth is somehow unknowable, and that theories are "mere instrumentalities." Scientists in the laboratory do not behave like Pyrrhonists or Social Relativists. They behave as if they are in the process of finding out what is true and have no pretensions of foreseeing the ultimate results of their investigations.

Scientists use discoveries to make more discoveries. For this reason they are both users and producers of capital goods. As such, they enjoy a proprietary interest in, and a partial monopoly of, their discoveries. A scientist can retain control over his discovery by keeping it a "trade secret." However, he is induced to make that discovery public by a reward system that gives him credit as the discoverer. This motivates him to make as many discoveries as he can, and to get as much credit (whether deserved or not), for doing so as fast as possible. Thereby a system of exchange with reciprocity arises. Discoveries, time, and other resources interact as elements of an economy with imperfect competition and much incertitude. From such simple considerations, much that has seemed problematic can be seen as perfectly reasonable. If this be so, then the empirical data upon which the irrationalists have argued for their thesis must be dismissed as irrelevant.

For example, it has been suggested that a paradigm shift does not occur until long after the antecedent paradigm has broken down. More generally, scientists may fail to falsify an hyopothesis in the face of anomaly or evidence that the hypothesis is false, contrary to Popperian ideals. When we realize that a paradigm or an hypothesis is a valuable resource, one that is hard to obtain, and one in which there are proprietary interests, it stands to reason that a scientist will not abandon it unless he hopes to gain a great deal in the transaction. Adopting a new paradigm may involve prohibitively expensive costs of retooling—one may have to learn new skills and obtain new equipment. One's intellect may be an antiquated plant that cannot profitably be converted—except perhaps by becoming an administrator. On the other hand, and again contrary to expectation, the ability to change is not simply a function of age. Older scientists who stand to gain do change their minds, and it is not simply a matter of persons with vested interests dying off.

Conversely, many scientists adopt a paradigm or an hypothesis without first undertaking a serious effort at testing it. Again, this seems to run counter to refutationist or Popperian ideals. However, testing is costly in terms of time and effort. The possible return on getting into the market from the start is often felt to outweigh the possible loss that results from what turns out to have been a bad investment. It may be that scientists change their views on the basis of the kind of evidence they accept personally, but which the scientific community in general rejects. A quick and unpublishable feasability study is hardly unreasonable from an economic point of view, even if it does not get one tenure. One would expect those scientists who have much to gain by a shift to be more inclined to do so than others—for example, the discoverer, who enjoys credit for founding the paradigm as well as for developing it. There may also be an advantage to operating as a "contrarian." Sometimes backing what everybody else considers the "wrong" hypothesis pays off handsomely, though often only after some time. A developing economy may be populated by a succession of entrepreneurs with different techniques. Thus, in the mining industry we have prospectors, claim-jumpers, and heavily-capitalized industrialists. Much the same occurs in science, with its creative thinkers, priority disputants, and grantsmen. Different considerations lead each of these types to embrace a paradigm under rather different circumstances. An original thinker may not possess the resources necessary for following up a discovery, or may be better off making another discovery instead. Scientists often speak of "skimming the cream" off a new development, and the economic metaphor here is very apt.

Another pseudo-problem has to do with the shady marketing practices of many scientists. Feyerabend (1975) provides some good examples from Galileo, but comes to conclusions that would please only an irrationalist philosopher. Any effort allocated to marketing has to be subtracted from that allocated to research. It makes perfectly good economic sense, therefore, when scientists try to get their views accepted with minimal effort. Even a very able scientist might well be expected to cut corners in marketing if it meant greater output in the laboratory. Furthermore, and this is especially the case with such figures as Galileo, the conditions under which one must market a commodity are not always determined by anybody's ideals.

Competition can be intense for a place in what are considered the "best" journals—those everybody cites and occasionally even reads.

Therefore great effort is devoted to getting published in the "right" place, whether or not this is justified by the content of the paper. A common practice, especially among the less creative intellects, is to multiply titles. This leads to a curious form of product homogeneity, one which has obvious disadvantages for the consumer, but may get the producer such rewards as free trips to meetings.

I take a rather different position on authority than some philosophers do. In my experience scientists denounce authority when it is against them, but appeal to it whenever doing so advances their own interests. Nonetheless it must be agreed that the only legitimate authority in science is reason and fact. Science could not exist otherwise, and it happens that this objectivity constitutes much of its humanistic and cultural appeal. Science has rightly come to symbolize the ideals of justice and personal liberty. The notion that science is "public" is reasonable in the sense that intersubjective judgment is requisite, but it is often perverted into the notion that subjective judgment should be exercised by a committee of experts. We are often told that scientific work should be evaluated by the scientific community. To the contrary, scientific judgment is, and should be, exercised by individual scientists, who bear full responsibility for the judgments they pass. A scientist who comes up with the correct answer is rewarded by virtue of making further contributions, or at least for having made them possible. When scientists reward their predecessors, it is always for having been, in some objective sense, "right." Nobody is ever praised for having pleased the authorities of his day. Quite the opposite is the case. People like Galileo and Mendel are worshiped as heroes—for the best of reasons. Authority, however, does play an important role in science: it is a cheap substitute for the real thing. An individual scientist does not have sufficient resources to check all the objective evidence for himself. Contrary to what such authors as Popper have asserted, it is indeed possible to do scientific reseach in complete isolation from society. The presence of colleagues may create pressures for objectivity, but only to counterbalance pressures against it.

Scientists are deeply concerned with priority of discovery, although many pretend to be indifferent to it. Priority is one basis for the reward system. Publication, or some equivalent of it, determines priority. It is not, ordinarily at least, a question of when a discovery was made. (This has to be qualified by certain conventions about publishing prematurely and the like.) The reason is that discovery becomes a useful resource only when it has been made public. A trade secret would give a monopoly restrictive of general progress.

An economic outlook also provides a useful criterion whereby we can decide when a discovery actually was made. The historical literature frequently discusses anticipations and independent discoveries, many of which I have found are more apparent than real (Ghiselin, 1976). A philosophical criterion might have it that a discovery has been made once an "idea" has occurred to somebody. A social science criterion would perhaps favor the recognition of the discovery by the scientific community (Brannigan, 1981). The issue of who made a discovery and when becomes crucial in certain marginal cases in which some author appears to discuss, say, natural selection, and this is used as a basis for questioning another's originality or integrity. With respect to Darwin and natural selection, it has been possible to show that alleged precursors did not understand the problems they were supposedly discussing (Ghiselin, 1969). It is one thing to devote a paragraph to some theoretical musing, but something else to drop what one was doing and devote years of research to elaborating upon it. In the latter case we have good evidence that the discoverer knew that he had discovered something important.

The place of scholarly communication is problematic here. Obviously a scientist should follow up his discovery at the writing desk. But is he to be denied credit if his contemporaries ignore his work? It is generally assumed that covering the literature is part of one's responsibilities as a scholar. Were this not the convention, anybody could get credit for merely repeating work that had already been done. It is notorious that, in many fields, work not published in English and within the previous few years is treated as if it were not part of the literature. Most of the excuses I have heard for this are transparently self-seeking, and I suspect that future generations will discount a lot of work. On the other hand, the cost of learning and using languages can be high, and one experiences diminishing returns when searching the literature. Such defective communication practices as writing badly and publishing in an obscure place can also be a way of passing costs on to the consumer.

The shady dealings of scientists are depressing, and I shall defer making Diogenes look like Pollyanna until later publications. A few remarks here about the cost-benefit analysis of cheating will suffice. Discussions of bogus data, plagiarism, grant-sabotaging, and the like, are generally moralistic rather than explanatory. Worse still, by labeling the rationalist ideal an ideology, they may be perverted into attacks upon reason itself (Broad and Wade, 1982). It is as if the pervasiveness of sin detracted from the effects of good works. I have no doubt that such virtues as a sense of honor and social responsbility, and likewise the more crass social pressures, help militate against unethical practices. However, more is involved than that. Sociologists (see Ravetz, 1971 for review) have pointed out that scientists rely upon one another's work when doing research. In economic terms, bad science is a bad resource. Therefore they descend upon cheaters in wrath and fury. Be this as it may, it would seem that the economic incentives for cheating are rather poor relative to the disincentives (see Tullock, 1966:151). The very best contributions are well-known. Hence they cannot readily be plagiarized. (Consider how far an economist would get, lifting whole chapters verbatim from *The Wealth of Nations*.) If one is a competent scientist one can always do a certain amount of low-grade hackwork without having to cheat. Therefore plagiarists will generally be submarginal scientists plagiarizing marginal work. There are of course pathological cases and others that do not fit this generalization. The kind of plagiarism one can get away with—stealing ideas from grant-proposals and unpublished manuscripts—is pervasive. One can substantiate this from the amount of effort invested by scientists in keeping the more valuable work a secret. For example, grants are awarded largely to fund research that has already been done, and used for other purposes. There are other reasons for this practice of course, not the least of which is to evade bias against originality.

One could say a great deal about how the academic and pecuniary economies interact with the scholary one. The lack of understanding here is suggested by the fact that so many of us fail to distinguish between the scholarly and the academic lives. Here I will only try to provide a simple rationale for what goes on. Scientists, academics and politicians seek to maximize rather different utilities. Scientists want to maximize discovery. Academics want to maximize such things as the budgets of departments and universities. Politicians want to stay in office. Taking these groups in reverse order, we would expect politicians to try to get the sort of research done that the public wants done. In general, this research will focus upon the putative "needs" of society. Academics will attempt to induce scientists to do the kind of research that costs a lot of money and requires the services of many administrators, graduate students, post-doctoral fellows, technicians, mice, etc., with the proviso, of course, that it can be funded. This research will satisfy the needs of those who like to run things, or at least like to get paid to run things. Scientists will allocate resources to projects that they hope will give them maximal return in terms of discoveries. If these interests coincide, all well and good. It is hard to say how often they do coincide. There is no particular connection between desired results and the opportunities. In science, demand does not create supply, or at least the supply is very inelastic. A failure to attend to this consideration can lead to a host of second-rate scientists pretending to do cancer research, and a lot of academics trying to believe that this is a good thing. The situation here is not as bad as one might think. Scientists, especially academic ones, are in a very good position to misappropriate funds, or time—as in neglecting their teaching in order to do research or get consultants' fees. Therefore they can siphon off some of the resources allocated externally for bad science, and apply them to good science. One way for politicians to get bad science done is to provide some resources for good science as a kind of institutionalized bribe. This arrangement, while it may have some advantages given the political realities, involves some obvious diseconomies. A wealthy amateur or a MacArthur Fellow can allocate funds so as to maximize discovery, but not everybody is so fortunate.

It does not seem likely that the aforementioned distortion will soon be ameliorated. It is much cheaper in terms of time and effort to trick the public into believing that a piece of research will have the short-term economic benefits that the public desires, than to persuade it to optimize scientific progress in general. It is better to pretend that scientists really are prophets. The public is ill-disposed to expend the effort needed to come to grips with such issues. The trouble is all the more difficult because treating scientists as prophets is acceptable pedagogy at all levels of instruction short of the doctoral orals. Students react more favorably to answers than they do to questions, and teachers supply what the market demands.

We often misrepresent the scientific enterprise to the layman in order better to get on with our research. To do so is considered no more reprehensible than is lying to children "for their own good." Yet we often misrepresent it to one another, and to ourselves. We have a standard model of how scientists are supposed to behave, and pretend to live up to it. Everybody tries to make his work conform to the contemporary idea of what is methodologically and philosophically correct. In *The Origin of Species*, Darwin tried to give an impression that he used an "inductive" approach. His private notebooks, correspondence, and other documents make him look much more like an advocate of the hypothetico-deductive approach (Ghiselin, 1969). Nowdays it is fashionable to be a Popperian, and everybody claims to be trying to refute his own hypotheses, and that those of the opposition are untestable. A superficial grasp of the Popperian jargon is cheap to come by and it may get the hoped-for results. It is notorious that scientists will have one philosophy for the laboratory, another for the writing desk. But there is nothing unusual about that. As with the businessman who has one morality for Sunday morning, another for the rest of the week, two kinds of enterprise are being optimized. Making a discovery is one thing, getting it accepted another.

So too with the history of science. Those who disagree with the dominant paradigm are very apt to appeal to Kuhn or Lakatos. One does not have to read much history of science before noticing that its pages abound in self-justification. Professional historians of course are immune to such problems—or rather may think their readers naive enough to believe that. But why should this be an exception to the general rule? The pursuit of knowledge "for its own sake" is nonsense at best and hypocrisy at worst. Science is fun; it may make one famous, or even rich, but we have reasons for engaging in it whether we know what these are or not. The question is not, whether we act out of self-interest, but how we act out of self-interest. In some cases self-interest leads to lapses of scholarly objectivity, in other cases it has the opposite effect. Contemporary historiography tends to emphasize the former. It stresses the influence of society. Were it only a matter of short-term interests, scientists would indulge in far more wishful thinking and conformity to external pressures than they do. There is a limit here. Our decisions as to what is true or false do not just affect our relationships with those now around us. They also determine whether or not we will make discoveries. We do not know what the future may hold, but we do know that opinion is ephemeral. Seeing the world as it really is puts one in an optimal position for making the discoveries yet to come. Whatever we must concede to irrationalism, reason exists because it has been useful in the struggle for existence. We do not abandon it without paying a heavy price.

NOTES

The author thanks the John D. and Catherine T. MacArthur Foundation for support, and Jack Hirshleifer and Gordon Tullock for advice on the manuscript.

1. I thank Jagdish Hattiangadi for drawing my attention to this point.

REFERENCES

Brannigan, Augustine, *The Social Basis of Scientific Discoveries*, Cambridge: Cambridge University Press, xi (1981).

Broad, William, and Nicholas Wade, *Betrayers of the Truth*, New York: Simon and Schuster (1982).

Campbell, Donald T., "Evolutionary Epistemology," in Paul Arthur Schlipp, ed., *The Philosophy of Karl Popper*, La Salle, Illinois: Open Court, 1 (1974) pp. 412–463.

Cohen, I. Bernard, *The Newtonian Revolution: with Illustrations of the Transformation of Scientific Ideas*, Cambridge: Cambridge University Press, xv (1980).

Dewey, John, *The Quest for Certainty: A Study of the Relation of Knowledge and Action*, New York: Minton, Balch (1929).

Feyerabend, Paul, *Against Method: Outline of an Anarchistic Theory of Knowledge* (1975).

Ghiselin, Michael T., *The Triumph of the Darwinian Method*, Berkeley: University of California Press, x (1969) [2nd ed. University of California Press, 1984].

————, "The Individual in the Darwinian Revolution," *New Literary History*, 3 (1971) pp. 112–134.

————, "A Radical Solution to the Species Problem," *Systematic Zoology*, 23 (1974a) pp. 536–544.

————, *The Economy of Nature and the Evolution of Sex*, Berkeley: University of California Press, xii (1974b).

————, "Two Darwins: History Versus Criticism," *Journal of the History of Biology*, 9 (1976) pp. 121–132.

Kuhn, Thomas S., *The Structure of Scientific Revolutions,* Chicago: University of Chicago Press, xii (1972) [Second Ed.: First Ed. 1962].

Lakatos, Imre, *The Methodology of Scientific Research Programmes,* Cambridge: (Cambridge) University Press, viii (1978).

Newton-Smith, W. H., *The Rationality of Science,* London: Routledge and Kegan Paul, xii (1981).

Popper, Karl R., *Conjectures and Refutations: The Growth of Scientific Knowledge,* New York: Basic Books, xi (1962).

Radnitzky, Gerard, "Progress and Rationality in Research," in M. D. Grmek, R. S. Cohen, & G. Cimino (eds.), *On Scientific Discovery,* Dordrecht: D. Reidel (1980) pp. 43–102.

————, "Popper as a Turning Point in the Philosophy of Science: Beyond Foundationalism and Relativism," in P. Levinson (ed.), *In Pursuit of Truth. Essays in Honour of Karl Popper's 80th Birthday,* Atlantic Highlands: Humanities Press (1982) pp. 64–80.

Ravetz, Jerome R., *Scientific Knowledge and its Social Problems,* Oxford: (Oxford) University Press, x (1971).

Tullock, Gordon, *The Organization of Inquiry,* Durham: Duke University Press, ix (1966).

COST-BENEFIT THINKING IN THE METHODOLOGY OF RESEARCH:

THE "ECONOMIC APPROACH" APPLIED TO KEY PROBLEMS OF THE PHILOSOPHY OF SCIENCE

GERARD RADNITZKY

I THE PRINCIPLE OF ECONOMY OPERATES IN ALL PROBLEM SOLVING

Scientific research is, to a large extent, rational problem solving. Research and economic affairs are the paragon of rational behavior. What is the relationship between the two? Economics deals with markets and situations where the various costs and benefits can be converted into monetary units. Recently concepts generalized from economics have been applied to fields of inquiry that have traditionally been thought not only to lie outside of the proficiency of economics, but to which the perspective of economics was thought to be inapplicable.[1] The fields of study include political science, sociology, ethnology, law, biology, psychology and history. The "economic approach" has given rise to the economic theory of politics, the economic theory of the family, the economic explanation of the evolution of law, and so forth. It has been applied successfully in the sense that it has produced testable consequences and new insights.

Is the application of the "economic approach," in particular, the application of cost-benefit analysis ('CBA' for short) to the methodology of research more than transferring a jargon? *The main goal of this essay is to explore the benefits to be gained from applying the CBA-frame in the methodology of research,* to ascertain whether it is more than a way of speaking or a metaphor, and more than a heuristic device. My conjecture is that making use of the CBA-frame does not solve any methodological problems, but that CBA provides an organizing schema that helps to clarify the nature of certain standard problems of methodology and sometimes also to clarify what exactly a particular methodological problem consists in. This claim will be illustrated with respect to two key problems of methodology: the problem of the *"empirical base"* and the problem of *rational theory preference.* In the first example the CBA-frame helps us to clarify the nature of the problem and to assess its relative importance for methodology; in the second example it helps us to see what exactly the methodological problem is.

If, as Popper's unified theory of knowledge has taught us, *all life is problem solving,*[2] the *principle of economy* is present in all living nature from the biological level to the most sophisticated human level. It is the principle of economizing, i.e., using given resources to realize as much as possible of a set of goals or realizing a given aim with as little of scarce resources as possible. This is why the results of epistemology may be transferred to biology while the results of evolutionary biology may stimulate epistemologial speculation.[3] Thus, in an important sense organs are problem solvers and perception is a protoform of knowing that economizes efforts and reduces risks, e.g., seeing versus exploring by locomotion.[4] The principle of economy also operates in consciousness: consciousness makes information processing more efficient and reduces the number of elements that are required in performing this task. In the course of evolution, natural selection is complemented, and in certain realms superseded, by conscious choosing. The traditions neous orders (and often as unintended consequences) constitute likewise epistemic resources, and so do many of the global assumptions that we make about nature. They can be thought of as an *economizing device* for dealing with a complex reality; they do so by reducing information—and decision costs. The CBA-frame itself is an epistemic resource.

Since in all rational problem solving the principle of economy is involved and successful research is basically a rational activity, I conjecture that concepts generalized from economics may be useful in the methodology of research. By *'methodology'* I mean, roughly, a set of rules—global rules, if they are rules of general methodology—which constitute hypothetical recommendations. A methodological rule may, typically, have the following form: If the research situation in which you find yourself is such and such, and if your aim is scientific progress, then by following rule M your chances of success will be greater than what they would be if you followed any rule which competes with M.[5] Methodology proceeds argumentatively; it deals with abstract entities: the objective content of theories, problems, arguments, criteria, etc. It does not attempt to describe or to explain the behavior of scientists. Rational methodology preference is likewise a problem of methodology. Underlying this essay is Popper's methodology. It is falsificationist, fallibilist (non-justificationalist) and evolutionary.[6]

The expression 'economic approach' is used here in the *wide* sense[7] which corresponds to Karl Popper's "situational logic," or "*rational problem-solving approach*" (as I would prefer to call it). I consider Popper's "situational logic," which stands in the tradition of "Austrian methodology," as a forerunner of the economic approach to *all* human action. Popper added the "method of situational analysis" to the manuscript of *The Poverty of Historicism* in 1938 and he regarded it as "*an attempt to generalize the method of economic theory (marginal utility theory) so as to become applicable to the other theoretical social sciences.*"[8] This method together with attention to unintended consequences should, according to Popper, be the focus of social science inquiry. Indeed, the rational-problem-solving approach/economic approach has enabled us to recognize that certain situations that we had come to regard as not market-like are in fact market-like, at least in certain respects. For instance, in the light of the economic theory of politics we can conceptualize democracy as a competitive vote-buying system, where the politician is an entrepreneur in votes, and the voter a consumer of competitively marketed political merchandise. It has enabled us also to produce interesting explanations of behavior in situations that are not market-like and, in the form of "as-if-rational" explanations, it is applicable even to animal behavior.[9] The core of the economic approach/rational-problem-solving approach is cost-benefit analysis.

COST-BENEFIT ANALYSIS ('CBA' FOR SHORT)—ITS PROMISE AND LIMITATIONS

Man is a chooser. *All* rational choices involve the weighing up of benefits and costs, rest upon the "opportunity cost principle." Strictly speaking, what is compared is not costs and benefits, but rather benefits and foregone benefits, because the opportunity cost of employing scarce resources in one investment project is the present value of the forgone net benefits of the "next best" alternative use of those resources. In economics the criterion of efficiency of allocation of resources is fulfilled if the marginal benefit of the project chosen equals the "marginal cost," i.e., the marginal benefit of the foregone "next best" alternative use. In economics the various benefits and costs (foregone benefits) associated with competing capital investments are made commensurate with one another by converting them to monetary units, and the net benefits in each time period are converted to their present value by discounting. But the key concepts of CBA can be *generalized.* Not only in business dealings but also in daily life we operate within the CBA-frame, most of the time. Insofar as we are not aware of this, we may, on reflection, have much the same experience as Molière's Monsieur Jourdain when he discovered that he had spoken prose all his life.

Since two or three decades CBA has become associated mainly with the *public sector economy.* One has hoped to be able to rationalize the use of taxpayer's money in projects in the public sector with the help of the CBA-method, in the (probably vain) hope that it might yield administrative rules that could simulate market processes. As one might expect, the application of the CBA-frame in public sector economy is full of problems. The CBA-method can meaningfully be applied only if a preference structure has been stated. The public sector decision-maker's objective function is said to be the maximization of "social welfare," which is a highly illusive concept. In that context it becomes problematic which benefits and costs are to be included, how they would be evaluated, how a discount rate should be chosen, etc., and the problem of externalities crops up in public sector economy in a way it does not in private sector economy. The value assigned to the sacrificed opportunities depends on the options and values of pecuniary and non-pecuniary benefits of the particular decision makers, i.e., it depends on what opportunity sets they take into account, and on how they evaluate the various expected benefits. Since these evaluations cannot be but subjective, opportunity costs for different individuals are not commensurable. Hence, a cost-benefit analysis in welfare economics that "pretends to base its arguments on inter-personal comparison of ascertainable utilities, lacks all scientific foundation."[10] Perhaps in the public sector economy a main benefit of CBA is that it may reveal to the decision maker, the areas of his ignorance and therefore caution the planner's optimism.

For *individual* actors and the *private sector economy* the application of the CBA is less problematic. For instance, for ascertaining *ex post*—with the benefit of hindsight—which of the investment projects that were in the individual's opportunity set at the moment of decision has so far been the "best," various tools are available, such as, e.g., the internal rate of profitability method.[11] Although CBA is a conceptual instrument for optimizing goal realization and, hence, implicit in all purposive action, it can be applied meaningfully only if the preference structure of the decision maker is given and several aims compete for scarce resources. That means that CBA is not applicable in situations where one single value is set absolute, in "ultimate" choices. In such situation, if means are scarce, the problem is not an economic but a technological problem.[12] It also follows that CBA is appplicable only if the expected benefits of the projects to be compared can be expressed in such a way that there is a reference basis common to all, i.e., if it is possible to compare the benefits to be gained from the project chosen and the benefits foregone. For an individual actor this requirement is fulfilled, because for an individual it is always possible to derive from his preference structure a criterion or measure that is intrasubjectively valid, i.e., valid for him. He can even choose between "incommensurable" benefits, because for an individual there is always a *tertium comparationis* which may simply consist in the *subjective* evaluation that he prefers this to that. Hence, the insurmountable problems of intersubjectively meaningful comparison that beset the application of CBA in public sector economy do not arise for the individual decision maker.

CBA APPLIED TO THE METHODOLOGY OF RESEARCH

Here we have to distinguish between the situation of a particular, individual researcher and the methodology of research as a special discipline—a discipline which, perhaps, is even more imperialistic than the economic approach, since it deals with methods, criteria, argumentations, etc., in *any* scientific discipline. In the case of an individual researcher—the researcher considered as a particular, concrete person—CBA faces the same sorts of problems as it does in any individual decision-making process. Whether or not the utility function of a real person includes scientific progress as an aim is irrelevant to our problem. It may very well be the case that his utility function includes such aims as to earn money, to get promoted, etc., but does not include producing new knowledge. However, it may turn out that he can realize his primary aims only by producing new knowledge and, hence, this becomes his interim aim; i.e., from his utility function and the constraints that obtain in the situation at hand it may follow that producing new knowledge is a suitable, or even an indispensible, means for realizing as much as possible of his primary aims. In this case, we get an *indirect* utility function, which includes scientific progress as a means. Since the means will be weighted by the utility function and may change when the constraints change, they are not on the same footing as the primary or "ultimate" aims. The evaluations of the actor are, of course, *subjective.*

The researcher as an ideal type is defined here as a being whose *ultimate aim* is scientific progress; this aim dominates all others. The fact that the property "being a researcher in the sense of the ideal type" may never be exemplified in real life is not a valid objection against the concept. To the extent in which a real person approximates the ideal type, achieving scientific progress constitutes his *intrinsic motivation.* Achieving scientific progress may, usually, be an interim aim. However, since scientific progress can be achieved only through research (a fact which belongs to the ubiquitous constraints), and the direct aim of research is discovery, scientific progress as a direct aim is constitutive of the meaning of research.

The researcher may be viewed as a *rational "discovery-maximizing producer,"* who selects and processes problems and problem solutions and, in particular, selects projects on the basis of their expected returns in new knowledge, in discovery. The problem of the choice of discount rate has a counterpart in the individual researcher's activity in the form of his planning and time schedule, his making of a science policy that is internal to science. The time preference or "impatience" exactly corresponds to the choice of the discount rate. However, the problem does not arise when we consider basic science as the activity of the idealized researcher, because basic research is an open-ended process. One of the problems of the use of CBA in economics is the problem of which benefits and costs are to be included in the analysis. In the application of CBA-thinking in methodology this problem has a counterpart which leads to the problem of theory appraisal, and in particular, to the problem of rational theory preference. Also the economic problem of the valuation of benefits and costs has a counterpart in the application of CBA in methodology, which likewise leads to the problem of theory preference. In economics any market rate of interest also contains a risk premium. In economic life there sometimes occur situations with completely uncertain outcomes and also situations in which the outcomes themselves may be unknown. In basic research this is the normal situation.

The preference scale of the individual researcher includes, by definition, scientific progress as value or aim. That means, if scientific progress is not among the aims of a particular person, we, *eo ipso,* do not consider him to be a researcher. But the preference scale of any individual will, besides scientific progress, also contain many other values or aims, some of which may not jibe perfectly with the aim of achieving scientific progress pure and simple. Moreover, in the case of an individual, the alternative benefits forgone at the moment of choice are not actually experienced. The decision maker has to imagine them. He compares descriptions or representations of possible situations with expected payoffs. Hence, as already mentioned, the expected effects of the sacrificed alternatives are *subjectively* evaluated, when the comparative evaluations are made "vicariously," when imagined or expected benefits are being compared in thought experiments. It is illustrative to distinguish two types of success, viz., success in the sense of an increase in one's reputation and success in the abstract sense, i.e., achieving scientific or intellectual progress, where progress is valued independently of whether or not this achievement will result in an increase in one's reputation.[13] Hence, an action may be recognized as rational, from the viewpoint of a particular researcher, even if it does not realize the scientific progress that the researcher would have been capable of achieving in the long run. Moreover, outlays for having learnt a technique are certainly *past* outlays (and in this sense bygones are forever bygones). However, they are *not neccessarily sunk* costs relative to the current decision making of the individual researcher, but may influence his entrepreneurial choice, in particular, if past outlays are high. Thus, it may be rational for him to stick to the old "paradigm,"even if he recognizes that the new "paradigm" holds more promise in the long run. Retooling to the new techniques may be too time-consuming for him, so that his reputation is best served by continuting to work with the old "paradigm." All this holds good, because, for the individual, the effects of the sacrificed alternatives are *subjectively* evaluated.

When CBA is applied to the methodology of science as a discipline, the situation is different. Then, the actor is a construction, an *ideal type*, viz., the researcher *qua* researcher. Personal preference scale and psychological motivation of any particular individual are irrelevant to the methodological issues. Methodology does not aim at describing or explaining the actions of particular scientists or of the scientific community, but it deals with methodological problems. *In research, the basic aim of the activity is given and, hence, the preference structure of the researcher as an ideal type is also given.* The basic aim is scientific or intellectual progress. *This aim is constitutive of the meaning of research* and, hence, it cannot be put into question in that context. Therefore, methodological rules, criteria, decision, etc., are appraised in terms of their *instrumental* value for an approximation to the basic aim, to scientific progress. An outside observer can estimate the subjective evaluations of particular agents, of particular scientists. This falls within the competence of the history of science or the sociology of science. Methodological appraisals are involved, but if they are used, i.e., a certain position in methodology is applied to a particular case. It is the task of methodology critically to examine the competing methodological appraisals and the criteria that are being used by various historians or sociologists of science. Methodology as a sort of technique for increasing the chances of scientific progress proceeds argumentatively. Like scientific research, it stands under the regulative principle of approximating the truth and of solving problems that are "scientifically important" in the objective sense. The methodological appraisals associated with the ideal type of researcher, or, speaking less metaphorically, with methodology as discipline, as a sort of technology, are objective evaluations. The changing body of scientific knowledge evolves like a spontaneous order (in F. v. Hayek's sense), and through the continuous whittling away of problem solutions that are less good than their competitors, it can achieve progress. It is claimed that CBA applied to the methodology of research may be based on evaluations of opportunity costs that are *objective*, in spite of the fact that CBA in personal decision making is bound to the fact that cost as it influences choice is subjective (and the fact that CBA in "welfare economics" appears to lack all scientific foundation, as F. v. Hayek has pointed out).

II ON THE CONCEPT OF RATIONAL ACTION

Since in methodology the key questions are of the form: "When is it *rational* to do X?" (e.g., when is it rational to prefer a particular theory to its rival?), it is advisable to clarify the concept of rationality. Rationality as used here is predicated primarily of actions, not of actors; it refers to the efficient use of means to achieve given ends. Although rational criticism of ends is possible and neccessary,[14] it is in the interest of clarity to distinguish between rationality and reasonableness. Reasonableness refers to the art of living, which, as Aristotle has taught us, must be based on the experience of life. I propose a prescriptive model which I call "good reason assay."[15] A good reason assay examines whether or not there are (or have been) good reasons for a particular actor to act (or to have acted) in a certain way, given his perception of the situation; it defines rational problem solving, given that perception of the situation. Its core is an explicatum of the idea of "rational action," the *"rationality principle"* ('*RP*' for short). On the basis of a good reason assay we can construct an historical explanation of individual actions; it focuses on the initial conditions. We need such explanatory patterns for answering such questions of the history of science as, e.g., whether a particular scientist acted rationally, given the state of his information, when he preferred a particular theory to others, when he accepted a particular explanation, and so forth.

According to the rationality principle or rational-choice principle (*RP*) an action is evaluated as *rational* if it meets the following requirements: IF 1. x perceives the situation to be of the type S; 2. x wants to realize the goal G; 3. x believes that, in situations of type S, M constitutes an effective and efficient means for realizing G; 4. x evaluates the total costs (all sorts of costs, monetary and non-monetary, even pangs of conscience) of using M in situation S, including also those "negative" side effects that are foreseen by x, lower than the marginal utility to be obtained from using M, i.e., an implicit or explicit cost-benefit analysis has convinced x that in the situation S the use of M is preferable to the non-use of M (which would also result in certain costs); 5. using M is within the capabilities of x, and 6. x is not prevented from using M, THEN x uses M. In sum, given the actor's perception of the situation, he has *good reasons* for doing M—i.e., he should do M—indeed, if he does not, he behaves irrationally.

In order to construct an historical explanation (or prediction) on the basis of the above good reason assay we need the following *empirical* hypotheses, which describe the initial conditions: *E-1:* The person a at time t did perceive his situation to be S; *E-2:* a wants (or wanted or will want) to realize goal G; *E-3:* a believes that procedure M is an effective means for realizing G; *E-4:* a believes that the marginal utility of using M is higher than the costs; *E-5:* a is capable of doing M; *E-6:* a is not prevented from doing M, and—this is the decision point—*E-7:* a is a rational agent in the sense of *RP* at least for the critical period of time. From the empirical premises it follows logically that a did (or will do) M. As in any empirical investigation we compare the conclusion derived from the premises with a description of what actually happened. If the conclusion is falsified, then at least one of the premises must be false. This type of historical explanation (or prediction) takes into account only the actor's perception of the situation.

If we wish to explain (or to predict) the *effect* of a's action, we have to take into account the *objective* situation, and the effect will at least be in part due to unintended consequences of a's action.

HOW CAN SUCH AN HISTORICAL EXPLANATION (OR PREDICTION) AND THE GOOD REASON ASSAY UNDERLYING IT BE CRITICIZED?

If the conclusion of the argument is falsified, the question arises where to put the blame. Any of the empirical premises may be modified, provided only that the proposed modifications rest upon empirical information that is *independent* of the new explanandum, of the correct description of what happened, i.e., modifications must not be made *ad hoc*. For reasons of economy it is advisable to question in the last place the empirical premise (E-7), the hypothesis that the actor at the moment of decision is (or was) a rational agent in the sense of the rationality principle *RP*. If we have empirical reasons for withdrawing premise (E-7) that are independent of the falsification of the derived description of *a*'s action, then the task will be to construct other sorts of explanations, e.g., a psychoanalytic explanation, a latent function explanation, a rule-following-behavior explanation, a conditioning-reinforcement explanation, and so forth. In these explanations the use of a good reason assay may again become pertinent, although on another level.[16] For example, one may argue that in a certain type of situation it was rational for the agent to act according to the rule-following model, because of the special character of the situation, e.g., if the action occurred in a tribal society or in the context of routinized or etiquette-governed behavior. In sum, there are no methodological differences between the rational procedure in the explanation of an individual action and the rational procedure in any other empirical investigation.

With respect to premise (E-3) it may be asked whether it was rational for the agent to rely on the information at his disposal when he made the decision. This is a separate problem, which has to be approached in exactly the same way as the problem of explaining the action. The good reason assay will essentially contain a cost-benefit analysis taking into account the estimated marginal utility of additional knowledge relevant to the decision and the information costs, the cost of acquiring or transferring knowledge to the decision maker, and also the subjective evaluation of the risks involved when acting on the basis of insufficient or perhaps partly false information. (This already anticipates the problem of the "empirical base.")

At least in some cases we can, with the benefit of hindsight and of the knowledge which is at our disposal now, but which was not at the disposal of the agent when he acted, construct a good reason assay that takes into account the *objective* situation instead of the actor's perception of the situation. However, if we have to concede that it would not have been possible for the agent to acquire all the relevant knowledge or that, considering the information costs, it would not have been rational for him to invest more in improving his knowledge base, then we have to concede that he acted rationally in not making any extra effort to improve his knowledge base, even if he did not succeed in realizing his goal. Error or failure do not by themselves preclude that an actor acted rationally.

HOW CAN THE RATIONALITY PRINCIPLE BE CRITICIZED?

Since *RP* introduces an explicatum of the intuitive idea of rational action, the relevent criticism is either that the explicatum is not sufficiently similar to the explicandum, or that it is not fruitful as a conceptual instrument in the sort of problem solving for which it is intended[17]—in the present case, for the explanation or prediction of individual actions. The proposal of an explicatum of the concept of rational action—the rationality principle or rational choice principle— does *not* imply any sociological hypothesis about how people behave all of the time or most of the time. Hence, *empirical* criticism leveled against it is irrelevant.

III WHEN IS IT RATIONAL TO QUESTION A POSITION AND WHEN RATIONAL TO "ACCEPT" IT, I.E., TO REGARD IT AS UNPROBLEMATIC, AT THE MOMENT?

THE IMPORTANCE OF THE CONTEXT IN WHICH THE METHODOLOGICAL PROBLEMS ARE PLACED

Following W. W. Bartley III, the expression '*position*' is used here as an umbrella term for theory, hypothesis—e.g., the hypothesis that a certain theory is closer to the truth than its rivals—viewpoint, criterion, value judgment, and so forth, provided that these abstract entities (Popper's W-3 entities) are linguistically formulated.[18] The researcher has continuously to decide whether to "accept" a particular position, i.e., whether to regard a descriptive statement, a particular theory preference, etc., as unproblematic at the moment, or to attempt to improve it, or to put it into question, i.e., to regard it as problematic (but worthy of consideration), or even to reject it.

Before applying CBA to key problems of methodology it behooves to specify the context in which these problems will be considered, the pertinent environment, so to speak. For, if the methodological problems we wish to examine are placed in the *justificationist context* (the metacontext of true belief)[19] then the road to their solution is blocked. This holds for both varieties of justificationist philosophy, for overt justificationism in the form of logical positivism or "probabilistic empiricism/verificationism" and for covert justificationism in the form of "philosophies of the framework" (in the wake of Wittgenstein's later philosophy). A promising treatment of the central problems of methodology is possible only if these problems are placed in the *non-justificationist or criticist context.*[20] Hence, I wish to insert a brief comment on that context.

The master principle of comprehensively critical rationalism, or, if we adopt Bartley's apt phrase, *pancritical rationalism*, is the maxim that forbids immunizing positions against criticism. It enjoins us *to keep ALL positions in principle open to criticism, i.e., not dogmatize anything— INCLUDING this very maxim.*[21] W. W. Bartley III has demonstrated that self-application of the maxim does not lead to semantical paradoxes, that, hence, there are no logical reasons which would force us to dogmatize the maxim, to exempt it from criticism in principle. The master principle follows from the concept of rationality, or more accurately speaking, it constitutes part of the explicatum of the concept of rationality. The master principle needs a complement, which likewise belongs to the explicatum of the idea of rationality: the general prohibition of immunization against criticism has to be complemented by the maxim *"prudenter dubitare"*: While rationality demands that all positions be in principle kept open to criticism, *calling into question a particular position is rational ONLY IF there are concrete reasons for doing so.* Also this complementary maxim follows from the concept of rationality (which includes the principle of economy), because resources are always scarce, in particular the resource time, and that, therefore, opportunity costs have always to be taken into account, and, while the costs of a critical discussion are much less than the costs of empirical testing, they are never nil. That means that CBA is indispensible if the maxim *"prudenter dubitare"* is taken seriously.

Hence, the important question is what qualifies as a good reason for putting a position into question, for problematizing it. There is always reason for *internal* criticism if one discovers that a position is inconsistent. That every argument contains assumptions which are not questioned in that argument is often thought to constitute a principal limitation of criticism. However, this view is mistaken, because each of the assumptions can be questioned in another argument, provided only that it has been made explicit. The problem is analogous to the problem of the criticizability of logic. We can, in principle, criticize any element of any logical system, but we can do so only with the help of other parts of logic, which we have to presuppose, at the moment.[22]

However, the crucial question is whether *external* criticism is more than an objection from a different point of view, i.e., the problem of whether the criticism of tradition is really possible. The revival of relativism in various fields of intellectual endeavor—in the philosophy of science evidenced by the enormous influence of Thomas Kuhn, but also by the influence of Paul Feyerabend, Stephen Toulmin, etc.— makes critical scrutiny of this position imperative. The relativistic philosophers arrived at their position because they recognized that the justificationist program had failed, that the search for secure knowledge, which fuses criticism with justification, is a will-o'-the-wisp, but were unable to free themselves from the justificationist ideal of knowledge according to which only secure knowledge is genuine knowledge. Relativism and theory instrumentalism in the methodology of research are but covert forms of justificationist philosophy.[23] At the center of modern relativism is the position that Popper has aptly labeled the *"myth of the framework."*[24] This view claims that the form of life, the "language game" in which we participate and which surrounds us much like a "natural" environment, cannot be criticized by us, and that, hence, external criticism is not possible. This is said to be so because that form of life sets the standards of criticism: if we want to engage in a certain sort of activity, be it science or theology, then we have to accept uncritically the standards that regulate that activity. All "meaning" depends upon the rules of a given tradition or community, on the rules of a given speech community or of the users of that tradition. Within that tradition or form of life, meaning and action can be criticized only by a reference to those rules, to the "logic" of that language game. Hence, a blunder, according to Wittgenstein, is always a blunder in the context of some rule system, but never a blunder as such. Following these general lines, e.g., Sir Alfred Ayer, Hilary Putnam and others claim that one cannot do science without accepting the "inductive" method— much as Karl Barth claims that one cannot do theology without accepting uncritically the Bible.[25] The "myth of the framework" has led to the "sociology of knowledge," which, more accurately should be called "the sociology of belief." This "sociological denigration of the rationality of science"[26] grows out of the form of life contextualism of Wittgenstein's later philosophy, which views knowledge as a function of a language game and social configurations as the determinants of knowledge.[27] Acting rationally then means nothing more than acting in accordance with what a community of scientists at the time deems appropriate.[28] With this view, knowledge, theory preference, etc., tend to become the subject matter of sociology. The relativist context limits the question "When is it rational to criticize a particular position?" to internal criticism.

If the problem of the "empirical base" is placed in the context of overt or covert justificationism, this leads to pseudo-problems; if the problem of rational theory preference is placed in that context, it becomes impossible to come to grips with it, because in that context there is no way of weighing the relative merits of alternative paradigms. Karl Popper, W. W. Bartley III, and Peter Munz have decisively criticized relativism in philosophy and in methodology.[29] Nonetheless, the "philosophy establishment" is still dominated partly by logical positivism (overt justificationism) and partly by form of life contextualism/relativism (covert justificationism).

In Popper's methodology and epistemology the quest for knowledge that is certain has been abandoned, and the various methodological problems have been placed in a non-justificationist or criticist context. Its pillars are a realist view of theories and a fallibilist view of knowledge, the claim that, in all his attempts to solve problems, man is fallible. It follows that the basic question of epistemology is: Which problem solution should be rationally preferred in a particular situation? In methodology this question leads to the problem of appraising competing problem solutions and hence, to the problem or rational theory preference. Bartley has then improved upon Popper's position by explicitly declaring the master maxim of critical rationalism to be self-applicable. Having placed the various methodological problems in a *non-justificationist or criticist context* these problems can get a solution, and *Popper's methodology can be seen as a special case of the application of the CBA-frame to espistemic situations.*

IV CBA APPLIED TO THE PROBLEM OF THE EMPIRICAL "BASIS"

WHEN IS IT RATIONAL TO "ADOPT" A SIMPLE DESCRIPTIVE STATEMENT (A "BASIC STATEMENT") IN THE SENSE OF REGARDING IT AS UNPROBLEMATIC, AT THE MOMENT?

The question of the rationality is now raised, not with respect to decisions relating to a particular position, but with respect to a particular sort of action, the handling of a particular *sort* of position: in this section the handling of simple descriptive statements and in the following section the handling of theories that compete with each other. When critical rationalists speak of "adopting" or of "accepting" a position they usually add the qualifying adverb "provisionally" or "pro tempore" in order to counteract the association to something final or incorrigible. For a Popperian to "tentatively accept" a statement means that he regards the statement to be worthy to be subjected to further criticism, to severe empirical testing.[30] I shall argue that "accept," "reject," etc., which give association to a decision process, are misleading if used with reference to the practice of research, but, with some caution, are applicable in the methodological reconstruction of that practice.

THE CONCEPT OF "BASIC STATEMENT"

The rational handling of very simple descriptive statements, of observation reports, constitutes one of the key problems of methodology and of epistemology. The program of logical positivism is to make the propositions of science more certain by constructing them from statements formulated in an epistemologically privileged primary language, i.e., a language whose descriptive predicates are simple "observation predicates." In all varieties of justification philosophy (*Begründungsphilosophie*) we find analogous programs. If the problem of the rational handling of very simple descriptive statements is placed in the justificationist context, then it is insoluble. Hence, the first step to a satisfactory problem solution is to place the problem in the non-justificationist context. Popper has solved the problem of the empirical "basis," at least in principle.[31] Yet, certain formulations or aspects of his solution have been criticized by some of his disciples. The most important criticism comes from W. W. Bartley III.[32] I hope that by applying CBA to the problem of the empirical "basis" we can improve our grasp of the problem.

A *"basic statement"* or a *test-statement*—a central concept of Popper's methodology—is a *report of observation* asserting that an observable event is occurring in a certain region of space and time.[33] Since the event must be individuated (the region of space and time specified), a basic statement is, *formally*, a singular existential statement or a statement that can be rephrased in this form; moreover, it must be able to contradict a universal statement, i.e., be able to constitute a potential falsifier of a theory. The *material* requirement is that the statement itself be intersubjectively testable by observation: it must be possible that the event is observed by others.

From the *viewpoint of epistemology* there is *no qualitative difference* between a basic statement and a general statement, i.e., a law statement or a law-like hypothesis, or a theory. All are fallible in principle, conjectural, criticizable and revisable. In this sense there is nothing "basic" about the so-called basic statements. However, there is a difference of degree: a singular statement is less problematic than a universal statement, simply because it describes or represents just one event while a universal statement describes an indefinite or infinite number of events. From the *viewpoint of methodology* there is a striking difference between basic statements and theories: basic statements are *easier to test* than theories; in this sense they are *closer to experience.* "Experience" has to be understood here in the sense in which we use the expression in everyday speech, e.g., when we say we have experience of cows or computers. Those who, at this juncture want to problematize the concept of experience, propose a problem shift and would abandon the problem of basic statements. Perceptual experience constitutes the "cause" and the "evidencing reason" for our believing and asserting a basic statement, and the linguistically formulated reports of a perceptual experience play the key role in the good reasons brought forward in order to defend such an assertation when it is questioned.

Our perceptions are colored by our "background knowledge,"[34] by the *assumptions* we make about reality—assumptions that can be seen as indispensable *economizing devices* for dealing with a complex reality. The linguistic formulations of our perceptual reports and the basic statements for which they constitute "evidencing reasons" are influenced also by the *linguistic medium* in which the perceptions are expressed, by the preconceptions built into that linguistic framework.[35] In this sense, as Popper pointed out in 1934, "every statement has the character of a theory, of a hypothesis."[36] *How strong is this dependence of a basic statement upon theories, and what is its import for methodology?*

The philosophical tradition has given two extreme answers to these questions.[37] Classical empiricists and their followers the logical positivists or probabilistic empiricists hoped that reports of perceptions or "protocol sentences" would be independent of theories—a psychologistic alternative to basic statements—and, therefore, would provide a *secure* source of knowledge, an ultimate foundation of empirical knowledge. "Protocol sentences" do not qualify as basic statements since perceptual experience is subjective. The positivists wished to dogmatize protocol sentences. Those who recognize that the positivists' program has failed but are unable to free themselves from the justificationist ideal of knowledge tend to fall into the other extreme: they claim that basic statements are accepted by *arbitrary* decision or by conventions.

POPPER DISSOLVED THE ALLEGED DILEMMA: EITHER BASIC STATEMENTS PROVIDE AN EPISTEMOLOGICAL ROCK-BOTTOM OR THEY ARE NOTHING BUT CONVENTIONS.

Popper's solution is not a middle way as some observers believe.[38] He demonstrates that the dilemma is spurious, and that it arises only in the context of justificationist philosophy—overt or covert justificationism. He *restructured the problem situation*, and he shows what a rational attitude to basic statement is.[39] However, as W. W. Bartley III has argued, Popper's formulations are at some places misleading.[40] Popper rightly stresses that observation is used to *test. Basic statements* may function as potential falsifier of a theory; in research their main function is to *provide a point of departure for producing a description of a reproducible effect*, i.e., of a statement that may function as falsifying hypothesis of a theory. Basic statements can themselves be tested by deriving from them (in combination with other statements that we assume at the moment) other basic statements or test statements. *The process of testing is potentially infinite;* but since no attempts are made to prove a theory or a basic statement to be false (let alone to be true) no infinite regress need arise.

If we wish *to test* a theory, the strategy is the following: find out what sort of events would be incompatible with the theory, i.e., would be "outlawed" by it; then, set up an experimental arrangement with a view to trying to produce such events and report the result of the test; finally, in order to facilitate criticism, get more than one observer and let the test be repeated by other experimenters.[41] From the viewpoint of logic, a single singular statement can falsify a theory. Claiming this is nothing more than asserting that a particular basic statement may be incompatible with some universal statements. From the viewpoint of methodology, a theory T is falsified by a statement that describes a reproducible event, a *type* of event that is "outlawed" by the theory or law-like hypothesis. That means that T is falsified if the falsifying hypothesis and the statement of the initial conditions are "accepted," i.e., regarded as unproblematic at the moment, and only so long as this is the case. Expressed more cautiously: If a falsifying hypothesis B is less problematic than the theory T (and the statement of the initial conditions)—an assertion about the objective situation—then T is falsified by B. Since B is conjectural, falsification, of course, is conjectural, too.

In the *practice of research*, as well as in everyday life, the handling of basic statements does not constitute any problem.[42] From a certain moment we regard, in research as well as in daily life, a particular basic statement as *unproblematic*—simply because we are convinced. (For instance, after a thorough check, I am convinced that at present there is no full-grown rhinoceros in my office.) I cannot decide to be convinced. One may verbalize one's conviction. Normally one will do so only when the truth of the statement under consideration has been challenged. *Experienced certainty is, of course, epistemologically irrelevant:*[43] each and everybody may be wrong, as already the skeptic philosophers of antiquity knew. If a basic statement is not unproblematic at the moment, then, as in all rational problem solving, a *cost-benefit analysis* is pertinent, which, however, in the practice of research remains implicit. How much effort is invested in re-checking a particular statement—whether "basic" (singular) statement or universal statement—will depend upon the agent's *subjective valuation of how much is at stake.* The valuation of the estimated costs if one should be wrong is subjective and will depend upon character traits of the agent, his attitude toward risk-taking, his personal valuation of the disutility of failure, and so forth. Popper made it quite clear that, insofar as the agent acts rationally, in all those cases where he does not, or not yet, regard a particular basic statement as unproblematic at the moment, it depends upon "the logic of the situation" whether he re-checks the statement or turns his attention to other areas.

The individual researcher's valuation of costs is subjective. However, it may be hoped that in the critical discussion with other researchers the individual differences that influence the subjective valuations of costs and risks may cancel out each other. Since, as has been argued above, even the simplest descriptive statement is theory-laden, i.e., exists within a web of general hypotheses or theories which are presupposed at the moment, there is ample opportunity for empirical criticism of a basic statement, for testing it by deriving further test statements from it (in combination with those theories that we presuppose at the moment). These remarks attempt to describe what goes on in research practice. *To describe research practice is not the task of methodology.* Methodology is a set of hypothetical prescriptions designed to increase the researcher's chances of realizing the aim of his activity: scientific progress.

Let us now turn to the METHODOLOGICAL problems.

It was claimed above that basic statements are less problematic than universal statements. That a given basic statement is unproblematic at the moment means that "at the moment nothing is known that speaks against it."[44] 'Known' is to be interpreted in the sense of Popper's concept of objective knowledge; it refers to an objective situation, not to mental states of a subject. However, *a statement can be unproblematic in this sense only because other statements are taken to be unproblematic at the moment,* viz., the relevant part of our background knowledge. We have to stop somewhere. Although, since we do not search for an Archimedian point, there is no danger of an infinite regress, the question arises why it should be rational to stop just at certain statements or positions, not to question them at the moment. In my opinion, this question can be answered only by having recourse to the *cost-benefit* frame.

A descriptive statement contains at least one descriptive or universal predicate. Since 1934 Popper has stressed that every descriptive predicate is *theory-laden* and that, therefore, every descriptive statement, however simple it may be, *transcends observation.*[45] A descriptive predicate, a universal term, is theory-laden—it carries a "theoretical halo," so to speak—because it figures not only in singular statements but also in some universal statements or theories. Theory-ladenness is a matter of degree. The so-called *observation predicates* or low-level descriptive terms such as, e.g., ' . . . is water,' ' . . . is broken,' ' . . . is heavier than . . . ' are *less* theory-laden than others that play a role in scientific theories such as, e.g., 'magnetic field,' 'electron mass,' 'nuclear mass,' 'W$^{\pm}$ boson,' 'Fermion,' 'handedness of a single molecule of alanine,' 'Hubble parameter.' The logical positivists' dichotomy between observation terms and theoretical terms is completely wrong and has created many pseudo-problems (e.g., the problem of theoretical terms).

In many cases there is *a special relationship* between a *concept of ordinary language* and a particular *concept of scientific theory.* In the literature the process that produces this relationship is often referred to as "explication of an intuitive concept." An *explication* is essentially a proposal to replace, in certain contexts, the original concept, which is less theory-laden (the "explicandum"), by another concept that constitutes an improved successor of it (the "explicatum"). The explicatum is claimed to be a better conceptual instrument in connection with certain cognitive tasks. It is more theory-laden than the explicandum; it is related to the explicandum concept by the requirement of "sufficient" similarity between the two in the sense that the exemplary positive (negative) cases of the extension of the expression designating the explicandum must also be positive (negative) cases of the extention of the explicatum term. However, the explicatum does not replace the explicandum in everyday speech; it replaces it *only* in certain scientific contexts.[46] An explication of a less theory-laden concept by another one that is related to it but is more theory-laden, i.e., a proposal in certain scientific contexts to use an improved successor of the original concept instead of that original concept, occurs always as a by-product of the development of a *new theory* of *scientific discovery.*[47] Concepts do not occur in isolation; "knowledge is propositional."

In science as well as in everyday life *a descriptive statement is of interest*, not in isolation, but *only in a certain problem situation*. Consider Popper's classic example "Here is a glass of water" (S)[48] in a problem situation where the problem is to ascertain whether this glass contains water or wine. The predicate "Water" is theory-laden. The observation report transcends observation; it has certain predictive implications. This is so because the predicate "Water" figures not only in statements of this sort but also in universal statements, in simple theories such as, e.g., the theory that water, if drunk, quenches thirst, that water has a certain taste, and feels to one's touch in specific ways. These are expectancies which, if formulated, can be expressed only by universal statements. Hence, when asserting that this glass contains water, *we also assert, by implication*, that its contents, if drunk, will quench thirst, and so forth. In this case all the concepts involved are at the level of explicanda, of the intuitive concepts of everyday language.[49]

If the statement S is unproblematic at the moment, this is so because the various theories which, in the problem situation at hand, we presuppose are themselves unproblematic. *These theories are unproblematic at the moment, because of previous methodological decisions.* Our background knowledge is not normally questioned. The theories constituting it are unproblematic at the moment, because they have been "adopted" as unproblematic *(pro tempore)* on previous occasions, because the researcher then considered them as better corroborated than their rivals. Some of these theories or assumptions are very general—e.g., the world-view assumption that the world will continue to exist tomorrow, that the sun will rise tomorrow, that the various laws of nature will hold good, that my lifespan is limited. Some of them are trivial, but they are assumptions, theories, nonetheless. These theories are not questioned at the moment, because at the moment there are no concrete reasons for doing so. All statements are fallible, but retesting a particular statement is rational only if there are concrete reasons for doing so. This is *the second precept of (pan)critical rationalism;* it is itself but an expression of the principle of economizing, of having recourse to the cost-benefit frame. If the occasion arises, we may question any particular statement or position at any time. This is what is commended by the *first maxim of (pan)critical rationalism:* in principle, to keep all our positions open to criticism and not to dogmatize anything.[50] A statement that is not falsified, but on the other hand, is not unproblematic at the moment—that is to say, it is known that some objections to the statement exist but not (yet) known whether they are really to the point—could be marked 'problematic' in the sense in which W. W. Bartley III, speaks of "marked knowledge."[51] The idea is that it would be *uneconomical* to delete too quickly a statement, theory, etc., before we have got out of it what it might have to offer.

In sum, while in the practice of research the handling of basic statements does not involve any conscious decision, in the *methodological reconstruction* it is recommendable to reconstruct that handling *as a decision process*. The decision is about whether or not a particular statement is unproblematic at the moment. However, a statement can be unproblematic only *in the light* of certain other statements that are presupposed, and they are presupposed because on previous occasions it was decided that they were unproblematic and no concrete reasons for revising these decisions have appeared so far. Since we do not search for an Archimedian point, this need not lead to an infinite regress. *The decision process may be suitably reconstructed as a cost-benefit assay,* in which account is taken of the estimated marginal utility of rechecking the statement and of the costs involved, in particular, the opportunity costs of the rechecking. When it has been decided that a statement is unproblematic at the moment, the estimated utility of an additional rechecking diminishes drastically and may perhaps, in some cases, drop to zero.[52]

When we, with the help of our reconstruction, wish to ascertain whether the actor acted rationally when handling a particular basic statement, we will have to construct a good reason assay that takes into account the various initial conditions, the actor's relevent beliefs and his subjective evaluation of the costs. If a person rechecks an observation sentence in excess of what appears to be rational according to *our* cost-benefit analysis of the *objective* situation, this falsifies our original assumption that he acted rationally in that situation. For instance, the person in Popper's example who repeatedly rechecks how many fingers he has,[53] will be diagnosed as a compulsory neurotic.[54] This shows that—since man is fallible—some risk-taking is considered obligatory, part and parcel of the human condition.

From the *methodological* point of view the important questions are: *How can a particular basic statement be criticized? What are the costs of defending a statement (whether singular or universal) that is "problematic"?* I propose to discuss these questions with the help of a few examples. However, before doing so, it behooves first to clarify the relationship between the concept of "unproblematic at the moment" and the concept of the "predictive implications" of a statement.

Every descriptive predicate is theory-laden. The *theory-ladenness, the "theoretical halo," of a predicate considered in isolation (in the vocabulary of the language) depends upon the state of development of the discipline to which the theories belong in which that predicate figures.* Consider, for instance, the statement 'This bone is broken' ($'b_d'$ for short, $'d'$ for 'diagnostic') asserted as the result of an examination without instruments. In ordinary language the word 'broken' as applied to bones has a sufficiently fixed meaning so that we know what we mean when we assert b_d. The "theoretical halo" of the predicate depends upon the state of the medical art. For instance, when X-ray diagnostic techniques have been developed, new ways of testing statements of type b_d have become available; 'broken' has *not* changed its meaning in everyday speech, but it has become more theory-laden than it was before, at least in a context where these new techniques are known (objective situation). This is so because the explicata of the concept "broken" are pertinent to the problem at hand. This also shows that it is somewhat artificial to speak of the "theoretical halo" of a descriptive predicate out of the context. It is the problem situation that determines *which* part, or how much, of the "theoretical halo" of a predicate which is available at a particular time, is relevant for the case at hand, i.e., *the problem-situation determines the predictive implications of a basic statement.* From b_d in combination with the *empirical* theory of X-ray diagnostics, test statements can be deduced which describe how a broken bone looks in an X-ray picture (let us call them 'statements of b_x-type'). If a predicted b_x statement is falsified, at least one of the premises of the argument, the conclusion of which is b_x must be false. In this case, unless we claim that the particular X-ray apparatus is defective, b_d has been falsified. The bone appeared broken, but luckily is not. Defending the basic statement b_d in this situation would force us to *reject* some of the other premises. If a checkup shows that the X-ray apparatus used is in order, then we would have to reject the empirical theory that underlies the X-ray diagnostic technology and eventually question the physical theory which made possible the construction of X-ray apparatuses. The methodological reconstruction of this case—*guided by the cost-benefit frame*—shows that the valuation of the *costs* is *objective*, and that, in the case under discussion, the *costs of defending the falsified basic statement b_d constitute costs in an objective sense* and that these costs would be unbearably high.

In this case we have corrected, with the help of the explicatum concept, a statement in which the concept "broken" is used at the explicandum level. However, the predictive implications that the ordinary language statement gets, in combination with certain scientific theories, do not form part of the *meaning* of the descriptive predicate *in everyday speech*, i.e., they do not change the explicandum, let alone replace it; the relationship between statements like b_d and statements using the explicatum is empirical and not analytical (explication being a by-product of discovery). For instance, we may reasonably suppose that—to consider our first example—both Aristotle and a modern chemist sometimes were right when they asserted tokens of the statement 'This glass contains water and not wine,' and that in the relevant sense they even meant the same thing. We may suppose this in spite of the fact that in certain cases disputes about the truth of a descriptive statement couched in ordinary language can be resolved by using the testing methods provided by the theories that underlie the explicatum concept—as it is the case in the present example. To believe that the meaning of the explicandum has changed means subscribing to the theory of "meaning change," a doctrine that eventually leads to idealism.

With respect to the "problem of the empirical base," the main methodological problem is the decision whether or not to *invest* time and effort *into producing a falsifying hypothesis* for a theory T by using a certain *basic statement as a point of departure*. Basic statements are indispensable in testing a theory T; they provide a point of departure for producing a falsifying statement for T (cf. top of p. 299). In order to maximize criticism and thereby the chances of error elimination (an analogue to the working of the selection principle in evolution), it is required that basic statements are *intersubjectively testable*. Such testability is a matter of degree. A simple example can facilitate exposition. Consider a report of a pointer-reading, e.g., the statement 'At t on this dial, the pointer is opposite Figure 2' ('b_0' for short). A certain perceptual experience is the motive for asserting b_0 (psychological description), and a statement that reports the experience may serve as "evidencing reason" for regarding a particular token of b_0 as unproblematic at the moment and for the decision to work with it (level of methodological reconstruction). Not only seeing is involved, but seeing *that*, seeing the object *as* a dial of a certain instrument, i.e., not only seeing, but observing in the context of a concrete perceptual task. The statement b_0 is unproblematic in the light of certain assumptions, e.g., that the observer's visual faculty is normal, that he is not suffering from optical illusions, that parallaxes, glare and other factors which may influence pointer-readings are under control, and so forth. If the above-mentioned assumptions about the initial conditions are not rejected, then to reject b_0—as not being a veri-dical report of what is observed—would be tantamount to questioning the general theory of perception that is used to analyze the phenomenon of perception. This would constitute *costs* in an *objective* sense, unbearably high costs unless there are concrete reasons for questioning the theory of perception.

A statement of the level b_0 possesses some degree of intersubjective testability if more than one experimenter can observe the dial. The time indicator t must not refer to a moment, but to a period of time the length of which depends upon the measuring technique used. Statements of the type b_0 are but *raw material;* they are not incorporated into the (evolving) body of scientific knowledge. They are of interest only in problem situations in which from b_0, in combination with statements about the initial conditions of the experimental arrangement and universal statements about the functioning of the measuring apparatus used in the experiment, further test statements are derived such as, e.g., the statement 'At t the pressure in atmospheres in this container is 2' ('b_1' for short). The predictive implications of a b_1 statement depend upon the state of the art. The pressure in the container can be measured by various measuring techniques. In the realm where more than one of such techniques are applicable, those techniques that are applicable must yield the same results.[55] If there is a discrepancy, this constitutes an objective problem—an unintended consequence of repeating the experiment.

Rejecting b_1, while retaining b_0, would force us to reject one or more of the other premises of the argument, e.g., to claim that the particular specimen of the instrument used in the experiment did not function properly. To uphold this claim one has to produce independent evidence for it. If b_1 is rejected while b_0 is retained, and it is also claimed that the instrument functions properly, then one would be forced to *reject* the physical theory that underlies the technology in accordance with which the measuring instrument has been constructed. In most, if not all cases, this would constitute a *cost* in an *objective* sense—again, an unbearably high cost.

What does it mean to test a basic statement like b_1? It will mean having another look, getting others to look again, rechecking the functioning of the measuring apparatus, and perhaps measuring again with another measuring technique. However, all this is meaningful only in the context of a repetition of the experiment, because what matters in science are not statements of the b_1-type—they, too, are nothing but raw material—, but a report of a *reproducible effect,* a statement of the form: '*Whenever* certain initial conditions are realized (with experimental arrangement X), then b_1' ('B' for short). A statement of B-type is of interest in science if it contradicts the theory that we wish to test. First the B-type statement possesses sufficient *intersubjective testability.* If a test statement cannot itself be tested in a way that demonstrates its intersubjective testability, the falsifying effect cannot be reproduced; therefore, in order to falsify a theory, the falsifying statement must describe a reproducible effect (or a repeatedly observable phenomenon, a type-event).[56] Describing a non-reproducible single event is not enough, and a statement that cannot be "re-controlled" is of no significance in science. *Hence, the methodological problem of the "empirical base" turns out to be essentially the problem of whether or not (when we wish to test a particular theory T) to invest time and effort into producing a falsifying hypothesis for T using a particular basic statement as a point of departure, that is, whether to invest into processing a particular singular statement into a statement which describes a reproducible effect and which may contradict T.* As in any investment decision, in any allocation of given scarce resources of time and effort to maximize scientific progress, that decision can rationally be made only on the basis of a *cost-benefit analysis*—only that perhaps 'cost-benefit analysis' is a high-flown title for something we always do when behaving rationally.

Finally, a passing remark in the sociology or history of science may be allowed. If a falsifying hypothesis of a well-known theory is "unproblematic" at the moment, in the sense that there is nothing known that talks against it, then it will gain wide acceptance by the scientific community. A positive *consensus omnium* is not required, because, if it were, probably no statement would get (through methodological decision) the temporary status of being "unproblematic."[57] No persuasion needs to be involved, and no amount of persuasion will get a falsifying hypothesis that sort of recognition by the scientific community in the long run if it does not deserve it for objective reasons.[58] A particular falsifying hypothesis may get recognition in the sociological sense much against the wishes of certain members of the scientific community. If this is the case, the situation might have some analogy with the emergency of a spontaneous order through mechanisms of cultural selection. However, in retrospect we can understand, by means of methodological reflection, why a particular hypothesis has survived severe criticism. The sociological hypothesis asserting that a particular hypothesis *B* has been generally "adopted" by the scientific community is, of course, itself fallible as everything else. A person can use it as a good reason for regarding that statement as unproblematic only if he places himself in the role of the layman. As a researcher he has to examine critically the objective reasons that, according to the claims made by its proponents, make it rational to regard a certain statement as unproblematic at the moment.

In sum, in the *practice* of research, the traditional "problem of the empirical base" is *no* problem at all. On the level of *methodology*, the rational handling of basic statements is reconstructed as a process that involves essentially an *investment decision*, and hence, *cost-benefit thinking*. The problem of the empirical base does not constitute a major problem of methodology; it is an epistemological problem. It cannot be avoided, because we test theories, falsifying hypotheses for theories, and test statements themselves, by deducing from them other test statements (basic statements). Hence, methodology assumes that the epistemological problem has been solved or is solvable. Within the fallibilistic context, the problem of the empirical "basis"—of what Popper 1930/33 also calls 'elementary statements of experience' (*elementare Erfahrungssätze*)[59]—can be solved. Knowledge in the objective sense is "possible" only because there are basic statements, test statements, that are "unproblematic" at the moment.[60]

V WHEN IS IT RATIONAL TO PREFER A PARTICULAR THEORY TO ITS RIVAL(S)?

IN THE PRACTICE OF RESEARCH AS WELL AS IN METHODOLOGY THE ISSUE IS THEORY PREFERENCE AND NOT ACCEPTANCE OF A THEORY.

In everyday life and in the technological application of scientific theories, the pertinent question to ask is indeed whether or not to accept a theory, i.e., whether one may reasonably expect that the technology based upon the theory will help one to realize a particular practical goal; the good reason for such an expectancy is that the theory is considered to be sufficiently well-tested and corroborated for the practical purpose at hand; it need not be the best theory—for economic reasons.[61]

In scientific research the situation is different. It does little harm to speak of "accepting" or "adopting" a basic statement in the sense of regarding it as unproblematic at the moment and, in the context of testing a theory *T*, to regard it as worthy of being used as point of departure for producing a falsifying hypothesis for *T*. After all, basic statements are but raw material in research and are not incorporated into the growing body of scientific knowledge (conjectural but objective knowledge). To speak of "accepting" with reference to theories, or to universal statements, is innocuous only if the phrase is used to state that we regard the theory as worthy of being subjected to further criticism, in particular to severe empirical tests. Even in this case, the theory in question has not been appraised in isolation, but has been selected from a number of theories which competed for the researcher's attention. However, this use of 'acceptance' is Pickwickian. It is very likely to be misunderstood. Using "acceptance" in the ordinary sense places the methodological problem of theory appraisal in a *justificationist context*, and in that context the problem is formulated in such a way that the road to a satisfactory solution is blocked. In that context, the question, "When is it rational to accept a theory?" will be clarified by asserting that the problem is to decide whether a particular theory—considered *per se*, in isolation, so to speak—can be *accepted* (at a certain level of acceptance), and that this decision has to depend upon the degree in which the theory is *probabilified by the evidence*. However, a look at scientific research would have demonstrated to the logical positivists how false their image of science is—if it is intended as a descriptive image—and Popper's criticism has shown how misleading their tenet is, if it is taken as a methodological prescription.

In science, and also in everyday problem situations, we always start with some preconceptions, some assumptions about the sort of phenomena to be explained; they may in most cases turn out to be false, but they constitute nonetheless some theory or a first step towards a theory. We never start from nothing, and in this sense *there is in every problem situation some competition among theories*. Competition among possible problem solutions is the growing ground for intellectual progress. This is one reason why with respect to theories the key issue is theory *preference* and not the "acceptance" (or rejection) of a theory *per se*.

Of course, the question of whether a particular theory is preferable to another particular theory arises only if the two theories are competitors. Theories are *competitors* if they are not only logically incompatible but can replace each other. For instance, Darwinian theory of evolution and nineteenth-century thermodynamics are conflicting theories, but not competing theories since they cannot replace each other. Theories compete relative to explanatory problem situations. Theories are competing in the *narrow* sense of the word if they offer incompatible solutions to the same, or highly overlapping, sets of explanatory problems; if an *experimentum crucis* is possible. Theories are competing in the *wide* sense if, although talking about the same sort of phenomena and not contradicting each other, one theory can explain certain phenomena while the other cannot, i.e., if the realms of applicability of the theories overlap partially, but one theory has greater explanatory power.

There is another reason why theory preference is the methodologically relevant issue, and not "acceptance" of a single theory. Scientific progress can be achieved, if at all, only through the interplay of creative imagination and criticism, and we learn from our errors. If a new problem solution has been proposed, a new theory has been created, the rational next step is to criticize it, to test it with a view to possibly improving it, last not least through error elimination. *So long as a theory is taken seriously as a possible solution to a scientifically interesting prob-*

lem, it has to be tested. Theories are tested by deriving from them, in combination with statements of initial conditions, testable consequences.[62] Hence, in basic research predictions are but a means of testing a theory. Insofar as the predictions, the deduced singular statements, are an end in themselves, that piece of research is, by definition, applied research and not basic research.[63] That means, that excepted from retesting are only theories that, at the moment, are used as instruments, e.g., as auxiliary premises in a deductive argument or as theories that underlie the hardware laboratory equipment we use in testing the theory we hope to improve or to replace by a better one. The aforesaid regulative principle of Popper's methodology urges the scientist to investigate whether the theory that has withstood severe tests so far also holds in areas in which it has not yet been tried out. If it does not hold there, he gets, as an unintended consequence of his action, some new objective problems: to explain why the theory does not fit the new area of application, while it is successful in the "old" area of application, what other theory might do better in the new area, and so forth. In this way, solved problems create new problems.

Thus, the question of when it is rational to stop problematizing a particular position is a pertinent question when asked with respect to basic statements, because basic statements are but raw material of science. But, if the question is asked with respect to theories, it is misleading, because it is based on the false assumption that research has a "natural" end. *Research is open-ended, because solved problems create new problems.*[64] *So long as we attempt to improve a theory, we subject it to severe testing, and in this way the theory is either improved or replaced by a better one.* In basic science theories do change steadily, often in deep and fundamental ways. As Popper expressed it succinctly (in his debate with Kuhn): science is "permanently revolutionary." Popper's methodology may, therefore, be labeled "preferentialist methodology." He replaced the question, "How can we prove?" by the question, "How can we improve?". In sum, in basic science we are continuously confronted with the problem of comparing competing theories: the "champion" theory with a modified version of it (is it really an improvement?), the "old" theory with a new one that is proposed as replacement, because the "old" theory has met with certain objections that have to be taken seriously, and so forth.

To appreciate the restructuring of the problem situation when the problem of theory appraisal is moved out of the justificationist context and placed into the non-justificationist context, it may be worthwhile to cast a glance at the positions taken on the issue of theory appraisal by those styles of thought that still dominate the philosophy establishment. The picture we find is analogous to that which emerged when we surveyed the two extreme positions with respect to basic statements. Operating in the context of justification philosophy, the logical positivists projected an ideal of science according to which progress consists in probabilifying a theory more and more. The central problem then is how to establish the degree of confirmation of a theory relative to a particular empirical base. Those who were impressed by Popper's criticism of inductivism,[65] but could not free themselves from the justificationist ideal of knowledge, again turned scepticists. To the view that basic statements are arbitrary or conventional correspond the following views of theories. Those who wished to continue working in the style of logical positivism adopted the *instrumentalist* view of theories. One of its latest versions is the so-called "non-statement view."[66] Theories do not make statements about aspects of reality, they do not describe, they are nothing but instruments. The instrumentalist view of the theories is often combined with a realist view of basic statements. Theory change is rational insofar as it is based on the relative success of the "applications" of the two theories. Kuhnians hold that what matters is "paradigm change," and they conceive "paradigm changes" roughly as due to changes of fashion—the *sociological turn* in the "philosophy of science" and at the same time a relativist turn in the so-called "sociology of knowledge." What matters is success in the sociological sense, there being no other criterion, because the theories that belong to one "paradigm" are incommensurable with the theories developed under another "paradigm." Thus, the problem of rational theory preference has been lost or abandoned, at least for major scientific developments.

THE PROBLEM OF RATIONAL PREFERENCE INCLUDES PART OF THE PROBLEM OF RATIONAL PROBLEM PREFERENCE AND LEADS TO PROBLEMS OF SCIENCE POLICY THAT IS INTERNAL TO SCIENCE.

Let us first examine *what happens after a falsification and see whether the CBA-frame can be relevant in that research situation.* The result of a successful falsification attempt of a theory T is summarized by stating a logical relationship: from certain premises, which we regard as unproblematic at the moment, it follows logically that non-T. *This is all logic can tell.*

The researcher now finds himself in a problem situation that is characterized by two determinants: by the aim of the activity—the *basic aim* of research is scientific progress—and by the result of the falsification attempt, viz., the above-mentioned logical relationship. The rational response to this sort of problem situation can be expressed by a methodological rule—the "logic of the situation" demands, so to speak, a certain response. The rule says: If you find yourself in this situation, you have to search for a new problem solution, i.e., to use creative imagination in order to propose a theory that is distinct from T and is not hit by the falsification that forced you to conclude that non-T; moreover, whatever you do, you must not attempt to repair the situation by reducing the empirical content of the falsified theory, e.g., by simply eliminating from it that section which you blame for the falsified prediction, (because, as we shall argue, the costs would be too high). *This is all methodology can tell.*

The researcher now confronts a problem of research policy that is internal to science. By *'research policy internal to science'* we refer here to the decision problems which confront the researcher after he has embarked on a particular field of study and has to allocate scarce resources such as his time and effort *within* this area of endeavors, problem cluster or discipline.[67] These decision problems refer mainly to rational problem selection, to investment decisions. In the example under discussion, the problem is whether it is more profitable, in terms of returns in new knowledge, to invest in an attempt to replace the "old" theory by a modified version of it or to invest in an attempt to replace it by a theory that is "new" in a conspicuous or even dramatic sense. *This sort of decision is a risky investment decision for which it is impossible to give a methodological rule,* if only because it is logically impossible to know whether or not we will get fruitful new ideas, whether we will be able to create a radically new problem solution. In this problem situation, the CBA-frame can provide a certain guidance for the researcher. It can help him to see which sorts of questions should be taken into account when comparing competing investment projects. I hope to be able to illustrate this a little further on.

WHAT GOOD REASONS CAN BE GIVEN FOR THE METHODOLOGICAL DECISION THAT A THEORY *T'* IS TO BE PREFERRED TO A THEORY *T*?

In the practice of research, the handling of basic statements does not involve any decision. Rational theory preference always involves a conscious decision by the researcher. Hence, every researcher has to act part of the time as methodologist of his own.[68] The methodological decision that a particular theory *T'* is to be *preferred to* its rival *T* is based on good reasons for conjecturing that the problem-solving capability of T' is greater than that of T. To clarify what we mean in this context by the phrase 'good reasons' we have to do three things: 1. We have to explicate "T' is better than T in respects . . .", i.e., make explicit the dimensions of criticism and the criteria to be used.[69] 2. We have to produce arguments for the claim that it is these criteria that matter. 3. We have to provide empirical support for the hypothesis that T' fulfills these requirements in a higher degree than T does. To solve the first problem, one has to state what the relevant concepts are: "relative content of empirical information," "relative truthlikeness" (zutreffender als), and "relative scientific importance" of the problems that can be solved with the help of the theory, etc. The second task consists in showing that the various desiderata such as increase in empirical content and increase in truthlikeness, follow from the basic aim of scientific research: to find interesting truth, i.e., theories with higher and higher explanatory and predictive power, theories that answer "deeper" and "deeper" questions. To support the hypothesis that T' meets these desiderata in a higher degree than T does, we have to refer to the relative performance to date, i.e., we have to compare the two balance sheets of past performance. All available information should be used in the criticism of theories, including appraisals of the "scientific importance" of the problems the theory can solve or has failed to solve. The key idea in Popper's methodology is that T' is superior to T if T' has survived more of our severe tests than T. On the basis of a comparison of the performance of the competing theories in the past, we make a fallible but objective conjecture about their relative capabilities. This conjecture is methodologically interesting only if it is more than a summary of past performance, only if it licenses a prediction about future performance which is risky but not unreasonable.

How risky such a prediction is can be illustrated by an analogy with sports events. There too we use information about performance in the past in order to make forecasts about the competitors' performance in the contest. Such forecasts are based essentially on physiological theory. In the case of the methodological forecast, there is no counterpart to physiological theory. However, this methodological procedure has nonetheless nothing do do with a "whiff of inductivism"(as the late Imre Lakatos thought): First, since the problem is no longer placed in the context of justification philosophy, we make no attempt from past performance to deduce predictions about future performance, no attempts to make an inference from the evidence (positive evidence and/or negative evidence) to an assertion about the degree of inductive support of a single theory, or to the conclusion that one theory is "more probabilified by the evidence" than its rival. Second, we have not looked for positive evidence (which is easy to come by) as inductivists would, but we have systematically searched for possible negative instances, and, only on the basis of the result of severe empirical testing, we *conjecture* that the theory that has so far survived the tests, all the tests or more of the tests than the rival theory, possesses a greater problem-solving capability than the rival theories that did not survive the tests. On a realist view of theories, we assume, moreover, *that this greater problem-solving capability of the theory* that survived all tests, or more tests than its rival, *is due to its being closer to the truth*, to its greater capability of *describing* certain aspects of reality. It is a risky conjecture. If the logical problem of induction could get a positive solution, then and only then the risk could be reduced. However, since this is not the case, it is imposssible in principle to reduce the risk involved in making conjectures about the future performance of theories on the basis of past performance. Hence, the risk involved in theory preference is unavoidable.

To decide which of two competing theories to prefer, the CBA-frame provides an ordering schema that helps the researcher to see which sorts of questions should be taken into account, such as, e.g., the question of the costs of defending a theory whose record, at the moment, is less good than that of its competitor. The practical consequences of the decision to prefer a theory T' to T is the decision to invest time and effort in the attempt to improve T' still further. This project will essentially involve a continued testing of T', e.g., by applying T' to realms of phenomena to which it has not yet been applied. The selection of problems—which in basic research is, by definition, made on the basis of their objective "scientific importance"—and, hence, the selection of research projects is the key issue of a science policy that is *internal* to science. Thus, the researcher as entrepreneur in discoveries is continuously confronted with the problem of the allocation of scarce resources of time, effort, etc., with the problem of the costs of acquiring certain epistemic resources such as methods, skills, conceptual frames, and so forth—costs which are mainly opportunity costs: what could have been achieved if the time had been devoted to other projects or activities. In particular for science policy is that internal to science, the CBA-frame itself constitutes an epistemic resource for the researcher. As in the market process, where the consequences of decisions are imposed on the decision makers, in science, returns in new knowledge, success and failure, all accrue to the researcher who made the decision. Research is basically a highly competitive enterprise which immanently involves, however, a considerable amount of cooperation, if only because the results of one researcher constitute an epistemic resource for other researchers, and the criticism of other researchers is an indispensible corrective and challenge to the productive researcher.

Since in a methodological appraisal the logical point of view is not the only relevant consideration, it would not be rational to consider as equivalent, a failure to explain or to predict—even if it involves a falsification—a fact that is scientifically fairly unimportant, and such a failure with respect to an observed regularity of great scientific importance (assuming, of course, that both belong to the theories' realm of proficiency). Hence, successes and failures should be weighted by the relative scientific importance of the problems concerned.

In order to weigh successes and failures by the scientific importance of the problem concerned, it is neccessary to provide an explicatum of the notion of a question Q_2 being of "greater scientific importance" than question Q_1, which competes with it for scarce resources of time, talent and effort within the same field of study. This explicatum has to be an objective concept, which has nothing to do with the subjective interests or predilections of individual scientists.[70] Hence, *the problem of rational theory preferences*, through the *ex post* appraisal of the relative performance to date, *includes part of the problem of rational problem preference* (namely an appraisal *ex post* of the relative importance of competing problems), *and it leads to the problem of rational problem preference where the assessment has to be made ex ante*. Rational problem preference *ex ante* is the key issue of research policy that is *internal* to science, to the efficient allocation of scarce resources of time, talent, and effort among competing research projects within a discipline. As mentioned, the allocations are risky investment decisions. However, since budgetary frames of a discipline are limited, this allocation problem cannot be avoided. The problem of rational problem preference has to be tackled also by every scientist who works independently, i.e., who himself plans how to allocate his time.

THE RATIONAL OPTION FOR ONE OF TWO COMPETING THEORIES IS BASED UPON A COST-BENEFIT ANALYSIS, WHERE THE EVALUATION OF BENEFITS AND COSTS IS OBJECTIVE. LIKEWISE, THEORY CHANGE IS AN OBJECTIVE PROCESS.

The main theses of this section are that opting for one of two competing theories is a rational decision only insofar as the appraisals involved are objective, that the relevant appraisals can be objective, and that, hence, theory change also can be and should be an objective process. At least in the long run this holds also in the history of science.

In all those research enterprises in which theorizing is closely linked to, and monitored by, empirical testing, theory change is indeed a process that is *objective*. In such fields of study, *a better theory eventually drives out a less good one—for economic reasons.*[71] Science, in the pursuit of truth about the natural world, *transcends* scientists, individually and collectively, here and now.

The best way of arguing for these theses is to *illustrate them by a simple example*. I can think of no better and simpler example than that used by George Schlesinger in a recent review of Kuhn's *The Essential Tension*.[72] It is the example of the round-earth theory superseding the flat-earth theory. In the beginning, the round-earth theory offended common sense in a way the flat-earth theory did not. However, there were observations that provided the material for a falsifying hypothesis of the flat-earth theory, e.g., the observation that may be summarized by the statement "A person standing on the coast sees the sails of an approaching ship before he sees the ship's hull." This statement is sufficiently neutral with respect to the competing theories to serve as a crucial observation. The observation can be made (*pace* Kuhn, Feyerabend, Hübner, etc.) by anybody independent of his world picture, the nature of the language he uses, etc. Indeed, a person who denies that this is the case can be disregarded without thereby doing any damage to the intersubjective testability of the statement in question. With the help of the round-earth theory the observation is easily explained. With the help of the flat-earth theory the phenomenon can also be explained, but only at the price of introducing certain *ad hoc* hypotheses about the bending of light rays, i.e., only at a certain cost. ('Explaining' means here that an argument is constructed whose conclusion is a description of the phenomenon in question.) The flat-earth theorist can *immunize* his theory against this falsification, *but only at a certain cost*, because his assumption about the behavior of light rays is purely *ad hoc*.[73] With the help of the round-earth theory one can easily explain why lunar eclipses are round. In order to defend his theory, the flat-earth theorist has to take costly measures; he may, e.g., deny that lunar eclipses are due to the shadow that the earth casts upon the moon. The objective cost of such a gambit is that, as a consequence of this move, the defender of the flat-earth theory has also to reject the theory which explains why lunar eclipses occur in the middle of the lunar month (when the lines from the sun to earth and from earth to the moon form an angle of 180 degrees). This pattern repeats itself again and again. The round-earth theory turns out to have a considerably higher explanatory power than its rival, the flat-earth theory. The first sailing voyage around the earth, with return to the point of departure from the opposite direction, can easily be explained by the round-earth theory, while in order to defend the flat-earth theory, it will be neccessary to explain why the phenomenon in question did not really constitute a circumnavigation, in spite of all appearances, i.e., it will be neccessary to explain it away. Eventually, *the accumulated costs of defending* the flat-earth theory, e.g., when one is confronted with pictures of the earth taken from satellites, have become *unbearably high. The relevant valuations of the costs are objective, and the costs eventually lead to a theory change in an objective process.* The examples that can be used to illustrate this are legion: the Ptolemaic theory versus the Copernican, the hollow-earth theory versus the Copernican theory, the theory of the ether (at least in the form given it within a Newtonian framework) and the theory of relativity, and so forth. By analyzing the example of the hollow-earth theory versus the Copernican theory, Roman Sexl demonstrates that experimental results *alone* cannot force a decision between two competing theories, not even in this case, because the defenders of the falsified theory can always make their theory "fit" the new discoveries by adding *ad hoc* assumptions or by certain mathematical transformations.[74] *The decisive question is what is the cost of such strategies that immunize a theory against falsification.*

That a rational response to falsification is guided by the CBA-frame can also be illustrated by what very likely are the two most often-mentioned examples of the history of science: the deviation of Uranus and the deviation of the perihelion of Mercury.

If a theory T is falsified, i.e., if T is regarded more problematic than the falsifying hypothesis of T, then the scientist has the problem of ascertaining which of the premises to blame. Popperian methodology gives him only the following advice: First, never attempt to repair the situation at the cost of reducing the empirical content of T—these sorts of costs are, in principle, unacceptable. Second, if you attempt to repair the situation by introducing an *ad hoc* premise merely as a temporary heuristic device, then that assumption has to be testable. You are obliged to test that premise and you must not retain it unless it has withstood empirical testing. Consider first *the example of the deviation of the orbit of Uranus from the orbit calculated with the help of Newton's theory* (taking into account Jupiter and Saturn). The postulating of an additional planet (christened 'Neptun'), the mass and orbit of which were calculated from the *observed* orbit of Uranus with the help of Newton's theory was completely *ad hoc*. Yet, the *ad hoc* assumption was testable and when, in 1846, it was corroborated, what had appeared to be a falsification had turned out not to be a falsification. Defending the champion theory had not resulted in costs, but rather in the gain of new knowledge (even if that knowledge concerns only the initial conditions). No subjective evaluation is involved; the development is an objective process.

The second example is the orbit of Mercury. Since the middle of the nineteenth century, it was known that its perihelion deviates (by 43 seconds of an arc per century) from what is calculated, given the initial conditions about the planets and the Newtonian theory. A correct deduction of Mercury's orbit can be obtained by introducing either the *ad hoc* assumption of an additional planet (analogous to Uranus's case), or the *ad hoc* assumption that the mass in the sun is distributed unevenly (*nicht streng kugelförmige Massenverteilung der Sonne*). Each of these assumptions is testable, but neither could be corroborated. In 1916, an accurate description of the orbit of Mercury was deduced from the statement of the initial conditions of the planetary system, without *ad hoc* asumptions with the help of the general theory of relativity. Hence, the falsification of Newton's theory, through the orbit of Mercury, was regarded as genuine; Einstein's theory superseded Newton's. The above-mentioned *ad hoc* assumptions offered a possible solution, since they were testable, but they did so only until they were falsified themselves. After 1916, to uphold the explanation of the deviation of Mercury's perihelion by means of Newton's theory in combination with one of the above-mentioned *ad hoc* assumptions would have involved *objective costs:* Besides the costs of the *ad hoc* assumptions (having in the premises a testable, but not corroborated or even falsified, assumption), one would have to reject not only the explanation given with the help of the general theory of relativity, but, by implication, *to reject also the theory that changed our world view.* Hence, in this case the objective costs of defending that one of the two competing theories which is less good are dramatic.

When a new theory begins to challenge the theory that has hitherto dominated the field of study, there may be, and probably most often there will be, an *initial period* of time during which it is *not* possible to rationally prefer one theory to the other. In this case the rational decision is to postpone decision and to limit oneself to describing the problem situation as exactly as possible. Even in our simple example, the round-earth theory appeared to imply such strange things as our antipodes to be walking upside down, and thus offended common sense. Paul Feyerabend has convincingly argued that, in the beginning, the Copernican theory had as much, if not more, difficulties or "anomalies" than the Ptolemean theory. However, *this is not a valid objection against the thesis that the evaluation of the costs of defending a falsified theory are objective* and that the costs of defending the less good theory eventually become unbearably high, in an objective sense. The situation may be seen in analogy with a newly established firm or industry. A theory or, more accurately speaking, one important aspect of theories, may be thought of as a sort of workshop for producing a certain sort of maps over a certain territory, which can be used for explaining and predicting. If the theory has just been created, the maps may contain many errors, but their quality may gradually improve. A newly-established firm may in the beginning only have costs, but if the enterprise is successful, it will, from a certain point in time, balance profits and losses and from then on the profits may increase acceleratingly. If so, a risky investment has proved successful in the long run. In many cases of newly-created theories the situation may be similar.

To summarize: The cost of defending a falsified theory or a theory for which the balance sheets of successes and failures is less good than that of its competitors is evaluated objectively. This case, incidentally, illustrates that the concept of cost may be useful even if we cannot measure costs. These costs are opportunity costs in the wide sense, i.e., in the sense of *epistemic resources forgone*, resources which would have been available if one had opted for the competitor of the theory. *These costs are twofold*: (1)—*The costs of immunizing moves*, such as introducing *ad hoc* hypotheses as additional premises or as part of a modified version of the falsified theory, consist in *loss of empirical content*. High empirical content is an epistemic resource, insofar as the theory is truthlike, or a potential resource if the theory has not yet been tested. The more the empirical content of a theory is reduced, the less its scientific interest, until, in the extreme, it may become an assertion that is empirically empty. (2)—The second category of costs is, firstly, the *loss of the good explanations that can be constructed with the help of the rival theory*. More importantly still, the rejection of these explanations (in the above example, e.g., the explanation of why lunar eclipses are round) forces the defender of the falsified theory *also to reject the theory with the help of which these phenomena can be explained. The loss of theories with high explanatory power constitutes the loss of most valuable epistemic resources.*

In rational theory preference a *cost-benefit analysis* has to be used. Of course, in an important sense, we always use cost-benefit analysis in everyday life, at least so long as we act rationally. Invoking the cost-benefit analysis framework helps us to conceptualize the problem situations; it enables us to articulate the various steps in the decision-making process and, hence, to make them more criticizable. The introduction of cost-benefit thinking does not solve any methodological problems. But it helps us *to recognize what exactly the problem is*. Thus, it has helped us to recognize, e.g., that the problem of the basic statements is *not* a serious methodological problem, while rational theory preference *is* a key problem of methodology, which involves evaluations of the costs of defending a theory, those evaluations being objective, and that hence, theory change too should be, and in the long run will be, an objective process.

A theory, once created, has, when taken together with other theories which we also assume, an infinite number of logical consequences. Most of them are unknown to its creator and his followers. They are unintended consequences. Also in this sense science *trancends* scientists, individually and collectively. The tradition of knowledge in the *objective* sense (knowledge, not as true or warranted belief, but as abstract entities in the sense of Popper's "World-3") is what gives science its continuity.

NOTES

1. Michael Ghiselin formulates the underlying assumption succinctly: "Resources, scarcity, and competition, together with the laws of nature that govern them, apply to all organisms everywhere, not just to ourselves." (Ghiselin, in this volume, p. 2).

2. E.g., (Popper, 1967) *U.Q.* p. 178: "I conjecture that the origin of *life* and the origin of *problems* coincide."

3. Popper has emphasized the continuity between problem solving at the biological level and the achievements of science ("from the amoeba to Einstein") since 1928. (Popper, 1928), MS p. 69, (Bartley, 1984b).

4. Cf., e.g., D. T. Campbell in (Schilpp, 1974) Vol. I, esp. p. 424; (Bartley, 1986a), (Radnitzky, 1986c).

5. On the concept of methodology see, e.g., (Radnitzky, 1981), (Radnitzky, 1982d), (Radnitzky, 1985c)—arguments for the support of methodology are outlined in (Radnitzky, 1983a) pp. 248 f.

6. Cf., e.g., (Popper, 1934/1959), (Popper, 1972), (Bartley, 1982), (Radnitzky, 1981), (Radnitzky, 1982b), (Radnitzky, 1985a).

7. This is in line with John Gray's contribution to this volume.

8. (Popper, 1976) *U.Q.* pp. 117 f., ital. in the original. Cf. also (Petroni, 1981).

9. Cf., e.g., (Ghiselin, 1974), (Heinrich, 1979). For explanations of other phenomena at the level of biology cf., e.g., M. T. Ghiselin's "economy of the body" (Ghiselin, 1978), (Hirshleifer, 1977), (Hirshleifer, 1978a), (Hirshleifer, 1978b).

10. (Hayek, 1979) p. 201. On the possible use of CBA as a formal ordering schema associated with rational decision-making see, e.g., (Kirsch, 1971) p. 59, and (Brown and Jackson, 1978) p. 175.

11. Cf., e.g., (Radnitzky, 1964).

12. (Kirsch, 1971) p. 70.

13. This aim, scientific or intellectual progress—*intellectual* success or success in an abstract sense (of Popper's W-3 entitites)—is not the same as success in the *sociological* sense, e.g., increase of a scientist's reputation, a type of success for which sociologists are fond of offering various measures such as citation frequency, prizes, etc. However, an inference from sociological descriptions, e.g., citation frequency of a theory, to its scientific merit (a methodological appraisal) is a case of naturalistic fallacy, and basing good

reasons for such an appraisal on sociological statements would presuppose that there always exists a strong correlation between intellectual success and success in the sociological sense. This is not so. The two types of success will converge and eventually conincide only in the long run and only in those disciplines where theoretical work is closely linked to *empirical* testing. This is certainly the case in the physical sciences. The natural sciences constitute one pole, and philosophy, with its many schools and fashions, the other pole on a dimension of "empirical control" of theory preference. In economics there exists a lot of "Platonism with respect to models" (H. Albert); sometimes authors entertain their models because their models entertain them. Moreover, the "success" of a particular economic theory in the *sociological or popular sense* will to a large extent depend upon the "vested interests" of special-interest groups, of politicians and bureaucracies, etc., and on ideological forces, and hence, it may often depend more on rhetorics and intellectual climate than on the scientific merit of the theory.

14. Cf. (Andersson, 1984a); (Bartley, 1984) p. 222 ff. (enl. 1984-ed. of *Retreat*, App.4).

15. (Radnitzky, 1968, 1973) Sect. IVF6b.

16. Cf., e.g., (Radnitzky, 1968/1973) Sect. IVF6.

17. On the concept of explication see, e.g., (Radnitzky, 1986d).

18. On "position," "context," and "metacontext," see (Bartley, 1982) pp. 124 f.

19. (Bartley, 1982) pp. 128, 137–142, 148–152.

20. (Bartley, 1982) pp. 157–161, cf.; also Bartley's two contributions to (Radnitzky and Bartley, eds., 1986).

21. (Bartley, 1982) pp. 157 f.; (Radnitzky, 1986b) Sect. 2.3 (Radnitzky and Bartley, eds., 1986). Presents an overview of the debate about the self-applicability of that maxim.

22. On criticizability of logic cf., e.g., (Bartley, 1982) pp. 174–178; (Radnitzky, 1986b) Sect. 2.3.3; (Radnitzky, 1985a) pp. 101 f.; (Bartley, 1984a) pp. 247–260.

23. For a concise overview of relativism and the instrumentalist view of theories in the methodology of research cf., e.g., (Radnitzky, 1982b) pp. 68–75 (with references to the pertinent literature). For a concise overview of theory instrumentalism see, e.g., (Andersson, 1979) pp. 8–10.

24. Cf., e.g., (Popper, 1970) p. 56; (Andersson, 1984a) p. 6; (Andersson, 1984b), (Bartley, 1982), (Radnitzky, 1986b).

25. (Bartley, 1982) pp. 126, 157.

26. (Grove, 1982).

27. Cf. the devastating criticism of the sociology of knowledge in (Grove, 1982); (Munz, 1985) examines and rejects the Wittgenstein option especially in the forms in which it has appeared in contemporary thought in Kuhn and Rorty, and contrasts this view with Popper's evolutionary epistemology.

28. (Grove, 1982) p. 552.

29. Bartley has criticized relativism and related views from his early classic *The Retreat to Commitment* to (Bartley, 1962) and to the new Appendices of monograph length in the revised and enlarged 1984-edition of *Retreat*. (Munz, 1985)—cf. fn. 27 above—examines in detail also the influence of relativist thinking on the historiography of science.

30. (Popper, 1959) New App.* 9, p. 419.

31. In *Grundprobleme* (Popper, 1979 [MS 1930–33]), (Popper, 1934/1959).

32. Cf. (Bartley, 1982) pp. 167 f. and Bartley's 2nd and enlarged 1984-edition of *Retreat* App. 3, pp. 213 f.

33. (Popper, 1979 [1930–33]) pp. 122, 127, 132: "Basissätze der Wissenschaft (die 'elementaren Erfahrungssätze')"; (Popper, 1957) *LdF* Ch. 5; (Popper, 1963) *CR* pp. 386–388; (Bartley, 1982) pp. 162–168; (Bartley, 1984a) pp. 132–216; (Andersson, 1984b) pp. 54, 57, 62.

34. To my knowledge the deepest treatise on perception is (Heelan, 1984).

35. Even the simplest statements of everyday speech illustrate this dependence. E.g., 'The sun sets in place k at time t' shows that a particular theory—in this case the Ptolemean theory—is built into our vernacular. However, the problem situation in which the ordinary language statement is normally used is such that this theory does not belong to the statement's predictive implications.

36. (Popper, 1959) pp. 94 f.—transl. from (Popper, 1934) p. 61.

37. A survey of the historical development and a critical assessment is given in (Andersson, 1984b).

38. E.g., (Shearmur, 1984) p. 694: " . . . Radnitzky suggests that Popper's philosophy is important in providing a middle way between the idea that there are firm foundations for knowledge and skepticism or relativism." This I do not wish to suggest.

39. See, e.g., (Andersson, 1984b) for a penetrating study of basic statements.

40. (Bartley, 1982) Sect. XIV and (Bartley, 1984) *Retreat*, App. 3 esp. p. 214.

41. (Popper, 1934); and, e.g., (Bartley, 1982) p. 167; (Bartley, 1984) p. 215.

42. (Popper, 1959) p. 93; (Andersson, 1984b) p. 58.

43. E.g., (Popper, 1979 [1930–33]) p. 126: "The important thing is that these *subjective convictions* do not enter into the *scientific procedures of* testing . . ." (italicized in the original, transl. GR).

44. Popper calls a basic statement "unproblematic" if there is no reason to test it (" . . . Bassisätze, die nicht weiter überprüft zu werden brauchen,")—(Popper, 1979 [1930–33]) p. 132. W. W. Bartley III places the distinction problematic/unproblematic in the center of his study of basic statements. Cf. (Bartley, 1982) sect. XIV and (Bartley, 1984a) pp. 213–216. He dispenses with the concept of decision with respect to basic statements. However, I doubt—for the reasons stated in the text—whether in the *methodological reconstruction* we can do without the notion of decision.

45. (Popper, 1934), (Popper, 1959) pp. 94 f., 423–5; (Popper, 1963) pp. 118 f.

46. For instance, we continue to use phenomological concepts like "Warm," ". . . Warmer than . . . ", etc., in everyday speech, although there exist a series of successor concepts such as, e.g., "Temperature in degrees Kelvin," and explicata of that concept in terms of thermodynamics and statistical mechanics.

47. For an aperçu of the concept of "Explication" cf., e.g., (Radnitzky, 1986d); for an example of an explication in economics, see, e.g., (Radnitzky, 1964).

48. (Popper, 1959) *LScD*, p. 95—'Here is a glass of water.'

49. Popper's famous example 'Here is a glass of water' ('*b*' for short) is theory-laden, but much less so than, e.g., statements of chemical thermodynamics. To make up our mind whether or not to regard *b* as unproblematic, simple tests will suffice, because in the problem situation at hand the layman and the chemist will mean the same thing when they assert a token of statement *b*. This holds even for the chemist who claims that liquid water is supposed to be a pure chemical substance but that so far nobody has yet been able to support this claim by a sound molecular argument and that, since from a molecular point of view we do not even know how to characterize a liquid, "we do not really know what water is," i.e., that we do not possess a fully satisfactory explicatum of the concept "Water" for certain scientific contexts. Also people with a false view of the nature of water may sometimes make accurate assertions about the contents of glasses. In particular, we have to beware of the essentialist temptation: the view that there is such a thing as *the* correct definition of a universal term like 'water.' What we have is the explicandum idea "Water" used in everyday life and a set of explicata of the original concept which are designed for use in special scientific contexts only.

50. Popper has not taken out this step. *"Pancritical rationalism"* is due to W. W. Bartley III, and it became presentable only after Bartley had shown that

there are no logical reasons that would force us to dogmatize anything, that making the maxim *self-applicable* does not lead to semantical paradoxes (as Popper probably feared before 1962).—Cf. (Bartley, 1982). (Radnitzky, 1986b), and (Radnitzky and Bartley, 1986), Part II.

51. On "marked knowledge" cf. (Bartley, 1984a) p. 208.

52. This is analogous to the situation in which a particular test is repeated provided it is really the "same" test.

53. (Popper, 1972) p. 79.

54. If we wish to explain his behavior, we will have to replace the assumption that in the situation in question he behaved rationally by the assumption that he behaved like a compulsory neurotic. We have then got a new problem: the problem to explain why this is the case. If we attempt to construct an explanatory pattern with the help of, e.g., psychoanalytic theory, a new cost-benefit assay—now at another level, taking into account psychological costs—may play a role.—Cf., e.g., (Radnitzky, 1968/72) pp. 235–243.

55. Incidentally, this already exposes the "operationalist fallacy": that it is wrong to believe that a quantitative concept can be defined by specifying a measuring technique. It is the other way round, the explanandum concept governs the production of the various measuring techniques. The operationalist confuses concept and the procedures by means of which the absence or presence (or partial presence) of the concept or property can be ascertained in a concrete case.

56. (Popper, 1979 [1930–1933]) p. 132: " . . . and this is the decisive point— that what matters in it (in scientific method) . . . is primarily not particular, *singular statements (besondere Sätze)*, but *general regularities (allgemeine Gesetzmäßigkeiten)* i.e., statements that . . . can and must be tested again and again in a deductive manner (by deducing many and very different singular statements)." (*italicized* in the original transl. from the German). See also (Andersson, 1984b) p. 63.

57. (Popper, 1979 [1930–33]) p. 131.

58. Paul Feyerabend overrates the power of persuasive techniques in much the same way as some economists (notably K. Galbraith) have overrated the power of techniques of advertising. The demand for goods and services that are valued only as instruments will eventually depend upon objective reasons, upon the results of tests of efficiency in practical use. For example, not even the most expensive advertising campaign will make people buy electric drills which are obviously more expensive and work less well than other brands. On the other hand, with such items as clothes, fashions, art, or ideologies, there are, of course, no limits to sheepishness.

59. (Popper, 1979 [1930–33]) p.124.

60. (*Ibid.*) p. 132.

61. On the relationship between science and technology see, e.g., (Radnitzky, 1983a) pp. 235–243; (Radnitzky, 1986a) pp. 666 ff.

62. In practice, theory testing appears to be localized. Physicists do not test general theories; they test either the least corroborated part of the theory or that part which is regarded as crucial for the calculation of the results. Theories, if they are powerful, condense so much information that one has to proceed in this way: to extract (by constructing deductive arguments) from them packages of empirical information that are so small that the information can be handled experimentally, that the derived hypotheses can be tested empirically.

63. On the distinction between basic and applied research cf., e.g., (Radnitzky, 1983a), (Radnitzky, 1986a) pp. 656 ff.

64. (Popper, 1959) p. 104; (Popper, 1934) pp. 69 f.

65. Cf. Popper, from (Popper, 1934) to (Popper, 1983) and (Popper, 1984).

66. E.g., L. D. Sneed, W. Stegmüller; cf. (Andersson, 1979), esp. pp. 8–10, for a concise critique of instrumentalism.

67. Science policy that is *internal* to science must be clearly distinguished from science policy that is *external* to science: the political decisions allocating financial and other resources among fields of study, among disciplines or groups of disciplines, of setting budgetary frames for basic science or budgetary frames for applied research according to "social merit," etc. For an overview cf., e.g., (Radnitzky, 1983a).

68. Cf., e.g., (Radnitzky, 1981) *PRR* pp. 45–50. Incidentally, those who deny that they operate within some methodological framework and claim that they do not need any methodology are as a rule adherents of naive positivism.

69. On the dimensions of criticism of theories, cf., e.g., (Radnitzky, 1974), esp. Fig. 4 on p. 90; (Bartley, 1982) pp. 161–177. The various dimensions of criticism have to be stated and ranked in a way that fits the particular problem situation. Space does not permit me to elaborate this. Let me only mention that the basic pre-testing criterion is relative content of empirical information—how much a theory says. Popper recommends bold conjectures, theories that have a high empirical content, are highly falsifiable, and, hence, also corroborable in principle, i.e., he recommends an entrepreneurial spirit in research. As in business, risk and possible gains are also correlated in science. The basic post-testing criterion is whether what the theory says, or how much of what it says, is accurate—the relative degree of truthlikeness. Has it so far withstood severe testing better than its competitor? If so, this is a good reason for conjecturing that it is closer to the truth. The concept of comparative truthlikeness is applicable also to cases where both of the competing theories are falsified. However, this approach bears no resemblance to the positivists' attempt to prove that a particular theory is more probabilified by the evidence than another.

70. Cf., e.g., Radnitzky in (Radnitzky and Andersson, 1979) pp. 244–249; (Radnitzky, 1980) pp. 221–227.

71. An analogy from economics could be that in a free market for money, high-confidence-money would drive out low-confidence money.

72. (Schlesinger, 1981) pp. 458 f.

73. On *ad hocness* cf., e.g., (Radnitzky and Andersson, 1979) pp. 242–244.

74. (Sexl, 1983).

REFERENCES

Albert, H., *Traktat über rationale Praxis*, Tübingen: J.C.B. Mohr Verlag (1978).

Andersson, G., "Presuppositions, Problems, Progress," in (Radnitzky and Andersson, 1979) pp. 3–18.

———, "Naive and Critical Falsificationism," in (Levinson, 1982) pp. 50–63.

———, "Creativity and Criticism in Science and Politics," in (Andersson, 1984c) pp. 1–14 (1984a).

———, "How to Accept Fallible Test Statements? Popper's Criticist Solution," in (Andersson, 1984c) pp.47–68 (1984b).

———, (ed.), *Rationality in Science and Politics*, (*Boston Studies in the Philosophy of Science*, Vol. 79), Dordrecht: Reidel, 1984 (1984c).

Antiseri, D., *Teoria unificata del metodo*, Padova: Liviana (1981).

Bartley, W. W., III. *The Retreat to Commitment*, New York: Alfred A. Knopf (1962); 2nd ed., rev. and enlarged, La Salle, Ill.: Open Court (1984a).

———, "On the Criticizability of Logic," *Philosophy of the Social Sciences* 10 (1980) pp. 67–77.

———, "The Philosophy of Karl Popper: Part III: Rationality, Criticism, and Logic," *Philosophia* (Israel) 11 (1982) pp. 121–221.

———, "Knowledge is a Product Not Fully Known to its Producer," in Leube and Zlabinger, 1984), pp. 17–46. (1984b).

————, "Philosophy of Biology *versus* Philosophy of Physics," in (Radnitzky and Bartley, 1986) as Chapter 1. (1986a).

————, "A Refutation of the Alleged Comprehensively Critical Rationalism," in (Radnitzky and Bartley, 1968) as Chapter 15. (1986b).

Brown, C., and P. Jackson, *Public Sector Economics*, Oxford: Martin Robertson, (1978).

Demsetz, H., "Information and Efficiency: Another Viewpoint," *The Journal of Law and Economics* 12 (April, 1969) pp. 1–22.

Ghiselin, M., *The Economy of Nature and the Evolution of Sex*, Berkeley: University of California Press (1974).

————, "The Economy of the Body," *The American Economic Review* 68 (1978) pp. 233–237.

Grmek, J., R. Cohen and G. Cimino (eds.), *On Scientific Discovery. The Erice Lectures 1977*, (*Boston Studies in the Philosophy of Science*, Vol. 34), Dordrecht: Reidel (1981).

Grove, J., "The Sociological Denigration of the Rationality of Science," *Minerva* 20 (1982) pp. 550–556.

Hansmeyer, K.-H. (ed.), *Das rationale Budget. Ansätze moderner Haushaltstheorie*, Köln: Kölner Universitäts-Verlag (1971).

Hayek, F. v. "The Use of Knowledge in Society," *American Economic Review* 35 (September, 1945) pp. 519–530, repr. as pamphlet, e.g., by the Institute for Humane Studies, Menlo Park, Cal. (1977).

Hayek, F. v. *Law, Legislation and Liberty*, 3 vols, London: Routledge and Kegan Paul (1973, 1976, 1979).

Heelan, P., *Space Perception and the Philosophy of Science*, Berkeley, Cal.: University of California Press (1984).

Heinrich, B., *Bumblebee Economics*, Cambridge, Mass.: Harvard University Press (1979).

Hirshleifer, J., "Economics from a Biological Viewpoint," *The Journal of Law and Economics* 20 (April, 1977) pp. 1–52.

————, "Competition, Cooperation and Conflict in Economics and Biology," *The American Economic Review* 68 (1978, 1978a) pp. 238–243.

————, "Natural Economy versus Political Economy," *Journal of Social and Biological Structures* 1 (1978, 1978b) pp. 319–337.

Kirsch, G., "Die Cost-Benefit-Analyse: Ein Katalog von Fragen," in (Hansmeyer, 1971) pp. 55–104.

Kuhn, T. S. "Logic of Discovery or Psychology of Research?" in (Lakatos and Musgrave, 1970) pp. 1–23.

Lakatos, I., and A. Musgrave (eds.), *Criticism and the Growth of Knowledge*, London: Cambridge University Press (1970).

Leube, K. and A. Zlabinger (eds.), *The Political Economy of Freedom: Essays in Honor of F. A. Hayek*, München: Philosophia Verlag (1984).

Levinson, P. (ed.), *In Pursuit of Truth. Essays on the Philosophy of Karl Popper on the Occasion of His 80th Birthday*, Atlantic Highlands, N.J.: Humanities Press (1982).

Munz, P., *Our Knowledge of the Growth of Knowledge*, London: Routledge and Kegan Paul (1985).

Pähler, K., *Qualitätsmerkmale wissenschaftlicher Theorien*, Tübingen: J. C. B. Mohr (1986).

Petroni, A., *Karl R. Popper: il pensiero politico, Critiche e proposte del grande teoretico liberale in una ricostruzione antologica*, Firenze: Le Monnier (1981). (Introduction by A. Petroni pp. 5–112).

Popper, K., *Zur Methodenfrage der Denkpsychologie*, Dissertation (Universität Wien, Sommersemester 1982) *in manuscript*.

————, *The Poverty of Historicism*, London: Routledge and Kegan Paul (1957) 10th impression (1979); originally published in *Economica* (1944/5).

————, *The Logic of Scientific Discovery*, London: Hutchinson (1959) 11th impression (1982); originally published as *Logik der Forschung*, Wien: Springer (1934).

————, *Conjectures and Refutations*, London: Routledge and Kegan Paul (1963) 7th rev. ed. (1978).

————, "La Rationalité et le statut du principe de rationalité" in Classen, E. (ed.), *Les fondements philosophiques des systèmes économiques*, Paris: Payot (1967) pp. 142–150; shortened Engl. transl. in Miller, D. (ed.), *A pocket Popper*, London: Fontana (1983) pp. 335–365.

————, "Normal Science and its Dangers," in (Lakatos and Musgrave, 1970) pp. 51–58.

————, *Objective Knowledge*, Oxford: The Clarendon Press (1972) 5th rev. ed. (1979).

————, *Unended Quest, An Intellectual Autobiography,* London: Fontana, (1976).

————, *Die beiden Grundprobleme der Erkenntnistheorie,* Tübingen: J. C. B. Mohr, (1979).

————, "A Proof of the Impossibility of Inductive Probability," *Nature* 302 (1983) pp. 687–688.

————, Against Induction: One of Many Arguments," in (Andersson, 1984c) pp. 245–248.

Radnitzky, G., "The Internal Rate of Profit as a Measure of Profitability," *Erhversøkonomisk Tidskrift* (Copenhagen) 28 (1964) pp. 195–211.

————, *Contemporary School of Metascience,* New York, N.Y.: Humanities (1968) rev. and enl. ed. Chicago: Regnery (1973); from (1977 Chicago: Gateway Editions).

————, "From Logic of Science to Theory of Research," *Communication and Cognition* 7 (1974) pp. 61–124.

————, "From Justifying a Theory to Comparing Theories and Selecting Questions," *Revue Internationale de Philosophie* 34 (1980) pp. 179–228.

————, "Progress and Rationality in Research," in (Grmek *et al.,* 1981) pp. 43–102.

————, "Entre Wittgenstein et Popper, Philosophie analytique et théorie de la science," *Archives de Philosophie* (Paris) 45 (1982, 1982a) pp. 3–62.

————, "Popper as a Turning Point in the Philosophy of Science," in (Levinson, 1982) pp. 64–80 (1982b).

————, "Knowing and Guessing. If All Knowledge is Conjectural, Can We Speak of Cognitive Progress?" *Zeitschrift für allgemeine Wissenschaftstheorie* 13 (1982, 1982c) pp. 110–121.

————, "Teoria della scienza," *Enciclopedia del Novecento,* Roma: Istituto della Enciclopedia Italiana, Vol VI (1982) pp. 370–386 (1982d).

————, "Science, Technology, and Political Responsibility," *Minerva* 21 (1983, 1983a) pp. 234–264.

————, "Die ungeplante Gesellschaft. Friedrich von Hayeks Theorie der spontanen Ordnungen und selbstorganisierenden Systeme," *Hamburger Jahrbuch für Wirtschafts- und Sozialpolitik* 29 (1984) pp. 9–33.

————, "Réflexions sur Popper—Le savoir, conjectural mais objectif, et indépendent de toute question: Qui y croit? Qui est â son origine?" *Archives de Philosophie* (Paris) 48 (1985, 1985a) pp. 79–108.

————, "Responsibility in Science and in the Decisions About the Use or Non-Use of Technologies," *The World & I. A Chronicle of Our Changing Era.* Washington DC, 1 (May, 1986, 1986a) pp. 649–675.

————, "In Defense of Self-applicable Critical Rationalism," in (Radnitzky and Bartley, 1986) as Chapter 14 (1986b).

————, "Erkenntnistheoretische Probleme im Lichte von Evolutionstheorie und Ökonomie," in (Riedl und Wuketits, 1986). (1986c).

————, "Explikation," in (Seiffert und Radnitzky, 1986). (1986d).

————, "Wissenschaftstheorie," in (Seiffert und Radnitzky, 1986). (1986e).

————, and G. Andersson (eds.), *Progress and Rationality in Science, (Boston Studies in the Philosophy of Science* Vol. 58), Dordrecht: Reidel (1978).

————, and G. Andersson (eds.), *The Structure and Development of Science, (Boston Studies in the Philosophy of Science* Vol. 59), Dordrecht: Reidel (1979).

————, and W. W. Bartley, III (eds.), *Evolutionary Epistemology, Rationality, and the Sociology of Knowledge,* LaSalle, Ill.: Open Court (1986).

Riedl, R. und F. Wuketits (eds.), *Die evolutionäre Erkenntnistheorie,* Hamburg and Berlin: Paul Parey (1986).

Seiffert, H. und G. Radnitzky (Hrsg.), *Handlexikon zur Wissenschaftstheorie,* München: Ehrenwirth Verlag (1986) *forthcoming.*

Sexl, R., "Die Hohlwelttheorie" in *Der mathematische und naturwissenschaftliche Untenricht* 36 (1983) pp. 453–460.

Shearmur, J., "Review of P. Levinson (ed.), *In Pursuit of Truth,*" *Technology and Culture* 25 (1984) pp. 694–696.

Schilpp, P. (ed.), *The philosophy of Karl R. Popper, (The Library of Living Philosophers),* 2 vols., LaSalle, Ill.: Open Court (1974).

Schlesinger, G. "The Essential Tension: Selected Studies in Scientific Tradition and Change," by Thomas Kuhn, The University of Chicago Press (1977) *Philosophia* (Israel) 9 (July, 1981) pp. 455–467.

Part V

THE ECONOMIC APPROACH TO CONFLICT

JACK HIRSHLEIFER

In racing for a prize you can better your chances by running faster yourself, or by making your opponents run slower. More generally there are two main classes of strategies in life's contests: improving your own performance, or hindering your competitors. When one or more competitors adopt hindrance strategies, the result is *conflict*. The term conflict does not necessarily imply actual violence—for example, we speak of industrial conflicts (strikes) and legal conflicts (lawsuits). But my discussion will mainly be directed to the use of violence.

A rational decision-maker, the economist presumes, will engage in conflict whenever doing so represents the most advantageous way of competing in a world where prizes are scarce. My primary concern will be to show that economic analysis—i.e., models of rational choice on the decision-making level, and of equilibrium on the level of social interaction—can do much for the study of conflict. But it is also true, and this is my secondary theme, that the study of conflict can do much for economics. Attending to the darker aspects of how humans might and do compete is absolutely essential even for a proper understanding of the relatively benign nature of market competition.

Returning to my primary theme, I want to show how the economic approach to conflict sheds light upon questions such as:

(1) What circumstances lead the parties to engage in conflict, i.e., to "agree to disagree"?

(2) In conflict interactions, when do we observe an interior or balanced solution, and when a tendency toward corner outcomes—total victory for the one side, unrelieved defeat for the other?

(3) Is conflict always or largely a mistake on the part of one side or the other, so that better information can be relied upon to promote peaceful settlement?

335

Table 5.1   Sequence of Topics

I. ELEMENTARY STATICS OF CONFLICT AND SETTLEMENT
II. DYNAMICS AND EQUILIBRIUM—THE UNSOPHISTICATED
    CASE
III. APPROACHES TO SOPHISTICATED EQUILIBRIUM
    1. TIT FOR TAT as Optimal Strategy in Repeated Prisoners'
       Dilemma Games
    2. Contingent Strategies and Commitment
    3. First Move vs. Last Move
IV. ON THE TECHNOLOGY OF CONFLICT
V. CONFLICT, ECONOMICS, AND SOCIETY

In this brief presentation I cannot actually answer all these questions, or even resolve any of them very adequately. I want only to show how the economic approach may permit us to effectively address them. The sequence of topics that I will follow is indicated in Table 5.1.

I ELEMENTARY STATICS OF CONFLICT AND SETTLEMENT[1]

Let me plunge right in with some extremely simple pictures designed to illustrate the interacting decision problems of two individuals as a function of their (1) opportunities, (2) preferences, and (3) perceptions.

Figure 5.1 illustrates alternative "settlement opportunity sets" QQ, drawn on axes representing consumption incomes c_B and c_R for Blue and Red, respectively. (Note: These are the *non-conflictual* opportunities—what the parties might achieve in the absence of fighting.) Three possible shapes for QQ are illustrated: positive complementarity (dashed curve), neutral complementarity, i.e., the constant-sum case (solid 135° line), and negative complementarity (dotted curve).

Turning now to preferences, in Figure 5.2 the trio of indifference curves U_B suggests Blue's alternative possible patterns of "tastes" regarding interpersonal distributions of income. Similarly, the curves U_R show Red's possible "tastes." The normal-looking dashed curves in each case apply when each party has some degree of *benevolence* toward the other; the solid curves (a vertical line for Blue, a horizontal line for Red) indicate merely neutral preferences, where each of the two simply values his own consumption income; finally, the positively-sloped dotted curves indicate *malevolence*.

Finally, we need to display the parties' *perceptions* of the outcome

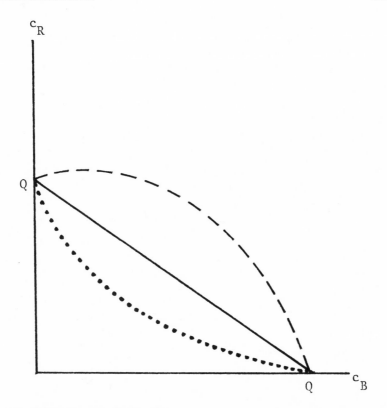

FIG. 5.1: **Alternative opportunity sets.**

in the event of conflict. Figure 5.3 puts together a particular settlement opportunity set QQ (complementary in this case), indifference curves for the two parties (both pictured as displaying a degree of benevolence), and two "conflict perception points" designated P_B and P_R, respectively. Then the shaded area is the "potential settlement region" (PSR), the set of possible income combinations representing improvements over what each perceives as attainable by conflict.

Under the plausible hypothesis that the larger the PSR the greater the likelihood of peaceful settlement, it will be evident that this likelihood is increased by: (1) greater complementarity of the settlement opportunity set QQ, (2) greater benevolence on the part of both parties, and (3) less "optimistic" perceptions of the likely outcome of conflict.

Several other possible combinations are shown in the diagrams. Fig-

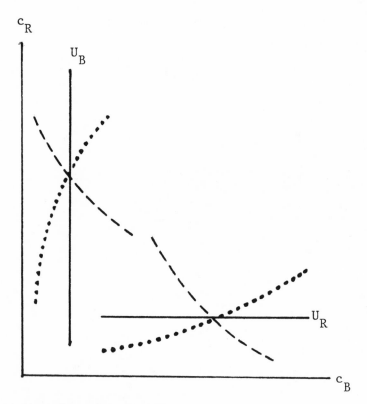

FIG. 5.2: **Alternative preference patterns.**

ure 5.4 illustrates how, in a situation with complementary opportunities and agreed conflict perceptions (i.e., P_B and P_R coincide), malevolent preferences compress the size of the PSR. Figure 5.5 illustrates how anti-complementary opportunities (concave curvature of QQ) also tend to constrict the shaded PSR region, in a situation of neutral preferences together with agreed perceptions. As for the effect of differential perceptions, Figure 5.6 illustrates how in the situation of the previous diagram, a shift of P_B to a new position P'_B (P_R remaining unchanged) has enlarged the PSR by the dotted area—Blue has become more *pessimistic* about the outcome of conflict. On the other hand, as illustrated in Figure 5.7, when each party is optimistic about the outcome it may well be that the PSR entirely disappears, suggesting that conflict has become inevitable.

The effect of complementarity on the international level has recently

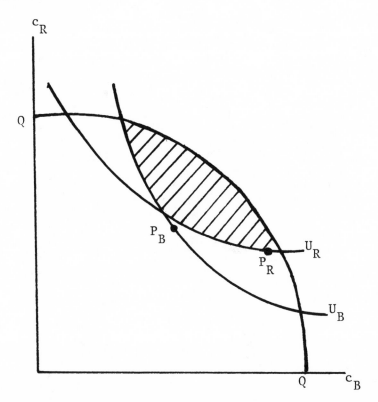

FIG. 5.3: **Mutual benevolence with pessimistic perceptions.**

been documented by Polachek (1980). His data indicate that those country-pairs with the most to gain from trade tend to engage in the least conflict.[2] And of course there are many other instances on the human and animal levels. For example, some small cleaner fish operate actually inside the jaws of their bigger-fish clients; the latter forego a quick and easy meal in return for the benefits of trade in the form of grooming services.

As for interpersonal preferences, individuals and nations with close ties of culture and kinship that lead to mutually benevolent preferences very likely do less frequently engage in conflict—but again, only in an "other things equal" sense. In particular, since brothers are often close competitors for resources, fractricidal conflict is not uncommon despite the closeness of kinship ties.[3]

As an instance displaying the role of changing perceptions and

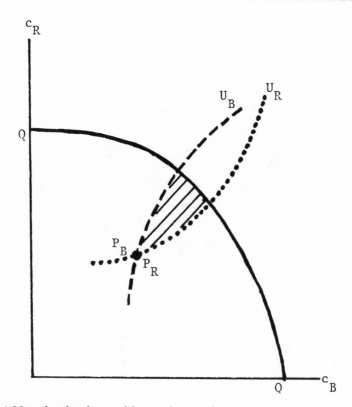

FIG. 5.4: **Mutual malevolence with agreed perceptions.**

beliefs, some authors (e.g., Blainey [1973] on war, Ashenfelter and Johnson [1969] on strikes and lockouts) make the important point that conflict is in large part *an educational process*. Struggle tends to occur when one or both of the parties is overoptimistic (see Figure 5.7). The school of actual struggle teaches the parties to readjust their conflict perception points to more realistic levels. Eventually, a potential settlement region PSR emerges (or an existing region grows larger) so that conflict tends to end by mutual consent.

Two qualifications must be kept in mind, however. First, as Wittman (1979) emphasizes, while the results of continuing struggle may lead the losing party to more realistic (pessimistic) perceptions, the winning party is likely to revise his perceptions upward. The loser becomes more willing to settle but the winner tends to increase his demands—so that the conflict may well continue.[4] Second, the damage due to

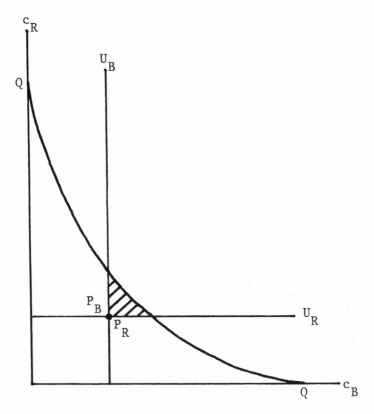

FIG. 5.5: **Anti-complimentary opportunities with agreed perceptions and neutral preferences.**

struggle may impoverish both parties and impair the settlement opportunities as well. The effect on prospects for settlement could go either way, depending upon the new relative positions of the perception points P_B and P_R and the revised QQ curve.

There is more to be said about elementary statics, for example, introducing *asymmetries* in the parties' preference functions (one may be benevolent, the other malevolent), or in the shape of the settlement opportunity set (Blue's non-conflictual activities may confer benefits on Red, while Red's impose costs on Blue). But I must set this topic aside in order to move on. How small a slice of our topic has been even touched on so far is suggested by Table 5.2, which indicates *some* of the directions in which the analysis needs to be extended.

In what follows, I will only be able to address the first of these topics

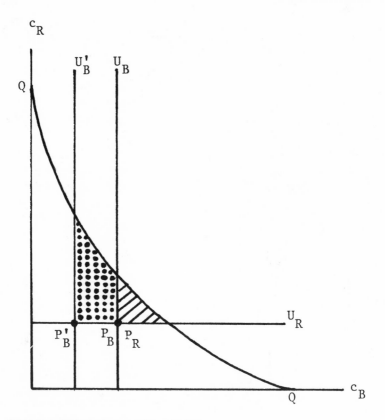

FIG. 5.6: Effect of Blue's increased pessimism.

in any detail. Among other things, I will be asking, granted that a mutually advantageous settlement opportunity exists, under what circumstances can conflict actually be avoided.

II DYNAMICS AND EQUILIBRIUM (THE UNSOPHISTICATED CASE)[5]

Under the heading of elementary statics I indicated how preferences, opportunities, and perceptions combine to influence individual decisions. But I did not progress very far toward showing how an *equilibrium* emerges when the parties' decisions interact. The nature of the equilibrium turns out to depend critically upon the detailed dynamics of the interaction—or, I shall sometimes say, upon the "protocol" that

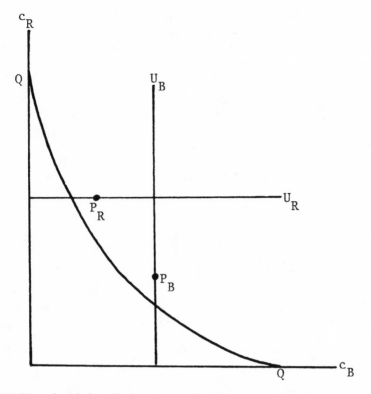

FIG. 5.7: **Mutual optimism eliminates potential settlement region.**

specifies how and in what sequence the parties make their choices. These specifications are most clearly expressed in the language of game theory. This language is adopted at a cost, since game theory drastically compresses the separate categories of preferences, opportunities, and perceptions into a single numerical tabulation representing the net *payoffs to alternative strategies*. But I will pursue this approach for the moment.

Table 5.2   Directions for Fuller Analysis

1. From statics to dynamics and equilibrium
2. From individuals to organizations
3. From 2-party to n-party interactions
4. From a-temporal to intertemporal analysis
5. Allowing for risk and uncertainty
6. Conflict at varying levels—"escalation"

The familiar game matrix, then, is taken as summarizing the players' decision environment. I will begin with a comparative discussion of three famous elementary 2 x 2 games—Battle of the Sexes (BOS), Chicken, known also in the biological literature as Hawk-Dove (HD), and Prisoners' Dilemma (PD)—shown in Tables 5.3, 5.4, and 5.5. These are non-zero-sum interactions; each represents a somewhat different combination of complementary versus anticomplementary elements. While the abstract game representation fails to distinguish between *conflict* as such versus other types of cooperation failures (for example, those associated with "externalities"), I will assume here that whenever efficiency is not achieved, the explanation is the adoption of a conflict strategy by one or both parties.

The most common solution concept for the non-zero-sum game is the "Nash non-cooperative equilibrium" (NE)—sometimes called the "equilibrium point." The key idea is that there is no equilibrium so long as either player can gain an advantage by shifting his strategy. (The pure-strategy NE's are marked with asterisks in Tables 5.3, 5.4, and 5.5, the first two cases having also a mixed-strategy NE not shown in the Tables.) The NE equilibrium concept might or might not be objectionable, depending upon the assumptions as to the players' capacities or the dynamics of the interaction. I want to make these assumptions quite explicit.

To divide the difficulties I first consider equilibrium in "unsophisticated" play. The players may perhaps lack the ability to reason stra-

Table 5.3   Battle of the Sexes

He		She C_1	C_2
	R_1	*10,5	0,0
	R_2	0,0	*5,10

Table 5.4   Chicken or Hawk-Dove

	C_1 (DOVE)	C_2 (HAWK)
R_1(DOVE)	4,4	*0,10
R_2(HAWK)	*10,0	-24,-24

Table 5.5   Prisoners' Dilemma

	C_1 (LOYAL)	C_2 (DEFECT)
R_1(LOYAL)	-2,-2	-20,0
R_2(DEFECT)	0,-20	*-10,-10

tegically—i.e., to conceptualize that "if I do this, then he will do that, in which case I would respond by. . . . " More interestingly for the economist, unsophisticated play might be appropriate even for intelligent parties in certain environmental situations, especially those associated with large numbers of players (as in the standard pure-competition model). Specifically, think of a "war of all against all," in which members of a large population encounter one another randomly in one-time pairwise interactions. This leads to a concept I shall call *evolutionary equilibrium* (EE). If the average return to each strategy depends upon the population proportions adopting one or the other, a dynamic process is set up leading eventually to an equilibrium distribution of strategies in the population. This evolutionary equilibrium could be either pure (one strategy eventually drives out all the others) or else mixed. It can be shown that the evolutionary equilibria are a subset of the Nash equilibria; to wit, the EE's are the "dynamically stable" NE's.

The dynamic process and the EE's for our three cases are pictured in Figure 5.8, in terms of the population proportion p characterized by the strategy in the first row and column of each table. Starting with Battle of the Sexes (BOS), as the directions of the arrows suggest there are two EE's—at the limiting proportions, $p = 0$ and $p = 1$. The mixed solution at $p = .5$ is an NE, but not being dynamically stable it is not an EE. The simplest interpretation is as follows. Assume that in each encounter the He and She roles are randomly assigned. In the initial population there are a fixed number of players having permanently chosen Strategy #1, the remainder playing Strategy #2. However, the population fractions will evolve in accordance with the relative success of the two strategies. It follows that if more than half the population is already committed to the first strategy, that strategy will be more successful and will multiply further, and similarly in the opposite case.[6] A possible application would be the struggle for language dominance in an initially bilingual population, there being a strong tendency toward a corner solution despite the *comparative* disadvantage suffered by native speakers of the losing language.

In contrast with the very mild "battle" involved in Battle of the Sexes, the game of Chicken or Hawk-Dove (I will usually employ the latter designation) can entail serious conflict. When one HAWK encounters another, a lot of feathers may fly. For the payoff numbers in Table 5.4, the diagram indicates a single EE at $p = .8$, a mixed solution. That is, the equilibrium strategy is to play DOVE eighty percent of the time and HAWK the other twenty percent. (Or else, there will

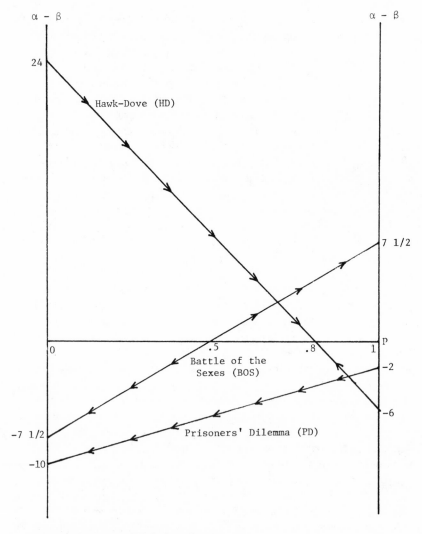

be a mixed population, eighty percent Doves and twenty percent Hawks.)[7] The HD game is sometimes thought to describe industrial or international conflict, the idea being that sometimes you have to play tough, for example, go out on strike, or else the other party will know you are a DOVE and take advantage of you. This interpretation, involving strategy in repeated games, does not really belong under our "unsophisticated play" heading, although the analogy is suggestive. A more precise interpretation is as follows. If there are only a few tough people around, it pays to be aggressive—only rarely will you get into costly fights. But when most of the population is aggressive, the smart play is to be quiet and stay out of trouble.

As for the Prisoners' Dilemma, Figure 5.8 indicates that there is a unique EE, in which everyone adopts the DEFECT strategy.[8] The international arms race is often described as a Prisoners' Dilemma, though once again this is only an analogy; the arms race corresponds to a repeated-play rather than a one-time-only game. A more accurate interpretation would be the famous "commons" problem, where it pays to impose costs upon one's neighbors whether or not they refrain from doing the same to you.

In the EE (and NE) solution to the Prisoners' Dilemma, the players are trapped in their third-best (i.e., next-to-worst) outcome, even though it seems that they should be able to achieve their jointly second-best outcome (which is on the settlement opportunity frontier) by mutually LOYAL play. What prevents their doing so is assumed *nonenforceability of agreements*. Similarly in Hawk-Dove, there is a potential mutual gain on average (in comparison with the mixed-strategy equilibrium) if the parties were to agree: "In each encounter one of us will be randomly designated to play HAWK, the other to play DOVE." To escape some real-world conflictual encounters it *is* sometimes possible to make binding agreements, but not always. Lawsuits can be settled without going to trial, via an agreement that the court may (perhaps) be relied on to enforce. But, except perhaps for small nations both subject to a common suzerain, no such outside enforcement is available in international conflict. More generally, enforceability of agreements is a matter of degree, depending in part upon the motives of the "enforcer"—which means that a three-party game is being played. Sometimes, however, agreements are said to be *self-enforcing*. This can only be the case, under HD or PD environments, when some kind of expanded game is being played. Such considerations lead to the topic of "sophisticated" equilibrium, the subject of the next section.

III APPROACHES TO SOPHISTICATED EQUILIBRIUM[9]

While the very unsophisticated models so far discussed are by no means devoid of applicability, to make further progress we have to consider more complex types of conflictual encounters. I can only address here topics associated with three types of complications:

(1) When there are repeated plays of the game, so that the parties can modify their choices in the light of opponents' earlier moves.

(2) When one or both parties can *commit* to a strategy.

(3) As a generalization of the preceding, when there are different "protocols,"for example when one party or the other has the first move, or when one or the other outcome is the *status quo ante*.

1 TIT FOR TAT AS OPTIMAL STRATEGY IN REPEATED PRISONERS' DILEMMA GAMES

The topic here considered is: In the repeated-play Prisoners' Dilemma, can the "trap" outcome be escaped by having one or both parties adopt the strategy of rewarding the other for LOYAL play and punishing him for playing DEFECT?

It is a well-known result in the theory of repeated games ("super-games" in the unfortunate current jargon) that the PD trap cannot be escaped for any finite numbers of plays. For, DEFECT surely will always be optimal on the last round. But then LOYAL on the next-to-last round cannot be rewarded and thus will not rationally be chosen, and so on back to the very first round. The prospects are somewhat better for an infinite number of plays, or where there is merely some positive probability of play always continuing for another round. Each of these cases involves heavier mathematics than I want to get into here, however.

In a recent volume, Axelrod (1984) (see also Axelrod and Hamilton [1981]) summarizes a number of his researches concerning the repeated-play Prisoners' Dilemma. By now quite famous are the two computer round-robin tournaments among candidate strategies submitted by various experts. In the first tournament each of fifteen different strategies was paired against every other (and against itself) in 200-round interactions. In the second tournament there were sixty-two entries; this time, instead of each pairwise interaction lasting a fixed number of rounds, a probability of continuation was chosen which worked out to make the average contest length 151 rounds.

The two tournaments were both "won" by the simple conditional-cooperation strategy known as TIT FOR TAT. Against any opponent the TIT FOR TAT player initially chooses LOYAL, but thenceforth simply mirrors his opponent's choice in the previous round. Thus, an

opponent who plays DEFECT at any point is punished, but in a proportionate eye-for-an-eye way that leaves open the possibility of
mutual reversion toward more cooperative play. The success of TIT
FOR TAT was due primarily to its "robustness." Even though TIT FOR
TAT never outscored any single opponent strategy in a one-on-one
encounter in these tournaments, it piled up points by doing quite well
against almost every opponent (and very well indeed when paired
against itself).

The claim has been made, on the basis of these tournament results,
that mutually profitable adoption of TIT FOR TAT is *the* explanation
for the evolution of cooperation.[10] Put another way, the contention is
that—if social cooperation evolves at all—it will be because populations initially pursuing a variety of strategies for coping with the
repeated-play Prisoners' Dilemma have ended up in an evolutionary
equilibrium in which everyone plays TIT FOR TAT. This claim must
however be treated with some reserve, and certain cautions will be
indicated here:

1. First of all, Prisoners' Dilemma is only one of a vast number of
mixed-incentive payoff environments in which cooperation might or
might not emerge. Battle of the Sexes and Hawk-Dove as discussed
above are two other such environments. Notice also that each of these
three patterns is a two-person game characterized by two strategy
options for each player. More generally, of course, there are games
with any number of players, and any number of strategies for each
player. In fact, there is a multiple infinity of payoff environments that
pose cooperation problems, and which do not take the special form of
a repeated-play Prisoners' Dilemma.

2. A *round-robin* tournament is also a very special type of contest. In
many circumstances, particularly if we are thinking of evolutionary
selection, the competition among strategies might be better charcter-
ized by an *elimination* tournament. TIT FOR TAT would do very badly
in elimination tournaments, since (as has been noted) it rarely if ever
can defeat any other strategy in a one-on-one encounter.

3. Finally, there is a flaw in the logical development which will be clarified by an example. Consider the strategy triad consisting of LOYAL,
TIT FOR TAT, and DEFECT—which may respectively be termed
Golden Rule, Silver Rule, and Brass Rule. Should the population ever
evolve to one hundred percent TIT FOR TAT, followers of the Golden
Rule (LOYAL) can successfully invade, as LOYAL and TIT FOR TAT
players would then be indistinguishable. This suggests that there will
be an indeterminate equilibrium involving only these two strategies ,
but such a conclusion is unwarranted. Because, once LOYAL becomes

sufficiently numerous, DEFECT becomes profitable again! The upshot is a mixed or cyclic equilibrium.

The "proof" that TIT FOR TAT would be the evolutionary equilibrium (Axelrod [1984], Appendix B) rests upon an assumption that, in order to enter, the invader strategy must actually *do better than* the incumbent. This is an unwarranted requirement; *doing equally well* suffices to permit entry, and in any case precludes extinction if there are any representatives already present in the population. Furthermore, even if definite superiority were required for entry, it can be shown that the EE still would not be a one hundred percent TIT FOR TAT population—if allowance were made for the fact that TIT FOR TAT is a demanding strategy. Specifically, TIT FOR TAT requires ability to discriminate between experienced behaviors, to remember which individuals among those encountered have displayed each type of behavior in the past, and to recognize those individuals when encountered again. Since they do not require these capacities, both LOYAL and DEFECT are less burdensome to adopt and live by. Once a proper accounting is made for the *cost* of the extra abilities that TIT FOR TAT requires, the economics of the situation will preclude the population evolving toward one hundred percent TIT FOR TAT.[11]

2 CONTINGENT STRATEGIES AND COMMITMENT

TIT FOR TAT was an example of a *contingent strategy* in a repeated-game context. It is also possible to have contingent strategies even with single-play games, which leads to what is called the theory of "meta-games" (another unfortunate choice of terminology).

Commitment represents the ability to foreclose one's own future freedom of choice, to guarantee to your opponent that you will not diverge from a specified chosen strategy. (Since one can only achieve any useful effect from commitment by communicating that fact to the other party, I will always be assuming that such communication occurs.) Particularly interesting results ensue from *commitment to contingent strategies*, which correspond to what we call in ordinary language "threats" and "promises." But commitment to a simple strategy is also entirely possible.

Consider Battle of the Sexes (Table 5.3). If He can commit to Strategy #1, the only rational response for She is also to play #1, allowing the committer the higher return. Correspondingly, She would like to commit to Strategy #2, forcing He to go along. In either case, the one with power to commit reaps the greater benefit from the interaction (10 versus 5).

Commitment to a contingent strategy makes sense, as has been emphasized by Thompson and Faith (1981), only in a situation of *sequential play*—where the parties move in some definite order over time. Such a protocol opens up a route of escape from the trap outcome of the Prisoners' Dilemma. It is important here to distinguish between "strategy" and "move." By assumption, the only actual *moves* are those available to the players in the original matrix—LOYAL or DEFECT. A *strategy* is a plan for playing the moves in a context of a particular sequential protocol, the governing rules of the game. The "Expanded Prisoners' Dilemma" of Table 5.6 illustrates such a situation.

In Table 5.6 we suppose that Row has the power to commit to a contingent strategy, Column being limited as before to his simple LOYAL versus DEFECT options. The interesting contingent strategy for Row is CONCUR: threaten DEFECT if Column's move is DEFECT but promise LOYAL if Column plays LOYAL. (But for completeness the rather illogical DIVERGE strategy is also shown.) Row's optimal play is to *commit* to CONCUR, in which case Column will surely play LOYAL—the result being (-2, -2). Thus, the Prisoners' Dilemma has been escaped; the parties achieve their second-best outcomes, as compared with the third-best (i.e., next-to-worst) results that constitute the trap solution. It is also interesting to note here that having the power to commit has not led to any comparative advantage for Row over Column.

The significance of commitment for the problem of *deterrence* is illustrated by Tables 5.7 and 5.8. Table 5.7 is another version of the

Table 5.6   Expanded Prisoners' Dilemma

	C_1 (LOYAL)	C_2 (DEFECT)
R_1(LOYAL)	$-2, -2$	$-20, 0$
R_2(DEFECT)	$0, -20$	$-10, -10$
R_3(CONCUR)	$-2, -2$	$-10, -10$
R_4(DIVERGE)	$0, -20$	$-20, 10$

Table 5.7   Deterrence Without Commitment

	C_1 (REFRAIN)	C_2 (ATTACK)
R_1(FOLD)	3,2	1,3
R_2(RETALIATE)	3,2	2,1

Table 5.8   Deterrence Requiring Commitment

	C_1 (REFRAIN)	C_2 (ATTACK)
R_1(FOLD)	3,2	2,3
R_2(RETALIATE)	3,2	1,1

Expanded Prisoners' Dilemma just discussed. In the deterrence context, for the party with the first move (the Column player), DEFECT in Table 5.6 becomes ATTACK in Tables 5.7 and 5.8, while LOYAL in Table 5.6 corresponds to REFRAIN in Tables 5.7 and 5.8. For the responding (Row) player, two strategies have been deleted. DIVERGE has been omitted because of its evident irrationality. Also, ATTACK (= DEFECT) has been dropped, since if Row can consider attacking regardless of what Column does we do not have a deterrence situation. Thus, the implication is, Row is incapable of attacking *except* in response. Responding to attack is, of course, the RETALIATE strategy. Failing to do so is the FOLD strategy, corresponding to LOYAL in the original Prisoners' Dilemma. (The actual numerical values given in the Table represent the *ranking* of the outcomes in the underlying Prisoners' Dilemma matrix, 1 being lowest and 3 highest.)

It is evident that deterrence succeeds *even without commitment* in Table 5.7. If attacked, Row prefers to RETALIATE, and this suffices to deter attack. But Row in Table 5.8 is more pacifically inclined, and if attacked, really would prefer FOLD to RETALIATE. Unfortunately, that guarantees he will be attacked! Here is where the power to commit provides an escape. If Row can guarantee in advance that RETALIATE will occur, despite his aversion to that course of action, deterrence succeeds. If he can reliably threaten to do what he does not want to do, he won't have to do it!

An interesting question is: What are the mechanisms of commitment in cases like this? Here we can go back to our fundamental categories of *opportunities, preferences,* and *perceptions.* If Row is pacifically inclined, as pictured in Table 5.8, he can try to shift the situation toward Table 5.7. If possible, he might alter his preferences in the direction of bellicosity. Alternatively, he could try to manipulate elements of the opportunity set. For example, he might make a wager with outsiders, staking a considerable sum that he will *not* choose FOLD. Or, he could make the current encounter into a visible precedent and test case, it being clear that his choosing FOLD here and now will invite future costly confrontations. Or, Row might work on Column's perceptions by putting out misleading indicators of bellicosity.

The emotion of *anger*, which might otherwise seem to be only a "primitive" hindrance to human rationality, appears here in a new light. Anger provides the needed commitment to RETALIATE. My psychological "loss of control," that leads me to punish aggression even where it is not to my short-run material advantage to do so, may be just what is needed to deter invasions.[12] And by a reverse argument, the same may hold for *love*. "Unselfish" willingness to share gains, even when not required to do so, can be not only psychologically but materially rewarding when cooperation on the part of others is elicited thereby.[13] Thus, both anger and love can serve as "enforcers" of implicit contracts between two parties.

3 FIRST MOVE VERSUS LAST MOVE

With outcomes specified by a given game matrix, quite different results may ensue depending upon whether the players choose simultaneously or sequentially—and if the latter, depending upon which moves first and which moves last. The latter topic has some suggestive implications for the choice between offense and defense in war, or pre-emptive moves in diplomacy. Without getting into these applications here, it will be of interest to look at some of the advantages and disadvantages of priority.

Consider a sequential-move single-round game. In such a game it may pay a player to follow a so-called "dominated" strategy of the corresponding simultaneous-move game. (Since the Nash equilibrium NE cannot involve playing a dominated strategy, it follows that the NE will not be an appropriate solution concept here.)[14] In Table 5.9 Column is supposed to be the first-mover. His strategy #2 is clearly dominated by strategy #1. Nevertheless, he does better at the sequential-play equilibrium R2, C2 (marked with a +) than at the Nash equilibrium R1, C1 (marked with an asterisk) that would be reached had he played his dominant strategy.

Table 5.9 "Dominated"-Strategy Equilibrium

| | | First-mover | |
		C_1	C_2
Second-	R_1	*4,2	2,1
mover	R_2	1,4	+3,3

A more central question for our purposes is, who has the advantage, first-mover or second-mover? In Battle of the Sexes (BOS), as has already been noted, first-mover can force achievement of the common-strategy outcome that favors him or her (see Table 5.10). And in Chicken or Hawk-Dove (HD) also, by playing HAWK the first-mover can force his opponent into DOVE with an inferior outcome (Table 5.11). Can last-mover ever have the advantage? Yes, as illustrated in Table 5.12. Here, if Column has the last move he can force R2, C2, with outcome (2,3)—whereas Row having the last move leads to R1, C2 with returns (3,2). Thus, the last-mover here has the advantage.

Interpreting these results, notice that both BOS and HD are characterized by strong parallelism of interest between the players. In contrast, Table 5.11 is a constant-sum case (if we interpret the tabulated numbers as cardinal magnitudes). The players' interests being strictly opposed, the first-mover knows that his opponent's final move will be entirely adverse to his interests. Hence, the non-terminator is induced to settle for a "safe" but relatively unsatisfactory intermediate payoff; that is to say, he must accept the bad to avoid the worst. But when the parties' interests are not strictly opposed, first-mover can commonly adopt a strategy such that he will benefit more by second-mover's optimal response than second-mover can gain himself.

A nice illustration of the relative advantages of first-move versus last-move arises in oligopoly theory. In the homogeneous-product duopoly case, with *quantity* as the decision variable, the first-mover has the advantage—the so-called "Stackelberg solution." Being able to

Table 5.10   Battle of the Sexes

		She	
		C_1	C_2
He	R_1	3,2	1,1
	R_2	1,1	2,3

Table 5.11   Hawk-Dove (Or Chicken)

	C_1 (DOVE)	C_2 (HAWK)
R_1(DOVE)	3,3	2,4
R_2(HAWK)	4,2	1,1

Table 5.12   Last-Move Advantage

	C_1	C_2
R_1	1,4	3,2
R_2	4,1	2,3

predict and therefore allow for his competitor's subsequent constrained optimization, the first-mover can produce a level of output such as to pre-empt most of the joint duopoly gain. If, however, *price* is the decision variable (as might be the case if the duopolists' products were not identical), then the last-mover clearly has the advantage. For, regardless of the price selected by his opponent, the last-mover can undercut it so as to engross most of the joint sales. Thus, once again the first-mover tends to have the advantage where there is strong parallelism of interest—the case where quantity is the decision variable, the parties having a strong joint interest in keeping the common price high. But the last-mover has the advantage where interests are more strictly opposed, as when he can largely deprive the other of sales by undercutting on price.

IV   ON THE TECHNOLOGY OF CONFLICT[15]

Conflict is a kind of "industry"—a way in which economic agents compete for resources. Just as the economist without being a manager or an engineer can apply certain broad principles to the processes of industrial production, so, without claiming to replace the military commander he can say something about the possibilities for "producing" desired results through violent conflict.

Under this heading I will only address one topic here: *increasing versus decreasing returns in the sphere of conflict*.

As an historical generalization, *battles* generally proceed to a definitive outcome—victory for the one side, defeat for the other. *Wars*, while sometimes terminating in complete overthrow of one side or the other, are somewhat more likely to end inconclusively or with a compromise settlement. I argue that this is related to the scope of increasing versus decreasing returns to the application of violence. A related phenomenon is the fact that the world is divided into a system of nation-states: while each government has a near-monopoly of power within a limited region, the struggles that continue to take place along the frontiers reveal that there is typically a periphery along which forces are about equally balanced.

Thus, there seem to be two general principles at work. (1) Within a given geographical region, as the scale of military effort grows there tend to be *increasing returns*— and hence a "natural monopoly" of military power within each sufficiently limited base area. (2) But in attempting to extend military sway over larger regions, *diminishing returns* are encountered to the projection of power away from the base—hence, we do not see a single universal world-state.

What is it that underlies the scope of the increasing-returns principle? Simply that the stronger contender can steadily inflict a more-than-proportionate loss upon his opponent, thus becoming (relatively) stronger still. In a situation where only pairwise relative strength counts, this process tends to proceed to the limit of total annihilation (unless flight or surrender intervenes).

Simple yet important special cases of this process are modeled in Lanchester's equations. In linear warfare, for example, the military units (soldiers, ships) arranged in line distribute their fire equally over the enemy's line. Symbolizing the Blue force size as B and the Red force size as R, the relevant process equations are:

$$dB/dt = -k_R R$$
$$dR/dt = -k_B B$$

where k_B and k_R are the respective attack efficiencies (reflecting factors like vulnerability versus accuracy of fire). The condition for equality is:

$$k_B B^2 = k_R R^2$$

Thus, military strength in linear warfare varies proportionately with force effectiveness but as the square of force size. Even where this exact rule does not apply,[16] it still is quite generally the case that in the combat process the strong become stronger and the weak weaker, ending in total victory for the one side and defeat for the other.

The logic of this is so compelling[17] that we may well wonder why it sometimes fails to hold. Among the possible complicating factors are:

1. Force effectiveness may not be uniform in time or in scale. The initially more powerful army may fatigue more rapidly. Or, the initially losing commander may turn out to have a comparative advantage in handling the smaller forces that remain once both sides have suffered attrition.

2. Actual battle is of course typically too complex to be modeled in a simple linear way. For one thing, the field of combat may be inhomogeneous: the losing side may have an "area of refuge" within which it retains sufficient strength to avoid annihilation.

3. In the fog of war, sometimes the winning general does not know he has won. Hence, he may withdraw the forces capable of achieving total victory.

4. While battles are almost always two-sided interactions, wars normally are at least potentially multi-sided. Rather than suffer further losses in order to annihilate a defeated enemy, the winning commander may choose to conserve the forces needed to meet other opponents.[18]

5. But by far the most important of the disturbing factors is the fickle finger of Fate. Recognizing the multitude of unpredictable chance-events in warfare that sometimes favor one side, sometimes the other, the prudent commander may be happy to settle for "good enough" rather than push matters to the extreme.

Allowing for these moderating factors, Figure 5.9 illustrates the applicability of the increasing-returns principle. There will be some critical ratio of forces, indicated by the dashed vertical line, where the probabilities of victory are equal. In the neighborhood of this critical ratio, small changes in the balance of forces tend to bring about disproportionately large effects upon the chances of victory.

My second broad generalization, that *decreasing returns* apply to the

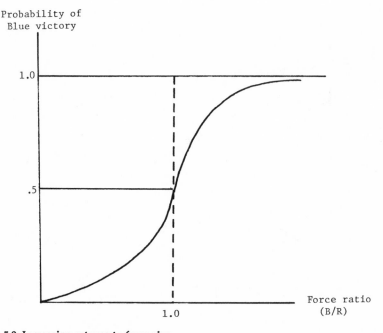

FIG. 5.9: Increasing returns to force size.

geographical extension of military power, is pictured in Figure 5.10.[19] Writing the military strengths at the parties' respective home bases as M_B and M_R, for a balance of power over distance to exist the following must hold:

$$M_B - s_B d_B = M_R - s_R d_R$$

Hence, s_B and s_R are the loss-of-strength gradients in geographically projecting power. And d_B and d_R are the respective distances from base over which each of the two has dominant power, where $d_B + d_R = D$, with D being the total distance between the two bases.

This analysis suggests that the size of nations, for example (on this, see Friedman [1977]), will depend upon two somewhat distinguishable abilities: (1) to organize power at the base and (2) to project power over distance. Major historical trends in the partition of the earth's surface— into independent city-states in some eras, huge superpowers in others—could be analyzed in terms of changes in factors like population sizes, technology, and organizational forms that affect the parameters of the equation.

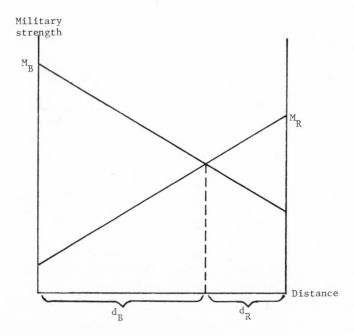

FIG. 5.10: **Decreasing returns to extension of power.**

This simplistic discussion of the decreasing-returns principle once again requires a long list of qualifications, parallel to those which hedge the applicability of the increasing-returns principle. I will mention here only one additional factor—the crucial distinction between offensive and defensive power. In technological environments where the defense is relatively strong, decreasing-returns to distance are intensified while increasing-returns to force size tend to be moderated. So a stable system of smaller sovereign states tends to emerge. But where offensive technology overbalances the defensive, as in present-day strategic warfare, the world appears to be in a fragile, if not downright unstable, equilibrium—the driving tendency being toward a single world-state dominated by whichever power is sufficiently ruthless to use its offensive strength.

I must leave the topic of the technology of conflict here, having discussed only one of the many crucial factors involved in the "production" of desired outcomes through exercise of violence. Some of the omitted factors are listed for reference purposes in Table 5.13.

V CONFLICT, ECONOMICS, AND SOCIETY

So far I have been able only to drop hints about what I described as my secondary theme—to wit, that the study of conflict is important for economics. I can only expand a little bit on those hints here.

We have seen that the technology of conflict helps explain the size and shape of nations. Apart from the overwhelming importance of that fact, the underlying principle has even broader applicability. Many types of competitions among individuals and organizations have conflictual aspects, and violence always remains as a coercive threat in the background. While the law may attempt to prevent thieves from steal-

Table 5.13 Illustrative Additional Topics in the Technology of Conflict

1. Offense versus defense forces and weaponry
2. First-strike versus second-strike moves/Counterforce versus countervalue targets
3. Trade-offs: Mobility versus fortification, accuracy versus rate of fire, forces in being versus mobilization potential, etc.
4. Maintaining organizational integrity under stress—military and civilian
5. Risk and its control

ing, business firms from sabotaging competitors' premises, attorneys from filing groundless lawsuits, or trade unions from intimidating non-members, control of such behaviors will never be perfectly effective. And in consequence, even entirely law-abiding individuals and organizations must, at the very least, plan on devoting some resources to extra-legal (not necessarily illegal) ways of protecting themselves. It will be evident that these invasive and counter-invasive efforts surely absorb a very substantial fraction of society's resources.

A related set of implications concern the internal structures of organizations. Thompson and Faith (1981), for example, make the extreme assertion (to put it mildly) that democracy is always an illusion, that every state is ultimately a military dictatorship (p. 376).[20] But inspection of the world reveals an enormous range of social structures adopted by animals and humans—ranging from extremes of hierarchical dominance to highly egalitarian systems. A more profitable line of inquiry is to ask what the factors are that affect the steepness of the social dominance gradient. Where there is a single concentrated key resource, as in the irrigation systems of ancient empires, we might expect the struggle for its control to lead to a highly hierarchical social structure.[21] In addition, concentrated populations can be dominated without excessive diminishing returns to the geographical projection of military power. On the other hand, more broadly distributed resources and populations, as in the pioneer days of America's settlement, conduce toward egalitarian social systems. It is also well-known that *external* conflict promotes the adoption of internal command economies and dictatorship. The explanation of this fact is, I believe, connected with the increasing-returns aspect of war and the consequent urgency of controlling free-riding, but unfortunately space does not permit development of this theme here.

My main message can be simply summarized. The institutions of property and law, and the peaceful process of exchange, are highly beneficent aspects of human life. But the economist's inquiries should not be limited to such "nice" behaviors and interactions. Struggle, imposing costs on others, and downright violence are crucial phenomena of the world as we know it. Nor is the opposition between the "nice" and the "not nice" by any means total. Law and property, and thus the possibility for peaceful exchange, can only persist where individuals are ultimately willing to use violence in their defense.

NOTES

The author would like to express his grateful thanks to the Earhart Foundation and to the GSM Research Center for Political Economy for support of this research. The author also had the benefit of helpful comments from Robert Axelrod, Craig McCann, Gordon Tullock and Donald Wittman.

1. The discussion in this section builds upon Boulding (1962, Ch. 1), Friedman (1980), and Wittman (1979).

2. Of course, any such uni-causal explanation must not be taken too far, lest we fall into the error of Angell (1910) who argued just before World War I that the growing web of international commerce had made war impossible.

3. This type of consideration leads to the very interesting question of just what are the factors that tend to generate benevolent versus malevolent interpersonal attitudes. The possible sources of human "altruism" have been much discussed by biologists and to some extent by economists (see, for example, Hirshleifer (1977, pp. 17–26), but for our purposes here, it is more instructive to look at the other side of the picture—malevolence or hatred. While it is quite possible to have "cold-blooded" fighting without hatred, there seems to be a feedback between the two in the human psyche. It appears that the ability to hate one's enemy has been selected in the evolution of the human species, a factor that leads to "hot-blooded," less rationally controllable warfare.

4. Sparta, after her defeat by the Athenians at Cyzicus (410 BCE), offered peace on moderate terms, and did so once again after Arginusae (406). But the overconfident democratic party controlling Athens rejected both offers. The war continued until the irremediable naval disaster at Aegospotami culminated in the total capitulation of Athens (404).

5. The discussion here develops certain ideas in Hirshleifer and Riley (1978) and Hirshleifer (1982, pp. 13–20).

6. Let the average returns to following the first and second strategies be a and b, respectively. In Battle of the Sexes a follower of the first strategy will be in the "He" situation one-half of the time and a "She" situation the other half. Thus:

$$a = .5(10p) + .5(5p) = 7.5p$$

Similarly, for a follower of the second strategy:

$$b = .5[10(1 - p)] + .5[5(1 - p)] = 7.5(1 - p)$$

Since $a - b$ is positive for $p > .5$, whenever more than half the population is initially pursuing the first strategy, that strategy will be the more suc-

361

cessful and the population will evolve toward an EE at p = 1.0. In the opposite case similarly, if p is initially less than .5 the population will evolve toward p = 0.

7. In Hawk-Dove, the payoff a to DOVE will be: $a = 4p + 0(1 - p)$. And for Hawk the payoff b will be: $b = 10p - 24(1 - p)$. The two strategies have equal payoffs when p = .8. In contrast with Battle of the Sexes, in Hawk-Dove this interior p is an evolutionary equilibrium EE. Whenever the DOVE proportion exceeds .8, $a - b$ is negative; HAWK being now more profitable, the DOVE population proportion p will retreat back toward .8— and similarly in the opposite case.

8. In Prisoners' Dilemma the respective returns are: $a = -2p - 20(1 - p)$
$$b = 0p - 10(1 - p)$$
Here $a - b$ is negative for any value of p between zero and unity, and hence, the population will evolve toward p = 0, so that the only EE is an all-DEFECT population.

9. This section builds especially upon Schelling (1960), Axelrod (1984), Thompson and Faith (1981), and Hirshleifer (1982) and (1983).

10. The common title of the Axelrod volume and the Axelrod-Hamilton paper—"The Evolution of Cooperation"—does indeed suggest such a sweeping claim. However, at various points, appropriate qualifying disclaimers do appear in the cited works.

11. For further details on these points see Hirshleifer (1982, pp. 20–35).

12. On this, see Simmel (1955 [1923]). More generally, an outraged sense of justice which leads to "moralistic aggression" (Trivers, 1971) by third parties may be an important force in maintaining the possibility of social cooperation. Again, it is essential that justice be pursued even where *not* in accordance with cost-benefit analysis. ("Let justice be done though the heavens fall.").

13. The "Rotten-Kid" paradigm (Becker, 1976) is a famous instance under this heading. Benevolent willingness of a parent to share the mutual gains can induce a merely selfish Kid to act in the overall family interest—with material benefit to all concerned.

14. It is true that if the choice situation were written in expanded-matrix form, allowing second-mover to employ contingent strategies, the correct solution would always be *one* of the Nash equilibria. But since these equilibria rapidly become excessively numerous with larger ranges of strategy choice, the NE remains not very useful as a solution concept. (On this, see also Brams and Wittman, [1981]).

15. This section makes use of discussions by Tullock (1974, Ch. 9), Boulding (1962, Ch. 12–13), and especially Lanchester (1956 (1916)).

16. Lanchester shows, for example, that where forces *occupy areas,* rather than *extend in lines,* relative strengths vary linearly with force sizes rather as the square of force sizes.

17. Exactly the same logic underlies what is known as "Gause's exclusion principle" in evolutionary theory: when two species compete to occupy any single niche, the more effective competitor must drive the other to extinction. This principle is subject to much the same qualifications as those which limit the scope of increasing returns in conflict interactions (see text below).

18. Harold II of England, having totally defeated the invading Norwegians at Stamford Bridge on September 15, 1066, was left with insufficient strength to avoid disaster at Hastings on October 14.

19. Such a diagram appears in Boulding (1962, p. 230).

20. This conclusion only very doubtfully follows from their analysis, which is, in any case, of a highly special sequential-play game protocol. The games being played in the network of associations that comprise a society are many times more complex than they allow for.

21. This point is the key theme of Wittfogel (1957).

REFERENCES

Angell, Norman, *The Great Illusion* (1910).

Ashenfelter, Orley A. and George E. Johnson, "Bargaining Theory, Trade Unions, and Industrial Strike Activity," *American Economic Review,* 59 (March, 1969).

Axelrod, Robert, *The Evolution of Cooperation,* New York: Basic Books, Inc., (1984).

————, and Hamilton, William D., "The Evolution of Cooperation," *Science,* 211 (March 27, 1981).

Becker, Gary S., "Altruism, Egoism, and Genetic Fitness: Economics and Sociobiology," *J. of Economic Literature,* 14 (Sept., 1976).

Blainey, Geoffrey, *The Causes of War,* New York: The Free Press (1973).

Boulding, Kenneth E., *Conflict and Defense,* New York: Harper & Bros. (1962).

Brams, Steven J. and Donald Wittman, "Nonmyopic Equilibria in 2×2 Games," *Conflict Management & Peace Science*, 6 (Fall, 1981).

Friedman, David, "Many, Few, One: Social Harmony and the Shrunken Choice Set," *American Economic Review*, 70 (March, 1980).

―――――, "The Size and Shape of Nations," *J. of Political Economy*, 85 (Feb, 1977).

Hirshleifer, J., "Economics From a Biological Viewpoint," *J. of Law & Economics*, 20 (April, 1977).

―――――, "Evolutionary Models in Economics and Law: Cooperation Versus Conflict Strategies," *Research in Law and Economics*, 4 (1982).

―――――, "Equilibrium Concepts in Game Theory," UCLA Dept. of Economics Working Paper #291 (May, 1983).

―――――― and J. Riley, "Elements of the Theory of Auctions and Contests." UCLA Economics Dept. Working Paper #118B (revised, August, 1978).

Lanchester, Frederick William, *Aircraft in Warfare* (1916), extract reprinted as "Mathematics in Warfare," in James R. Newman, ed., *The World of Mathematics*, 4. New York: Simon & Schuster (1956) pp. 2138–57.

Polachek, Solomon W., "Conflict and Trade," *J. of Conflict Resolution*, 24 (1980).

Schelling, Thomas C., *The Strategy of Conflict*, London: Oxford University Press (1960).

Simmel, Georg, "Conflict," (tr. Kurt H. Wolff) in *Conflict and the Web of Group-Affiliations*, New York: The Free Press (1955). (Original German publication, 1923).

Thompson, Earl A. and Roger L. Faith, "A Pure Theory of Strategic Behavior and Social Institutions," *American Economic Review*, 71 (June, 1981).

Trivers, Robert L., "The Evolution of Reciprocal Altruism," *Quarterly Review of Biology*, 46 (March, 1971).

Tullock, Gordon, *The Social Dilemma: The Economics of War and Revolution*, Center for the Study of Public Choice, Virginia Polytechnic Institute and State Univ. (1974).

Wittfogel, *Oriental Despotism: A Comparative Study of Total Power*, New Haven: Yale University Press (1957).

Wittman, Donald, "How a War Ends: A Rational Model Approach," *J. of Conflict Resolution*, 23 (Dec., 1979).

AUTOCRACY

GORDON TULLOCK

It is said that an ancient Hebrew, if he were to be a good Hebrew, would know that there were false gods, but should know nothing else about them. I don't know whether this myth is correct, but I think we have a modern example. The average citizen or scholar of democratic countries knows that there are undemocratic governments around, but all he really knows about them is that they are "false gods."

I don't want to quarrel with the view that these various forms of autocracy are indeed undesirable, but I think that it is worthwhile studying them. First, in the world today, most governments are dictatorships; most people live under dictatorships. Second, if we look over the sweep of history, this condition has been normal. There have been occasional upsurges of democracy. The Greek and Roman republics were one wave.[1] This was, of course, succeeded by an autocratic government in Rome itself, and then foreign conquest by autocracies.

There was, in medieval times, an upsurge of democratically controlled city-states, one of which, Venice, actually lasted one thousand years. But these again, in general, were brought under control of undemocratic rulers around the time of the Renaissance. Third, an upsurge in democracy essentially came out of English roots and expanded, reaching its high point, I believe, in 1914, and has been contracting since then. This brief summary of the expansion and contraction of democracy is intended as a way of pointing out that democracy has been, and is today, a rather rare government form. We may deplore this fact, but we should not deny it.

Let us then turn to a consideration of one particular form of undemocratic government, indeed, the commonest one: the form that I call "autocracy." This form of government takes in both what is normally thought of as monarchy and dictatorship.[2] I take it that most people know in general the kind of government that I have in mind, even if they oftentimes don't have much idea of its details.

There are, of course, differences between the hereditary monarchy and the ordinary dictatorship. Indeed, as a rough rule of thumb, historically, dictatorships are transitory, with the eventual switch to heredity control being likely. The transmission of the Duvalier "Presidency" of Haiti and the apparent transfer of the Kim dynasty in North Korea are, I believe, merely the precursors of what will in time become the normal procedure. That is to say, the usual situation is a hereditary succession interrupted by periodic dynastic overthrows.

But there are differences between the hereditary-king system and the dictatorship. First, the change of dictator is apt to be a fairly disturbing event and occasionally large numbers of people are killed. There have been some technical ways of avoiding that, which I will discuss later, but, normally, transmission form one dictator to another is a rough period. Succession in the royal dynasty usually is not so difficult, although quarrels within the ruling family, or between it and other families, can cause a good deal of bloodshed.

The second major difference here, is that the kings, through accidents of gene selection, can be fairly stupid and inept people. Louis the Sixteenth, of course, is a good example. Dictators, on the other hand, although they may not be nice people, are invariably talented. They tend to be intelligent, tough, and aggressive. They also tend to be much less secure than a hereditary monarch. Napoleon is sometimes quoted as having said that a hereditary monarch could go out every summer for ten years, lose a battle, and then return to his capital and live quite happily; but that he, Napoleon, would be finished if he lost one battle. This is a slight exaggeration, but it does point in the generally correct direction.

In this paper, I'm going to talk about the dictator rather than the hereditary monarch, mainly because they are much commoner in the present-day world. In addition, I'm going to restrict myself to discussing one particular problem; how the dictator stays in power. I'm willing to argue that this is the most important problem for a dictator once he has gotten in power. It dominates almost everything else he does, including, as we shall see below, his choice of policies. Nevertheless, there are many other aspects of dictatorship [3] which are of interest, but which cannot be dealt with in a paper of this length.

Having said that I'm going to talk about how dictators stay in power, I must now frankly confess that I do not have a general theory of dictatorship or a general theory of how dictators stay in power. I've been concerned about the problem of dictatorship for almost as long as I've been interested in Public Choice. Indeed, my first work on what now is thought of as Public Choice, was undertaken while I was in Communist China, and I was thinking more of the government *there* than

I was of democracies. The reasons that my writings have mainly been concerned with democracies is simply that dictatorship turns out to be a very difficult subject.

One objective of this paper, and I hope, of my forthcoming book, is to inspire other people to turn their attention to this important, and I would even say, vital, problem. I hope that it will be the first step towards the development of a general theory of this form of government. Unfortunately, it is a rather faltering first step. I hope that the audience will concentrate on further developments which might be made in the theory of dictatorship rather than on pointing out quite truthfully that I haven't gotten all that far.

The existing literature on dictatorship is sparse and, in my opinion, very poor. It is heavily dominated by moral considerations and, in fact, to a considerable extent, consists of simple attacks on the whole idea. These attacks can be rather restricted. It's an intriguing characteristic of communism that it does not have any political science at all for its own governments (which are, of course, always dictatorships), but that it does have an elaborate attack on other governments, all of which are accused of being dictatorships—this being an accusation that is apparently intended to hurt. But even there, they have no theoretical structure.

If we turn to the few things that I can find in Western sources, Machiavelli is perhaps the most informative. A mixture of moralistic attacks on dictators, moralistic advice to dictators (i.e., they're told to be good) and occasional discussions in terms of the class structure of the dictatorship, are almost all we find. In my opinion, all of these things are beside the point.

If we look at real-world dictatorships, the first thing to note about them is that they actually don't do very much. For a number of years, I have been challenging students in my graduate class to produce a discriminate function by which you can tell dictatorships from non-dictatorships by looking at the international statistics of the well-being of their citizens. I, of course, rule out such standard dictatorial functions as the size of the secret police or censorship. It's interesting that we have yet to find a genuine discrimination function, although the awards I've offered to my students are quite high.[4] One of these papers has been published in *Public Choice* (Laband).

This is not to say that dictatorship is a good form of government, but that most dictators really don't do very much in the way of policy. Such mass murderers as Hitler, Stalin, Mao Tse-tung, and Pol Pot are decided exceptions. It is not that dictators are necessarily nice people, but that they are deeply preoccupied with the problem of staying in power and the people that they fear most are not the masses, but high officials of their own regime.

Theoretically, the problem of maintaining power in a dictatorship is really very similar to that of maintaining a majority for redistributional purposes in a voting body. It is easily demonstrated, of course, that it is always possible to build a majority against any particular program of redistribution by offering something to the "outs" on the original program and fairly high payment to a few of the "ins."

The situation in a dictatorship is similar. It is always possible, at least in theory, to collect together a group of people which is more powerful than the group supporting the status quo. This group will be composed of other important officials of the regime and whoever could benefit from its overthrow and the replacement of the dictator by someone else. The reason for this is that the rewards now being received by the supporters of the status quo—keeping in mind that the dictator himself usually is very well paid—are available for redistribution to their opponents.

As an example, which doesn't really fit most dictatorships, but nevertheless may be familiar, suppose that Reagan is a dictator in the United States and his cabinet are in complete control of everything. The ambitious Secretary of State, shall we say, offers to Undersecretary of Defense a promotion to Secretary of Defense, and makes similar offers to other officials. Since the dictator himself and his prominent supporters are to be removed, there is clearly plenty of room for promotion of other people. This is like the circulating majority problem in a democratic voting body.

It should be said here that it's something of a mystery why the voting bodies do not behave in the highly unstable way that the Arrow Theorem would imply they should. Indeed, I have been conducting a long debate on this subject under the title, "Why So Much Stability?" in my journal. The purpose here, however, is not to contribute to that debate, but to think about the dictatorial counterpart.

How then, does the dictator avoid this problem. The first thing to be said is that most of them don't avoid it permanently. There have been many dictators who have died peacefully in office and over time, the tendency for dictators to pass the throne on to their son has been strong. Although there have been many such dictators, the number who have been overthrown is much larger. Thus, the problem I have stated, although successfully solved by some dictators, has not yet been solved by all. Even those who are overthrown, however, have usually a number of years of success before the overthrow occurs.

Traditional discussions of dictatorships, rarely bring this matter up. The problem, however, surely dominates the activities of the dictator. To quote an American euphemism: "In order to be a great Senator, one must first of all be a Senator." Similarly, if you are to do anything as a dictator, you must first of all be a dictator. You live under the Sword of Damocles permanently, and worrying about the thickness of the thread is apt to be a continuing preoccupation.

I am not here discussing the overthrow of the dictator by popular forces. If the police and army are even reasonably efficient and willing to shoot to kill, that won't happen. Indeed, I'm not positive there is any clear-cut case of a popular overthrow of the government. Generally speaking, it is a fight within the government itself, although the government may have democratic aspects. In the United States, for example, the local governments of the original thirteen colonies were already elected governments with the exception of the governor himself, who was appointed by the King. The elected legislatures threw out the appointed governors which, although done by a democratic process, clearly indicated a squabble within the government rather than a rising against the government. I believe that most other cases in which you have what appears to be democratic overthrow of a dictatorial regime will be shown to have the same pattern, although I cannot claim to have made a careful study of all of them.

Characteristically, however, the overthrow of the dictator simply means that there will be another dictator. This second dictator will normally announce that he has popular support and, for that matter, he may well have it at the beginning. Basically, however, it is one dictator replacing the other and the policies they follow will probably not be radically different. If we look at the world, we quickly realize that these policies will not be radically different from those that would be followed by a democracy either.

Here we must point out once again that the modern totalitarian dictators—Hitler, Stalin, Mao Tse-tung, Pol Pot—are exceptional and unusual people and I'm not talking about them here. I suggest that the reader think of Francisco Franco, a more normal dictator, even though he periodically maintained that he was a follower of either Mussolini or Hitler. It's hard to find any policy, other than keeping power, which he followed throughout his reign. Although he, of course, prevented centers of opposition from developing, his government was not violently oppressive. During most of his reign, for example, Spain had no death penalty. The reinstitution of the death penalty in his last year came after extremely severe provocation in whch his political opponents had "executed" something like one hundred of Franco's supporters. Even here, when they murdered his prime minister, instead of striking back hard, he chose to make concessions and select as new prime minister a man who was thought to be more acceptable to his opponents. All of this is not intended to argue for Franco's regime; in fact, I think it was a very poor government. Nevertheless, it was not a violently repressive regime. Franco in no way compares with Hitler, Stalin, Mao Tse-tung, or Pol Pot.

But this has been a digression. Let us return to our main topic of how the dictator holds his power, in spite of the fact that he will inevitably be in a position where a coalition of, let us say, the commander of his army and the chief of the secret police, could jointly remove him while benefiting themselves.[5] Hume pointed out that, although a ruler could rule the people by the power of his police and army, he could not rule the police and army by that power. As Hume put it, rule depended on opinion. It seems to me that this insight of Hume, like most of Hume's other insights, was an extremely good one. Hume did not, however, properly describe the opinion.

I should like to repair this deficit and say that the opinion that a dictator must maintain among the people around him is not so much that he is a good, just, or God-ordained dictator, but simply, that if it comes to an effort to overthrow him, he will win.

A more modern social scientist than Hume, Schelling (1960) had pointed out the situation in which people can agree without discussing the matter in advance. If there are a number of people, all of whom will gain a great deal if they make the same choice, and all of whom will lose if they do not make the same choice, there may be certain characteristics of the environment which act as cues and lead them to, in fact, make the same choice. On the other hand, of course, there may not.[6]

For a political example, let us consider the Brams and Riker (1972) view of what happened in American nominating conventions back in the days when the convention was not a mere puppet of pre-existing primaries. All of the people attending the convention were professional politicians who hoped very strongly to be rewarded because they had provided support for whomever was nominated as president. On the other hand, usually they didn't know when they arrived who was going to be nominated. There was then a cautious feeling-out of the situation, with individuals moving to the support of whomever they thought was, in fact, going to win. The early movement tended to give more information to others, and very quickly, everyone was rushing to get on the bandwagon of the winner. Those who waited too long, of course, were not rewarded because their vote had not been necessary.

Further, those who failed to get on, or who pushed too hard for one of the losers, would not be rewarded. The result here is a combination of Hume and Schelling. The opinion which counted here was the opinion as to who was likely to win. The decision had to be made while it was still uncertain who was going to win, because if you waited too long, you would get no reward. The result was at first caution and then a cascade of people rushing to join whomever they thought would win.

Efforts to overthrow a dictator have somewhat the same structure. The basic difference is that everything is much more concealed than it would be at a convention, and second, if the dictator himself wins, as he usually does, over efforts to overthrow him, the thing may proceed so rapidly that we don't even see the early stage at all.

The basic problem can be seen from the following line-graphs. Figure 5.11 has on the vertical axis the probability that a dictator will be overthrown and on the horizontal axis the number of people who have joined the conspiracy against him. Note that, although I say the *number* of people, the individuals would have different lengths along the axis, with a private in a provincial garrison taking up very little space on the axis and the chief of staff a great deal.

The extreme example of this disproportion is seen in the events in France in 1958. Before De Gaulle decided to overthrow the government of France, there was substantially no chance of it being overthrown, but as soon as he had made up his mind, the government collapsed. In essence, he himself occupied a space on the horizontal axis which perhaps extended from point A to point B.

The vertical line which extends down from the top of Figure 5.11 through all the other graphs, cuts the line on Figure 5.11 at a point where the probability is 50/50. In other words, anything to the right of that line has a better-than-even chance of overthrowing the dictator and anything to the left has a worse-than-even chance.

On the second graph, we continue the same horizontal axis, but the vertical axis is the reward from successful participation in the overthrow of the dictator. Note that I have drawn this line and the other lines not on the basis of empirical evidence, but more or less the way I think they should be. The reader is invited to experiment with other lines if he doesn't agree with these.

The third line, which is actually on the second quandrant of the Cartesian axis of Figure 5.12 shows the punishment which the individual is likely to receive if he joins the revolutionary effort and it fails. The bottom graph simply shows the net present discounted value of joining the revolutionary conspiracy, for some individual contemplating such an action. It is computed from the first three line-graphs. The

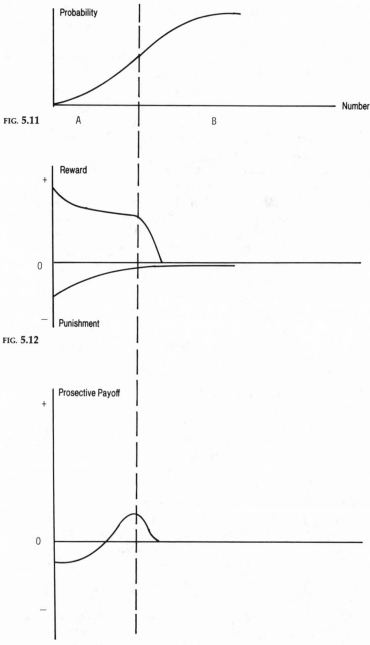

FIG. **5.11**

FIG. **5.12**

FIG. **5.13**

problem of the dictator is in making certain that everyone thinks that they are currently well to the left on this diagram. The problem of the person attempting to organize conspiracy is to convince people that the present discounted rewards of joining the revolution are positive.

This rather simple set of diagrams is, of course, intended for heuristic purposes and is not intended as an empirically accurate measure of probabilities, etc. Nevertheless, I think the diagrams do represent quite accurately the type of calculation that must be undertaken under these circumstances.

Suppose then, that the commanding general of the third army corps suddenly announces that the government is corrupt, wicked, etc., and that he will save the country from these depraved rulers. He tries to make this announcement as convincing as possible and what he is trying to convince people of, in general, is not that he is good, just, etc., but that he is strong and will win. Of course, there is no reason not to claim virtue and he, no doubt, will, but this is less important. He will try to obtain control of communications (this means the TV or radio stations), because he wants *his* message, which is "I am strong and will win!" concealed under "I am virtuous," to be transmitted and not the current dictator's message.

At this point various other people in the country, particularly the higher officials, are presented with a difficult problem. Is it better for them to jump on the revolutionary bandwagon or join with the dictator in suppressing the revolution? Further, it's very dangerous to show hesitation. This is particularly true if you consider that the dictator himself might win because he is likely to regard hesitation or neutrality in these cases as treason. Strength comes from an appearance of strength, but strength also gives an appearance of strength.

The discussion of how dictators are overthrown is extremely brief. I have not, for example, even dealt with the not particularly uncommon situation in which the attempted overthrow is strong enough so that it seizes part of the country physically and that there is then a protracted civil war. Here again, the real point of the civil war is to convince people that one side or the other is going to win.

But how does a dictator prevent this kind of overthrow? He must always have, as one of his primary objectives, the presentation to the world of a picture of strength. Note here that the world is not the average citizen, although the dictator should try to convince them too. The world is actually his higher officials. An impressive-looking, but actually hollow, armed force, may frighten the citizenry, but it's not likely to frighten the higher officials who know how hollow it is. On the other hand, the hollowness of this force may mean that the officials feel they cannot rely on it in an effort to overthrow the dictator.

Before turning to our discussion of how the dictator gives everyone the impression that he is strong and will win, let me deal briefly with a precaution that he will normally take—stringent enforcement of the law against treason. Any conspiracy, even discussion, of overthrowing a dictator is apt to be severely punished if the dictator finds out about it, and he'll make every effort to do so. His reasons are simple. Things which indicate his strength are plainly visible. He has guards, police, and the military, to say nothing of possible public demonstrations. People involved in these various activities are apt to feel that the other people involved in the same activity are loyal to the dictator unless they have some positive information to the contrary. By making it illegal to even discuss overthrowing a dictator, the dictator makes it difficult for such positive information to develop. Thus, the dissatisfied lieutenant in the dictator's personal guard is apt to feel that his dissatisfaction is a limited phenomenon and not to realize that there are a great many other people who'd be delighted to overthrow the dictator. On a more cold-blooded level, even if the lieutenant in the dictator's guard realized that it must be true that there are a large number of people who could benefit by overthrowing the dictator and moving upward themselves, he is unable to safely communicate with them and hence, insure his own future in the revolutionary movement.

This prevention even of the discussion of overthrowing the dictator is an important precaution which any sensible dictator will take. It has, however, a serious defect. Machiavelli said that it was astonishing that any overthrow of a prince ever occurred because of necessity; the conspiracy was risky and there was a safe alternative, which was to betray the conspiracy to the prince (Machiavelli, p. 96). The prince would then, naturally highly reward the person who had betrayed the conspiracy and take care of those members of the conspiracy that had not informed.

In general, Machiavelli correctly identified the phenomenon. He overlooked, however, another problem here. One of the ways of rising in the entourage of any dictator, Machiavelli's "reward," is to denounce a conspiracy. It's not necessary that there actually be a conspiracy there to be denounced. The dictator is apt to be surrounded by skilled and subtle courtiers, all of whom are trying to convince him that all of the others are disloyal to him. Their reason is simply a desire to rise in his favor. Thus, the dictator has very strong motives to suppress conspiracies against himself, and to highly reward people who inform him, but the reward system in and of itself tends to generate false alarms.

All of this makes life difficult for the dictator and, indeed, it is by no means the only thing that makes it difficult. He can neither trust his officials not to conspire against him nor can he necessarily trust reports of such conspiracies. It should be said that in recent years the development of very small recording devices had made it somewhat easier for the person who wants to betray a genuine plot to do so. Unfortunately, most of the people who are in a position to plot (i.e., the higher officials) are rather subtle individuals who are accustomed to communicating by allusion and indirect methods, and hence, recording their conversation is not all that helpful. A general conspiracy may not at all be spoken of like one and, on the other hand, even casual conversation may possibly be interpretable as a conspiracy.[7]

But if the ruler cannot prevent subtle conspiracies among the people of high rank around him, he pretty surely can prevent any widespread conspiracy from developing. Thus, higher officials may feel that there are enough of them antagonistic to the current dictator so that a conspiracy would work, but there is no way that they can assure themselves that their subordinates will follow their orders. It was, of course, this problem that stopped coups and attempted coups by the German military against Hitler. In this way, firm enforcement of the law against treason is certainly highly desirable on the part of the dictator, but he will find it very difficult to do and it is certainly not a firm and final reliance. In practice, dictators tend to respond to reports that one particular official is conspiring against them, not by killing him, but by appointing him ambassador to some far off place. He can then be brought back later. Stalin, of course, followed the policy of simply killing and it must be admitted that he was an extremely successful dictator.

Let us now return to the positive methods that the dictator has for demonstrating strength, for convincing all the people around him that, in the event of any effort to overthrow him, he will be successful in suppressing it. The first of these, of course, is simply seeing to it that any group of people that he particularly suspects are kept physically from doing anything about it. The current King of Morocco has suffered several efforts by military men to replace him. In consequence, at the moment, the army is almost entirely kept out of Morocco proper and engaged in a war against the Polisaro. When they are in Morocco, they are not allowed to leave their base without police permission and are escorted by the police whenever they do leave the base. This offers a good deal of protection against the army, although the possibility that it might decide to march into Morocco cannot be totally ruled out. It doesn't offer any protection against the police. The current dictator of Syria has chosen to balance matters. His brother commands a special,

very well equipped military force which, in essence, guards the dictator. The dictator does not permit this force to get large enough so that
his brother could safely take on the current dictator and the army.[8]
Such balancing is more common than the kind of thing the King of
Morocco is doing.

The problem here is that, in a real sense, a dictator lives in a state of
nature. He is not the owner of important assets in a well-run state.
There is no overwhelmingly powerful state which can protect him.
What he needs to be protected from is parts of the state. All of this
makes his life dangerous and in some ways unpleasant, but presumably the dictators regard the advantages greater than the
disadvantages.

The situation is analogous to a very typical Public Choice problem—
the self-enforcing constitution. It's fairly easy to design a constitution
for a state which would lead to at least a reasonably good government.
The problem is designing this constitution in such a way that it
enforces itself. How do you, to give but one example, prevent a
supreme court from deciding that it should be supremer than the
designers of the constitution intended? At the moment we don't have
very much of a solution to this problem in democratic politics and the
dictator must face it every day. The Gang of Four in China lost their
position of power because the commander of their guard force chose
to arrest them rather than guard them. Arevalo, a dictator of Guate-
mala, was assassinated by one of his own guard while he was walking
towards the dining room of his house with his wife.

But this problem, which we have not solved in democracy, and
which is so important for a dictator, can to some extent be mitigated in
a dictatorship by attempting to enforce the law against treason, and by
a variety of other techniques to which we will now turn.

The first of these is simply preventing others from getting positions
of firm power. The dictator should practice what Mussolini called
"Changing of the Guard," i.e., he should move his high officials
around so that they never develop firm personal following in whatever
job they hold. This is particularly important in the case of the army
and police force, and it is, of course, in those areas where most modern
states rotate higher officers with regularity. First, this shifting around
demonstrates the power of the dictator. Any individual knows that at
any time he can be removed. Second, it provides a way of quietly
rewarding services.

The dictator, if he's well-advised, will not only rotate people from
one military command to another but will at least occasionally remove
individuals from command totally, and then a few years later bring

them back. It should be said here that, in Mexico, the "Party of Revolutionary Institutions" was originally just a coalition of military men, and the conversion of a rather disorderly state to one which is rather orderly, as dictatorships go, largely involved imposing rotation on the higher military officials, all of whom were, in fact, bandit chiefs with their own little armies. This imposed rotation was one in which the troops, loyal to particular military chiefs, were not rotated with their chiefs.

There are many cases of this. When Mao Tse-tung seized control of China, he actually was the head of an organization in which there were in essence five armies, all of which had been built up by one leader from practically nothing, and which were to a considerable extent loyal to that leader. Mao might have been able to deal with this by ordinary methods, but the Korean War gave him a wonderful opportunity. He basically drafted from each of these armies specific units to send to the Korean War. These units were then rotated back to China on a regular basis, but were not returned to their original army. As a result, at the end of the Korean War, the five major armies had been melded into one. Mao Tse-tung was able to remove the four most important generals from their positions of personal power.

One thing that most dictators should at least give careful thought to is personal command of the army. At the least, the dictator must devote a lot of attention to who commands it, and if possible, should fix it up so there is no true commander but instead, a number of officials with titles like Minister of War, Chief of Staff, etc. He can, however, take direct command himself and this frequently is very helpful in retaining power.

Another technique is collegial control (i.e., putting a board or commission at the head of almost everything). The Lords of the Admiralty are an example of this from the present day. Cabinets and councils are yet other examples. A group of this sort cannot effectively conspire because somebody will almost certainly talk, nor is any individual likely to be able to use it to build up a personal following.

Another technique, a very traditional one, is "cutting off the head of the tallest flowers," or disposing of people who are rising in power and influence. When the Great Captain returned to Spain after having won most of Italy for the King of Spain, he was almost instantly exiled to his estates and prevented from having any influence in the government of Spain. Khrushchev, who disposed of Zhukov right after Zhukov had made Khrushchev a success in the "Anti-Party Plot" affair, is certainly another example.

As a minor, but, nevertheless, possibly important aspect of keeping power, a lot of pompous ceremony surrounding the dictator is a good idea. It should be noted here that the dictator no doubt also enjoys this. It is particularly helpful if the dictator can arrange to have himself surrounded by a great deal of pomp and ceremony while putting on an appearance of being a very simple man himself. Lord Montgomery during World War II insisted that all of his staff officers be perfectly dressed, with shoes shined, etc., while he himself, wore less-than-perfectly tailored uniforms. His public relations officer made quite a bit out of this contrast. This is the kind of thing that frequently pays off for a dictator.

There is another important aspect which is that the dictator should always get his way. In order to always get his way without making a lot of mistakes, the dictator has to be careful. Machiavelli said, "a dictator should continuously solicit advice, but never take unsolicited advice." (Machiavelli, p. 117) In my opinion, this is still a good bit of advice for any dictator. Second, the dictator should normally make up his own mind late in the public discussion of any particular problem. Lastly, if he runs into a singularly difficult problem, he should push the whole thing off on an inferior. He can blame the inferior if things work out badly. Once he has taken a position, however, it is generally dangerous for him to change. A dictator can get away with this sometimes, but not frequently.

The basic problem here is one which has been discussed in connection with nuclear war, a problem called "escalation dominance." The dictator should be surrounded by people who all feel that opposition to the dictator has less chance as it proceeds to a higher level. In other words, the individual courtiers should realize there is no point in starting a serious argument with the dictator because the dictator will win, that if any of these courtiers tries to arrange a coup, the dictator will win, and that if they actually start a civil war, the dictator will win. As long as the courtiers think all of these things are true, the dictator is safe.

Earlier I promised to deal with the problem of peaceful succession. Most dictators are against having any kind of succession arrangements set up because they're aware of the fact that whoever is selected as their successor has: a) a very strong motive to kill them, and b) a very good chance of getting away with it. Indeed, South American dictators, when they finally decide that they want to retire, very commonly organize a temporary democratic succession because that is the only safe way of retiring.

There have been, however, two methods of replacing the dictator peacefully which have, at least in some cases, been successful. The first of these is what I call the Catholic procedure, although the communists also use it. There is a dictator who appoints an advisory board. When he dies, the board performs its only real governmental function; it selects his successor. The Catholic church has used this system for a long time although there have, of course, been difficulties. The communist states use this system also. I don't know whether they're aware of the Catholic precedent. They have so far avoided a genuine civil war although there have been coups in both Russia and China.[9]

The second technique which, as far as I can see, was invented by the Mexicans, although it does have some antecedents in Rome, is simply the dictator who rules for a fixed period of years; six years in the case of Mexico. He then appoints his successor and retires. This system has been going on in Mexico now since the 1930s and was copied by Brazil in the 1960s. I am inclined to the view that this system is fundamentally unstable and only very special circumstances have permitted it to successfully continue this long; but that may be mere prejudice on my part.

So much for this rather brief introduction to the problem of how dictators stay in power. It is, of course, fundamental to the dictator's activities and it shapes almost everything else he does. I have found that when I talk about dictators in the way in which I've been doing now, that I get two responses. One is that I'm obviously wrong, and the other is that everybody has always known these things. I'm inclined to believe that the latter is right in the sense that, at any event, all dictators have always known these things. Yet, so far as I know, this approach is not in writing anywhere else. I believe that is not because it involves any great intellectual penetration, but simply because scholars in general have not studied dictatorships. Acknowledging the commonness of this form of government, it assuredly deserves study.

NOTES

1. Although it's not of great importance to this paper, I normally define democracy as a government which is controlled by the vote of a considerable number of people. I do not require that everybody be permitted to vote or that various parts of the American Bill of Rights be accepted.

2. The current constitutional monarchies, in which the king, or in the case of Japan, the Emperor, is essentially a decorative part of the state rather than a functional ruler, should be referred to as democracies rather than monarchies, or in the particular case of Thailand, a dictatorship rather than a monarchy. The King there is also restricted to ceremonial roles. The dictator, whoever he is, runs things.

3. I am currently in the process of writing a general book on the subject.

4. A guaranteed "A" for the course.

5. It's very hard to tell who will remove you. Batista was a mere sergeant when he staged his first successful revolution. He and his fellow non-coms removed all of the regular officers of the Army and appointed themselves in their place. The current dictators of Surinam and Liberia did somewhat the same thing.

6. Schelling's first example involved two people who would be highly rewarded if they met in New York without prior consultation. He (a professor at Yale) reasoned each would independently go to the information booth in Grand Central Station.

7. Ssu-ma Chien, grand historian of China, was castrated because as a high official in the court, he made what superficially appears to be a completely casual remark which was interpreted by the Emperor as deploring the appointment of the brother of his favorite mistress as commander of an army which had just been routed by the barbarians. It is possible that this is what Ssu-ma Chien in fact had in mind, but it's certainly not clear.

8. At the time this page was actually written, Damascus was an armed camp with different military factions pointing their guns at each other and occasionally engaging in light gunfire. This is a more overt expression of the normal situation in the Syrian Dictatorship or indeed in any dictatorship.

9. The fact that there have been coups in these countries seems to be concealed simply because reporters don't use the magic word "coup." The arrest of the Gang of Four, for example, is not normally referred to as a "coup" or attempted "coup," although obviously it was.

REFERENCES

Brams, Stephen J., and William Riker, "Models of Coalition Formation in Voting Bodies," *Mathematical Applications in Political Science*, University Press of Virginia: Charlottesville, Va., Vol. 6 (1972).

Hume, David, *Essays, Literary, Moral and Political*, Ward, Lock & Co., Warwick House: London, England, n.d. [1870's] p. 23.

Laband, D.N., "Is There a Relationship Between Economic Conditions and Political Structure," *Public Choice Journal* 42 (1), (1984) pp. 25–38.

Machiavelli, Niccolo, *The Prince*, The Oxford University Press ("World's Classics" translation by Luigi Ricci, revised by E.R.P. Vincent): New York & Scarborough, Ontario, Canada (1968) pp. 96, 117.

Schelling, Thomas C., *The Strategy of Conflict*, Harvard University Press: Cambridge, Mass. (1960).

A GENERAL CONSTITUTIONAL POSSIBILITY THEOREM

PETER BERNHOLZ

I INTRODUCTION

The specter of Arrow's General Impossibility Theorem (Arrow, 1963) has haunted social scientists for about thirty years (Sen, 1970; Plott, 1967; McKelvey, 1976; Kramer, 1977; Mueller, 1979; Bernholz, 1980, 1982; Schwartz, 1981). The impossibility of aggregating individual preferences in non-dictatorial societies into a consistent social pattern seems still to disturb many people (Tullock, 1981; Koford, 1982) in spite of the many efforts to escape Arrow's results by weakening his rather plausible assumptions. The situation looks even worse since Sen's theorem about the impossibility of a Paretian Liberal (Sen, 1970) has been found to be valid for all non-oligarchical organizations of society (Bernholz, 1980). Indeed, intransitive or cyclical social preferences possibly containing non-Pareto-optimal outcomes side by side with others within the same cycle are certainly not appealing.

In this paper we propose to look at the consistency problem of non-oligarchic societies from a different perspective than that taken by Arrow and the authors interpreting and enlarging his work by weakening and changing one or the other of his assumptions. First, we are concerned with the possible assignments of the rights to decide among different pairs of outcomes and the decision rules used, i.e., with different organizational settings of non-oligarchic societies. The members of society decide within an institutional framework and this may result in mutually inconsistent decisions and in non-Pareto-optimal outcomes which have not been wanted by anybody. This is the meaning to us of expressions like "intransitive" or "cyclical social preferences" containing non-Pareto-optimal outcomes. The existence of a "social welfare function" or a "social preference ordering" would thus convey the idea that the decisions taken by the members of society lead to a consistent pattern and to Pareto-optimal outcomes, if individuals have complete, weak, and transitive preferences.

Second, Arrow and the literature starting from his theorem mostly take some non-oligarchic assignment of the rights to decide among pairs of outcomes and the decision rules applied explicitly or implicitly as given, and ask whether such an assignment allows, in the presence of certain plausible additional assumptions, a transitive social ordering to be generated for all or some configurations of the possible preference orderings of the members of society. The non-oligarchic assignment of decision rights is thus, in a sense, taken as a parameter, whereas the individual preference orderings are taken as variables. Of course, this does not preclude the validity of the theorems derived for the different parameter values, i.e., for different non-oligarchic assignments of decision rights.

I suggest that this way of looking at the problems of non-oligarchic societies has precluded the discovery of some important results, and that a modified approach may lead to a quite different evaluation of the relevance of the General Impossibility Theorem for such societies. This paper will not take individual preference orderings but, rather, the assignment of decision rights to different subsets of society as a variable, and then start from some configuration of individual preference orderings as a parameter. By proceeding in this fashion, we will be able to prove that there exists for any collection of preference orderings of the members of society some non-oligarchic allocation of decision rights to different subsets of society, implying

1) a transitive social preference ordering;

2) a Pareto-optimal outcome "preferred by society" to all other outcomes, including all other Pareto-optimal outcomes (if not all members of society are indifferent among all Pareto-optimal outcomes).

Result 2) allows, moreover, for any configuration of individual preferences an assignment of rights which lets society "prefer" any Pareto-optimal outcome to all other outcomes, and hence, is "superior" to all other Pareto-optimal outcomes.

Moreover, by taking this different approach, it can be shown that results 1) and 2) can be derived for some purely liberal assignments of rights but that there can be cases in which such an assignment is oligarchic. Results 1) and 2) do not hold, however, for total direct democracy, i.e., an organization of society in which all members have the right to decide among all pairs of outcomes by simple or qualified majority voting.

Some people may argue that these results are either not surprising or not of much significance. Indeed, one may feel that it is not surprising that there exists at least one non-oligarchic assignment of rights for any collection of individual preference orderings, which implies transitive social preferences. I am not sure, however, whether this feeling is justified — First, no such constitution may exist for majority voting of all members of society on all pairs of outcomes. Second, purely liberal constitutions of this kind may be oligarchic. Finally, if one argues in this vein, Arrow's theorem would seem to be trivial, too. For who would have expected that *one and the same non-oligarchic constitution* (or assignment of rights to subsets of the members of society) should imply intransitive social preference orderings for all kinds of individual preference orderings, e.g., for those in a medieval Christian, a modern Western, or a traditional Islamic, society?

If we accept these judgments, then the results of the present paper suggest two important questions: First—which sets of collections or profiles of individual preference orderings allow which non-oligarchic constitutions in the sense of excluding intransitivity of the social preference orderings? (or better: which sets prevent the problem of inconsistent decisions?) Second—which changes of profiles necessitate which kind of constitutional reform? It is obvious that these are important but difficult problems. But they cannot be dealt with in the present article.

II NOTATION AND DEFINITIONS

We consider a set V of m $\geq$ 2 individuals with weak, ordinal, complete, and transitive preferences over a finite set U of n $\geq$ 3 outcomes x_i (i = 1, 2, ..., n). Further, define $U_1 \equiv U - \{x_1\}$, $U_2 \equiv U - \{x_1, x_2\}$, ..., $U_k \equiv U - \{x_1, x_2, ..., x_k\}$. Moreover, call U^P the set of Pareto-optimal outcomes in U and U_i^P the set of Pareto-optimal outcomes in U_k (k = 1, 2, 3, ..., n − 1).

For each pair of outcomes x_i, x_j ε U let there exist a nonempty set V_{ij} c V of one or more individuals who have the right to decide according to some non-stochastic decision rule d_{ij} among these outcomes. Since x_i, x_j are treated as an unordered pair, we obviously have $V_{ij} = V_{ji}$ for all i,j. Note that only one decision rule is used to decide among each pair of outcomes. Otherwise, contradicting results might be reached.

Decision rule d_{ij} has the following properties:

1) there exists at least one non-empty winning coalition $C_{ij} \subseteq V_{ij}$ ($C_{ij} \neq \phi$) such that if for all $k \, \varepsilon \, C_{ij}$, $x_i P_k x_j$ is true, "society prefers" x_i to x_j, i.e., $x_i P x_j$.

2) If $C_{ij} c V_{ij}$ and if $x_i \, P_g x_j$ for $g \, \varepsilon \, V_{ij} - C_{ij}$, and if the preferences of all other members of V_{ij} are unchanged, then $C'_{ij} \equiv C_{ij} \cup \{g\}$ is a winning coalition, too, such that $x_i P x_j$.

It is obvious that there may be many winning coalitions C_{ij}, C'_{ij}, C''_{ij} ... for each pair of issues x_i, $x_j \, \varepsilon \, U$.

If no winning coalition for x_i against x_j is present, because there are not enough individuals $k \, \varepsilon \, V_{ij}$ for whom $x_i P_k x_j$ is true, then a blocking coalition B_{ji}, for all of whose members $k \, \varepsilon \, B_{ji}$ $x_j R_k x_i$, holds, does exist. In this case we will write for society, $x_j R x_i$. Again, usually several blocking coalitions B_{ji}, B'_{ji}, B''_{ji}, ... , exist. On the other hand, if a winning coalition C_{ij} exists, then no blocking coalition B_{ji} can be present. If neither $x_i P x_j$ nor $x_j P x_i$ are valid, i.e., if neither a winning coalition for x_i against x_j nor for x_j exists, society will be said to be "indifferent" between these outcomes, $x_i \, I x_j$. In this case, at least two blocking coalitions B_{ij} and B_{ji} exist. It is important to realize that, for each pair of outcomes, either relationship P or I must be present, since a V_{ij}, V_{ji}, B_{ij} or B_{ji} exist for any pair x_i and x_j. Moreover, we use D_{ij} to describe if either a winning or a blocking coalition for x_i against x_j exists. Note that either D_{ij} or D_{ji} must be present, whatever the individual preferences of the members of V_{ij}. Since there may be several winning or blocking coalitions, there may be several D_{ij}, D'_{ij}, D''_{ij}, ...

Finally, we shall denote by a *profile of preference orderings* for the m members of society an m-tuple of individual preference orderings, one for each member. Obviously there are many such profiles, since individuals can have quite a number of different preference orderings.

Let us mention that the above definitions allow all kinds of oligarchic and non-oligarchic decentralized institutional arrangements of society, including the extremes of dictatorship, "pure liberalism," where $V_{ij} = \{k_{ij}\}$ (for all $i, j = 1, 2, \ldots, n; i \neq j$), and $\bigcap\limits_{\substack{i,j \\ i \neq j}} V_{ij} = \phi$, and

"total direct democracy," where all members of society together have the right to make all the decisions, i.e., $V_{ij} = V$ (for all $i, j = 1, 2, \ldots, n; i \neq j$), by using simple majority voting.